# ORTONA

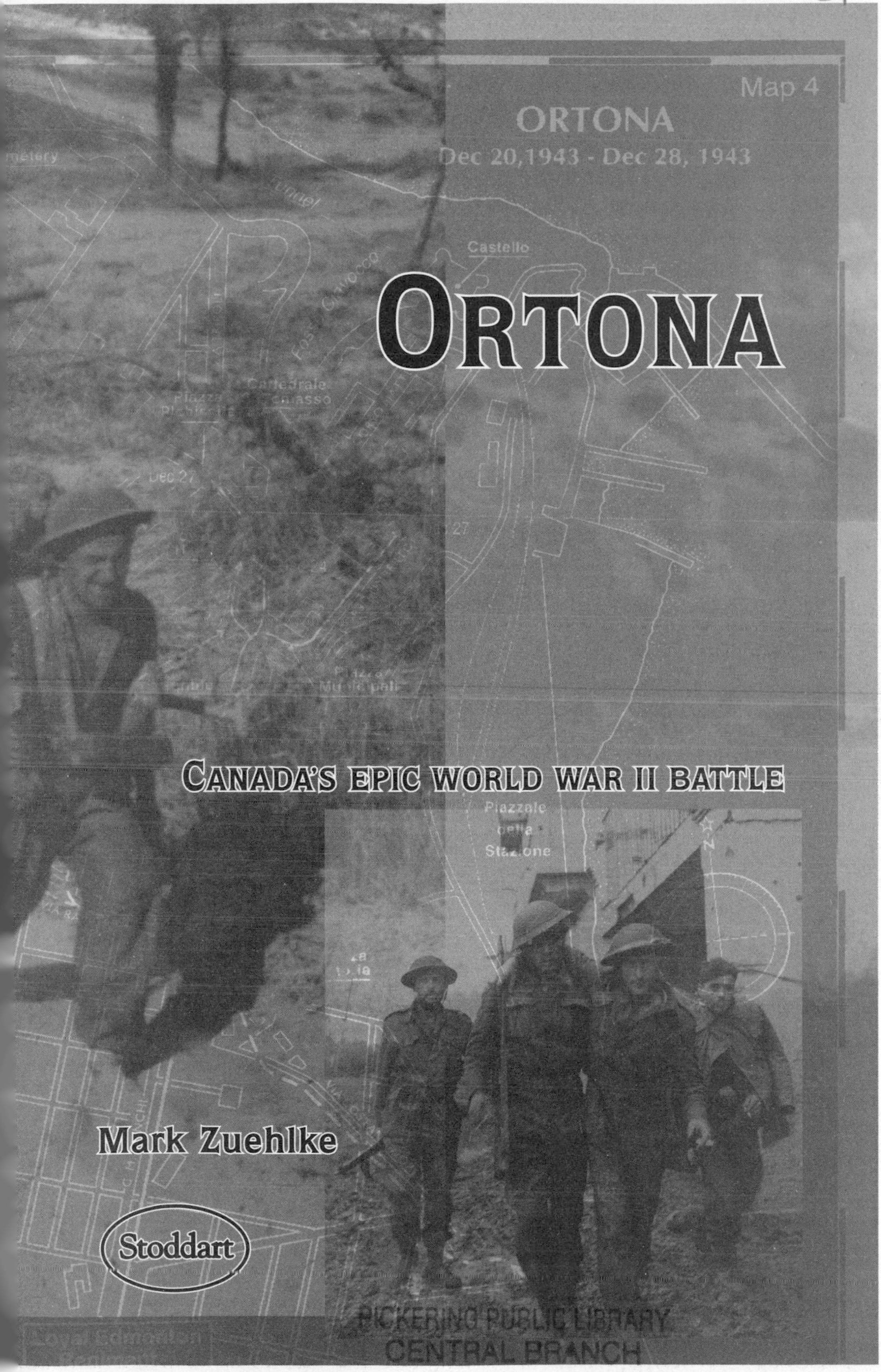
Map 4
ORTONA
Dec 20,1943 - Dec 28, 1943
Castello
ORTONA
CANADA'S EPIC WORLD WAR II BATTLE
Piazzale
della
Stazione
Mark Zuehlke
Stoddart

Published in 1999 by Stoddart Publishing Co. Limited
34 Lesmill Road, Toronto, Canada M3B 2T6
180 Varick Street, 9th Floor, New York, N.Y. 10014

Distributed in Canada by General Distribution Services Limited
325 Humber College Blvd., Toronto, Ontario M9W 7C3
Tel. (416) 213-1919    Fax (416) 213-1917
Email Customer.Service@ccmailgw.genpub.com

Distributed in the U.S. by General Distribution Services Inc.
85 River Rock Drive, Suite 202, Buffalo, New York 14207
Toll-free tel. 1-800-805-1083  Toll-free fax 1-800-481-6207
Email gdsinc@genpub.com

03 02 01 00 99 1 2 3 4 5

**Canadian Cataloguing in Publication Data**

Zuehlke, Mark
Ortona: Canada's epic World War II battle

Includes bibliographical references and index.

ISBN 0-7737-3198-9

I. Ortona (Italy), Battle of, 1943. 2. Canada. Canadian Army —
History — World War 1939–1945. I. Title.

D763.I82077   1999     940.54'215713     C99-931465-3

Jacket design: Bill Douglas @ The Bang
Jacket illustration: Stephen Quick
Part title photo: Sarah Jane English
Design and typesetting: Kinetics Design & Illustration

Printed and bound in Canada

We acknowledge for their financial support of our publishing
program the Canada Council, the Ontario Arts Council, and
the Government of Canada through the Book Publishing
Industry Development Program (BPIDP).

*The next dreadful thing to a battle lost
is a battle won.*

— *Arthur Wellesley,
Duke of Wellington*

# CONTENTS

# PREFACE

WRITING a history dedicated exclusively to a single battle fought more than fifty years ago presents an enormous challenge for the modern historical writer. Documentation is often lacking, the physical landscape is changed, the memories of the veterans who survived may be fading, and there are far too few veterans left. Yet that collective veteran memory became the essence of this book.

I was privileged to interview or correspond with many an old soldier, as well as Italian civilian. I was able to access the interviews that Major Michael Boire conducted with German soldiers who fought at Ortona. Each veteran reached into the web of personal memory to pull forth compelling stories, often little more than a snapshot, of a horrific experience. My debt to them all is immense. They are all listed in the bibliography.

There are some historians who argue that the memory of participants in events that have been filtered through the passage of fifty or more years is suspect. They argue that writers should only march down the official record when stating what is or is not a fact. Fact. What a conundrum for a non-fiction writer. Norman Mailor has argued that nothing can be factual — that everything is coloured through the eyes of the recorder and therefore no interpretation of events can be called "true."

I confronted this problem daily. The war diaries of the battalions featured in this book are rife with errors and sometimes blatant revisionism to protect commanders from just criticism for decisions that led to unnecessary deaths. The official histories are laden with inaccuracies that the war diaries illuminate. Individual soldiers point out errors and omissions in the official record, while the war diaries may contradict both. So where is truth?

To address the problem, I used a somewhat unscientific solution based on gut instinct. I cross-checked where possible. If two or three veterans say the same thing, it seems probable that this is what happened. Sometimes I was forced to consider the middle road between accounts of an event and make decisions, based on terrain and other military factors, to arrive at what likely transpired. Seldom did these decisions contradict the memory of veterans relating the story more than fifty years after the fact. Rather, their memory often corrected the official version.

War, as the esteemed psychologist Abraham Maslow contended, is a peak experience. There are only about three peak experiences possible in Maslow's world. They involve a heightening of sensation that transcends the normal flow of life. The experience is so intense that it will never be forgotten. It is not surprising then that the veterans still carry these memories and that some are unable to discuss them at all because they remain so alive to them. For others, the memories are beginning to fade. Many times veterans either wrote or said, "I don't remember the details." They often referred to things being "a blur." Yet through this fog of time, many incidents were starkly illuminated in their descriptions. The distant gaze in Bert Hoffmeister's eyes, as he described the caked blood on the hands and faces of the wounded in the San Vito hospital, is mute evidence of how vivid such memories remain. When a bullet meant for Jock Gibson only clipped his ear, but struck the young runner behind him in the face, the image of the boy's dead body lying on a cobblestone street in San Leonardo stuck. Those are the type of memories reflected in this book. Usually it was not too difficult to verify memories against the official documentation. Often, through interviewing other veterans, I was able to see the same incident through many eyes, and their stories were usually in agreement.

I tried wherever possible to confirm the memory of the veterans with the historical record as contained in the National Archives of Canada, the Directorate of History of the Department of National Defence, the Canadian War Museum, and the published official histories. At times the accounts conflict. For example, George Garbutt's experience before Villa Rogatti was completely at odds with that recorded by the war diary and then immortalized in the Princess Patricia's Canadian Light Infantry official history. It takes a special courage to point out that the heroism assigned to you never actually occurred and that, in fact, you were in a different part of the battlefield at the time.

Largely, however, I believe the official records are accurate. And mostly the veterans agreed with those records. What the official records often don't include are the mistakes made at every level of command. War is an exercise in confusion. Based mainly on the analysis of veterans, I have tried to capture and reflect the many errors of strategy and tactics that occurred. These men had to bury comrades as a result. So I gave them the last word.

# ACKNOWLEDGEMENTS

WHILE researching this book, I was assisted by many helpful staff at the National Archives of Canada and National Library of Canada, the Department of National Defence's Directorate of History, the Canadian War Museum reading room, the Canadian Broadcasting Corporation's Radio Archives (special thanks to Debbie Lindsey), the City of Edmonton Public Archives, and the University of Victoria Special Collections.

Many people were extremely generous with their time and in sharing resources that helped bring this book to completion. Wayne Langton, whose father died at Ortona while serving with the Saskatoon Light Infantry, was always enthusiastic with his support. Oral historian Ken MacLeod both physically and metaphorically opened doors to interviews with various veterans. Dr. Reginald Roy provided some helpful suggestions of where to look in his papers for information.

In Italy, I was fortunate to stay with Sue Leoni and family in Rome. Nicholas Serafini was a helpful guide in Ortona and also a capable translator. Fabio Dell'Osa and everyone at the Ristorante

Miramare in Ortona did much to help ensure that the Italian story of the battle could be included. The food was wonderful, too.

My debt to Major Michael Boire is great. He contributed immensely to my understanding of the physical nature of the battle-field in and around Ortona. Michael's subsequent efforts in interviewing German veterans of the battle and sharing the resulting interview transcripts and translated diary entries contributed a dimension to this book that would otherwise have been absent.

The regimental associations mostly went out of their way to try to link me up with surviving veterans. The Seaforth Highlanders of Canada and the Loyal Edmonton regimental associations were particularly helpful. The Loyal Edmonton Regiment was also a great host at two reunions, which opened doors for more interviews.

A full list of the veterans either interviewed or corresponded with is included in the bibliography. Without their participation this book would have lacked many compelling eye-witness accounts. I am indebted to them all. Some veterans went to great lengths to help me connect with others. Victor Bulger, Wilf Gildersleeve, and Bill Worton particularly went beyond the call of duty for a stranger. So, too, did Peggy Turnbull and her family. Jerry Richards and Jack Haley not only helped with other contacts but also took an active interest in bolstering a writer's flagging morale as the book grew in both size and complexity. It was a welcome lunch. Fred Gaffen read the manu-script and offered helpful clarification of several points regarding Canadian military organization and events at Ortona.

A grant from the British Columbia Arts Council helped make writing this book feasible. Literary agent Carolyn Swayze found a home for it. Thanks, Carolyn. Elizabeth McLean provided her metic-ulous editing and, as always, was a pleasure to work with.

I was blessed to have the unfailing support and companionship of Frances Backhouse during the research and writing of this book. She also spent long hours reading the manuscript and offering many sug-gestions for needed changes. Any remaining errors and omissions are mine.

As this book was being researched, several old soldiers who fought at Ortona died. The stories they did not tell are lost now. If there is a veteran in your family, I urge you to help him write or tape his memories. With each passing on, a wealth of historical memory is forever lost.

The many battles of World War II in which Canadians fought have largely gone ignored by historians as individual subjects worthy of in-depth attention. This book has been an effort to redress that neglect with regard to the Battle of Ortona. This is a work of remembrance. I hope it also contributes to our collective understanding of both the experience of battle and its inevitable human costs.

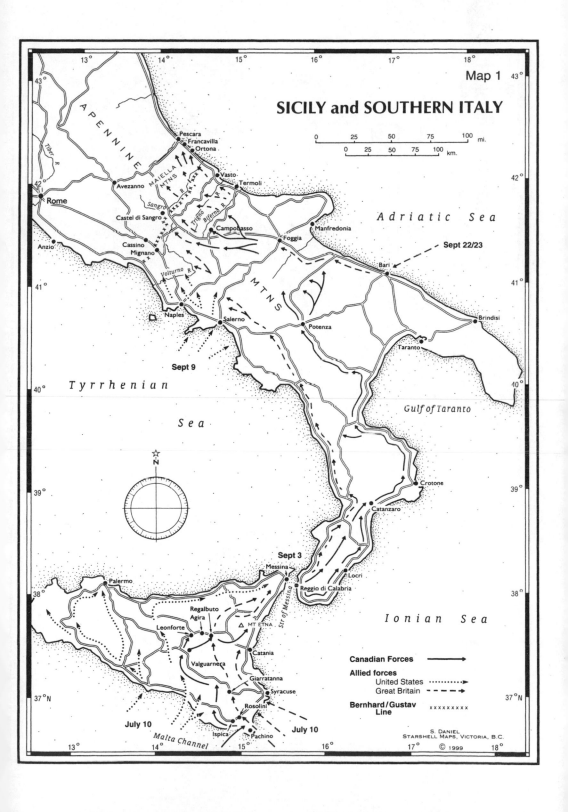

**Map 1**

# SICILY and SOUTHERN ITALY

43°

42°

*Adriatic Sea*

Sept 22/23

41°

Sept 9

*Tyrrhenian*

40°

*Sea*

*Gulf of Taranto*

39°

Sept 3

*Ionian Sea*

38°

37°N

July 10

July 10

*Malta Channel*

**Canadian Forces** ——→

**Allied forces**
    United States ·········→
    Great Britain – – – →

**Bernhard/Gustav Line** xxxxxxxxx

S. DANIEL
STARSHELL MAPS, VICTORIA, B.C.
© 1999

### Place labels

APENNINE · Tiber R. · Pescara · Francavilla · Ortona · Vasto · Termoli · MAIELLA MTNS · Avezanno · Trigno R. · Biferno R. · Sangro · Castel di Sangro · Campobasso · Foggia · Manfredonia · Rome · Anzio · Cassino · Mignano · Volturno R. · MTNS · Bari · Naples · Salerno · Potenza · Taranto · Brindisi · Crotone · Catanzaro · Messina · Locri · Reggio di Calabria · Str. of Messina · Palermo · Regalbuto · Agira · Leonforte · MT ETNA · Catania · Valguarnera · Giarratanna · Syracuse · Rosolini · Ispica · Pachino

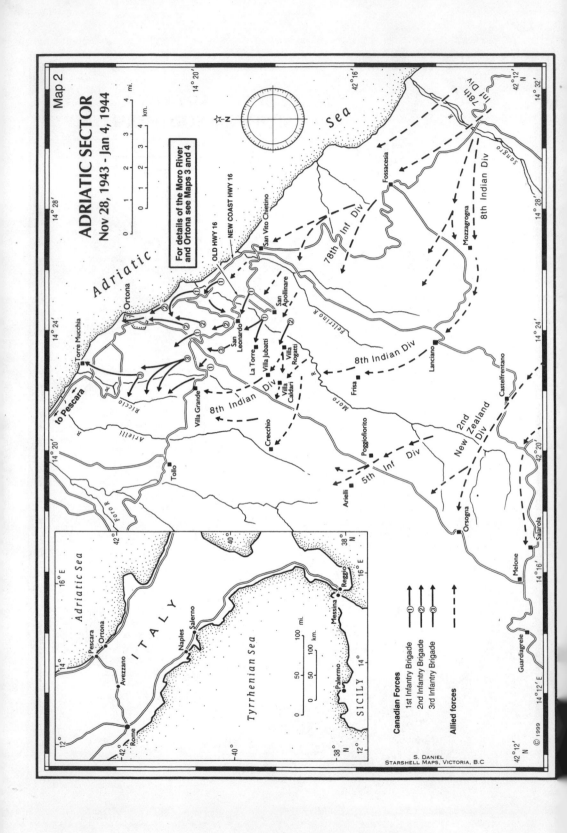

Map 2

## ADRIATIC SECTOR
### Nov 28, 1943 - Jan 4, 1944

For details of the Moro River and Ortona see Maps 3 and 4

**Canadian Forces**
1st Infantry Brigade
2nd Infantry Brigade
3rd Infantry Brigade

**Allied forces**

S. DANIEL
STARSHELL MAPS, VICTORIA, B.C

© 1999

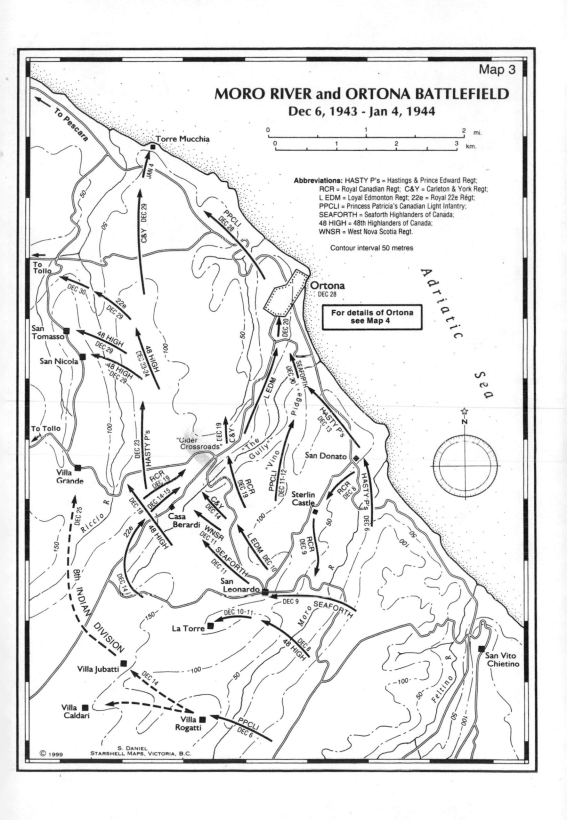

Map 3

# MORO RIVER and ORTONA BATTLEFIELD
## Dec 6, 1943 - Jan 4, 1944

0          1          2   mi.

0     1     2     3   km.

**Abbreviations:** HASTY P's = Hastings & Prince Edward Regt;
RCR = Royal Canadian Regt; C&Y = Carleton & York Regt;
L EDM = Loyal Edmonton Regt; 22e = Royal 22e Régt;
PPCLI = Princess Patricia's Canadian Light Infantry;
SEAFORTH = Seaforth Highlanders of Canada;
48 HIGH = 48th Highlanders of Canada;
WNSR = West Nova Scotia Regt.

Contour interval 50 metres

To Pescara

Torre Mucchia

JAN 4

C&Y DEC 29

PPCLI DEC 28

To Tollo

DEC 30

22e DEC 29

San Tomasso

48 HIGH DEC 29

48 HIGH DEC 23-24

San Nicola

48 HIGH DEC 29

Ortona
DEC 28

*Adriatic Sea*

DEC 20

**For details of Ortona see Map 4**

L EDM

SEAFORTH DEC 20

To Tollo

HASTY P's DEC 23

RCR DEC 19

"Cider Crossroads"

DEC 19

C&Y

"The Gully"

PPCLI DEC 11-12

Vino

HASTY P's DEC 13

San Donato

Villa Grande

RCR DEC 19

DEC 18

C&Y DEC 14

Casa Berardi

48 HIGH

WNSR DEC 11

SEAFORTH DEC 11

L EDM DEC 10

Sterlin Castle

RCR DEC 8

HASTY P's DEC 6

DEC 25

Riccio R.

22e

DEC 14

RCR DEC 9

San Leonardo

DEC 9

Moro SEAFORTH

**8th INDIAN DIVISION**

150

DEC 10-11

La Torre

DEC 8

48 HIGH

San Vito Chietino

Feltino R.

Villa Jubatti

DEC 14

100

Villa Caldari

Villa Rogatti

PPCLI DEC 6

© 1999

S. DANIEL
STARSHELL MAPS, VICTORIA, B.C.

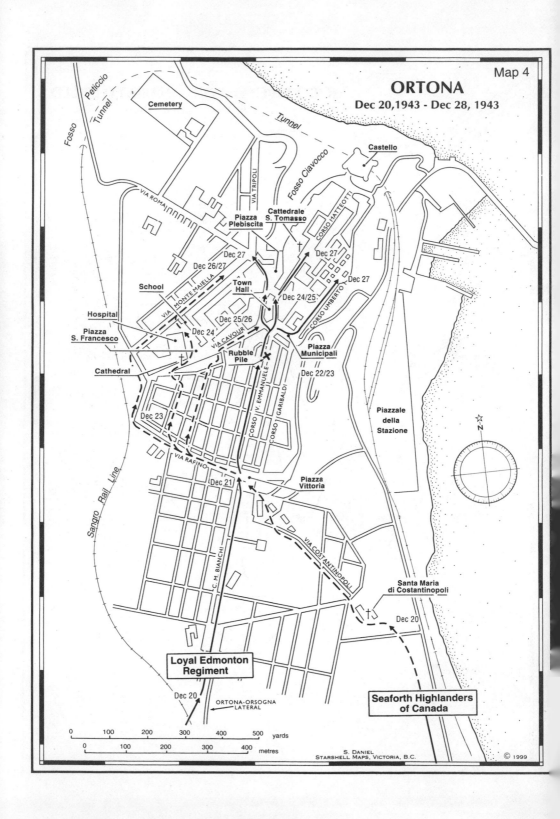

Map 4

**ORTONA**
Dec 20, 1943 - Dec 28, 1943

Cemetery

Castello

Fosso Peticcio Tunnel

Tunnel

Fosso

VIA ROMA

VIA TRIPOLI

Fosso Ciavocco

CORSO MATTEOTTI

Piazza Plebiscita

Cattedrale S. Tomasso

Dec 27

Dec 27

Dec 26/27

School

VIA MONTE MAIELLA

Town Hall

Dec 24/25

Dec 27

Dec 27

Hospital

Dec 24

Dec 25/26

VIA CAVOUR

CORSO UMBERTO

Piazza S. Francesco

Rubble Pile

Piazza Municipali

Cathedral

Dec 22/23

CORSO V. EMMANUELE

CORSO GARIBALDI

Dec 23

Piazzale della Stazione

N

VIA RAFINO

Dec 21

Piazza Vittoria

C. M. BIANCHI

VIA COSTANTINOPOLI

Sangro Rail Line

Santa Maria di Costantinopoli

Dec 20

**Loyal Edmonton Regiment**

Dec 20

ORTONA-ORSOGNA LATERAL

**Seaforth Highlanders of Canada**

0    100    200    300    400    500    yards

0    100    200    300    400    metres

S. DANIEL
STARSHELL MAPS, VICTORIA, B.C.

© 1999

# INTRODUCTION

# THE WAY
## TO ORTONA

WHEN Canada declared war against Germany on September 10, 1939, the nation had a professional army numbering 4,500 and a partially trained militia of only 46,000. By October, 70,000 Canadians wore soldier's khaki. In December, 15,911 sailed for Britain as part of the 1st Canadian Division. Poland had fallen. A spring invasion of France by Germany was certain. Britain was at risk.

For the next three and a half years the Canadian army in Britain grew ever larger — reaching 500,000 by 1942. The soldiers trained and they waited. Meanwhile Canadians fought in two major battles, each ending disastrously. On December 25, 1941, Hong Kong was surrendered to Japan. Two Canadian battalions were among the vanquished defenders — 290 dead, 493 wounded, 1,184 sent to slave labour camps. Then came Dieppe on August 19, 1942. The Canadian debate over this battle's purpose and execution will never cease. In a single dreadful day, 907 died, 1,946 surrendered, and a nation was left with a legacy of shame and glory.

All this time 1st Canadian Division waited. The soldiers joked that theirs was the only military formation in history whose birthrate was higher than its deathrate. Many a soldier had come to Britain at twenty and was now a father at twenty-four. Then the waiting and the fun abruptly ended.

The delay in committing Canadian divisions to battle resulted from Ottawa's initial desire to keep its volunteer army together. But as the war dragged on, popular opinion at home called for Canadian troops to fight. Where mattered little, so long as it was sooner rather than later. The decision was made to split the army. The 1,851 officers and 24,835 enlisted men of the newly redesignated 1st Canadian Infantry Division and the 1st Canadian Army Tank Brigade were sent to the Eighth Army, commanded by General Sir Bernard Law Montgomery. Along with the U.S. Fifth Army, the Eighth Army was to invade what British Prime Minister Winston Churchill called Europe's soft underbelly. Sicily first, Italy second, then through the back door into Austria, and perhaps right into Germany. That was the plan at its most optimistic. At the least, it was hoped, they would knock fascist Italy out of the war and divert thousands of German troops from the Russian front and France's Atlantic coast. Already the massive buildup for an invasion across the English Channel was underway; a 1944 invasion of France was inevitable.

Most of the 26,000-strong Canadian contingent waded ashore in Sicily on July 10, 1943. In thirty-eight days the island fell. Canadians marched 120 miles, fought several small, fierce engagements, and took 2,310 casualties. Of these 562 died. The nation now had the bloody battle honours it had sought.

When on September 3 the Allies invaded Italy, Canadian troops were in the Eighth Army vanguard. The Italian army was in tatters after suffering massive losses in Africa and Sicily, so offered little opposition. On September 8 Italy surrendered, but German divisions quickly advanced and engaged the invading Allied forces. Through the fall of 1943, the Eighth Army fought its way up Italy's eastern coastline, while the American Fifth Army followed the western coast. Between the two armies stood the Apennine Mountains. Every dusty mile had to be hard won.

December 1943 brought the Canadians to the southern bank of the Moro River. Beyond lay the coastal town of Ortona. In Sicily the Canadians had been blooded, on the march up Italy's boot they had become veterans of the long campaign. During the entire month of December, the Canadians in Italy would endure one of the most bitter battles in the nation's history. This is their story.

# ONE

## MARCH TO THE MORO

# 1

## A Colossal Crack

RIDICULOUS that a piece of paper should leave him feeling so uneasy. Lieutenant Jerry Richards knew this, but the unease remained, forming a lump in his gut. November 25, 1943, and the weather was growing ever colder and wetter in the Apennine foothills where most of the 1st Canadian Infantry Division was assembled in and around the medieval town of Campobasso.

The twenty-one-year-old lieutenant commanding the three-inch mortar platoon of the Princess Patricia's Canadian Light Infantry Battalion thought the weather would prove no friend to soldiers on Italy's narrow Adriatic coastal plain. Yet the warning order accompanying the rather unusual Order of the Day from Eighth Army commander General Bernard Law Montgomery directed the Canadians to prepare to embark by convoy down the rough tracks running from the mountains to the coast. The divisional move would bring the Canadian infantry division, its supporting artillery regiments, and what was now known as the 1st Canadian Armoured Brigade together south of the Sangro River for what promised to be the first major battle fought by a combined force of all Canadian units in Italy.

Richards figured this battle would prove more bitter than those seen since the invasion of Sicily five months earlier. The promised soft underbelly was proving instead to be a pelvis of steel.[1]

Yet Monty appeared to have no doubts that the Germans were almost done. His Order of the Day promised that the Eighth Army would support the American Fifth Army's efforts to take Rome via an offensive up the western flank of Italy. The Eighth Army, he said, would do its "part in a manner worthy of the best traditions of the Eighth Army and the Desert Air Force. . . . The enemy has been out-fought by better troops ever since we first landed in Sicily, and his men don't like what they are getting. The Germans are in fact in the very condition in which we want them. WE WILL NOW HIT THE GERMANS A COLOSSAL CRACK."[2] Rather than infusing him with patriotic fervour, the blustery rhetoric of Monty's Order of the Day depressed Richards. It seemed a strange conceit to the young soldier to broadcast intentions so openly as to cast aside all element of surprise. With every soldier in the Eighth Army hearing the order read aloud by his commander there was scant hope German intelligence would remain in the dark for long about Montgomery's intentions.

The "colossal crack" was meant to shatter the Bernhard Line stretching across Italy's waist from the east coast to the central Apennines, where it linked up with the Gustav Line extending to the Tyrrhenian Sea. Both the Gustav and Bernhard lines were part of the vital defensive network the Allies had dubbed the Winter Line. If either one was breached by Allied forces, a road leading to the capture of Rome could be opened. The Gustav and Bernhard lines were each heavily fortified and designed to be defended in depth by German Generalfeldmarschall Albert Kesselring's Tenth Army.

It was clear that this time the Germans were determined to put up a fierce defence rather than slip away soon after, or even before, battle was seriously joined. The German strategy had so far been to conduct a slow, carefully controlled withdrawal up Italy's boot. Utilizing the defensive characteristics of the rugged terrain to their limit, Kesselring's divisions would dig into fortified positions. To break through whichever German line they faced at the particular moment, the Allies had to fully deploy their forces and prepare a major offensive operation. When the assault went in, the Germans would usually hold for only a very brief time before retreating in good order to a new well-prepared defensive line. This strategy slowed the Allied advance to a crawl. It also ensured that German casualties and loss of precious war matériel remained tolerably low. The opposite was true for the Allied forces. Losses absorbed were always out of proportion to the ground gained and the casualties inflicted on the defender. Kesselring had drawn the Fifth and Eighth armies into a costly war of attrition which he and his divisions fought exceedingly well.

For the past few months, Richards all too often had witnessed the costs the German strategy exacted on the Eighth Army. Only the month before, his mortar platoon had been advancing in its trucks toward a village called Cercemaggiore not too far south of Campobasso, where a small action was underway at an intersection of Highway 17 dubbed Decorata Crossroads. Richards's truck was leading the platoon convoy of six vehicles, each loaded with the five men of a mortar section and their weapon. His truck was a leftover from the African campaign, its roof cut off to keep the cab cooler. Richards was fearfully worried because his driver drove like a man possessed. The truck hurtled down the narrow dusty track past columns of marching infantry also using the road to reach the fight. Any second, Richards was sure, the truck would hit one of these soldiers or career out of control into the ditch. After unsuccessfully ordering the driver to slow down several times, Richards realized the truck's lower gearing barely worked and the brakes weren't very good either. He was just absorbing this information when there was a deep crumping sound and he suddenly soared upward.

He came to in the ditch alongside the road, unsure how long he had been unconscious. Blood ran down his face from a scalp wound and, fingering it, he realized he must have landed in the ditch directly on his head. His helmet had probably saved his life. Staggering out of the ditch, disoriented, with no idea where he was, Richards wandered about for several moments on the road until some of his men ran up from the following trucks and hurriedly bandaged his head. By the time they finished, Richards had become aware of his surroundings and saw the truck nearby, its badly twisted front end standing directly over the crater left by a German land mine. Richards staggered shakily over to the truck and saw the unconscious driver still behind the wheel. His legs were torn off above the knee, both stumps spurting blood into a rapidly growing pool on the cab's torn floor. Richards crawled into the wreckage and hastily put a tourniquet on each stump to keep the man from bleeding to death. Then he and the other soldiers carefully loaded the driver into a jeep along with the other troops who had been in the back of the truck and suffered broken legs when the blast threw them to the ground.

After a long delay when the jeep driver got lost and nearly strayed into what Richards believed was the German lines, they reached a field dressing station. By this time Richards thought the wounded driver looked like hell. The medical team went to work, putting him on intravenous fluid drips and rebandaging the stumps, but there was little else they could do. Blood loss and traumatic shock rendered the outcome inevitable. Richards stood beside the wounded soldier for the fifteen to twenty minutes it took him to die. Dispirited and still woozy from his scalp wound, Richards then lay down on a stretcher beside the body of his driver and fell into a troubled sleep.

The driver's death seemed typical of the insanity of war in which Richards and the other Canadians of 1st Infantry Division found themselves. Yet it was a war to which most of the soldiers seemed addicted, driven by a sense of duty to their regiments and responsibility to their comrades. Two days after his wounding and the driver's death, the young lieutenant was resting outside the field hospital when he saw a truck from the Princess Patricia's Canadian Light Infantry driving by. Richards ran over and asked the driver, "What's happening up there? Are we in action?" The driver nodded his head. Richards told him to wait, ran into the hospital, and told the chief medical officer he was leaving. "You can't do that," the doctor said. Richards replied, "Well, they need me up in battalion. My platoon's already short-handed. I can't lie around here when I'm not badly hurt." His head wrapped in a large khaki bandage that looked like a turban, Richards grabbed the little gear he had, jumped into the cab of the truck, and raced back to war.

In fact, Richards seemed to have been racing toward war ever since the Canadian declaration on September 10, 1939. The then seventeen-year-old had been working part-time at the *Calgary Herald* as a cub reporter and completing a trigonometry course to finish his high school education. On September 1, he and the other reporters had logged hours of overtime issuing an extra edition of the paper devoted to coverage of Germany's invasion of Poland. Nine days later, they repeated the effort with an edition on the nation's declaration of war. Full of indignation about what Adolf Hitler was doing in Poland and lured by the excitement war promised, Richards decided the day after the declaration to enlist in the local militia regiment, the Calgary Highlanders. Lying about his age, he was accepted as a private. Within a year, Richards was in Britain and had been promoted to the rank of sergeant. He then passed an officer's qualification test, was shipped back to Canada in the early days of the Battle of the Atlantic for training, and returned to Britain with the rank of second lieutenant in February 1943.

As the Calgary Highlanders had a surplus of lieutenants, Richards found himself languishing in a replacement depot waiting for a spot in his regiment to open when a call was issued for volunteers to transfer to 1st Canadian Infantry Division. In the words of the colonel issuing the call, this division was "expecting some wastage." Richards, fully aware that "wastage" was an inelegant euphemism for battle casualties, volunteered along with many of the other officers in the replacement depot. Days later, he and a platoon of infantry reinforcements under his command were en route in the invasion fleet sailing for Sicily. Richards now wore the unit insignia of the Princess Patricia's Canadian Light Infantry, one of three regiments designated as battalions in the division's 2nd Canadian Infantry Brigade.

Still a replacement, Richards missed the July 10, 1943, amphibious invasion of Sicily and remained in reserve until the battle for Sicily was almost won. By early August, there had been sufficient wastage for him to be called to the regiment. He joined the PPCLI's line units at Mount Seggio, in the foothills of Mount Etna, where he took command of a rifle platoon. By then the fighting for Sicily was largely ended and Richards's contribution to the victory was to lead one uneventful patrol up the slopes of the massive volcanic mountain.

Richards also missed the initial fighting in the invasion of Italy when he was first designated Left Out of Battle — a precautionary measure that saw a small number of officers, non-commissioned officers, and lesser ranks for each line unit held in the rear. In the event that the regiment was wiped out, the LOB troops would form a core nucleus around which the regiment could be rebuilt. Being LOB put

Richards in the vicinity of battalion headquarters, where the battalion commander assigned him to brigade headquarters as the battalion liaison officer.

For most of the initial advance up Italy's boot, Richards spent his time as a glorified errand boy, riding a motorcycle from one place to another to bring back information to the brigade command about what was transpiring at the front. Although it was dangerous work, the main threat to life and limb was posed by Canadian tanks and trucks competing with him for a place on the dirt tracks that passed for roads in southern Italy. Richards hated the duty, longing to rejoin the battalion and be a line soldier again. He also intensely disliked the brigade's commander, Brigadier Chris Vokes. Richards thought the big, red-haired man a pompous bully. He also didn't care for Vokes's apparent imitation of Montgomery, right down to carrying a fly whisk and speaking in an affected British accent.

Finally Richards obtained permission from the battalion commander to switch back to a rifle platoon if he could find his own replacement. He approached his best friend, who had taken some staff training courses. "You'll live a lot longer at brigade HQ than you'll ever do commanding a rifle platoon," Richards said. "Why don't you put your knowledge to work and switch with me?" His friend, who admitted to having seen quite enough combat, agreed.[3] Richards returned to the regiment and to commanding a rifle platoon but was soon switched to command of the mortar platoon when its officer fell sick. Since then, Richards had seen enough war close up to lose his taste for the excitement it provided. He was now solely concerned with fulfilling his responsibility to support the rifle platoons with fire from his six mortars and with doing his best to keep the men of his platoon alive.

These sometimes contradictory responsibilities plagued his thoughts as he issued the orders that set his mortar platoon troops to work preparing their gear and weapons for the impending move to the Sangro River. Every detail was vitally important and he carefully oversaw the soldiers as they cleaned the mortars, loaded the ammunition, and organized their personal battle kits and gear. Throughout the battalions, Richards knew, many other lieutenants issued similar orders and thousands of young Canadians from every part of the nation and every walk of life readied the division for a march toward battle. The order to move had not yet come, but when it did the troops would be ready. All that remained was for the British 78th Division, the 2nd New Zealand Division, and the 8th Indian Division to put in the main attack against the Sangro River defences and set Monty's "colossal crack" into operation.

◆ ◆ ◆

The Eighth Army offensive against the Bernhard Line was to be the first part of the kind of one-two attack favoured during the African campaign by British Field Marshal Herold Alexander, Deputy Supreme Commander, Mediterranean. The plan called for Montgomery's Eighth Army to push boldly over the four-hundred-yard-wide Sangro River, cross the mile-wide flat plain on the other side, and seize the low northern ridge overlooking the valley. Once control of the Sangro was achieved, the Commonwealth troops would advance briskly against a disorganized enemy to break into the wide valley that extended inland from Pescara on the coast through the Apennines to Avezanno, fifty miles east of Rome.

It was Alexander's strong belief that when the Eighth Army seized Pescara and broke westward to Avezanno, the Germans would have to shift divisions positioned along the Gustav Line facing the American Fifth Army in order to halt Montgomery's advance on Rome. With the line fronting the Fifth Army weakened, American General Mark Clark would be able to punch through the Gustav Line at Cassino and link up with a planned amphibious invasion behind the German lines at Anzio, just twenty miles southwest of Rome. Once the Americans had closed upon the city's outskirts, its surrender would be inevitable. Clark's part of the plan was designated Operation Raincoat. Its success depended almost entirely on whether Montgomery could not only capture Pescara but also advance up the valley to Avezanno before Christmas Day.

Outwardly both Clark and Montgomery, who privately despised each other, exuded nothing but supreme confidence in their ability to pull off their respective tasks. Clark blithely told Alexander, "Oh, don't worry. I'll get through the Winter Line all right and push the Germans out."[4] For his part, although promising a "colossal crack," Montgomery worried that Lieutenant General Charles Allfrey, whose V Corps divisions would bear the brunt of the Eighth Army's offensive, was the least capable of his corps commanders. Allfrey, Montgomery thought, was overly inclined to fiddle with details and demonstrably lacking in boldness. He was also increasingly anxious about the deteriorating weather. "I *must have* fine weather," Montgomery wrote. "If it rains continuously I am done."[5]

Worries aside, the generals manoeuvred their armies into position and began to unleash them against the Germans. Montgomery's first step was to initiate a diversion on the upper reaches of the Sangro River to draw German forces into the Apennine foothills and away from his planned main thrust near the river's mouth. Involved in the diversionary actions were the British 5th Infantry Division, elements of the 8th Indian Division, and the three battalions of the 3rd Canadian Infantry Brigade: the West Nova Scotia Regiment, the Carleton and York Regiment, and the Royal 22e Regiment — the French-Canadian regiment more commonly known as the Van Doos.

By November 25, when Montgomery issued his "colossal crack" Order of the Day, it was unclear whether the diversions had succeeded in luring German forces away from the river's mouth. Intelligence reports on the success of these diversions remained contradictory, but there was no option except for Montgomery to plunge ahead with the main offensive. On November 28, the Eighth Army's V Corps offensive centred on the advance of three divisions, the British 78th Division, 8th Indian Division, and 2nd New Zealand Division, supported by the British 4th Armoured Brigade. Their attack was preceded by a massive artillery barrage. Initial success put the divisions across the Sangro, advancing aggressively toward the ridgeline beyond. Montgomery boasted, "My troops have won the battle as they always do. The road to Rome is open."[6] Even as Montgomery spoke, the offensive was losing its impetus in the face of stiff counter attacks launched by a battle group composed of the 26th Panzer Division and the 90th Panzer Grenadier Division, which Kesselring had hurriedly shifted from the west to the Sangro River. Although the combined German armoured and infantry counterattacks failed to force back the Allied advance, they succeeded in blunting it, transforming the battle into a bloody punching match between two fairly evenly matched opponents.

The Germans grudgingly gave ground to the V Corps divisions, withdrawing toward the Moro River, about seven miles north of the

Sangro. Here, German engineers were busily constructing fortified positions on the northern ridge that overlooked the narrow river valley. In the distance, approximately three miles up the coast from the Moro's mouth, the small Adriatic port town of Ortona was visible. By December 4, the Germans were firmly entrenched on the northern ridge of the Moro valley while the British 78th Division held most of the southern ridge. But the British division desperately needed relief. Since the invasion of Sicily, the 78th had suffered more than 10,000 casualties, more than 4,000 incurred in the advance across the Sangro. The division was so whittled down by casualties to front-line troops that it was no longer combat effective.[7]

In anticipation of the need for the 78th to be relieved at some point in the Sangro River battle, Montgomery had issued orders on November 25 for the 1st Canadian Infantry Division to prepare for a move from the Campobasso area to the 78th's rear. That move started late on December 1, with the Princess Patricia's Canadian Light Infantry, Seaforth Highlanders of Canada, and Loyal Edmonton regiments of the 2nd Canadian Infantry Brigade in the vanguard.

Just over two months before, 2 CIB had undergone a major change in command when Vokes was promoted from brigadier to major general and assumed command of 1st Canadian Infantry Division. His promotion came after Major General Guy Granville Simonds, divisional commander since the preparation for the Sicily invasion, was confined to quarters on September 20 with a severe case of jaundice. On the 27th, Simonds was evacuated to a British casualty clearing station and Vokes took over his job.

The same day, 2nd Canadian Infantry Brigade held a sports day in the Italian town of Potenza, where it was enjoying a rest and recuperation posting. Lieutenant Colonel Bert Hoffmeister, then a twenty-six-year-old commanding the Seaforths, was sitting in the roughly constructed stands overlooking the sports field when he spotted a divisional runner approaching Vokes in another section of the stands. About three minutes later, a liaison officer tapped Hoffmeister on the shoulder and said, "The Brigadier wants to see you." Hoffmeister walked over to sit next to Vokes. Without preliminary, Vokes informed him, "As of now, you're commanding 2nd CIB. I'm going to take command of 1st Canadian Division. . . . Good luck to you."[8] Hoffmeister said he would let Major Doug Forin know that he now had command of the Seaforths and would meet Vokes within the hour at divisional headquarters.

Despite Vokes's rough exterior and unsophisticated manner, Hoffmeister considered the man a competent commander. He also genuinely liked the veteran soldier whom many considered a disagreeable and coarse bully. The two had worked well together within 2 CIB, and Hoffmeister had no doubt that both he and Vokes were up to handling their new jobs.

The question of Hoffmeister's competency was undisputed in the ranks of 1st Canadian Infantry Division. Soldiering ran in his blood. The Hoffmeister family had been military for generations. The man the soldiers of the Seaforth regiment affectionately nicknamed "Hoffy" had joined the regiment as a cadet in Vancouver when he was only eleven years old. By the time he was sixteen, Hoffmeister was cadet commander. In 1937 he became a commander in the regular regiment. In October 1942, following a staff training course, Hoffmeister had been promoted to lieutenant colonel and had assumed command of the Seaforths. In Sicily, and during the early months of the Italian campaign, Hoffmeister had proven himself to be a top-notch battalion commander and a fearless leader.[9] Major Thomas de Faye, who commanded the Saskatoon Light Infantry company that provided heavy weapons support to 2 CIB, thought Hoffmeister undoubtedly the most talented battalion commander in the Canadian army. Within days of Hoffmeister's assuming command of the brigade, de Faye thought him the army's best brigade commander as well. "Not only a very brave soldier, but also a compassionate man," de Faye said of him.[10]

The major was less impressed with Vokes, whom he had worked alongside when the red-haired brigadier had commanded 2 CIB. Adequate, de Faye commented: "A tough old bird, great boxer, tall, wide, and built like a bulldog, which also summed up his personality perfectly." Before the war, Vokes had served as district engineer officer of Military District No. 3 at Kingston and had been in charge of building Dundurn Military Camp with relief camp labour. Faced with a hostile labour force, Vokes had gained their respect and cooperation by offering to take any of the unemployed young men out behind the barracks for a boxing match. None took him up on the offer. Merely an adequate leader Vokes might be, but de Faye respected the man's courage and figured that guts was what it took to lead soldiers effectively during war.[11]

Although de Faye and some other officers in the division were not overly confident in Vokes's command ability, he was generally well regarded by the troops. Twenty-six-year-old Private Elwyn R. Springsteel, serving in No. 18 Platoon of the Loyal Edmonton's 'D' Company, was always glad when Vokes came up to visit upon the regiment one of his short, sharp speeches. Most of the time when Vokes arrived Springsteel and the other men would be paraded in full kit with packs on their backs, rifles strapped over their shoulders, helmets on their heads. Vokes would always immediately order the men to sit down and take off the tin hats. "I want to be able to really see you," he would say as the men settled comfortably before him.[12]

Lieutenant Don Smith of 'B' Company, Carleton and York Regiment, shared de Faye's contention that Vokes was merely competent as divisional commander, but he also found the major general's habit of imitating Montgomery irritating, especially the way Vokes insisted on swishing around his horsetail swagger stick. When he dropped in to visit the troops, he would always tell the officers to have the men "gather round the jeep" in an affected accent that sounded much like Monty, crisp and haughty. Usually he called such sessions immediately prior to the troops' going into battle and would end his brief address with the same words — "Go in there and kick 'em in the crotch." It was a line the men loved.[13]

Regardless of their opinion of Vokes, officers and men alike were glad that he was a Canadian — even if he did affect British mannerisms. Loyal Edmonton Lieutenant John Dougan, a platoon commander in the same company as Private Springsteel, had first seen Vokes when the regiment was going into an attack in Sicily. Vokes was standing on the side of the road talking to the men as they passed, giving them encouragement. Later the twenty-two-year-old officer realized that Vokes might not be the best divisional commander ever, but he and most of the men he knew would rather have an average Canadian commander than the best commander the British could offer. Dougan was proud to serve in an all-Canadian division where all the senior officers were also Canadians, which was not the case in World War I. He thought that most of the other young line officers and the troops they commanded felt the same. Not a soldier in the division, Dougan believed, would put up with any sharp criticism of those officers' abilities — particularly from anyone not asked to risk their lives in response to their command.[14]

Dougan and every other officer in 1st Canadian Infantry Division knew Vokes now faced his most difficult command challenge to date. Becoming divisional commander had come as something of a shock to Vokes, who was only second senior officer at the time. Brigadier Howard Penhale, commander of the 3rd Canadian Infantry Brigade, was senior to him. By tradition, when Simonds was relieved, divisional command should have fallen upon Penhale. Overweight, and a veteran of World War I, Penhale lacked Vokes's inarguable command presence, but that seemed insufficient reason for Vokes to be promoted over him. Vokes never learned why command fell his way. But shortly after his appointment to major general was confirmed as a permanent promotion in November, Vokes quietly shuffled Penhale out of the division. He gave Penhale's command to Brigadier Graeme Gibson, just transferred from England to Italy. He told the new brigadier it was his job to turn around what he considered the worst-run brigade in the division.[15]

Vokes's first major challenge was to quickly move the whole division about fifty miles from the Campobasso area to a rallying point at Termoli, and then another twenty miles up the coast to the south of the Sangro River's mouth. Given the dreadful condition of the roads in the region, it was a daunting task. During the first four days of December, 1st Canadian Infantry Division was to complete the move in its entirety. This included pulling the 3rd Canadian Infantry Brigade out of front-line positions in the upper Sangro River region near the base of the Apennines. Approximately 15,000 soldiers travelling in hundreds of vehicles started the difficult process at 0700 hours when 1st Canadian Infantry Brigade climbed into their vehicles and set off under a clear cold sky to pass through Campobasso and descend to the coast.

By early afternoon, 2 CIB had begun jockeying to crossroads and finding the snaking road that led from the mountains to Termoli plugged with 1 CIB and its supporting artillery vehicles. Formed up in a column in the twisted streets of the village of Busso, the PPCLI stared out at a seemingly endless line of vehicles rumbling past on the main road. At 1500 hours the road was still clogged with a solid traffic jam and the regiment's officers started muttering among themselves, wondering how in hell they would be able to cross the assigned start point as scheduled at 1530 hours. To their amazement, precisely as the minute hands of their watches ticked to the appointed moment of departure, the roads suddenly cleared and "the unit rolled on to the road dead on time."[16] So it went for all the battalions of the two brigades moving out of the Campobasso region that day.

Although the descent from the mountains to the coast proceeded in orderly fashion, this proved not to be the case once the division exited the mountain road at Termoli and entered Highway 16 — the coastal highway that provided virtually the sole supply and transportation route for the entire Eighth Army. Here they joined the long, winding column of vehicles from various divisions all advancing toward the Sangro River at about the pace of an ox cart. Quartermaster Sergeant Basil Smith of the Hastings and Prince Edward Regiment of 1 CIB had been happily enjoying the views as the column approached the coastal highway. No sooner had they managed to slip into the north-ward-moving stream of traffic, however, than a gale whipped up off the Adriatic and lashed the column with freezing rain. Smith scribbled in his diary: "The roads are damnably slippery, bridges are washed out up ahead and there is mile upon mile of transport, going both ways, lined up bumper to tailgate, this convoy is a driver's nightmare. Spent most of the night on the road, tried to grab a few winks of shut-eye but every time either Breakenridge (my driver) or myself dozed off, a limey red-cap would waken us, to proceed another fifty yards, or less. These red-caps certainly took a volume of abuse tonight, poor devils. We were at least in the cab of a truck, but they were out in the weather, trying to do a job. Finally pulled up into a field, about ten miles south of Vasto at 0200 hours of the 2nd and flopped in the seat until dawn."[17]

# 2

## WAITING, WAITING, ALWAYS BLOODY WAITING

FIRST Canadian Infantry Brigade dropped out of the column south of the Sangro in the early morning hours of December 2, while 2nd Canadian Infantry Brigade continued to lurch forward in the midst of the endless flow to a position close to the river. Here, the infantry climbed down from the back of their trucks, shouldered field packs and weapons, and marched to footbridges slung by the engineering crews across the Sangro. With the vehicles all jammed before the single pontoon bridge the British had got over the river, the infantry would make better time on foot and the battalions of the British 78th Division were up ahead waiting to be relieved. With few complaints, the men accepted the march forward in the rain with a stoicism born of months of forced marches up and down the rugged terrain of southern Italy. Vokes described the march of his soldiers as "a shuffle and the only resemblance to marching was that they shuffled along in step. It ate up the miles with the least expenditure of energy. It was almost as if each soldier were praying: 'Lord, you pick 'em up and I'll lay 'em down.' Soldiers on campaign are always tired."[1]

The infantry would have said none were more tired than themselves. While the gunners of the artillery regiments, the tankers of the armoured regiments, the engineers, and the many soldiers who constituted the Royal Canadian Army Service corps moved forward with an array of motorized transport, the infantry line units walked as often as they rode. They walked the sharp end at the front of this long, winding column, and they carried the weapons that an infantry company required to fight the enemy up close. The commanders might define war in terms of corps, divisional, brigade, and battalion manoeuvres, but for the infantryman, survival rested on his mates in the platoon and, above that, in the company. On paper, thirty-five men and one officer to a platoon. The reality since Sicily was that most platoons numbered barely twenty due to losses caused by illness, and the killed and wounded who had not yet been replaced. Reinforcements arrived in a continuous trickle that was never sufficient to bring the ranks to full strength.

The infantryman's primary weapon differed little from that his father might have carried in the trenches at Ypres, on the Somme, before Vimy, or during the slaughter of Passchendaele: Lee Enfield Rifle, No. 4, Mark 1. The fastest-operating bolt-action rifle in the world, which, in the hands of a trained soldier, could pump out ten rounds of .303 ammunition a minute loaded into the gun in box magazines. Weighing 9.06 pounds empty, the rifle was simply a slightly updated version of the same weapon that had been standard equipment for British and Commonwealth troops since its introduction on November 11, 1895.[2]

Unlike his father, a Canadian soldier in 1943 might also carry a Thompson submachine gun or a Bren light machine gun. Every platoon had at least one two-man crew armed with a Bren. With an empty weight of 22.38 pounds, this air-cooled, gas-operated gun was considered one of the most reliable and finest light machine guns made during the war, far superior to the American Browning M1919A6 (commonly known as the BAR) and a match for those carried by the Germans. The normal rate of fire from the Bren's thirty-round distinctively curved magazine was five bursts of four or five rounds a minute. It was generally fired from a prone position with the barrel resting on a bipod, the gun tucked into the firing man's shoulder, the assistant crouching nearby to provide fresh clips as the one in use emptied. A good firing team could put out 150 rounds a minute in measured bursts or 500 on full automatic.[3]

Officers and troops alike were fond of the Thompson submachine gun, especially for close-up fighting where its short firing range was irrelevant. The troops of the Eighth Army considered the Thompson about the only weapon the Americans designed and manufactured that was worth the money paid. Its only drawbacks were that it was a heavy clunker, weighing 10.62 pounds empty, and that it fired .45-calibre ammunition, whereas the Lee Enfield and Bren both conveniently shared the same ammunition. Because its ammunition was, however, heavier than just about any other used on the battlefield, the Thompson proved devastating when its bullets hit a target. An enemy soldier struck by a .45 slug from a Thompson usually went down and stayed down, either dead, dying, or badly wounded.[4]

When the Canadians had been preparing to deploy to Sicily, they had been provided with some 9-millimetre Sten submachine guns, a British-designed weapon that was stamped out like metal cookies from a cutter. Inexpensive to make and popular with the commandos and European underground, the gun was held in disdain by the Canadians and generally ditched as quickly as possible. All too often its primitive safety switch came off and the gun accidentally discharged, causing friendly casualties. By the time the Canadians reached the Sangro River, hardly any Stens were in use by front-line units.

The other weapon the infantry carried was the Type 36 grenade. Its segmented metal exterior was thought by the soldiers to resemble a pineapple, so it became known as the pineapple grenade or simply a pineapple. Filled with high explosive that, upon exploding, turned the metal exterior casing into about eighty pieces of deadly shrapnel, the 36 was effective to the range a man could pitch it in an overhand throw. Once the fuse was activated, however, there was no deactivating it and the weapon was dangerous to thrower and immediate comrades alike if improperly used. Some soldiers hated and avoided grenades. Others, such as Seaforth Highlander Private Harry Rankin, loved them. Rankin loaded up all the grenades he could carry, used them whenever possible, and even kept notes in his pay book setting out the safe times that a grenade with each fuse length could be held and still be thrown out a safe distance.[5]

In addition to these weapons and their ammunition, each rifleman carried a bayonet, water canteen, some emergency rations, perhaps some extra socks, and a few personal effects, as well as a bandage for dressing a wound. It was not uncommon for a soldier's canvas pack to hold one hundred pounds of gear. In a haversack across his shoulder was also an anti-gas respirator that he hoped never to use. Two pouches attached to combat webbing held numerous five-round clips for the rifle, extra loose .303 cartridges, and normally a couple of thirty-round .303 magazines for the Bren gun. Secured on the webbing and stuffed into pouches would be a varying number of grenades based as much on personal preference as any standard requirement.

An infantry division's fighting strength depended on the number of riflemen fit for duty in the rifle companies. Seldom did this strength exceed what the army called light scale. Light scale dictated a company strength of 110, battalion strength of 440, and a total strength of 3,960 in a division's nine infantry battalions. These were the troops who went head to head against the enemy infantry. Bren carrier, mortar, and antitank platoons were left out of these calculations because they were seldom in the immediate front line. To keep each rifleman properly equipped, supplied, and medically cared for required almost a three-to-one-ratio of divisional support personnel for every front-line soldier.

Increasing the firepower of the infantry were support companies with various types of mortars; the artillery regiments with their twenty-five-pounder guns; the antitank units equipped with six-pound and seventeen-pound antitank guns; the reconnaissance regiment with its armoured cars; and the armoured regiments with their Sherman M-4 tanks. But always it was the infantry that had to go forward and root the enemy out of their holes, clear the buildings, sweep the dense stands of trees. The infantry led, and it was the infantry who most often bled and died.

◆ ◆ ◆

As the infantry trudged once more on foot toward new positions immediately behind the 78th Division, their transport and support vehicles continued to jockey across the Sangro. It took six hours of waiting and lurching yard by yard for the PPCLI's transport to finally get over the bridge. The trucks linked up with the infantry near the small hamlet of Fossacesia. And there, as was so often the case in the army, the soldiers were told to wait. Soon they learned that the fighting south of the Moro River was not yet concluded. The 78th was still trying to shove the Germans out of San Vito Chietino, a town just south of the Moro valley. Word came back that the 78th would not hand over the front to the Canadians until it had bloody well thrown the last German over the other side of the river. Few complaints about this turn of events were heard among the ranks. Nobody was that anxious to start mixing it up with *Tedeschi*, the Italian word for German, which the Eighth Army had quickly adopted as its favoured slang for the enemy.

Everywhere the Canadians looked they found innumerable signs of how bitter the battle for the Sangro had been. Loyal Edmonton Regiment platoon scout commander Lieutenant Alon Johnson, waiting his turn to cross the bridge, sat in his jeep and surveyed the detritus of war about him. Utility poles were down or tilted erratically and trailed wires, burned-out hulks of German tanks and antitank guns stood in the fields, shell craters were everywhere, dead horses and mules lay swelling on the roadsides. A British officer from one of the line units that were starting to trickle past stopped to chat with Johnson. "You must have had quite a battle here," Johnson said. The officer paused, looked reflective for a moment. "Yes, a bit of a do," he replied drolly and proceeded on to the rear.[6]

Dawn found many Canadian units still trying to get over the Sangro bridge. And with the dawn came sporadic German artillery shelling of the bridgehead. Shells thumped down on either side of the bridge, sending up geysers of water, and erupted on and around the road. As shrapnel sang through the air, men piled out of helplessly jammed trucks, Bren carriers, and jeeps to scramble into the dubious shelter of the ditch. When a barrage lifted, any vehicles damaged too badly to continue moving were pushed into the ditch to allow the rest of the column to advance.

Major de Faye and his Saskatoon Light Infantry troops were stuck in the column just before the bridge at about midday. He thought the bridge a bloody poor effort, a sagging pontoon construction that seemed on the point of washing out. Only two vehicles could cross at a time, explaining what the Canadians were finding to be the worst traffic jam of the war. The major's SLI unit was a mini-battalion of about 500 men divided into three companies. One company was composed of three platoons, each equipped with four medium Vickers .303 machine guns and loaded into tracked, lightly armoured Bren carriers. The second company was broken into two platoons each armed with four 4.2-inch mortars mounted in fifteen-hundred-weight trucks (15 cwt.), with Bren carriers for the forward observation officers, who went up to the line with the infantry and radioed back firing coordinates for the mortars. His third company was armed with single-barrel twenty-millimetre Oerlikon anti-aircraft guns organized in four platoons with four guns each. A single gun was loaded by hand into the back of a 15-cwt. truck.

Originally, most of the men in the SLI had hailed from Saskatchewan and many from Saskatoon. But a reorganization in England prior to the Sicily invasion had boosted the numbers of the battalion and now de Faye had soldiers and officers from all parts of Canada in his unit, although the majority of the men were still from the prairie provinces.

The major was a career soldier, who had joined the SLI as a sixteen-year-old private in 1934. He had lied about his age, so he could receive the full soldier's pay that would go to a man of eighteen. When war broke out, de Faye had gathered enough Canadian Officers Training Corps courses at the University of Saskatchewan to qualify for the rank of captain and, with a shortage of officers in the rapidly expanding army, found himself promoted to this position at the age of twenty-one. He was the first to admit that the idea of a twenty-one-year-old captain was ridiculous. What he did not know about soldiering "would probably have filled every military manual ever written."[7] But he had also the supreme self-confidence of youth, as did so many of the officers in Canada's amateur and entirely volunteer army.

And now he sat in a jeep, right up next to the damned bridge. His men were jammed up behind him in their vehicles, every man undoubtedly wondering if they would get across the Sangro and away before the next German artillery salvo arrived. Traffic was completely stopped. Minutes passed, as the tension mounted. Every man in the column grew twitchier and twitchier. Next to de Faye's jeep, a British dispatch rider was parked on the verge, lying back on his motorcycle with his feet up on the handlebars. "Waiting, waiting, always bloody waiting," he sang in a clear, high voice. The soldiers in the vehicles all laughed, breaking the tension. Moments later the convoy lurched forward again. In a few minutes the bridge was crossed, the moment of immediate danger past.[8]

◆ ◆ ◆

Throughout December 2 and the early part of December 3, as the rest of 1st Canadian Infantry Division started assembling in the 78th Division's immediate rear south of the Moro River, 3rd Canadian Infantry Brigade was engaged in the more complex manoeuvre of disengaging from its front-line positions in preparation to join the rest of the division. December 2 also saw 1st Canadian Armoured Brigade begin rolling its tank battalions across the Sangro to support the upcoming Canadian advance. Everything progressed relatively smoothly throughout the Canadian forces and it appeared that the scheduled takeover of all 78th Division positions by December 4 would proceed more or less as planned.

Third CIB's West Nova Scotia Regiment had withdrawn from its forward positions on December 1. The men were able to rest for a couple of days just back of the upper Sangro River line in the village of Agnone in billets that were complete with lights, running water, and a movie theatre showing the 1930 film *Gambling on the High Seas*. Meanwhile, the Royal 22e and Carleton and York regiments were still carrying out light patrolling along the upper Sangro front, the Van Doos hearing heavy enemy transport beyond the German lines. The Carleton and York, for its part, was unable to put patrols over the Sangro due to the presence of a network of German heavy-machine-gun posts that fired on anyone, including civilians, who tried crossing the river section facing its front. By December 3, both battalions had been relieved by the British 5th Division and were moving slowly over rough terrain and in worsening weather toward the coast, as were the better rested West Novas. The brigade was scheduled to link up with the rest of the division on December 4 and to move into a reserve position, while 1st and 2nd Canadian infantry brigades assumed the front-line positions being handed over by the 78th Division.[9]

Divisional headquarters had reason to be relatively well pleased with the organization and execution of its move to and across the

Sangro River. Despite the bottleneck on Highway 16, over which the division had no control, the Canadians had swiftly and with few logistical problems manoeuvred a total strength of approximately 1,850 officers and 24,800 other ranks of the infantry division and the armoured brigade seventy-five miles over difficult terrain in four days.

On the evening of December 4, the battalions of 2 CIB began relieving the last of the 78th Division troops on the southern ridge overlooking the Moro River. PPCLI Lieutenant Jerry Richards and his mortar platoon were parked at the side of a road, the men resting as well as they could in the gathering gloom as the troops of the 6th Royal Inniskilling Fusiliers marched past. Richards fell into conversation with the battalion's padre and the two were soon, as soldiers are prone to do, swapping impressions of their commanders and eventually of Montgomery himself. Both men wondered what the hell Monty was up to, trying to carry out a major offensive when the winter weather was closing in and soon the combination of cold and mud would effectively grind their advance to a halt. Even if they got over the Moro, there were many more rivers similar to it between here and Pescara.

The padre's description of what the Inniskillings had gone through sounded more like something out of the Great War than the present one, and Richards didn't think that boded too well for the Canadians. He recounted to the padre a story of the time when Monty came to visit the Canadians in Sicily, delivering a rousing speech from the back of a captured German jeep, known as a Kubelwagen. "There is no one better than my Canadians," he had declared. Although there had been some rousing cheers in response, Richards and most of the men he overheard talking afterward doubted his sincerity. The padre laughed at the story. "That's the very same thing he said to us. There's none better than my Irish." The padre shook Richards's hand and followed his men into the darkness. Richards started loading up his men to move forward and join the infantry companies already looking out from the slit trenches left by the 78th Division toward the German positions.[10]

◆ ◆ ◆

As 1st and 2nd brigades settled into their positions on the Moro River ridge without difficulty and with virtually no opposition from the Germans on the facing ridge, the situation to their rear fell into chaos. In the early morning hours of December 4, the Sangro River swelled in mere minutes by six feet. Floodwaters swept the precarious pontoon bridge away and reduced most of the footbridges to kindling. Third CIB and some divisional support units were stranded on the southern bank.

Montgomery was desolate, his dream of a breakthrough offensive carrying the Eighth Army to Rome shredded by the weather and V Corps's initial failure to rapidly carry the advance forward to Pescara. He berated V Corps commander Charles Allfrey for having commanded the offensive amateurishly and with "a lack of 'grip' and 'bite'" that was entirely unacceptable.[11] Of the damage caused by the Sangro flooding and the increasing rainfall he wrote, "I don't think we can get any spectacular results so long as it goes on raining; the whole country becomes a sea of mud and nothing on wheels or tracks can move off the roads."[12]

Only days before, Monty had boasted that he hoped to accompany the New Zealand division into Rome. Now, he cast about for some way to transform disaster into partial success. Forcing the Germans back from the Sangro meant little. Thousands of men had perished for nothing if the Eighth Army became bogged down for the winter months before the Moro River. This was not the Great War, where it was accepted that heavy casualties could be taken for no discernible gain except some strip of devastated farmland. The olive groves and vineyards of the Sangro valley, the small towns of Lanciano and San Vito Chietino meant nothing. They were of no meaningful strategic value.

If he could not have Rome, Montgomery would create a target that was closer, easier, and still of strategic significance. Pescara would be best and it was that objective he continued to cite in all memos as his goal.[13] But he was also looking at a nearer, more easily attainable target: Ortona. Since the Eighth Army had started its long march up the boot of Italy, the problem of supply had plagued its advance. The entire Italian campaign was of secondary importance to the massive buildup taking place in Britain preparatory to the planned spring or summer invasion of northern France. This meant that vital munitions, medical equipment, vehicles, and particularly amphibious vessels were too often either unavailable or in short supply. Reinforcements were also hard to come by and had to be transported from Algeria, so all the divisions were short-handed. Added to the problem of the lack of supply was the need for every man and every tin of food and box of ammunition to be hauled over poor roads from the heel of Italy to reach the ever advancing front-line units. With each German retreat, Montgomery's supply lines grew longer and more difficult to sustain.

Southern Italy's east coast was lightly populated, the shoreline rugged and hostile. The few ports that did exist were poor and incapable of harbouring ocean-going freighters. Not so Ortona. The town was small, but aerial reconnaissance photos showed that it possessed a serviceable and adequate deepwater port backed by a rail yard. Although the Germans destroyed every inch of rail line as they retreated with a kind of plow hooked to the rear of a steam engine that left ties and steel rails ripped to pieces, Commonwealth engineers followed behind restoring the tracks as best they could. The combination of a usable port and a potential rail line from the boot of Italy to the front lines was enticing. Montgomery would, of course, prefer Pescara, prefer to have his troops facing the valley leading to Avezzano for a spring offensive toward Rome. Failing that, however, Ortona would do. And it should not be too difficult a prize to win. Crack the hastily cobbled-together Moro River defensive line, sever the Ortona-Orsogna road to deny the Germans good lines of supply from the coast to their inland divisions, push forward from the road, and Ortona should fall easily. With the Canadian division pressing in and around Ortona's outskirts, the Germans would have little option but to fall back from the town to the Arielli River about three miles north of Ortona. Even with the dreadful weather, taking Ortona should require only a minor battle.

The reconnaissance pictures showed that the Germans had already taken measures to render the port unusable without some extensive repairs. Large holes had been blown in the northern mole, rendering the port unsafe for large vessels. To ensure the port was not further damaged by Allied action, and believing Ortona would also serve well as a rear-area rest base once the front line moved north to Pescara, Eighth Army command decided to spare the town the aerial bombing, followed by heavy artillery bombardment, that would normally be rained down upon a community possessing a serviceable railroad marshalling yard and port facility. There would be little value in capturing a harbour that required months of rebuilding.

Montgomery issued orders for Ortona's capture that same day. A chastened Allfrey signalled to Vokes, "You must get over River Moro as soon as possible."[14] With all the bridges destroyed by the retreating Germans, it was necessary for the Canadians to find a site where the Royal Canadian Engineers could build a ford or bridge capable of supporting the weight of tanks. Otherwise, the infantry would have to carry out the attack without the backing of armoured units. To find a crossing point, Vokes immediately ordered the three battalions of 2 CIB and elements of the British 38th Brigade to initiate patrolling into the valley, accompanied by engineering sappers. The 38th temporarily remained under Vokes's command until a full handover of the front from the 78th Division to the Canadians could be effected. Three possible areas for crossings held promise: on the right flank, along a new coast road that was missing from the Canadians' topographical maps; on the old highway which snaked down into the valley and up the other side to enter a village named San Leonardo; and down an older dirt track about two miles upstream from San Leonardo, where a yet smaller village, Villa Rogatti, perched on the ridge.[15]

While orders went down the line from the headquarters of 2 CIB's infantry battalions to the companies and eventually to the platoons that would send out the patrols, Major de Faye deployed his Saskatoon Light Infantry support companies along the ridgeline to provide covering fire for the infantry units. Periodically the Germans tossed over some desultory artillery fire that caused little harm, but the 78th had reported that the enemy were putting patrols of their own over the river to harass the forward positions. To counter these and provide anti-aircraft protection, de Faye set up his sixteen twenty-millimetre Oerlikons in a spaced line down the length of the brigade front. Several times during the day the anti-aircraft guns hammered away, tracers spewing into the sky on a low trajectory, as a single two-engined Messerschmitt 110 fighter bomber raced in from the coast to roar up the valley and drop a handful of small bombs in its wake. Neither the anti-aircraft fire nor the bombs seemed to do much damage.

Princess Patricia's Canadian Light Infantry Lieutenant Jerry

Richards had established an observation post in an abandoned German slit trench across the Moro from Villa Rogatti. A motley collection of enemy equipment lay scattered around the position. It appeared *Tedeschi* had pulled out in a hurry. Peering through his binoculars, Richards looked over at the opposite ridge in hopes of spotting a good target for the three-inch mortars. Down on the road leading up to the enemy ridgeline, a German Mark IV tank sat, stationary and apparently unoccupied. Richards saw little point in firing at what seemed an abandoned tank. Presumably it had broken down and its crew had been forced to flee on foot.

Villa Rogatti itself was quiet, seemingly empty of life. Once he caught a fleeting image of the field-grey uniforms of a squad of Germans as they raced across an open patch of land and into the dense cover afforded by a vineyard. They moved far too quickly for the mortars to zero in on them before they were lost in the vegetation. Soon after, one of Richards's mortar crews supporting a nearby infantry company started dropping rounds on some invisible target across the river. It looked to Richards as if the crew was simply wasting ammunition, but they ceased firing before he needed to order them to do so.

Even though it was not yet dark, a section from one of the infantry platoons slithered down into the valley to the river. They drew no fire and moved along the river for some distance, obviously searching for a ford, before beginning to head back up the slope. The patrol's movement along the river had taken it to where the battalion's outer left flank joined the 8th Indian Division's lines. Suddenly from the 8th's position, a Vickers machine gun began chattering, tracers arcing down toward the Canadians who were beginning to make their way up the slope. The soldiers scrambled into a ditch near the river and flattened down, bullets spitting up dirt in front of them. Richards grabbed his runner by the shoulder and told him to get over to battalion HQ and have someone radio the 8th Division to stop firing, that the patrol was Canadian, not German. The runner set off at a sprint and a few minutes later the Vickers ceased fire.

The Canadian patrol came up over the lip of the ridge right in front of Richards's position. None of them was hurt, but every man looked badly shaken by the experience of being fired on by his own side. "If it wasn't for that ditch," the corporal said, "I don't know what we'd have done. Been goners probably." He shook his head and led the men off to his platoon position.[16]

Richards went back to observing the opposing ridgeline and the valley below. Although it was December, the landscape looked more like that of a Canadian fall than winter. In the narrow valley, where the Moro was barely visible amid a dense line of trees, scrub brush, and occasional stands of bamboo, the leaves and much of the grass had turned yellow. He could see glimpses of the Moro, a river barely more than ten feet wide and running the muddy brown that was typical of Italian streams. The vineyards and olive groves blanketing the slopes of the valley and stretching off across the plain to the north were thickly vegetated and intensely green even on a heavily overcast and often drizzly day. The plain itself was corrugated with narrow gullies sharply dividing the terraced and cultivated land into defined sections. In Villa Rogatti, the two- and three-storey buildings were of rough grey-brown stone with red or black tile roofs. Behind the village he could see a number of hamlets identified on the map as La Torre, Villa Jubatti, and Villa Caldari. Each was separated from the other by deep gullies cutting sharply back from the Moro valley. If not for the war, it would have been a pretty scene. But there was always the war, and the rugged landscape before him appeared less a sight to enjoy than an obstacle that would be hard to cross.

◆ ◆ ◆

South of the Sangro, 3 CIB faced another obstacle that was impossible to cross by normal means. The river was still in full spate and showed no indication of dropping any time soon. British engineers laboured frantically to throw an all-weather bridge across its span, but that work would take until December 6 to complete. There was no option for the Carleton and York, Royal 22e, and West Nova Scotia regiments but to bivouac on the south shore of the river and await the completion of a bridge. Meanwhile, supply of the rest of the division and the armoured brigade across the river would be carried out by a handful of DUKW amphibious trucks, called "ducks." The American-made six-wheeled, two-and-a-half-ton trucks were capable of doing six knots afloat and also of operating on roads at about the same speed as the Commonwealth's standard three-ton lorry. A flotilla of these vehicles now set about shuttling supplies across the mouth of the Sangro, as well as critical medical and other units needed on the distant shore preparatory to the beginning of the Canadian offensive scheduled for the night of December 5–6.

The divisional attack would start without 3 CIB. To keep apprised of the situation at the immediate front, brigade commander Brigadier Graeme Gibson rode a DUKW across the Sangro on the morning of December 5. He planned to spend the night organizing the forward logistics for his brigade to settle in on the proper side of the river.[17]

The morning of December 5 also saw the infantry of 2 CIB preparing for a night attack across the Moro to seize the two crossings at San Leonardo and Villa Rogatti. The previous night's patrols had determined that the crossing close to the river's mouth, where the newer coastal road was located, was too deep and wide with floodwater for an easy crossing. The Royal Canadian Engineers were confident of building a bridge only in front of San Leonardo. Vokes decided consequently that the main attack would focus on seizing San Leonardo, while a secondary attack would be put in at Villa Rogatti. San Leonardo would be taken by the Seaforth Highlanders of Canada and the PPCLI would attack Villa Rogatti. The Loyal Edmonton Regiment would be in reserve, ready to move through the lines of whichever regiment opened the best opportunity for pushing toward the Ortona-Orsogna lateral road.

At the river mouth, 1 CIB would relieve the 38th Brigade in the morning. Despite the fact that constructing a bridge at this point was considered impossible under present conditions, Vokes planned for the Canadian brigade to launch a diversionary attack across the river as soon as the relief was completed. This way the Germans across the river would be forced to defend three positions, not knowing which was the primary target of the attacking Canadians.[18]

At the Loyal Edmonton headquarters, scout platoon leader Lieutenant Alon Johnson looked across the valley to Ortona in the distance. The town looked relatively nondescript to the twenty-three-year-old officer. Johnson's eye was caught by the large dome of a Roman Catholic cathedral standing in the midst of a cluster of old buildings. The dome shone as if coated in brass.[19]

# 3

# PEARL OF THE ADRIATIC

IN the summers of the 1920s and 1930s, workers and their families had come to Ortona from the factory towns of northern Italy, from Milan, Piacenza, Reggio, and Modena. To escape the torturous heat of Rome, mid-level bureaucrats had gathered up their wives and children and caught the train that ran through the wide valley stretching from Avezanno to Pescara. In Pescara they changed trains for the brief run down the blue Adriatic coast to Ortona's station. There they disembarked and looked up to the escarpment facing the water, where the town perched. Those who minded their *lire* waited for the bus or made the thirty-minute climb up the flagstone steps that zigzagged up the steep face. The more affluent vacationers usually paid to be whisked, along with their luggage, in the gondola that ran between the train station and the esplanade, Corso Umberto I.

From the gondola, they were rewarded with a fine view of the old castle perched precariously on the edge of the cliff. They also looked back down upon the harbour with its two recurved moles, looking like crab claws. The moles, built of rock and earth, sheltered the harbour from storms and prevented the basin from filling with silt.

To the immediate south of the harbour a white sand beach stretched clear to the ridgeline where San Vito Chietino was visible on the far side of the Moro River. Inland, lush green olive orchards and vineyards blanketed the surrounding countryside, dotted by farmhouses and the small timeless hamlets of San Donato and San Leonardo, little more than a half hour's walk away along the dusty, narrow lanes.

Long abandoned, the castle's thick sandstone block walls crumbled more with each passing year. Cracked by past earthquakes and undermined by two railway tunnels leading to the port, which ran under its foundations, the castle was slowly collapsing down the cliff. It was an ancient structure, dating back at least to the 1400s. Townspeople and even a few Italian historians claimed the origins of Ortona dated back to the thirteenth century BC, when escaping Trojans had landed here after the fall of Troy and founded a new city. Successive earthquakes had swept away all trace of these legendary roots, but buildings that were at least 500 years old were common along the town's streets.

In the southern part, more modern houses, some warehouses, and a couple of larger apartment buildings now stood; but in the older, larger quarters of Terravechia in the north and Terranova in the west, traditional brownstone buildings faced each other across cobblestone streets barely wider than an ox cart. The old buildings were primarily two or three storeys high, the lowest storey often possessing only a solid wooden door that provided entry to one large windowless room — traditionally a shop for a craftsman, grocer, or other shopkeeper. In the late 1930s, with a global depression, a war in Abyssinia, and so many dead from Il Duce's intervention in Spain, many of these dark caverns were transformed into homes for the poorest Ortona residents. About 10,000 people were crowded into the town and for many the living conditions were crude. Generally, even the residential quarters above the caverns were quite basic: a few stark rooms with front windows brightened by painted shutters and an iron rail balcony.

The tourists noticed little of Ortona's increasing poverty. They gathered each morning on the beach to the south of the town to worship sun and sea. The beach and Ortona's prospect over it were the reasons the town was known in many corners of Italy as the Pearl of the Adriatic. Swarms of children played in the gentle surf, while the fathers, mothers, aunts, uncles, grandparents, cousins, sweethearts, and friends gathered under their umbrellas — the younger ones in bathing suits, the older in ever darker and heavier-weight clothes — spaced tightly together in the manner favoured by Italians who sought not privacy but community on a beach. In the afternoon, after taking the main meal in Ortona's *trattorias* and *ristorantes*, they returned to the hotels and *pensiones* for the siesta. With the setting of the sun they rose to join the locals in the ritual promenade up Corso Vittorio Emanuele. The broad main street of Ortona was fronted to the north in Piazza Municipali by the two-storey municipal building, with its distinctive clock mounted just below the roofline. Before the bars and *trattorias* on the corso, cloth-covered tables were set out and waiters wearing starched white shirts and precisely pressed black pants fetched carafes of the rich red *montepulciano*, cappuccinos, *grappa*, and sweet cake. Later, when the evening darkness had settled in, the vacationers again filled tables in the *ristorantes* for their second main meal. They savoured the pasta smothered in black mussels or the lightly fried mullet, either of which had been drawn that very day from the sea before the town. Others preferred the grilled lamb brought to Ortona in the morning by the farmer from the highlands near Guardiagrele. When the meals were done and if the weather was still fine, as it usually was in the summer months, musicians played on Corso Umberto I. Dancing and much festivity would continue into the small hours.[1]

On Sundays, vacationers and townspeople alike gathered in the various churches of Ortona to take Mass. The main cathedral was San Tomasso, with its great frescoed dome and an adjacent watchtower that rose up almost as high as the upper reaches of the brass-roofed cupola. Cattedrale San Tomasso was so named because it purportedly housed a tomb containing the sanctified remains of the Christian apostle Saint Thomas, often referred to as Doubting Thomas because he initially questioned the truth of Christ's resurrection. When Thomas demanded physical proof of the resurrection, Christ appeared before him and asked him to touch his wounds. Stunned with the truth of the resurrection, Thomas said: "My Lord and my God," thereby explicitly acknowledging Christ's divinity. Legend held that pilgrims to Rome who viewed Saint Thomas's remains in Ortona would enjoy a safe journey to the Vatican City.

Cattedrale San Tomasso may have been the grandest of Ortona's churches, but the oldest was Santa Maria di Costantinopoli, believed to have been originally constructed in the fourth or fifth century AD, although it was heavily overlain with medieval construction and by the 1930s only the base foundation was authentic. According to local lore, this church was founded by Saint Mary Magdalene herself, prior even to the erection of the Byzantine-era structure — so that the ground upon which the church stood was among the most consecrated in Italy. This church was of narrow construction with a simple stone exterior and, by Italian standards, a relatively plain interior. It stood on the southern outskirts of Ortona, its back close to a steep embankment that fell away to the intersection where the coastal road and railroad met the Ortona-Orsogna lateral road.

◆ ◆ ◆

From the time of his birth in 1930, Americo Casanova lived near the old church. He was a happy child, but at just two years old one rather large shadow was cast over his life. His father left Ortona to seek a better income for the family by emigrating to the United States. Thereafter, Americo's only contact with his father was through letters and the presents sent regularly from Hershey, New Jersey, where his father worked in the famous chocolate factory. Before he left for the United States, Americo's father built a small four-unit apartment building for his wife Angela and the three children. The family lived in one apartment and drew income from the other three. Between the rental income and the money sent from America, Angela Casanova was able to provide well for her three children: Mario, the oldest; Maria, two years younger; and little Americo, who was six years younger yet. The apartment was in the town's new section to the immediate south of the old part of the town and close to Santa Maria di Costantinopoli.

Having an absent father did not make Americo unique in Ortona. Many of the men of the community were away. Ortona, being a port town, drew men to the sea — most as fishermen, but also many who left to crew the ocean freighters. There was little for a man to do for a living in Ortona in the 1930s if he did not fish the sea or till the surrounding soil. Unemployment was high and so the men left, some going north to the factories, others being pressed by the military into service, and a few, such as America's father, travelling overseas to America with the hope of eventually returning with enough money to set up a business or, sometimes, of bringing the family over to join them in a new land.

The fishermen and their families clustered in the oldest section of Ortona, the warren of narrow streets and passages adjacent to San Tomasso and set back from the esplanade. In the morning, the men descended the stairs from Ortona to the harbour where their boats were docked alongside the long northern mole. Here their nets were hung on large racks close to the shoreline. Sometimes Americo would look out at the water to where the small boats dotted the horizon, nets out, and wish his father were out there, soon to come home. But then he would look at all the fine things that decorated their home, the furnishings from America, and remember that this was made possible only by a father who worked in a chocolate factory in the United States.

As Americo grew older, tensions in Ortona also grew. Il Duce, Benito Mussolini, was calling ever more men to the services and then the war started. This one was bigger than the one fought in Abyssinia or the undeclared incursion of the army divisions into Spain to assist General Francisco Franco in crushing the godless Republic. As the war spread and finally the Americans joined against Italy, the flow of money and presents from America slowed and then ceased altogether. But there was still the apartment rental and the family lived comfortably enough, even with the growing food shortages that plagued all of Italy as the nation's fortunes worsened with each passing month.[2]

◆ ◆ ◆

Antonio Di Cesare, a couple of years older than Americo Casanova, was not so lucky. In 1942, his father had been one of the thousands of conscripted soldiers who surrendered in Africa to the British Eighth Army when Tunisia fell. Antonio's father was sent to a prison camp in South Africa, his meagre soldier's pay stopped coming as Italy fell into chaos, and Antonio's mother and the boy became entirely dependent on assistance provided to the families of prisoners by the International Red Cross. They lived in a little house 400 yards from the southern outskirts of Ortona in a community marked on no map but known locally as Porta Caldari. Able to grow some vegetables, the small family eked out a difficult life that might have bordered on starvation had it not been for the generosity of their extended family and neighbours. This was particularly true after the Italian government surrendered and the German army moved immediately to occupy most of Italy.[3]

On July 25, 1943, King Vittorio Emanuele III had accepted the resignation of the head of the government, his Excellency Cavalier Benito Mussolini, after an extraordinary ten-hour session of the Grand Fascist Council demanded that the dictator step aside so that Italy could sue the Allies for peace. Immediately after the king accepted Mussolini's resignation, Il Duce was taken into protective custody. The king then called upon seventy-one-year-old Marshal Pietro Badoglio to form a government, which promptly dissolved the Fascist Party. Until Mussolini's resignation, the German army presence in Italy was concentrated in Sicily, where the Axis forces were attempting to throw back the Allied invasion. On July 30, with the Italian government obviously poised for a surrender to the Allies, Hitler ordered the nation occupied by German infantry and armoured formations.

Throughout August, the Allies and the new Italian government undertook complex and secret negotiations to secure a peace accord that would not only remove Italy with honour from the war but also ensure the Germans did not arrest and remove Badoglio's government from power, replacing it with a puppet administration of its own choosing. Plans were hammered out for a strong Italian army force supported by the American 82nd Airborne Division, which would be parachuted near Rome, to protect the government on the day it was scheduled to announce Italy's surrender.

The date of September 1 was initially agreed upon for the armistice announcement, but it took two more days of secret haggling before the armistice was formally signed. Even then it had yet to be made public because the Italian government was not safe from German reprisal. On September 8, the 82nd Airborne was scheduled to land near Rome, dropping on airports supposed to be secured by Italian troops. But at the last minute, Badoglio radioed the Allies to cancel the operation, claiming that a public announcement of the armistice was impossible, as was the airborne operation, because of the presence of

German divisions in and around Rome. Stunned at first by this reversal in plans, General Dwight D. Eisenhower, Supreme Allied Commander Mediterranean, finally responded at 6:30 p.m. by proceeding with a planned broadcast announcing that the Italians had signed an armistice agreement. The Italian government was caught entirely by surprise. When Badoglio's foreign minister burst into his office and told him the news, Badoglio said, "We're fucked."[4]

Within a couple of hours of the broadcast, German divisions near Rome began encircling the city. Badoglio, his family, and the Royal Family locked themselves into the main Ministry of War building, while scattered skirmishes broke out between German and Italian troops at the gates of Rome. In the early morning hours of September 9, a convoy of five vehicles fled through Rome's eastern gate onto the highway from the city via Avezzano to Pescara. Having slipped through the tightening German net, Badoglio, King Emanuele, and their families and immediate aides spent a tense day hiding in the small mountain town of Guardiagrele before entering Ortona on the evening of September 10. That night they were taken aboard the Italian corvette *Baionetta* and whisked by sea to Brindisi, which had already been captured by Allied forces. The first the people of Ortona learned of the passage of their king through the community was the discovery the following morning of the vehicles abandoned by the northern mole.[5]

Only days after the surrender, the International Red Cross aid to the Di Cesare family stopped, as the Germans' tightened occupation of Italy disrupted the operations of the international aid organization. The Di Cesares' situation worsened, but so did that of most of the people of Ortona and all of Italy. As the Germans appropriated the transportation network for their military operations, and Allied aerial bombing began causing extensive damage to communication and transportation systems, normal movement of food and goods became virtually impossible. Each community was forced to draw in upon itself and look to its own limited resources of food and fuel to ensure the survival of its population. But making life more difficult was the absence of young men to work the fields and crew the fishing boats. Most were away, serving in the army, navy, and air force.

◆ ◆ ◆

The chaos that descended on Italy in the immediate wake of the surrender swept up twenty-eight-year-old Antonio D'Intino. In 1940 he had been called back to duty by the Italian navy, in which he had served from 1933 to 1935. D'Intino, a small, slight man, wanted only to stay on his family's land to the immediate west of Ortona and tend the olives and grapes, to find a good woman, to marry and establish a family. But the war cared little for his dreams, so he reported for duty. Initially he served aboard a destroyer, but by early 1943 Allied blockades had locked the majority of Italian ships in the two major naval harbours at La Spezia and Taranto, so he was set to work transporting naval shells from La Spezia to reinforced underground bunkers in the inland hills.

On September 11, his commander called D'Intino and the rest of the unit together and told them the war was over for the Italian military. "You're on your own now," the officer said. "If you stay here the Germans will probably imprison you or send you north to work in their factories."[6] He left quickly, without looking back, seeking his own safety. D'Intino and four other men, all from the Adriatic coastal regions of Abruzzo and Molise, decided to try to make their way home. La Spezia was south of Genoa, on the wrong coast, and several hundred miles from Ortona. The better part of two German armies stood between the two places. The men realized the journey would be hard, if not impossible. But they could see no alternative. If they could reach their homes, they might be able to pick up the threads of their lives and avoid capture and forced labour.

Still wearing their naval uniforms, the five managed to catch a train north to Parma, an inland city on the rail line that led to Bologna. From Bologna a line ran direct through Pescara. Arriving in Parma, the five were told by a sympathetic rail official that there were Germans in the city who were picking up anybody wearing a military uniform. The men found some civilians willing to swap a few ragged clothes for the good cloth of the uniforms. They also learned that no civilian trains were running out of Parma to Bologna. They would have to proceed on foot. Sticking to back country roads and trails recommended by peasants, the men slipped through the ever tightening German military net to Bologna. It took a week for them to cover a mere seventy-five miles.

In Bologna, luck was with them as they learned that a civilian freight train was preparing to depart from a station just south of the city. D'Intino and his friends rushed across country to the station and arrived in time to board the southbound train. Dirty, unshaven, hungry from seven days with barely any food, the men hid in a boxcar and passed a fearful journey as the train rolled slowly down the coast, passing through several cursory military checkpoints manned by bored German soldiers. It was night when the train reached Ortona. D'Intino bade farewell to his friends and jumped off onto the gravel siding. He walked home and slept outside the house for the remainder of the night because he did not want to waken his aging father. Despite his hunger, filthy state, and weariness, D'Intino was happy. He was home and determined to stay no matter what the war chose to visit upon Ortona.[7]

◆ ◆ ◆

On September 24, thirteen days after the flight of King Vittorio Emanuele III and Marshal Pietro Badoglio from Ortona and within days of D'Intino's return, German soldiers arrived to secure the harbour. An order was issued placing all port facilities under German control. Notices were also posted throughout the town that it was now illegal for anyone to possess radio transmitters and that all civilian property was subject to the use of the army as required. Over the next few days, the residents of Ortona watched with growing fear as German supply trains rolled by on the main line, carrying arms, munitions, and soldiers south to face the advancing Eighth Army.

Twelve days after the first arrival of German soldiers in Ortona, an engineering unit arrived. From trucks they unloaded twenty-eight tons of explosives and proceeded to blow about fifteen major breaches in the northern mole. Larger fishing vessels were sunk, as were several small freighters that were in the harbour when the Germans arrived. Within weeks, the destruction of the mole rendered the port too shallow for use as a deepwater harbour. At low tide, the tidal plain now stretched for several hundred yards out beyond the limits of its former extension.[8]

No fishing vessels were now allowed to put to sea. The few men of military age living in Ortona were subject to immediate draft for forced labour parties, as the Germans set about preparing fixed defensive positions on the ridgeline overlooking the Moro River and at key points between the Moro and Ortona. A risky cat-and-mouse game developed between civilians and Germans. Few young men willingly reported for duty when the Germans posted notices demanding workers for labour parties. The Germans, knowing there were some men who were fit and able, would begin searching houses. Antonio Di Cesare was still only a young teenager, but that was sufficiently old for the manpower-strapped Germans. So Antonio joined a clutch of men in playing the dangerous evasion. They would hide in one of the old buildings in the fishermen's district. When the Germans entered the house and started searching the lower floor, the fugitives would pass a wooden plank from an upper window across the narrow street into the facing window of a house on the other side. The hastily improvised bridge provided a catwalk over which the men could cross to the safety of the other house. Once all were across, the plank was pulled in, the windows shuttered. Short of soldiers to carry out an efficient search, the Germans seldom caught the men in the act of escaping. When they did it was not uncommon for them to fire upon the fleeing men. Some were wounded, a few killed. Most, however, were able to avoid being picked up by the German search parties.[9]

Although none of the men wanted to help the Germans by providing free local labour, this was not the primary reason they risked their lives to escape the searches. In an utterly random pattern, the German roundups sometimes had a more ominous result. Occasionally the drafted men found themselves facing the scrutiny of dreaded SS squads. A few of the men would be bundled into a truck and would disappear to the north, usually to work as slave labour in German factories. Others, possibly informed on by Fascist neighbours, were sent to the death camps because they were suspected of being Communists, Socialists, or Jews. An older friend of Americo Casanova, Pascuale Angelone, was arrested by the SS and shipped to Buchenwald. He remained there until his liberation in 1945 and never knew why the Germans had spirited him away to that slaughterhouse. He was not Jewish and was too young to have had the chance to know anything of Communism or Socialism in Fascist Italy.

Americo's mother Angela was afraid of the Germans for another reason. One day a squad burst into their apartment. Luckily Mario, old enough to work in the labour parties, was not home. Still, they had searched the house and taken particular notice of the family's American possessions and the letters from her husband that bore his address in Hershey, New Jersey. She explained that her husband had been caught overseas by the war, made it sound as if he would have come home had it been possible. Although they went away without damaging anything, the soldiers had seemed angry. Usually the soldiers were courteous in their treatment of the civilian women, but after they discovered the American possessions they had spoken to her in a coarse, rough manner.[10]

By November, conditions had badly deteriorated. Food was scarce. The men could seldom work the fields, there were no fish, and no meat reached Ortona from the foothill pastures. Antonio D'Intino avoided the work parties by digging five small holes in various corners of the family farm. Often, when the Germans started rounding up workers, someone would ring the bells in one of the churches in a manner that the soldiers mistook for Italian custom but which actually served to warn everyone that a search was underway. In the fields, men whistled warnings to each other when they saw soldiers approaching. As soon as a warning was given, everybody scattered and hid. D'Intino hunkered in the nearest of his holes, staying there until the bells either rang the all-clear signal or the other farmers again whistled to indicate the German patrol had passed. D'Intino's father was weakening with each passing day and he feared the old man would die if the Allies did not soon come, bringing food and medicine. His hope of impending liberation was pinned to the sound of the artillery in the far distance and the reports that there was fighting on the Sangro River. As the soft booming of the guns drew closer and sharpened, D'Intino dared to hope that the Germans would soon flee and the war would pass Ortona by.[11]

Such hopes were dashed suddenly at the end of November when the Germans issued an order for the immediate evacuation of all civilians from Ortona. Americo Casanova was taken by his grandmother and an aunt to Tollo, west of Ortona. His mother and the two older children defied the order, Angela fearful of leaving the apartment building unwatched. Signora Casanova was not the only citizen of Ortona who clandestinely refused to leave. The Germans had insufficient men to enforce the evacuation order. While Angela stayed naively in the hope of protecting her property, others remained simply because they had nowhere else to go and were afraid to become refugees.[12] Many hid from the Germans in the rail tunnels under the town or in the vaults of the cemetery. During the times when the German presence in Ortona was minimal, they would return to their homes and continue life as usual.

Perhaps because the Germans believed the town had been largely evacuated, they failed one day to post guards on a convoy of horse-drawn wagons left next to the train station. The wagons were filled with food. When the civilians realized the supply train was unguarded, they descended upon it like locusts. Within a matter of minutes every wagon was emptied. Antonio D'Intino was among the looters and was able to carry off several days' worth of precious food. To everybody's surprise, when the Germans discovered the wagons emptied of their stores they failed to exact punishment upon the community. Indeed, they seemed entirely preoccupied. It appeared that units of Germans were jostling with each other to go in opposing directions, some retreating, others rushing through Ortona on their way to a new front line established at the Moro River. Ortona itself remained largely unoccupied.[13]

In the meantime, Antonio Di Cesare's mother stashed all the family's best china, lace, and other valuables in the ceiling of their little home. She hoped this would save them from German looters. Then she and Antonio accompanied two uncles and their wives and children in fleeing to Villa Deo, a tiny hamlet outside the small village of Villa Grande, southwest of Ortona.[14]

The forced evacuation of Ortona was not the only sign that made Antonio D'Intino believe the Germans were planning a major defensive line fixed on the Moro River. First, there were the improved positions that the men had been forced to help build on the Moro ridgeline, some with concrete walls and roofs. Then there were the gun pits to the north of Ortona that the men had dug. The adjacent underground bunkers appeared designed to store artillery munitions. He saw the German command cars driving the dirt lanes on Ortona's outskirts and thought he understood the way the officers in the cars gestured at their maps and pointed out positions. D'Intino suspected the Germans were preparing firing lines and registering coordinates for map-based firing plans. With that thought in his mind, D'Intino dug his small holes deeper. He worked with his hands now because the Germans had taken the shovel when they also confiscated the few vegetables that had been growing in the small garden plot. His stomach rumbled with hunger. But he ignored his hunger and weakness and dug with tired fingers through the wet, heavy clay. He created shelter for himself and his father because he was now sure that there would be a battle and they would be caught in its heart.[15]

◆ ◆ ◆

On December 3, as the Canadians started deploying on the southern bank of the Moro River, the German 65th Division withdrew from the front lines. Like the British 78th Division against which it had fought during the Sangro River battle, the German division was in tatters; exhausted and greatly reduced by casualties. As the 65th withdrew, its positions were filled by troops of the 90th Panzer Grenadier Division. During the African campaign, the Eighth Army had often encountered the 90th Light Division and considered it one of the finest units in the Afrika Korps. The 90th had been all but destroyed in May 1943 during the closing days of the battle for Tunisia that marked the end of Germany's presence in Africa. In July 1943, the 90th was rebuilt as one of the new Panzer Grenadier divisions that Hitler had instructed his inspector-general of armoured troops, General der Panzertruppen Heinz Guderian, to create after the twin defeats in the early part of the year in Africa and at Stalingrad. Panzer Grenadier units were intended to be highly mechanized, capable of operating either independently or alongside the armoured Panzer divisions. The Panzer Grenadiers were thus sufficiently motorized to keep abreast of the German tanks during a blitzkrieg advance.

The soldiers of the 90th were selected from the 30,000 Germans withdrawn in a brilliantly executed and entirely unopposed sea evacuation from the Italian islands of Sardinia and Corsica in September 1943. A good portion of the division's men were veterans who had fought for the Wehrmacht since the September 1939 invasion of Poland. Among them were men who had participated in one or more of the massive German campaigns of the early 1940s, including the blitzkrieg through France in 1940 that had stunned the world, the battle for Africa, and the endless invasion and subsequent defensive withdrawal in Russia. Others were raw recruits with little or no battle experience and relatively little training prior to their assignment to garrisons in Sardinia or Corsica.

As a Panzer Grenadier division, the 90th was organized into two infantry regiments of three battalions each, supported by a Panzer tank battalion, an artillery regiment, an antitank battalion, and an engineer battalion. Each infantry battalion was generously equipped with fifty-nine light and twelve heavy machine guns, three 7.5-millimetre antitank guns, six 8-centimetre mortars, and four 12-centimetre mortars. The number of machine guns gave the 90th tremendous front-line firepower.

On paper, the 90th was to have 14,000 men in its two regiments but, as was true of all German divisions by 1943, the real number was significantly less. Germany was plagued with a serious manpower shortage due to the heavy casualties absorbed in nearly four years of war on two major fronts. Russia was proving a slaughterhouse unlike anything Hitler's generals had anticipated. This left the German army with essentially two groups of soldiers. The best were the veterans, mostly men who had seen combat on many different fronts. A U.S. War Department report described the typical German veteran as a "prematurely aged, war weary cynic, either discouraged and disillusioned or too stupefied to have any thought of his own. Yet he is a seasoned campaigner, most likely a non-commissioned officer, and performs his duty with the highest degree of efficiency."[16] In contrast, the same report described recruits by 1943 as being either too young or too old for active service and often suffering ill health. To a man they were poorly trained. The young recruits were viewed as the most dangerous, since most were so inculcated in Nazism that they were fanatics. The older recruits were fearful of what an Allied victory would wreak on Germany — and, more important, upon their families and communities — in revenge. This fear drove them to fight with a desperate courage.

In December 1943, the German army numbered 4.27 million men. Of these, more than 1.5 million were over thirty-four years old.[17] The average Panzer Grenadier private preparing to square off against the Canadians at the Moro River was about six years older than his Canadian counterpart. While his officers and non-commissioned officers, right down to the rank of corporal, were generally seasoned veterans, he and his comrades were usually either younger or older than normal for military service conscripts and had little or no combat experience. Although many of the younger privates had lived most of their lives under Hitler's government, the Panzer Grenadiers were not typically Nazi fanatics, as the majority of hardened party members served in SS units.

Young Antonio Di Cesare discovered the truth of this in his dealings with the Germans he encountered in Ortona and at Villa Deo. Most of the soldiers turned out to be friendly and generous to the boy. One Panzer Grenadier, who was about twenty-two years old, spent almost every free evening in the small Villa Deo home where the eight members of Antonio's family lived. Mostly the young man pined for his family in Germany. He talked longingly of his life back home and how much he wanted to return to his engineering studies. Sometimes the young man brought food, but not often. It was clear to Antonio that the Germans had little in the way of regular food supplies themselves. Antonio liked the young German and worried for his safety, as did the rest of the family.[18]

◆ ◆ ◆

The Panzer Grenadiers were well aware that they faced a stiff, bitter fight in the forthcoming days — one they probably couldn't win. Since the beginning of the Italian campaign, there had been little doubt that the Germans would be forced back by the Eighth Army's ongoing offensive advance. The best they could hope for was to make the Canadians pay in blood for every bit of ground and to slow the Allies long enough for the worsening winter weather to bring the advancing army to a halt until spring. Delay meant everything for the Germans. If this could be achieved with relatively light casualties on their side, that was the closest the German division could come to victory. There was no hope of the Eighth Army being routed and the Germans marching back to the toe of Italy in a blitzkrieg advance. Those days were gone for the Wehrmacht in Europe. There were not enough men, not enough tanks, no air superiority. But each day they postponed the loss of Rome, each day they prevented the Allies breaking through the back door that Italy opened to the rest of Europe, gave Germany more time to perhaps reverse its ill fortune in Russia and somehow stave off the disaster of defeat.

Outnumbered and outgunned by the Canadians, the 200th and

361st regiments of the 90th would have to make up for these handicaps through effective defensive tactics. The Panzer Grenadier's relied on initial heavy defence from fortified positions backed up by lightning-quick, violent counterattacks to throw the enemy back in confusion before it could solidify any gains won. Along the Moro River ridgeline, the Germans started digging into the reverse slopes of the many gullies and ravines that crisscrossed the heavily terraced farmland.

The Germans knew from long experience that fortified positions dug deep into reverse slopes were immune to virtually anything but a direct hit by a bomb or artillery round. It was also extremely difficult for either planes or guns to achieve a direct hit because of the angle of arc a bomb or shell must attain to strike the reverse-slope position. Moreover, when the bombardment ceased, the German soldiers could tumble out of their shelters and rush forward to prepared positions built near the edge of the slope. From there, they could catch the approaching enemy infantry in the open on the opposing side.

There was no doubt in the mind of 76th Panzer Korps General der Panzertruppen Traugott Herr, whose korps included the 90th Division, that the division would face heavy aerial and artillery bombardments designed to shatter its defensive positions. Montgomery's standard offensive tactic was to precede any major advance of infantry and tanks with the heaviest artillery and aerial bombardment he could deliver. This had been the key to Montgomery's success at El Alamein and it was an essential aspect of the British general's tactics. The "watchword for one and all," Herr told his commanders, is "into the ground."[19] While on one side of the Moro the Canadians prepared to attack, on the other side the Germans worked frantically with pick and shovel, burrowing deep into the Abruzzo clay.

# 4

## THE SHARP END

THE fear was in them all. Only a fool claimed otherwise and such a man would be considered a potential hazard by the others. Since July 10, 1st Canadian Infantry Division and 1st Canadian Armoured Brigade had been on campaign. Five months of fighting and marching. Moments of terror and horror interspersed with extended periods of boredom and the drudgery of the advance across Sicily and up Italy's boot. Now the battalions were strung out in a long line facing the Moro River and every man in the line companies knew that soon — in a few hours, or a day, or two, or three at the most depending on his brigade and battalion — he would again face directly the fire of German machine guns and rifles. In the slit trenches, waiting for the attack to commence, there was time to think — time for the fear to grow in his belly.

For most the fear was not crippling, but it gnawed the gut and rendered the rations tasteless or unappetizing. Hastings and Prince Edward Regiment Lieutenant Farley Mowat imagined it as a worm. Looking out over the Moro River, he felt the worm in his gut grow, enlarge, become harder to thrust away and ignore.[1]

Some found it no longer possible to quell the fear. Instead they collapsed under it. The day prior to the Princess Patricia's Canadian Light Infantry's move from San Vito Chietino to the battalion's Moro River position, Lieutenant Jerry Richards discovered one of his men cowering in a slit trench, gibbering, refusing to fall in. Richards was momentarily baffled. In his short tenure as a platoon commander he had not faced this situation. He thought of ordering the man at gunpoint to rise and join the ranks. Then the inanity of such an action struck him. Richards ordered two of his other soldiers to drag the man out of the hole. They grabbed the shaking soldier by the arms and yanked him to his feet, but he continued weeping and babbling. Richards ordered the soldier taken to the field dressing station for the medical officer to sort out. The man disappeared into the divisional medical system, never to be seen again. Perhaps he was evacuated, as was occasionally the fate of the worst battle-exhaustion cases. More likely he was reassigned to less hazardous rear-area duty, where the fear of dying at any moment was lessened.

It was military medical policy that first priority should be given to treating a battle-exhaustion case quickly so that the man could be returned to his unit. However, as the Italian campaign progressed, ever fewer soldiers so affected were returned to the front-line platoons. A major reason for this was that neither the officers nor the soldiers involved in the up-front fighting wanted these men at their side. Dr. Arthur Manning Doyle, divisional psychiatrist, found that infantry commanders sought to quickly get rid of any soldiers they deemed unstable or jittery in action. Such men were believed to pose a danger to themselves and a threat to their comrades. Doyle wrote of the normal attitude of the officers: "Though they frequently use such uncomplimentary terms as yellow they usually recognize that the soldier with an anxiety neurosis just can't help it. . . . The worst possible situation in the line is a body of troops led by a neurotic officer. Troops that have fought well under another break and run when under an officer they know to be himself abnormally nervous and vacillating."[2]

Saskatoon Light Infantry Major Thomas de Faye had faced such a situation in Sicily. During a routine check of his battalion positions, de Faye discovered that one heavy-machine-gun platoon commander had ordered his men to set up their Vickers guns in positions on a forward slope. This was a very dangerous position for the guns, and the men all seemed justifiably anxious. When he asked where the commander was, they shrugged their shoulders and said they had no idea. Searching about, de Faye discovered the officer huddled in a cave well behind the gun positions. "I can see so well from up here, sir," the man blathered. "I can maintain better control over the situation here." Whether simple cowardice or battle exhaustion, de Faye knew not; but he ran the officer back to the divisional commander with the message that he didn't want the man in his unit, that he presented a hazard to his men. The officer was shipped out of the division in twenty-four hours. The major later heard he was returned to Canada where, rumour had it, he was promoted and assigned to training duties.[3]

Cowardice. Courage. Two poles on a spectrum of behaviour. By December 1943, the soldiers in Italy knew that most of them were capable of either extreme. The hero today might break down completely the day following and the supposed coward might suddenly display a selfless disregard for his own safety. It all depended on circumstance and a man's physical and mental condition. Bravery was a consumable commodity, like water in a bottle. Eventually, if drawn upon too often without an opportunity for the bottle to be refilled, the last reserves of courage must inevitably be drained. For this reason, most of the troops and officers felt only pity and sympathy for the men who fell victim to battle exhaustion. It could happen to anyone. It could happen to them. It was a form of illness, not much different than the dysentery, the jaundice, and the malaria that had afflicted the division since it hit the beach in Sicily.

◆ ◆ ◆

Every army on campaign has been faced with dysentery, caused by the miserable hygienic conditions inherent in an environment where men cannot bathe regularly, where eating utensils are usually filthy, where sources of water are often polluted, and where the feces and urine of those already afflicted with dysentery remain unburied. Intensely painful and bloody diarrhea is the most noticeable symptom, accompanied by dehydration and exhaustion. As the malady progresses, victims become weak and usually lose their appetite. Most soldiers suffering dysentery were expected to tough it out, for the illness would usually clear up over time. Severe cases were generally treated with the drug sulphaguanidine. Rarely were dysentery cases taken into hospital. Of course, the presence in all the battalions of men experiencing dysentery contributed to its spread. But there was little alternative — the illness was too endemic to all the units for every sick soldier to be sent for hospital treatment.[4]

Another illness that persisted during the summer and fall months of 1943 was jaundice. More properly known as infectious hepatitis or hepatitis A, the disease reached near epidemic levels within the Canadian units in early September 1943. Doctors later determined that the troops were most likely infected almost immediately upon landing in Sicily, as the disease has a four- to six-week incubation period. During the first two to seven days of the infection's cycle, soldiers experienced "malaise, fatigue, lassitude, and loss of appetite, sometimes accompanied by nausea, vomiting, and diarrhea."[5] The loss of appetite was a particularly difficult aspect of the disease because it greatly weakened infected soldiers.

Loyal Edmonton Regiment Lieutenant Alon Johnson contracted jaundice shortly before the Canadians reached Campobasso. His skin turned a definite yellow and he was tormented by peculiar cravings for specific foods. "Boy," he'd say to himself, "if I could just have some chicken that'd taste so damned good." Presented with a platter of chicken, however, he would feel nauseated just looking at it.[6] Fatty foods were particularly intolerable because jaundice usually causes an inflammation of the liver and in some instances of the spleen, making fat difficult to digest. Fever was usually also present for at least a few days. Because of the severity of symptoms associated with jaundice, many infected soldiers were evacuated to hospitals well to the rear, even to Africa or Great Britain. In 97.5 percent of cases, it took fifty days from the onset of symptoms until a soldier was generally thought fit to return to full combat duty.[7] In Johnson's case he was never sent to the rear but remained at battalion headquarters.

Present throughout the summer of campaigning in Sicily and then in the lower parts of Italy were mosquitoes — a good many of which carried malaria. Allied high command had known this would be the case and initiated a plan to combat the disease. Quinine, a natural alkaloid extracted from the bark of the cinchona tree in Java, effectively masked the effects of malaria, while not curing it. But there was precious little quinine to be had by the Allies because Java had been captured in January 1942 by Imperial Japan. Fortunately, however, there were chemical substitutes for quinine that achieved the same effect.[8] While the Americans relied on a drug called atabrine, the British and Canadian divisions in Sicily took nepadrine.

Twenty-one-year-old Lance Corporal Jack Haley, a radio signaller with the Princess Patricia's Canadian Light Infantry, dutifully took his nepadrine each day and never suffered from malaria. As he marched across Sicily, Haley was always amused by the small bill-boards the medical units erected here and there which read: "If you pee a golden stream it means you've taken your nepadrine." Despite the propaganda campaign, many soldiers refused to take the drug because it was rumoured that the pills would render them perma-nently impotent or sterile. The rumour reached such a point that officers had to line their troops up and personally ensure that each man swallowed his daily pill.[9] Despite these precautions, malaria was common throughout the ranks and many soldiers were hospital-ized when their symptoms became too severe. Although new cases of malaria ceased once the Canadians had advanced far enough up the Italian boot, the disease typically recurs several times over a period that can run for several months or even years. The after-effects of passing through a malarial region continued to be felt for many months, and were still a problem when the battalions deployed before the Moro River.

◆ ◆ ◆

While illnesses wore men down and resulted in 1st Canadian Infantry Division and 1st Canadian Armoured Brigade always being well below strength, the short firefights and battles that typified oper-ations prior to the Moro River further decreased the troops as men were wounded or killed. "When you're killed in battle it doesn't really matter to you that the battle was a little one or not," Johnson would say.[10] Johnson had come to the division as a replacement, taking over the scout platoon after its officer had been shot dead by a German sniper when his jeep rounded a corner in the road. The jeep still had a bullet hole through its body near the passenger seat, serving as a reminder to Johnson of how easily death could come for you in this strange business of war. So far he had been lucky, but such was not the case for all the men who had accompanied him into active military service.

Johnson had reported to the enlistment office of the Loyal Edmonton Regiment in Edmonton on March 25, 1942, along with his friend and fellow University of Alberta Canadian Officers Training Corps cadet John Alpine Dougan. The recruiter recognized Dougan's last name and asked whether he might be the son of World War I cavalry veteran Jack Dougan. John said he was and added that his father now lived in Lethbridge. That was the extent of their pre-enlistment interview. They were offered positions in the regiment if they agreed to enlist as privates, rather than seeking a commission on the basis of their COTC training. Both agreed immediately. Over the next few days, three of their fellow COTC cadets — Keith McGregor, Jimmy Woods, and Earl Christie — also enlisted under the same terms.

The decision to enlist was easier for some than for others. Dougan suffered considerable anxiety over the possibility that enlisting might completely derail his dream of becoming a historian. It was just two weeks before the third-year exams of his honours history baccalaureate program. Would he lose the year? And when the war was over, would he have the opportunity to return to university? Dougan could only afford post-secondary studies because he had received a scholarship from the Imperial Order Daughters of the Empire. With these concerns in mind, he sought out the dean of the Arts and Science faculty to see what future might await him after the war if he were to interrupt his studies.

A veteran of the Great War, the dean assured the twenty-year-old Dougan that if he felt the need to enlist immediately rather than wait until completion of his schooling, the university would support his decision. Relieved, Dougan left the dean's office and headed off to war without further hesitation. He, like his friends, desperately wanted to get into it and do his duty. Later, Dougan received word from the university that he would be granted his degree in absentia due to having volunteered for military service.

The five cadets quickly revealed during training at the Edmonton barracks that they all had potential as leaders. Soon they were sent to Non-Commissioned Officer school at Currie Barracks in Calgary. All but Woods completed the course successfully. The four graduates were then shipped to Gordon Head Military Camp near Victoria as officer cadets. By June they had their second pips as lieutenants on their shoulders, Dougan had fallen in love and hoped to marry a woman he had met at a Victoria social, and they were back in Calgary completing the last stages of officer training. Johnson graduated second in the class, Dougan third. Then the four headed for Britain as replacement officers, slated to assume command positions in the Edmonton regiment as they became available.

No slot presented itself for any of them until after the invasion of Sicily, when the Eddies suffered heavy casualties in a vicious tangled battle in the streets of the small village of Leonforte. With several platoon commanders killed or wounded, Dougan and Christie were called out of the replacement depot and assigned to two platoons in 'D' Company. Christie took No. 17 Platoon and Dougan No. 16. A fifth-year medical student with a quick, inquisitive intelligence, Christie was older than Dougan. In Dougan's opinion, his friend was undoubtedly destined for an outstanding career in medicine.

Two weeks later, the Eddies went into an attack against a hill northeast of Regalbuto, designated Hill 736. To strengthen the lead force, Christie's and Dougan's platoons were attached temporarily to 'B' Company, commanded by Major Archie Donald. The entire lead element was nearing the crest of the hill when it came under intense German machine-gun fire. Dougan saw some of the enemy soldiers crouched behind one of the guns and then he felt as if a club cracked his skull. One bullet had hit him square in the centre of his helmet, another had struck his left forearm, and splinters from another had pierced his right forearm. He lay on the ground, knocked senseless for a few moments, then scrabbled to his feet. Unable to find his rifle, bleeding from both arms and a cut on his scalp, Dougan painfully dragged his service revolver out of its hiding spot inside his shirt, gripped it in both hands, and led the remnants of his platoon across 300 more yards of open ground in a wild charge to clear the summit.

In the aftermath, Dougan learned that Christie lay dead back on the slope. Dougan knew it was pure luck that he had not met the same fate. Canadian helmets were made of fairly thin steel and were not normally capable of repelling the strike of a machine-gun bullet. If the angle of the bullet had been slightly different, it would have pierced the steel and entered his brain instead of coursing a grooved circle around the outer edge and ricocheting away. Surviving was enough of a blessing, but he also had another reason for relief. One of his buddies had salvaged the helmet immediately after the hill was cleared, intending to mail it as a souvenir to Dougan's mother, but had lost it during a long march. Dougan did not like to think of the shock his mother would have experienced if she had unexpectedly received the macabre souvenir. As for Dougan, his wounds took several months to heal, and he did not rejoin the Edmonton regiment until it was resting in Campobasso in November.[11]

◆ ◆ ◆

Random chance often dictated who lived, who died. Since the invasion of Sicily, the three Turnbull brothers — Joe, Gord, and Bill — had seen enough buddies killed and maimed to feel nothing but amazement that they all still lived. The three were members of the 12th Canadian Armoured Regiment, known as the Three Rivers Tanks, all men on the sharp end who served in 'A' squadron. Joe and Gord were Sherman M-4 medium tank commanders, Bill a crewman in another Sherman.

Bill, the youngest, had been first to enlist. Barely eighteen years old, he enlisted in early October 1940. Gord followed him into service a couple of weeks later and Joe enlisted on October 23. The oldest at twenty-five, Joe had served for three years in the Mackenzie-Papineau Battalion during the Spanish Civil War, a fact he had not shared with the recruitment officer at Camp Borden, Ontario. A few weeks earlier, unemployed, discouraged by the way the world was going, and still full of hatred for Fascism, Joe had attempted to enlist in the Royal Canadian Air Force. When he mentioned that he had fought for the Spanish Republic and had only returned to Canada in 1939, the recruiters had conducted a furtive huddle. After a few minutes they returned and sternly rejected his enlistment application. Joe knew the cause. He had heard that other veterans of the 1,600-strong, all-volunteer Canadian force that had gone illegally from Canada to fight in Spain were being refused entry into the armed forces, because they were believed by the top brass to be Communists bent on fomenting revolution in the ranks. So at Camp Borden Joe conveniently forgot to mention his Spanish Civil War past and was welcomed into the regiment.[12]

The brothers had managed to stick together ever since and, through a combination of luck and determined effort, were assigned to the same squadron. They were close-knit, devoted to each other. Joe particularly felt a great responsibility to ensure that his two younger brothers got through this war safely. In Britain, the Three Rivers, like all the Canadian armoured regiments, had endured the long bleak years of seemingly endless reorganizations and re-equipping with one type of tank after another. Then came the Sicily invasion. In August 1943, eighty-four men in the regiment were killed or wounded. In one battle alone, ten of the thirty tanks of 'A' squadron were knocked out of action by enemy fire.[13]

Throughout the months of his early service in Sicily and Italy, Joe tried with little success to write regularly to Peg, his new wife in Edinburgh. He had met Peg in the autumn of 1941 when the three brothers had gone up to Edinburgh from their base on the Salisbury Plain to visit the "land of our ancestors," as Joe explained it to her. Peg was a friend of some of his Turnbull relatives in Scotland. She had been happy to help show the three men around the old city during their brief stay. Shortly after the brothers returned to duty Peg had received a letter. Joe wrote that she was going to come back to Canada with him when the war was over. They were married on November 29, 1942.

Joe knew that Peg desperately wanted to receive a letter that was more thoughtful and reflective than the curt notes he had previously sent her way since the Sicilian operation had begun. But how to find words that would be both truthful and yet still set her mind at ease. His reality was the noise and confusion of tank battle, the hammer of the 75-millimetre guns, Shermans broken, Shermans burning, the torn or immolated bodies of friends that had to be pulled from the tank wreckages in the aftermath of battle. He could not write the truth of that to Peg. On October 21, 1943, he finally mustered his nerve and put pen to paper. "We are not fighting Italians now," he wrote, "but the Germans, and they are in every sense equal to the toughest and finest soldiers in the world. They will not retire, they have to be killed. And there is only one way we can beat them, Peg, we have to be just a little bit tougher, and that leaves us lacking in any of the finer human feelings. If you understand this you will excuse the abrupt attitude in my letters and know it is not deliberate."[14]

He went on to describe how Bill and he had gone into an action recently with Bill acting as Joe's wireless operator. "We knew it was a bad thing to have two of us in the one buggie but we wanted to try it together."[15] Carefully sifting through the details of his daily life, Joe chose those stories that might bring a smile to Peg's face and make her less worried about the three of them. Among other things, he wrote of a battle where an enormous panicked dog had forced its way into the turret of Bill Stewart's tank, knocked the gunner out of his seat, and refused to be evicted until the fighting was over. In closing he wrote: "There are times when I'd let the whole job go to blazes just to see you for a wee while. But I still have a job to do and my little part of it is not finished. I don't know when it will end but I'll do my best until it is over."[16] Joe Turnbull knew, of course, that the end was far out of sight and many unforeseen dangers awaited the Canadians in their journey through Italy. By December 4, that journey had brought them all to the Moro River.

# TWO

## FOR LACK OF
## A BRIDGE

# 5

## Rush Jobs

At 1900 hours on December 5, the Hastings and Prince Edward Regiment of 1st Canadian Infantry Brigade completed taking over the positions vacated by the last of the British 78th Division's infantry on the southern ridgeline near the Moro River's mouth. Major A.A. Kennedy, known to his friends as Bert, was frantic with worry. Only a few hours before, the veteran militia officer and ex-artillery man had attended an Orders Group at brigade headquarters and discovered to his dismay that the Hasty P's were expected to put the first Canadian troops across the Moro.

The battalion's attack was intended as a diversionary exercise to draw German attention away from the main inland assault of 2nd Canadian Infantry Brigade's Seaforth Highlanders of Canada at San Leonardo, and a further secondary attack by the Princess Patricia's Canadian Light Infantry on the extreme left of the Canadian line fronting Villa Rogatti. While also undoubtedly rushed in preparing their plan of attack, Kennedy thought, the other two battalions at least had most of the afternoon to settle into positions, conduct some limited reconnaissance patrols down to the river, and had precious remaining hours to assign individual companies with defined tasks for the forthcoming assault. Kennedy faced attacking in the dark, with virtually no time for preparation, across terrain his men had been unable to reconnoitre in daylight. As acting commander of the regiment in place of Lieutenant Colonel John Tweedsmuir, who had recently been evacuated to North Africa with a severe case of jaundice, it was Kennedy's dubious honour to organize a full-scale battalion assault under some of the worst logistical conditions possible.

Consequently, Kennedy was in a dark mood when Lieutenant Farley Mowat, serving in the intelligence section, entered battalion headquarters. Mowat had been forward on the ridgeline trying to learn what he could about enemy positions from the Royal Irish Fusiliers. Unfortunately, the Fusiliers' intelligence officer was more eager to escape to the rear than to provide a thorough briefing. He took off almost immediately upon Mowat's arrival, leaving Mowat with nothing to do but lie in the cover of some heavy brush, getting slowly soaked by the persistent drizzle, while trying futilely to see some signs of enemy movement on the other side of the valley. Enemy artillery shells droned overhead and exploded in the battalion's rear areas. The coast road to the south of the blown bridge was also getting a pasting. As dusk settled in, Mowat returned to battalion HQ to report what little he had seen.

"Where the hell have *you* been?" Kennedy snapped as Mowat came through the door. "Goddamn it, we're to cross the Moro right away. No preparation. No support. What've you found out?"

Mowat told him the precious little he knew, doing nothing to improve Kennedy's mood. He ordered the lieutenant to take a scout platoon patrol out, find a usable river crossing, and to bloody well report back in the hour with some results. Taking three men, Mowat led a patrol down to the river. In the gathering gloom of evening, they waded along its overflowing banks until they discovered a crossable ford. Even as they returned to the ridge, they found 'A' Company's men shouldering guns and ammunition in preparation for leading the assault. Mowat remained with Kennedy, while the scout leader Lieutenant George Langstaff acted as 'A' Company's guide to the ford.[1]

◆ ◆ ◆

As was true for all three Canadian assaults that night, the Hasty P's were going in without the benefit of the Eighth Army's preferred tactic of first saturating enemy positions with intense artillery fire. At the last moment, Major General Chris Vokes had decided the attacks would have a better chance of success if they went in silently. He was banking on catching the Germans napping. Orders regarding this were, however, slightly confused. Lieutenant Colonel Cameron B. Ware, commanding the PPCLI, remained under the illusion that at least his attack would be preceded by a heavy bombardment of Villa Rogatti and the surrounding area on the northern bank of the river.[2]

Kennedy, for his part, was well aware that the Hasty P's were to receive no artillery or armoured support, which only reinforced his impression that the entire attack was confused and overly rushed. The plan he had managed to cobble together in a few frantic hours called for No. 7 Platoon of 'A' Company to cross the river by the sandbar ford discovered by Mowat's patrol. That platoon would set up a firm defensive position across the river and hold in place until the rest of the company came up in support. 'A' Company, still undetected, they hoped, would then wriggle up to the "lip of the valley." Once 'A' Company was established on the ridgeline, Kennedy planned to shove the rest of the battalion's line units over and spread them out along the edge of the ridge. They would then dig in for the rest of the night. While the infantry forced a crossing, the battalion's pioneer company, supported by Bren carriers mounting machine guns, would descend to the destroyed coast-road bridge and see if a crossing for tanks could be constructed with the minimal engineering equipment the pioneers possessed. Kennedy hoped by morning to bring tanks across to support his infantry units in repelling the German counterattacks that would inevitably come with the dawn.[3]

For the diversion to be effective in drawing Panzer Grenadier attention and personnel from the other two assaults, the Hasty P's had to go in shortly before the Seaforths and PPCLI started their stealthy crossing of the Moro. Consequently, the unit with the least time to prepare and the barest idea of terrain and enemy defences set off at 2200, just three hours after it had taken over the lines from the Irish regiment. 'A' Company's No. 7 Platoon, which Mowat had only recently handed over to a new commander when he was transferred to the intelligence section, descended into the valley, crossed the sloughlike stretch of river created by the sandbar, and managed to establish a forward position on the opposite bank without being discovered by the enemy. The thirty-man platoon had absolutely no idea what enemy positions or strength lurked ahead in the immediate darkness. Every man recognized the extreme danger of the situation and desperately tried to keep loose equipment from clinking, avoided even furtive whispers, and took every other conceivable measure to avoid alerting enemy soldiers to their presence.

Perhaps fearful of betraying the platoon's presence by sending a man splashing back over the river to report the first objective secure, the platoon commander neglected to send a report back by runner. Despite this oversight, the rest of the company moved off when its commander decided sufficient time had passed for the lead platoon to have reached its first objective. When the company came up on No. 7 Platoon's rear, this platoon swung to the left, where a gradual slope led up to the ridgeline. The main body of the company started to move forward, extending the company line with the lead platoon on the far left, so that the entire company would reach the top of the valley in an advancing line. While No. 7 Platoon made good time up its slope, the rest of the company bumped into a steep cliff. Stymied as to how to surmount this obstacle at night and without betraying its movement, the company came to a dead halt, soldiers either milling about along the cliff bottom or standing rooted in place, staring up its face. Meanwhile No. 7 Platoon disappeared into the blackness of the night.[4]

Barely had the two segments of the company become separated than the entire company was caught in a "violent crossfire from six or seven enemy medium machine-gun positions."[5] In seconds 'A' Company was pinned down and engaged in a fierce firefight, green and blinding-white enemy flares soaring high overhead to illuminate the Canadian soldiers for the German machine-gunners. Mortar bombs started to rain down on the company, worsening its already desperate situation. The Germans also quickly brought the pioneers under machine-gun and mortar fire, resulting in their quick withdrawal from the area of the blown bridge.[6]

No. 7 Platoon was in the worst situation, out of contact with the rest of the company and directly engaged with enemy machine-gun and rifle sections firing from well-dug-in positions. The Canadians could do little for shelter but squirm deeply down into the mud behind whatever bush or tree presented itself. The other platoons were helpless to get up and support No. 7 Platoon. With no idea where the platoon was, and under heavy enemy fire itself, any advance forward to the platoon's aid would likely result in an exchange of fire between the company and the isolated platoon. The only hope would have been for the rest of the company to come up directly on the platoon's right, so it was obvious who they were and so they could outflank the Germans firing on the platoon. But no route up the cliffs could be found. Both the lead platoon commander and the company commander recognized the hopelessness of the situation and started withdrawing back across the river. The Germans let them go, not risking an immediate counterattack in the darkness. When they got back to the southern shore, the troops learned that Kennedy had been trying to radio orders for them to withdraw and that he considered their casualties to have been "fairly light" considering the circumstances.[7] Mowat disagreed. He was horrified to see the casualties that No. 7 Platoon, particularly, had suffered. Its new commander was severely wounded, Sergeant Bates and several other men who had been in the platoon since Sicily were dead or dying.[8]

The attack might have failed, but Kennedy was already planning for the morning. After listening to the report of the 'A' Company commander, he decided it would be possible for an attack at the ford to succeed if it were properly supported with artillery and the logistics were in place to keep the infantry adequately supplied with munitions. He would, however, need approval from 1st Canadian Infantry Brigade commander Brigadier Howard Graham and probably Vokes himself. Whether he received authorization would undoubtedly rest upon the degree of success 2 CIB had in its attack, scheduled to get underway at midnight. Kennedy decided there was a good chance another attack on his front would prove worthwhile and set about organizing his units and getting the necessary preliminary permission.

An immediate problem that promised to plague any battalion successful in establishing a position on the northern bank of the Moro would be receiving ammunition resupply and evacuating wounded. With all the bridges out and no crossable fords yet constructed that were capable of supporting truck or Bren carrier traffic, resupply depended on what the men could carry on their backs. A wounded man who was unable to walk on his own posed a serious problem. In country this rough, it could easily take four men, one on each corner of a stretcher, to carry one casualty out. In the past under such combat conditions, 1st Canadian Infantry Division had turned to the Eighth Army's reserve of Indian muleteers and their animals. Already the PPCLI and Seaforths had mules on hand to carry headquarters' radio equipment, extra ammunition, and other equipment over on the heels of their assaults. The mules would then also be used to bring back the wounded. Kennedy, having been denied the time to make such arrangements earlier, now called up some mules to support his troops in the hoped-for morning attack.[9]

The presence of the muleteers presented some logistical problems of their own for Quartermaster Sergeant Basil Smith, who was rudely shaken awake just after turning in at midnight and advised to rustle up a meatless ration for a dozen Hindu muleteers. For a division fuelled on tinned meat, this was a tall order. Scrabbling about in his memory, Smith remembered seeing half a bag of rice lying in the back of one truck along with a few cases of kippers. Certain he had once heard that kippers were a Hindu delicacy, Smith gathered up the kipper cases and the rice, and tossed in a few tins of milk for good measure. That, he figured, would suffice until a proper Hindu ration — whatever that might be — was brought up from Eighth Army stores.[10]

While the Hasty P's organized for an anticipated attack in the morning, the regiment's war diarist noted that the failed night attack's objective to "create a diversion was certainly attained, enemy activity on our front being very great for the rest of the night."[11] Whether it was sufficient to divert German resources from the fronts facing the Seaforths and the PPCLI would soon be determined.

◆ ◆ ◆

Having enjoyed a few hours of daylight overlooking the Moro River, the Seaforth Highlanders of Canada's officers and men were able to gain a slightly better understanding of the terrain in which they were to fight during the night of December 5–6 than had been the case for the Hasty P's. Yet recently promoted Lieutenant Colonel J. Douglas Forin knew he still faced a rush job "and rush jobs have spelt to us unfavorable settings and advantage with the Germans. Zero hour was midnight, the Seaforths had to commit one company to the main road axis to ensure safety for the RCE's mine sweepers."[12]

The requirement to send one of his companies up the main road toward an enemy town in order to protect a planned mine-sweeping party of Royal Canadian Engineers particularly rankled. It seemed premature to think of putting RCE troops across the river before San Leonardo was seized. The requirement that he screen their activity denied him a great deal of freedom in planning his route of attack. He would have to put one company up the side of the road and support it with another company on its immediate flank. That meant committing two-thirds of his assaulting force to a line of attack Forin thought near suicidal. If he were a German officer, an attack up the road to San Leonardo would be precisely what he would expect.

To offset the difficulty he anticipated with the road assault, Forin decided to send his remaining forward company out wide on the left flank. A gully there offered a good route up the valley slope to a position between San Leonardo and the hamlet of La Torre. If successful, this company would be able to cut San Leonardo off from reinforcements out of La Torre. The whole plan was very risky, but he must proceed as ordered by 2nd Canadian Infantry Brigade commander Brigadier Bert Hoffmeister.[13]

Forin issued his orders to the company commanders. 'B' Company, commanded by Captain W.H. Buchanan, would carry out the left hook manoeuvre to get between San Leonardo and La Torre. 'C' Company, under Captain David B. Blackburn, would lead the assault up the road, with Major Tom Vance's 'A' Company supporting its flank. 'D' Company and battalion HQ would remain in reserve on the other side of the river, ready to move up and reinforce whichever attacking company achieved a breakthrough to San Leonardo. Two of the company commanders were inexperienced in combat. Buchanan, a Calgary Highlander exchange officer sent to gain combat experience in preparation for the northern Europe invasion, had just come to the Seaforths from Britain. Blackburn had been recently shifted from command of the support company to infantry company command.

The inexperience of the company commanders reflected the losses the Seaforths and other 1st Division battalions had taken from sickness, mostly the jaundice epidemic. Forin himself was extremely weak with jaundice. He kept on his feet only by taking some pills the battalion doctor gave him and by eating a restricted diet of boiled chicken and tinned salmon. Although he thought the jaundice was improving, it still affected his ability to lead because of the weakness he experienced.[14]

Forin's orders to the company commanders were that, in accordance with instructions from Hoffmeister, their specific task was to establish a bridgehead on the other side of the Moro River by capturing San Leonardo. Third Field Company of the RCE was standing by with the equipment necessary to build an improvised sixty-foot-long crossing constructed of steel cribs that would be capable of supporting seventeen-pounder antitank guns.[15] The purpose of the Seaforths' bridgehead was to push German infantry back from the destroyed bridge that crossed the river before the town. This would allow the engineers to construct a Bailey bridge without being subjected to small-arms fire. Therefore, if successful in seizing San Leonardo, the companies were not to advance forward but to dig in and await the completion of the bridge. Once the bridge was finished, it would be possible to move tanks up in support of the Seaforths and the bridgehead could then be expanded. Forin completed his briefing by admonishing each company commander to maintain regular radio contact with HQ, so he would know when and where to deploy 'D' Company.[16]

Precisely at midnight, 'B' Company set off. Accompanying it was Captain T. Lem Carter, a forward observation officer for the Royal Canadian Artillery's 2nd Field Regiment. His presence meant that 'B' Company had the use of two #18 field radio sets, the British man-carried standard radio for company-sized units. The other companies each had one of these radios. Within minutes of 'B' Company's departure, 'C' Company set off down the slope. Both companies were following narrow paths located in the afternoon by the scout platoon, which appeared to lead down to the river. Thirty minutes later, 'A' Company set off on another track. At the head of 'A' Company was scout platoon trooper Private A.K. Harris.

Harris's job was to get the company across the river. Once finished that task, he was free to return to battalion headquarters. Heavy clouds obscured the moon as Harris led the company along the ridgeline to the path they would use for the descent to the valley floor. In contrast to the men following noisily behind him, Harris wore rope-soled shoes and carried nothing metal other than his helmet and a pistol. Ahead, German shells started striking the ridge. Harris led the company off on a wide detour away from the ridgeline to avoid the artillery concentrations. He was moving slowly, carefully, the way a scout who wants to stay alive does. This was too slow, however, for Vance, who passed word along to Harris to pick up the pace. Reluctantly Harris did so and soon reached the path leading into the valley. Vance, Lieutenant J.W. Baldwin of the lead platoon, and Company Sergeant Major Angus Blaker joined Harris at the trailhead. Vance insisted Harris take a section of Baldwin's platoon with him to serve as a bodyguard. Harris initially protested, but finally realized he was caught in the age-old dilemma soldiers face when presented with questionable orders from an officer. With his unwanted bodyguard in tow, Harris started the descent. "The noise of the men with me seems more dangerous than their protection is worth," he later wrote.

Harris proceeded to "drop them off as guides at each turn in the trail. The brush was head high. Every few minutes a flare blossomed in the sky and sparkled brilliantly for a minute or so.[17] Each time a flare popped, Harris froze and surveyed the bleached landscape before him. There was no sign of German positions or that enemy soldiers had been using the trail. Safely at the river, which he considered little more than a stream, Harris waded across and up the steep bank on the other side. In a few minutes he was joined by Lieutenant Baldwin and his platoon. Harris's job was done, but he was unable to decide what to do next. His orders were to return to battalion HQ, but HQ itself was expected to cross the river during the night. If he returned, Harris would only face another river crossing. When the Germans started shelling the trail over which the company had just come, Harris decided to stay with 'A' Company until HQ came forward.

Baldwin's platoon led off, Harris now preceding it as the point man. Soon word came up that the rear platoon was missing, apparently having lost track of the rest of the column in the dark. By this time, Harris was in near panic about the noise coming from the men behind him. "Clinking equipment, boots squelching in the mud, and the odd muttered curse" carried clearly above the sound of distant battle. It seemed impossible that the Germans could fail to hear the company's approach. Harris later wrote that when he was about ten feet in front of the lead platoon, crossing a small gully, "a stream of fire flies arch . . . through the blackness. They grope for the muffled sounds of 'A' Company. The quiet is shattered by the rip of Spandaus. There are shouted commands behind and then the pop-pop-pop of the Brens." Harris, officially a guest at this battle, decided to "lay doggo."[18]

While Harris, armed with only a pistol, went to ground, 'A' Company strung out behind him was pinned down by a hail of fire from what seemed to be at least a dozen machine guns. In the first seconds of the fight, Major Vance was blinded by the brilliant flash from a high-explosive shell exploding right in front of him, Company Sergeant Major Angus Blaker was killed, and Lieutenant Baldwin wounded. Soldiers all along the line were down, some wounded, others dead or dying. Despite being injured, Baldwin tried to work small parties of his platoon forward but the enemy fire was too intense. His radio having broken down during the river crossing, the wounded Vance was unable to reach Forin to either request reinforcement or to seek permission to break off contact with the enemy and withdraw. After the battle raged on for some time and his unit absorbed still more casualties, Vance ordered a withdrawal back across the Moro.[19]

To Harris, hunkered in cover on the other side of the gully, it seemed the Canadians were engaged in a "much noisier night battle than the Germans. . . . There seemed to be much shouting back and forth from our side. In the short periods of silence it was possible to hear the quiet disciplined voices of the German machine gunners through the darkness. One got the unfair impression that they were the better soldiers." He realized, however, that the reality was that a unit caught in an ambush was more likely to break noise discipline. Had the tables been turned, Harris figured that the Germans would have appeared just as panicked as the Canadians.[20]

At 0200 hours, about one hour after 'A' Company broke contact with the enemy, one of its runners reported to Forin that the remains of two platoons were across the river and returning to battalion HQ with casualties.[21] No. 7 Platoon of 'A' Company, separated from the other two platoons shortly after the river crossing, was apparently still on the other side of the river.

Harris had listened to the soldiers withdraw, knowing it was impossible for him to safely join their retreat. Even after the company had gone, the Germans continued to rake the area with machine-gun fire. Finally, when the guns fell quiet, Harris crawled over to a haystack he had spotted earlier and wormed into its heart. Once inside he was able to stand and poke his head out for a good look around. He could see precious little, including any of the machine-gun positions that had fired on 'A' Company. Just as it started to turn light, Harris left the stack and retraced his steps to the south bank of the Moro.[22]

◆ ◆ ◆

While two platoons of 'A' Company were being cut up in an ambush on the right flank of the Seaforth attack, 'B' Company slipped through to its objective to the west of San Leonardo without a shot being fired. Buchanan set up his positions and waited for the dawn. Despite Forin's orders to report back, battalion HQ heard nothing from Buchanan. As far as Forin knew, 'B' Company had simply vanished on the other side of the river.[23]

As for 'C' Company, it advanced only one hundred yards beyond the river's edge before being struck by machine-gun fire from the facing high ground at 0100 hours. The guns appeared to be firing on pre-fixed lines with excellent overlap, so there was no chance of any platoon pressing an attack without being cut to pieces. The company went to ground, conserving ammunition and offering only token return fire against the German gunners.[24]

Throughout the rest of the confused night of fighting, Forin's radio stayed completely quiet. He could raise nobody. Lacking any idea of 'B' Company's whereabouts, able to see the volume of enemy fire raking 'C' Company, and with 'A' Company staggering back across the Moro in disarray, Forin saw little point in advancing 'D' Company into the fray. Meanwhile, the alerted Germans had started heavily shelling the area of the blown bridge. The RCE unit decided that work on throwing the bridge over the river could not continue and the engineers retreated to safety. It was clear to Forin that if anything tangible could be rescued from the night's attack it would have to wait until daylight. Perhaps then he would be able to bring supporting artillery and mortar fire in to break up the enemy resistance and enable the battalion to advance.[25]

# 6

## No Good, Johnny

Of the three regiments attacking across the Moro River on the night of December 5 and in the early morning hours of December 6, the Princess Patricia's Canadian Light Infantry had conducted the most thorough reconnaissance and planning. Early patrols had discovered a ford slightly downstream of Villa Rogatti. Thirty-year-old Lieutenant Colonel Cameron Bethel Ware, a permanent force officer before the war, decided to send his entire three-company attack force up this route. 'B' Company would lead at midnight, with 'A' Company following in thirty minutes, and 'C' Company crossing fifty minutes after the first company jumped off. 'D' Company would remain in reserve, scheduled to join the battle in the morning. Rather than spread his companies out and assault the village from differing flanks, Ware planned to attack on a one-company wide front, hitting Villa Rogatti from the southeast. The two following companies would then move through 'B' Company to exploit success or provide immediate reinforcement.

Ware had also managed to develop some concrete plans for the battalion's reinforcement in the morning by tanks of the British 44th

Royal Tank Regiment. Under cover of first darkness, PPCLI patrols, accompanied by some 44th tankers, had determined that tanks could negotiate a rough road that led down from the southern ridge to a destroyed bridge directly below Villa Rogatti. The river here was found to be fordable by tanks and unguarded by German sentries. Once across the river, the tanks could follow a circuitous route up to the ridgeline by driving along the valley floor to a point about a mile downstream, and winding up another narrow track to the ridge. From there, a road led back to the village. It would be a difficult task for the tankers to get through the mud of the river and follow the extremely rough and slippery tracks, but all concerned thought the plan should work.

At the same time as the patrols investigating tank routes went into the Moro valley, a 'B' Company patrol commanded by Lieutenant J.L. McCullough set off on a hazardous reconnaissance up the opposing ridgeline and into the rear of Villa Rogatti. McCullough's task was to assess the validity of Canadian intelligence reports on the defences at the village. The lieutenant and his small patrol managed to slip through the German defensive net, conducted a limited observation, and returned without a shot being fired. McCullough reported to Ware that Villa Rogatti was anything but an isolated German outpost. While the patrol had been on the other side of the valley, they had seen and heard almost constant movement of enemy troops passing in and out of the village. Further, McCullough said it was evident that German armour would be able to easily reach Villa Rogatti from rear positions.

The report confirmed Ware's suspicions. Assuming his infantry companies could seize Villa Rogatti during the night, he absolutely must receive early morning support from the British tanks to hold on when the Germans inevitably launched a strong counterattack supported by Panzer tanks. Success would hinge almost entirely on the tankers getting over the river and into the village before the enemy could organize and deploy a strong reaction force. [1]

First, however, Villa Rogatti had to be taken. Intelligence reports, relying largely on aerial reconnaissance photos, showed that the Panzer Grenadiers had heavily fortified the village. Gun pits had been dug in the surrounding orchards and vineyards; houses had been transformed into bunkers. The village itself presented a difficult obstacle, set on a point where the ridgeline was shaped roughly like a horseshoe with the two spurs facing the river. Villa Rogatti's small stone houses circled the edge of the horseshoe and were backed by a mixture of terraced vineyards and orchards interspersed with small, deep gullies. There was very little depth to the village, as most of the buildings bordered the edge of the ridge. The whole place was little more than two streets wide.

To disorganize and suppress the German defenders, an artillery barrage had originally been scheduled for just prior to the lead company's jump-off time of 2359 hours. Ware received no indication from either divisional or brigade headquarters of Vokes's decision that all the attacks that night would be made silently, without artillery support. At 2350 hours he was still anxiously awaiting the beginning of the barrage, thinking that if the barrage were delayed for some reason the shells would catch 'B' Company as it entered the valley on schedule. It was a hellish moment for the PPCLI commander as he had to decide whether to wait for a barrage which might or might not come, or plunge ahead with the attack. Ware gave his orders and at 2359 hours 'B' Company descended into the valley.[2]

◆ ◆ ◆

Without an artillery barrage, the only way for the PPCLI to capture Villa Rogatti would be to get as close as possible before the Germans realized they were being attacked. Captain R.F.S. Robertson led 'B' Company down the steep, slippery slope on a narrow donkey trail that cut through the olive groves to the river. The company waded across and moved downstream along the northern bank to a junction in the valley-bottom trail, from which two trails ascended to either spur of the village. Robertson's lead platoon set off on the trail heading up to the southeastern portion of Villa Rogatti. When the advancing soldiers entered a narrow defile leading to the village, a German machine gun started to fire from the high ground to their left. This was followed by a shower of stick grenades and another machine gun opening up on the right. 'B' Company faced an arc of enemy positions, well concealed in the dense foliage of the vineyards and olive groves.

Despite the intensity of the resistance, Robertson's unit immediately went on the offensive. Bren guns and the company's two-inch mortars were put into action, the latter firing at almost the minimum extent of their range on a virtually flat trajectory. Lieutenant J.G. Clarke was hit in the throat by a bullet, but 'B' Company succeeded in closing with the enemy positions and destroying them with bursts of small-arms fire and grenades. Some of the defenders abandoned their positions and retreated toward the village, others surrendered on the spot. Pressing forward, the company moved past the houses on the outskirts and found it had breached the Germans' primary defensive line. 'B' Company was now in the midst of the Germans, most of whom were staggering half-dressed and bleary-eyed out of their billets in the village's houses to become prisoners.

Following close on 'B' Company's heels was 'A' Company under the command of Major W. "Bucko" Watson. He swung his company to the right, heading for the most northerly reaches of the village. As the lead section rushed across a road leading into Villa Rogatti, a German motorcyclist roared out of the darkness toward the village yelling, "Achtung! Achtung!" at the men he obviously thought were Germans. Several of the Canadians raised their rifles and a volley of fire tore the soldier off his BMW motorcycle. The motorcycle barrelled into the ditch and the body rolled in next to it. The company pushed on, leapfrogging platoons as they swept through the buildings. More prisoners were taken and more Germans killed or sent fleeing into the darkness beyond Villa Rogatti. The village was essentially in Canadian hands. In some of the houses where Germans had been billeted, the Canadians discovered half-eaten meals abandoned on kitchen tables.[3]

◆ ◆ ◆

Although two companies of the PPCLI were now inside Villa Rogatti, the Germans still had numerous fortified positions on all sides of the village. 'C' Company was heading up a trail directly in front of Villa Rogatti, with Lieutenant George Garbutt's platoon leading. The path broadened slightly, and just as the first soldiers entered this ground a grenade exploded about fifteen feet to one side. The Calgary-born officer heard no prior challenge issued by the German sentries. Seconds later, another grenade went off ten feet away, followed almost immediately by a slight plopping sound directly behind Garbutt. He hunched over, waiting, and then the grenade detonated only three feet behind him. Shrapnel whizzed between his legs, one small piece biting into his calf. Realizing the trail was a preset killing zone, Garbutt plunged to the left, pushing up a slight rise through some bordering bushes, and found himself on open ground. Meanwhile, his men backed around a corner in the path. So far there had been only one man in the platoon significantly wounded. Corporal Ralph Andros had a small piece of shrapnel sticking from his boot that had penetrated about half an inch into his foot.

A machine gun positioned seventy to eighty yards ahead of the platoon started firing down the path. Pulling the pin on his one grenade, Garbutt threw it straight up the hill toward the gun, hoping to cause them some worry. He was sure the grenade failed to explode anywhere near the gun because of the throwing range. Still, the gun stopped firing and the platoon was able to use the lull to get off the path to safer ground.

Silence fell over the battlefield, the Germans practising excellent noise discipline so that Garbutt was unable to fix their position. He lay on the ground, searching up the hill for any silhouettes against the light from the village, but could see nothing. He thought that the grenade throwers were probably to his right, roughly in a position directly above the ambush point. Garbutt raised his Thompson sub-machine gun, intending to put a burst of fire where he guessed the Germans were. The gun snapped out one shot and then jammed. Garbutt cursed himself for carelessly loading the magazine and started scrabbling in his front-leg pockets, which were hard to reach lying prone as he was, for another magazine. Then he fumbled the jammed clip clear and replaced it with the fresh one. It seemed an eternity had passed since the gun jammed; he was damned scared, knowing the shot and resulting muzzle flash had betrayed his position.

Just as he was ready to open fire again, Garbutt heard a soft rustling on the path below him and then a quiet "Sir? followed by "Mr. Garbutt?" Recognizing the voice as that of his young runner, who had been cut off from him when the ambush started, Garbutt realized the man had crept back to the spot where he and the platoon had parted company in hopes of finding his commander. The officer slipped down to his runner and whispered to him to go back to the platoon and bring up some grenades. When the man returned with a satchel of grenades, Garbutt sent him back to the platoon.

Alone again, Garbutt started tossing grenades into the position from which he thought the Germans had sprung their ambush. When the grenades were used up, he crawled back to his men, who had now been joined by the rest of 'C' Company. A medical orderly quickly put a bandage on Garbutt's calf and then he led off again, taking his platoon about fifty yards to the left in hopes of getting up to Villa Rogatti by a different route. After going only a short distance, he heard a soft challenge issued in German, followed almost immediately by another grenade exploding harmlessly some twenty feet away. The platoon backed off, reported to 'C' Company commander Captain M. Cousins, and the entire company hunkered down to await first light.[4]

♦ ♦ ♦

Taking a slightly different line of approach than 'C' Company, Ware was advancing with his headquarters combat section, following closely on the heels of 'D' Company and the machine gun platoon of Saskatoon Light Infantry assigned to the battalion. Ware liked to lead from the front and he was determined to get into Villa Rogatti by dawn so he could personally direct the defence.[5] With him was Lance Corporal Jack Haley, his radio signaller. Haley and his assistant were using two mules to transport the heavy #22 radio set Ware used to communicate with brigade and divisional headquarters. The radio was usually transported by Bren carrier or truck, but neither of these vehicles was currently usable, so Haley had resorted to mules. The radio was slung on one mule and its two large rechargeable batteries were on the other animal, with wires running between. This gave him power and enabled the use of the radio while moving forward. The two mules were linked together by a chain running between their necks. A wiry Moroccan muleteer was along to handle the large beasts.

As Ware's group moved into the valley, Haley saw tracers arcing through the fading darkness. It seemed to be mostly German fire concentrated on fixed lines rather than a firefight. A lot of the firing came from Schmeisser 9-millimetre submachine guns. Just as Haley and his mules started heading directly down into the valley, one of these guns opened up with a long burst of fire into the brush some way off from the advancing column. The mule skinner jumped and took one long, wild-eyed look over at Haley. "No good, Johnny," he said, then scampered off up the slope and disappeared.

Haley was now a mule skinner. As they descended into the valley, the soldiers near the mules groused in whispers that the damned animals were making too much noise and were going to draw German fire. Haley could hardly blame them because it was true. The mules were blundering into the stabilizing poles the Italian farmers used to train their grape vines, and as every pole cracked underfoot the racket was terrific. With each outburst of noise caused by the mules, the German Schmeisser fire intensified.

Things suddenly went from bad to worse when the mules, led inexpertly by Haley, blundered one on either side of a tree, whereupon the connecting chain pulled them up abruptly in their tracks. Both mules started pawing the ground, snorting, and trying to bull forward. Haley and his assistant vainly attempted to guide the animals backward to untangle them from the tree. The German gunfire increased in volume and intensity, tracers searching along the hillside for the source of the noise. Then the chain snapped and the two mules crashed off down the hill, the one with the radio trailing electrical wires in its wake. The only consolation for Haley was that the German fire stopped creeping toward him.

Frustrated, sure he would never see the mules or his radio equipment again, Haley passed word down the advancing line of soldiers ahead for anyone seeing the mules to gather them in and wait. To his surprise, just before the river Haley caught up to the mules, with two hefty infantrymen holding them by their chains. The men handed over the animals and all too happily departed. Haley hooked the wires back to the battery, discovered he still had power and was able to go on the air, and then continued on to the river. As his mule team started across, he realized it was just about light. The river was shallow, barely boot-top depth, but daylight was coming surprisingly fast. "My God," Haley thought, "they'll see us for sure. Here we are on this riverbed and we'll get shot at." But the Germans, so eager to fire at any sound only minutes before, were inexplicably silent as the entire formation of soldiers crossed the river and started up the slope toward Villa Rogatti.

Things remained quiet the whole way up the main trail into the village. Once inside, Ware established his headquarters in a farmhouse overlooking the valley on the community's southeastern flank. Haley and his assistant quickly dug a slit trench next to the house, put up the radio aerial, and established an excellent link with brigade HQ.[6]

◆ ◆ ◆

While Ware's party crossed the Moro and came up on Villa Rogatti, 'C' Company had advanced at first light against the positions that had earlier blocked them. This time there was no opposition. About one hundred yards uphill from where the ambush had been sprung, Garbutt's platoon discovered a dead German lying in a slit trench. There was no indication of what had killed the man.

The soldiers pressed on and reached some relatively level terrain across which a number of empty slit trenches were scattered. Farther uphill, Garbutt saw a figure run across an opening and heard a man yell, "Herr Oberleutnant." Garbutt moved up quickly, expecting a fight, but found only two soldiers, who he thought were probably Poles, sitting in a slit trench. They immediately surrendered.

Continuing up the hill, Garbutt next saw a German soldier moving around near a machine gun only about seventy yards away. He seemed to be picking up things lying on the ground, shell casings perhaps. Garbutt and his platoon opened fire. The German dashed to his gun and started firing back, ripping off burst after burst toward the Canadians for a full minute or more. Then he must have realized that he was in trouble and outgunned, for he jumped away from the gun and ran uphill through some small brush and high grass. Garbutt's platoon kept shooting. Brens and rifles were pounding away but he disappeared apparently unscathed. "Amazing," was all Garbutt could think.[7]

From there, the advance into Villa Rogatti went unopposed and 'C' Company fell in just behind battalion HQ to serve as the reserve company. The other companies were dug in throughout the village and there seemed to be a lot of firing going on. But, with four rifle companies, its medium machine-gun platoon, and combat HQ section all in position, there was no doubt that the PPCLI had secured its objective and was determined to stay. Ware was even beginning to think it possible the battalion could achieve its next objective: to clear the way for an advance by the Loyal Edmonton Regiment through Villa Rogatti to the fortified villages of Villa Jubatti and Villa Caldari, and on from there to cut the Ortona-Orsogna lateral highway. Such a move would isolate the German west flank, which rested on the fortress position of Orsogna. This would open a route for out-flanking Ortona, perhaps allowing the town to fall to the Canadians without a shot being fired in its streets.[8] If the tanks got over and reinforced the PPCLI, Ware began to feel such an exploitation of his battalion's success was possible. First, however, he had to repel the counterattacks that were surely coming.[9]

◆ ◆ ◆

Morning skies over Villa Rogatti were clear, the sun's surprising warmth raising steam off the soggy clothing of German corpses scattered among the surrounding olive groves and vineyards and in the streets, backyards, and houses. But the fighting continued unabated. Shortly after dawn, it was evident that the 90th Panzer Grenadiers' 200th Regiment had recovered from the surprise that had caused it to lose the village the previous night to the Patricias. Mortar and artillery field guns started pounding the houses and streets; machine-gunners and riflemen opened up from the dense cover of the surrounding farmland.[10]

Crouched in his slit trench, bullets and shrapnel flying overhead, Lance Corporal Jack Haley hunkered over his radio, ensuring that brigade HQ was kept informed of developments in the battle. He was also passing firing coordinates to the supporting artillery regiment on behalf of its forward observation officer, whose radio was broken. The FOO's radio loss was actually good news to Haley because the set's batteries were still strong, giving him some badly needed spares. Haley's main concern was that, lacking any opportunity for resupply of fresh batteries, his radio would fail at a critical moment. Responding to orders from Ware, the FOO was concentrating artillery shoots from the gun companies at the town's edges to break up German formations trying to fight their way back into Villa Rogatti's streets. The intensity of the German counterbombardment and light-weapons fire seemed to keep increasing. Shrapnel flew all over battalion HQ's farmyard, snapping through the house's windows. Bullets scythed the air. Haley saw a young girl, not more than six or seven years old, run into the street between two buildings and abruptly tumble to the ground. A soldier rushed over, scooped her up, and carried her to cover. Later he saw the girl being treated by the medical officer, who told him she had miraculously been grazed across the lips by a bullet. Although both lips were severely swollen, she would be all right. This was not the case for Haley's recalcitrant mules. They were sprawled beside a building, legs up, bodies continuing to be mangled by shrapnel and shell blasts.[11]

For the rifle companies on the village edge, conditions were much worse. Fire coming into the west of the town was thicker than anything the PPCLI had yet seen in Italy. Having only the ammunition each man had carried across the river on his back, the soldiers were running desperately short. One Bren gunner refused to fire on enemy groups of "less than twenty," in an effort to conserve bullets.[12] 'B' Company Sergeant Major W.D. Davidson scrambled back to where 'C' Company waited in reserve by battalion HQ and begged three bandoliers of ammunition. Throwing the heavy load over his shoulders, he lurched back to his men with the vital resupply.[13]

Early in the morning, the Germans increased the pressure on the PPCLI by launching an all-out counterattack. Luckily for the PPCLI, the attack's execution was poorly organized. Obviously confused about the overall Canadian disposition, a platoon of Panzer Grenadiers began forming up behind a hedge directly opposite battalion HQ. Ware looked out a second-storey window and beckoned for the men around him to grab their guns. About five battalion staff, including Ware who carried a Thompson submachine gun, poked their guns out the window and broke up the German formation with an intense volley of fire. The Germans scattered back into the vegetation, leaving several dead.[14] One officer and a sergeant were pinned down in some brush, but ignored calls to surrender. A couple of soldiers were detailed to ensure the Germans were kept in place with rifle fire every time they tried to slip away.[15]

◆ ◆ ◆

Meanwhile, troops in the forward sections of 'A' Company watched helplessly as the Panzer Grenadiers manhandled an antitank gun up the hill to a firing position beyond the range of their weapons. Minutes later, shells from the gun started punching holes in the buildings they were using for cover. Infantry, supported by heavy machine-gun fire and the antitank gun, forced their way into the streets. Major Bucko Watson shifted his 'A' Company platoons to meet the threat, but one five-man section under the command of Lieutenant R. Carey found itself isolated and out of ammunition. The unit had to surrender and the Germans quickly led the Canadian soldiers away before a rescue could be effected. Casualties in the company were heavy and it was beginning to seem that the Germans might wipe out more sections.[16]

Realizing he could do little to influence events from battalion HQ, Ware dashed 300 yards across open ground raked by machine-gun fire to link up with Watson. The battalion commander took over command of the company and proceeded to reorganize its units to meet and repel the attack through effective counterassaults supported by fire from other sections. Slowly the Germans gave ground and withdrew into the tangled vegetation of the shell-torn vineyards.[17]

Repelling this attack brought the PPCLI no respite. The tired soldiers soon heard the distinctive roar of engines and the squeaking, clanking sound made by the tracks of German tanks. Supported by the 75-millimetre cannon and mounted machine guns of several Panzer Mark IVs, German infantry were soon in among the Canadian positions on the west flank of the village. Crouched in his slit trench, continuing to send orders that directed the artillery bombardment practically into the battalion's forward positions, Haley looked longingly toward the eastern road snaking up out of the Moro valley. He could hear tanks down there grinding and churning away. But it was obvious they were mired in the mud and having a rough time getting up. If they didn't arrive bloody soon, Haley worried the battalion might just be overrun.[18]

Ware, sharing this concern, sent Lieutenant W. Riddell sprinting back toward the river to find the tanks and guide them into the village. Rushing down the slope, Riddell jumped off a ledge and landed directly on top of a hiding German soldier. Hearing a groan from the man, the officer drew his pistol only to discover another German coming out of some brush with his hands up. Riddell's orders were to get to the tanks, not to mess about with surrendering Germans, but luckily his orderly was in tow. Handing off the surprisingly docile Germans — who outgunned Riddell's little pistol — to the similarly armed orderly, Riddell hurried on. A few minutes later, he linked up with the commander of the 44th Royal Tank Regiment squad. Four of the unit's tanks were hopelessly bogged down in the mud, but the other seven were able to advance into Villa Rogatti.[19]

"Just like the cavalry in the movies," Haley thought as the British tankers roared up over the lip of the valley. The tanks rolled past battalion HQ and drove directly into the battle raging on the west side of the village. With the appearance of the tanks, the German officer and his sergeant who had been hiding near headquarters came out with hands up and walked into the Canadian perimeter.[20]

The tanks reached 'A' Company at a critical moment, just as the unit was becoming increasingly disorganized, ammunition was rapidly disappearing, and casualties were mounting. Although the company had tried knocking out the German tanks with its PIATs, none of the unreliable and difficult-to-fire rounds from the hand-held antitank weapon had scored a crippling hit. Formally designated "Projector Infantry Anti-Tank," the PIAT was a thirty-two-pound shoulder-braced launcher, firing a 2.5-pound bomb that looked like a short-barrelled version of the more commonly recognized American bazooka. It required an extremely steady hand to aim and fire accurately. And, unless the firing soldier was lucky enough to score a hit on one of the more lightly armoured sections of a tank, the chance of doing significant damage was slight. Most Canadian soldiers hated the weapon, knowing that it was probably going to fail in knocking out the tank while also bringing the man firing it to the tank crew's attention.[21]

As the British tanks rolled up, almost everyone in 'A' Company from its commander to a number of lowly privates tumbled out of firing positions, rushed up to the tanks, and started pointing out targets for immediate attention. The British tank commanders leaned out to receive directions. Everybody ignored the incoming German fire, which Ware later described as "flying so thick it didn't matter whether one was laying down, standing up, or running." Within moments of the tanks opening fire, a green flare went up from the enemy lines and the German armour and infantrymen retreated from the village.[22] Ware estimated that this first counterattack had been launched by two Panzer Grenadier companies and a squadron of tanks. As the Germans withdrew, 'A' Company threw out a hasty fighting patrol to capture the abandoned antitank gun and drag it into the perimeter. It was 1130 hours. Ware ordered his companies to start digging in and to expect another counterattack at any moment. The British tanks slipped into hull-down hiding positions behind various houses, but the squadron's commander warned Ware that their ammunition was in short supply.[23]

At noon a mule train arrived, carrying medical supplies and precious munitions for the infantry. Nearly forty men, most from 'A' Company, were being given the best treatment possible by medical officer Captain W.L.C. McGill in the cover of a couple of buildings near the battalion HQ. It was impossible to safely evacuate them from Villa Rogatti to the other side of the Moro because of the continuous shelling. Shortly after the mule train arrived, a British tank rumbled in filled to the brim with more shells for the tankers.[24]

In the early afternoon the good weather turned poor. A light rain began falling and fog crept in. Haley, worried that the rain might leak inside the radio casing and short out the unit, sent his assistant to find a more sheltered position. The man located a small stone hut near battalion HQ with a narrow window that the aerial could be extended through. A few minutes after they lugged the radio gear to the new location, a mortar barrage dumped down on the farmyard and a direct hit turned his slit trench into a crater.

Haley began to wonder why the hell he had been in such a hurry to go off to war. There he had been at sixteen years old, standing in a line in the Seaforth Highlanders of Canada barracks with a lot of young, pimply boys obviously not far past puberty. The recruiting officer had come down the line asking ages and with each pronouncement of "Nineteen, sir," sent the boy back for his birth certificate. Haley had fled his home in Medicine Hat several weeks before, riding the boxcars to Vancouver, heading for the adventure and excitement of war. When the officer confronted him, Haley snapped, "Nineteen, sir!" and cracked his heels sharply together while assuming a stance of perfect attention. The officer grinned without humour. "I don't bloody believe you, boy, but you're in." Next the officers learned that the former Boy Scout knew Morse code. He was off to the Royal Canadian Signal Corps, then upon graduation from the signallers' school was eventually assigned to the PPCLI as Ware's personal radio signaller. Which had brought him to Villa Rogatti, where the excitement and adventure he had sought was just a little too immediate for his liking.[25]

At 1530 hours, 'B' Company's Captain Robertson signalled Ware that a German attack was coming his way. He estimated the Germans were sending in about seventy infantrymen in support of nine Mark IV tanks. The artillery fire that had continued to make any movement inside the perimeter a deadly undertaking suddenly increased, and the German machine-gunners hiding in the olive groves and vineyards cranked up their volume of fire. Ware again rushed from the battalion HQ across about 500 yards of largely open ground saturated by enemy machine-gun and mortar fire to reach the British tanks. Riding on the outside hull of one of the tanks, he guided them to a position that provided a perfect field of fire against the approaching armour. In conference with the tank commander, it was agreed the tanks should stay hidden until the enemy were very close. Ware then moved off across more hotly contested fire zones to reach 'B' Company and assist Robertson in mounting his perimeter defence.[26]

◆ ◆ ◆

The enemy tank company approaching Villa Rogatti was 7 Company, 26th Panzer Regiment, commanded by Oberleutnant Ruckdeschel. One and a quarter miles southwest of the village, Ruckdeschel linked up with an officer from the 200th Panzer Grenadier Regiment, but was unable to get a solid report on Canadian dispositions inside the town. The attacking force then advanced on line in a northeasterly direction to the left of the road entering the village. Infantry, formed on either side and to the rear of each tank, provided covering protection. The tanks ground along in low gear, pushing through the olive trees and vineyards, churning the ground beneath the tracks into deep, muddy ruts. Visibility for the tank commanders was zero due to the trees and high vines. The dense fog further restricted Ruckdeschel's vision to about 100 yards.

Two hundred yards outside Villa Rogatti, Ruckdeschel recorded in an after-action report, the tanks "were suddenly struck by a terrific bombardment. Tank 724 was hit, presumably in the fuel tank and immediately caught fire. The company thereupon responded with counter-fire from all vehicles."[27] Visibility was still so obscured that the German tankers could only fire at muzzle flashes from the British armour. Ruckdeschel thought his tanks faced superior massed tank fire, and seconds later an "intense and well directed" artillery bombardment started falling. Tank 725 had its right track shot off, 733 was knocked out by a shot through its gears. The remaining six tanks pressed forward in "a series of rushes, at the same time firing rapidly in the direction of the muzzle flashes. . . . In the village a house was on fire."[28] Tank 712 broke to the right and started ripping up a 'C' Company platoon with its machine gun. Cutting back to the road, the commander of this tank spotted a British tank on the edge of the village and knocked it out with three rapid shots.

   The rest of Ruckdeschel's company had continued advancing in rushes until it was within fifty yards of the village. The tanks were bringing the Canadian infantry in facing houses under fire with machine guns and their main cannon. Armour-piercing shells were opening holes in the walls, turning the heavy stone into splinters of skin-flaying shrapnel. Tank 721 took several shots from British tanks in its turret. Ruckdeschel noticed another British tank through the smoke and fog, standing silently with its turret directed toward his tank. He assumed one of his tanks had knocked the British machine out of action. Thirty yards from Villa Rogatti, 734's engine took a direct hit, followed by several other quickly delivered strikes. Ruckdeschel thought this fire came from an antitank gun, but he couldn't see where the weapon was located. The PPCLI's six-pounder antitank guns were shooting with amazing accuracy from positions several hundred yards away on the southern ridge of the Moro valley.[29]

   Although the Panzer Grenadiers managed to get inside the village, they faced intense fire and started withdrawing almost immediately. Ruckdeschel decided that continuing the tank attack could only result in the loss of the entire squadron. He ordered a retreat and started gathering in the wounded and "detanked and drifting crews." Two of the wounded, a radio operator from 721 and its commander Leutnant Meyer, who had been hit by shell splinters after abandoning the tank, were squeezed inside the safety of Ruckdeschel's tank. The rest of 721's crew, all slightly wounded by artillery fire, and another tank commander whose tank had been knocked out of action, clung to the outside of the tank's hull as Ruckdeschel made a hasty withdrawal. Attempts by one of the other surviving tanks to tow back damaged tanks 725 and 733 failed. Ruckdeschel ordered both blown up after being stripped of usable parts.

The tank squadron commander mounted a guard with his remaining force on the road north of Villa Rogatti, in case the British tanks and Canadian infantry attempted to advance. Ruckdeschel's force had lost five tanks. Three tankers were known to be dead, six were wounded, and five were missing.[30] The infantry had taken a worse mauling. All the Germans had to show for the attack was that the 90th Panzer Grenadier command believed the Canadians were now contained in Villa Rogatti and would be unable to break through the encircling, heavily entrenched German defensive line.[31]

Not that the PPCLI had any immediate plans to undertake a breakout. 'A' and 'B' companies had borne the brunt of the day's fight and accounted for most of the battalion's eight dead, fifty-two wounded, and eight missing. This was the heaviest daily casualty rate the battalion had suffered in the war to date. About half the wounded were capable of walking and plans were underway for evacuating the wounded after nightfall. The PPCLI also had about forty prisoners under guard at battalion HQ.[32] Ware estimated enemy dead at about 120.[33] Enemy weapons captured included the antitank gun, six 81-millimetre mortars, many machine guns, and three motorcycles, as well as masses of food and clothing.[34]

At 2130 hours, two officers from the Loyal Edmonton Regiment came forward to discuss with Ware a plan that would see the Eddies moving through Rogatti in the morning and advancing on Villa Jubatti. Two hours later, however, this plan was cancelled and Ware was advised by Brigadier Bert Hoffmeister that if a withdrawal proved necessary, the PPCLI was to fall back across the Moro River.

Ever since joining the PPCLI as a young lieutenant commanding a machine-gun platoon, Ware had dreamed of one day commanding this battalion. He had just led it to the battalion's hardest-fought victory of the war. He was optimistic the PPCLI could easily hold and expand the bridgehead won on the northern side of the Moro if adequately supported. He was baffled. It was the first thought Ware had given to retreating.[35]

# 7

# MIXED RESULTS

WHILE the Princess Patricia's Canadian Light Infantry was successful in throwing back German counterattacks and consolidating its hold on Villa Rogatti during the daylight hours of December 6, the situation for the Seaforth Highlanders of Canada remained stalemated. Finally, Lieutenant Colonel Doug Forin had received word from Captain W.H. Buchanan at 0715 hours that 'B' Company was on its objective to the left flank of San Leonardo and taking fire from German heavy machine guns. Had there been radio communication during the night, Forin could have put 'D' Company across the river, enabling the two companies to fight their way side by side into San Leonardo. That opportunity was lost. The movement of a company in daylight across the hotly contested valley would yield nothing but casualties.

Meanwhile, small-arms fire kept 'C' Company pinned down alongside the road leading up from the Moro to the village. The company, which was well dug in and had suffered no casualties so far, had ceased attempting to advance against the German resistance. Forin knew he was unlikely to break this impasse unless tanks were put over the river to support the infantry. With armoured support, the Seaforths could renew the advance up the road and win entry into San Leonardo. The Seaforth commander's emotions seesawed between frustration over lost opportunity and anxiety over the uncertain fate of the companies on the opposite shore of the Moro River.[1]

Everything hinged on tanks. But the British Armoured Brigade's Shermans, supporting the Canadians until the 1st Canadian Armoured Brigade units reached the forward lines, failed to locate a workable river crossing. Four times that morning the tanks attempted to cross, only to bog down in the soft muck of the riverbed, forcing the abandonment of some of the tanks. In the absence of a proper diversion constructed by the Royal Canadian Engineers, it was obvious that the tanks were incapable of reinforcing the Seaforths. As for the engineers, any daylight attempt to construct a diversion with their bulldozers was deemed suicidal. Instead, the balance of the tank squadron supporting the Seaforths took up position on the southern ridgeline and proceeded to hammer revealed enemy machine gun posts in and around San Leonardo with cannon fire. In the afternoon, when clear skies gave way to rain and low-hanging fog, the effectiveness of their fire was greatly reduced.[2]

Meanwhile Forin was amazed to receive a radio request from Buchanan seeking permission to set off and capture La Torre, which the company commander figured was largely ungarrisoned. Given that the hamlet was well to the west of San Leonardo — the objective target — and of no tactical value to the current situation, Forin refused. He ordered Buchanan to shift 'B' Company to the western edge of San Leonardo, where it somewhat threatened the Germans pinning down 'C' Company. A presumably disappointed Buchanan radioed back that he had prisoners and was sending these back to battalion HQ.[3] There was no indication whether 'B' Company was moving to 'C' Company's aid, but at 1000 hours Buchanan reported meeting enemy opposition and being "in the process of cleaning it up."[4]

Still unsure what exactly 'B' Company was up to and seeking some way to get 'C' Company back on the offensive, Forin consulted with 2 CIB commander Brigadier Bert Hoffmeister. He told Hoffmeister that if he was supported by a heavy artillery barrage from the 2nd Field Regiment's twenty-five pounders and the 4.2-inch mortars of the Saskatoon Light Infantry, he would advance 'D'

Company, what was left of 'A' Company after its hard fight of the previous night, and battalion HQ over the river. Once across, this force would link up with 'C' Company and make a determined drive into San Leonardo. The two men agreed on the plan, setting the start time for 1400 hours.

◆ ◆ ◆

Buchanan's reluctance to break off his advance toward La Torre was motivated by 'B' Company's spectacular achievements. Throughout the morning and into the afternoon the small unit had pressed forward against intense enemy opposition. The Canadian soldiers seemed, Buchanan later related, "inspired and protected." Time and again they went up against superior, heavily entrenched forces and broke the defences. By 1400 hours, Buchanan had captured fifty-nine prisoners, and killed or wounded more than seventy Germans.

One house attacked by 'B' Company had been defended by sixteen machine guns. As the Canadians closed on the building and prepared to blast the defenders out with grenades, a white flag attached to the end of a rifle barrel poked out a window. Buchanan ordered his men to hold their fire. Seconds later, a German officer appeared in the doorway. He and a soldier armed with a light machine gun started walking toward the Seaforth line. When they were very close the two suddenly opened fire with their weapons and the Canadians shot them down. This was the second time Buchanan's men had faced a flag of surrender used as a deadly shield by the Panzer Grenadiers. The remaining defenders of the building were either killed or driven off during the Seaforths' renewed attack.

No sooner had they concluded this fight than an Italian boy of about fourteen ran up and pointed out a haystack that he said was actually a bunker containing an enemy machine gun and an antitank gun. As the boy started walking back to cover, he stepped on the igniting prong of a German Schützenmine or S-mine, triggering the spring that caused a canister loaded with 350 ball bearings to jump three feet into the air before exploding. Buchanan and his men rushed to the boy, but he was dead — his body shredded by the deadly charge. Enraged, three of the Seaforths rushed the haystack position, overwhelmed the surprised defenders, and killed them all.[5] Buchanan's men continued to advance, capturing positions, taking prisoners, and suffering hardly any casualties while killing dozens more of the enemy.

◆ ◆ ◆

While 'B' Company's raid continued and 2 CIB set its plans to conduct a breakout attack against San Leonardo, 1st Canadian Infantry Brigade had also decided to launch another offensive across the Moro River. Major Bert Kennedy, commander of the Hastings and Prince Edward Regiment, convinced Brigadier Howard Graham that a bridgehead could be won at the coastal road to the east of the Seaforths' debacle. Kennedy's objective was to move 500 yards beyond the Moro River to seize a junction of the coast highway with a road leading east into San Leonardo. With the junction in Canadian hands, 1 CIB could advance westward to either take San Leonardo independently or support the Seaforth attack. Alternatively, the brigade could advance on Ortona by the coast highway. Major General Chris Vokes approved the plan and Kennedy started finalizing details.

Because they already knew the ground, Kennedy decided to put the Hasty P's across at the same point used in the night's abortive attack. This would, however, be no attack by stealth against a well-dug-in and alert enemy. Instead, the Hasty P's would move forward on the heels of a twenty-minute barrage laid on by 2nd Field Regiment artillery and the brigade's Saskatoon Light Infantry 4.2-inch mortars. 'C' Company would establish a bridgehead immediately upon crossing the river and 'D' Company would attack through its position. Once the bridgehead had been established, the rest of the battalion and supporting tanks would cross to expand the position on the north bank of the Moro. The time for the attack was set for 1400 hours.

At 1340 hours, the barrage began precisely on schedule. Twenty minutes later 'C' Company moved forward.[6]

◆ ◆ ◆

As the Hasty P's advanced, the Seaforths' assault stalled before it even began. Just as Forin and his attack force started off, four German tanks were observed rolling into the streets of San Leonardo. The British tank commander, whose guns were to have supported the infantry, informed Hoffmeister his priority was now to bring the enemy tanks under fire. No support could be given to the infantry. Hoffmeister told Forin to scrap the planned attack and prepare for probable withdrawal of his companies from the opposite riverbank.[7] The brigadier was now of the opinion that 2 CIB should concentrate its attention on exploiting the success won by the PPCLI at Villa Rogatti, rather than continuing to push forward against the heavy resistance concentrated around San Leonardo. While this discussion was underway, the nearby tanks embarked on a pitched battle with the German armour, both sides ineffectually chucking shells back and forth in the gathering fog.[8]

Forin was little distressed by the attack cancellation. While the plan had been the only one possible, he had not been optimistic of success. Assuming the Seaforths had managed to take San Leonardo, they would only have been able to hold the village if the engineers managed to build a tank diversion over the Moro during the night. Were the engineers to fail, the battalion would be hard pressed to defend the village against the inevitable counterattacks that would be accompanied by strong armoured support. Unlike at Villa Rogatti, the German tankers would be blessed with some excellent level terrain over which to come directly into the village.[9]

However, Forin now faced the probability of having to disengage his companies across the river under fire. Further weakened each hour by jaundice, he grew ever more gloomy as he awaited final orders from brigade after Hoffmeister consulted with divisional command. Forin's depressed demeanour did not go unnoticed by Hoffmeister.[10]

◆ ◆ ◆

San Donato was nothing more than a loosely gathered scrabble of stone huts, a small chapel on an escarpment facing the Adriatic, and farmland interspersed between the homes of the twenty or thirty families who called this place home. The coast highway passed through San Donato, which also served as a crossroads for a road branching off to San Leonardo. For the past week, the sound of explosions had increased and sometimes the very earth under fifteen-year-old Anna Tucci's feet had quivered as if an earthquake threatened. The people of San Donato had looked south toward the distant sounds, wondering if and when the battle would reach them.

As the rumble of the guns crept closer, a few families loaded their belongings into carts, hitched up donkeys or mules, and set off as refugees through Ortona and north toward uncertain safety. Most, however, remained. Where was there to go? Where would be safe? This was their home; if they left, would return be possible? They looked south, made furtive preparations, and waited. At 1340 hours on December 6 the time of waiting ended. War came to San Donato and swept Anna Tucci into its maw.

It started with a hideous banshee wail, followed by an explosion in the fields near one of the houses. Clods of dirt flew up out of the black smoke and flame. Then the shriek of more shells filled the air and explosions blossomed all through San Donato. Immediately south of the Tucci house, the road junction appeared to be literally hurled to the heavens by a terrific bombardment. Anna heard invisible objects hissing through the air outside her family's home. Everyone in San Donato had made earlier preparations for this moment.

Anna and her family rushed from the house, ran into a narrow nearby gully and followed this to caves riddling the escarpment face. The escarpments had always been a warren of caves, a place where children played and parents warned darkly of the danger of being buried in a collapse. In the caves they had hidden food, blankets, and water. The people of San Donato crowded into the small caverns and hunkered there as the ground shook and trembled. Trickles of dirt showered down from the cave's ceilings and coated them in a light, chalky dust. A few villagers failed to reach the safety of the caves. Their bodies lay like discarded black rags amid the vegetable gardens, olive groves, and vineyards of San Donato.

After twenty minutes, the savage bombardment ended as abruptly as it had started. In its wake was no deathly stillness. Instead, the shriek of falling shells and thunder of explosions was replaced by the distant rattle of machine guns and the softer thump made by firing mortars and tank cannon. Anna huddled in the cave, terrified.[11]

◆ ◆ ◆

'C' Company of the Hasty P's was first across the Moro River, following closely in the wake of 4.2-inch mortar fire laid down by the Saskatoon Light Infantry. On the ridge behind, British tanks and self-propelled guns stood ready to pound opposing machine-gun positions as soon as they revealed themselves by firing on the infantry. The battalion's three-inch mortar company was dropping bombs down the firing tubes as fast as the gunners could work. Two forward observation officers from 2nd Field Regiment were on hand with radios to direct the twenty-five pounders onto enemy concentrations and strong points. The fog was thickening, and visibility was worsening.

'C' Company reached the far bank and started across the open ground leading to the ridgeline. From straight ahead and from the left flank, sudden thick concentrations of machine-gun and rifle fire struck the advancing line. Several men fell screaming. The rest quickly went to ground. What had started out like a Great War infantry assault, where men advanced in orderly lines, deteriorated in seconds to the norm of war in the 1940s. Soldiers crawled forward in small groups, while others covered them with rifle and Bren fire. Some men froze, clawed a hole in the earth, and refused to move. Others dashed about, exposing themselves recklessly to fire. The enemy resistance was fierce. 'C' Company's advance slowed, then stalled almost entirely.

Across the river, Kennedy, seeing the attack losing steam, directed 'D' Company into action. Its orders were to destroy the enemy positions on 'C' Company's left. To shield the company's advance, the mortars ceased firing high explosives and dropped a screening blanket of smoke bombs between the Canadians and the German positions. A troop of British tanks was dispatched to cross the river near the demolished coast highway bridge.[12] 'D' Company got very close to the enemy gun pits before running into what seemed a wall of fire. Kennedy saw the men scatter, many clawing into whatever cover they could find. A number appeared to fall, either wounded or killed. Radio communication with the company was lost.[13]

Disaster loomed as Kennedy received word that the tanks going to the infantry's support were hopelessly mired in the river mud. He knew the Germans had tanks nearby. It could not be long before they were deployed into the battle.[14] Reluctantly, at 1540 hours, Kennedy ordered a withdrawal. The Bren carrier platoon was to provide cover fire with its machine guns and the three-inch mortar platoon was to lay down smoke to blanket the infantry's movement back over the Moro. While 'C' Company withdrew easily, 'D' Company, either failing to receive the radioed order or being unable to break off contact with the enemy, remained in its position.[15] If not soon withdrawn, Kennedy feared the company would be overrun. Unexpectedly the fog engulfing 'D' Company cleared, and Kennedy saw that its soldiers had actually penetrated into the German defensive positions, which appeared to have been largely abandoned. What had looked moments before to be a minor defeat now offered the slightest glimmer of hope for a victory.

For five minutes Kennedy hesitated. To switch from withdrawal to hasty attack meant to risk most or all of the battalion, but the fate of many a battle has been decided in favour of the bold gamble. Kennedy ordered the nearest troops, the carrier platoon, to dismount and cross the river as foot infantry to support 'D' Company. He sent 'A' and 'B' companies forward to seize the objectives originally assigned to 'C' Company.[16] Kennedy led the two companies across himself, with Lieutenant Farley Mowat accompanying 'A' Company.

The fire that had slackened after 'C' Company's withdrawal immediately sprang back to life. Both advancing companies were caught in the open by the fire of heavy artillery, armoured fighting vehicles, mortars, and intense machine-gun fire. Casualties were surprisingly few given the concentrated fire, but still the regiment was taking many dead and wounded.[17] Retreating in the face of the German fire was impossible; the two companies could only continue forward.

On the left flank, the combined force of 'D' Company and the carrier platoon troops pressed upward and managed to cut through the German positions on the slope to reach the ridgeline itself. There the unit was pulled up abruptly by a well-organized counterattack that forced it back over the lip of the ridge. Here 'D' Company was joined by the rest of the battalion, now including 'C' Company.

Kennedy, realizing infantry could not possibly advance into the open ground beyond the ridge to face down German tanks without armoured support, ordered his men to dig into the slope of the ridgeline.[18] This position was known as a reverse slope, and enemy tanks could not depress their gun barrels sufficiently to bring the soldiers hiding below the ridgeline under fire. Nor could German mortar or artillery fire be easily directed against the position, as it was invisible to the gunnery officers and required too steep a trajectory for delivery of accurate fire.

As darkness closed over the battlefield, the battalion's tenuous toehold on the northern bank of the Moro remained hotly contested. Total casualties for the day's assault stood at twenty-three wounded and, surprisingly, only five killed.[19] In their shallow slit trenches, the soldiers knew they faced a desperate night. As Kennedy had committed the rifle companies of the entire battalion, there was little or no chance of a withdrawal under fire without the battalion being cut to pieces. Their only option was to dig in and hold, no matter what the enemy threw their way.

# 8

# THE IMPOSSIBLE
# BRIDGE

As December 6 drew to a close, Major General Chris Vokes faced a crisis of decision. The original plan to breach the Germans' Moro River defensive line by forcing a crossing fronting San Leonardo lay in tatters. The bridgehead position won by the Seaforths' 'C' Company and a platoon of 'A' company was untenable. 'B' Company had enjoyed remarkable success in its assault on the German left flank, piercing the boundary line between 200th and 361st Panzer Grenadier regiments, but it was impossible for the Seaforths to capitalize on Captain Buchanan's gains. Slowly reports trickled back from 'B' Company that it had taken about sixty prisoners, overrun sixteen enemy positions, and killed or wounded many other Panzer Grenadiers, while taking casualties of only two killed and six missing.[1] Unfortunately, 'B' Company's exploits amounted to little more than an aggressive raid due to the inability to reinforce its success with infantry and armoured support. By about 2200 hours, Vokes was informed by the Royal Canadian Engineer commander, Lieutenant Colonel Geoff Walsh, that building a Bailey bridge over the Moro at the site of the demolished bridge below San Leonardo was impossible because the road turned sharply at right angles on reaching the river.[2]

Faced with this news, Vokes decided on the spur of the moment to abandon the thrust at San Leonardo and shift 2nd Canadian Infantry Brigade's entire effort west to exploit through Villa Rogatti. "A cardinal rule of tactics is to exploit success and ignore failure," he noted. If successful, switching the division's main thrust to the left flank would win a clear run from the lip of the ridge "without any intervening natural obstacles to the Ortona-Orsogna lateral road. Having cut this road the direction of attack could then be swung towards Villa Grande or Ortona." But the attack routes across the valley that had been used by the Princess Patricia's Canadian Light Infantry and its supporting tanks were too poor to facilitate a major offensive. Vokes realized that "feasibility would hinge on whether the demolished road bridge could be restored with a Bailey Bridge as the road exit up the far escarpment was necessary for movement."[3]

Decision made, Vokes directed Lieutenant Colonel Jim Jefferson to ready the Loyal Edmonton Regiment to move through the PPCLI's lines in the morning. The Seaforths would withdraw all units from the northern side of the Moro and shift westward into reserve behind the other battalions of 2 CIB.[4] Meanwhile, 1st Canadian Infantry Brigade would continue expanding the Hastings and Prince Edward Regiment's bridgehead near the river's mouth. That action would, however, remain a diversionary effort, unless the 2 CIB breakthrough at Villa Rogatti faltered.

◆ ◆ ◆

The movement orders reached the Seaforths none too soon. Forin received final orders to initiate the anticipated withdrawal shortly before a runner sent by Buchanan, whose #18 radio had broken down a couple of hours earlier, reported that the captain requested permission to withdraw. The runner told Forin that 'B' Company faced a strong counterattack out of La Torre of between 200 and 300 German infantry. Buchanan was giving ground slowly, each platoon supporting the other in a measured withdrawal that was costing the Germans casualties; but the company could not possibly hold against such a superior force. Forin told the runner to tell Buchanan to bring his men home.[5]

Meanwhile 'C' Company and the platoon from 'A' Company withdrew easily. 'C' Company had come through the entire battle without suffering a single casualty, which impressed Forin not at all. He roundly chastised Captain Blackburn for failing to lead the company effectively or aggressively. It seemed to Forin that, from the moment the company had come under fire the previous night, it had done nothing except stay under cover. Forin further thought the "performance of neither 'A' or 'C' company was in any way outstanding, nor was it up to the standard of previous performances of companies in the attack."[6]

At 1000 hours on December 7, 'B' Company slipped across the river and rejoined the rest of the battalion. It was, however, missing one section of about half a dozen men and 2nd Field Regiment forward observation officer Captain T. Lem Carter. The artillery officer and this section had become separated from the rest of the company when Carter was severely wounded in the legs, rendering him unable to walk. Carter and several Seaforth infantry troops had covered the company's withdrawal, Carter laying down intense fire with his Thompson submachine gun. He then urged the handful of soldiers to leave him behind. "If I'm no good to fight the enemy, I might as well give him the trouble of looking after me," the officer said.[7]

While the soldiers hesitated over whether to follow Carter's order to leave him behind, Lance Corporal John H. Teece observed the small clutch of men from a spot 200 yards away. Realizing the section was in imminent danger of being cut off, surrounded, and either captured or killed, Teece turned back. Crawling skillfully through the thick brush past the closing German line, he linked up with the soldiers. He then took charge, ordering the men to rig a stretcher for Carter and cutting short the man's demands to be heroically abandoned. In an ordeal that would continue until well past first light on December 7, Teece and the other men wormed their way through the thickest vegetation they could find, dragging Carter on his stretcher. At times German soldiers were moving or standing guard within mere feet of their passage, yet Teece's careful guidance enabled the men to avoid detection. Teece and his small force were the last Seaforths to abandon the San Leonardo bridgehead.[8]

◆ ◆ ◆

While the Seaforths spent the night of December 6–7 withdrawing, the PPCLI set about consolidating its position at Villa Rogatti. Accordingly, Lieutenant Jerry Richards was summoned to the rear battalion HQ and ordered to raise a party of volunteers from his mortar platoon to cross the Moro and bring out wounded. Of fifty-two men who required evacuation, about half were ambulatory. Richards left HQ feeling slightly bemused that his men were to be asked to volunteer, while he was ordered to lead the evacuation party. As far as Richards was concerned, every man in the PPCLI was a volunteer, so why ask for volunteers now? He told his platoon sergeant major to call for volunteers as instructed, but that everyone had better bloody well be a volunteer.

For Richards, the previous day had been fraught with frustration and a sense of helplessness. Not once had the mortar platoon been called upon to fire across the valley, nor had he received an antici-pated order to move the firing tubes across to Villa Rogatti. Consequently, he was pleased to be leading the resupply and evacua-tion party. It gave him a sense of purpose.

Around midnight, Richards set off with his platoon in tow. Accompanying the men was a herd of ammunition-laden mules and their Moroccan muleteers. As the party descended toward the Moro, Richards saw a column of Germans coming his way and started to raise his Thompson before realizing that these were some of the pris-oners taken during the earlier fighting. The two columns passed each other in uneasy silence.

The crossing was uneventful. Richards brought the entire party up to the farmyard where Lieutenant Colonel Ware had established his forward HQ. Richards went in to report and found Ware sound asleep in a corner. Looking down on the sleeping man, the twenty-one-year-old thought Ware had turned grey overnight and perhaps, at thirty, was too old for this kind of job. Hating like hell to wake the man, he bent over and gave his shoulder a little shake. Ware roused instantly and received the report that Richards had ammunition for the companies, as well as men and mules to evacuate the wounded.

One element of 'A' Company was on the far flank of the village with two burning buildings between itself and the rest of the bat-talion. Moving ammunition by mule to this position was going to be dangerous, so Richards went alone with one mule and its muleteer.

The only way over to 'A' Company was to walk in front of the flames engulfing the buildings. This perfectly silhouetted the two men and the mule. They passed into the firelight and back into the darkness without the enemy firing a shot, which perplexed but relieved Richards. As he passed the building next to those on fire, however, his heart leapt at the sound of a Vickers machine-gun firing bolt being jacked back. Turning to look in the window he was passing, Richards stared down the muzzle of a machine gun manned by a wild-eyed Saskatoon Light Infantry gunner.

Entering 'A' Company's area, Richards saw no sign of life. Searching around for someone to receive the ammunition, Richards passed under a building and heard a soft voice above his head say, "Bubble." Again Richards's heart leapt, as he scrambled through his memory for the countersign reply of the day. "Squeak," he squeaked. Looking up, he saw the guard pointing his rifle out the window directly into Richards's face. The man gave him directions to the front line where, he said, a sergeant would take the supplies.

Heading off, Richards was grateful the day's passwords had been relatively sensible. As all passwords came from Eighth Army Headquarters, many involved the names of famous British cricket players or cricket rules and were unintelligible to the Canadians. Richards wondered how many soldiers got shot by friendly guards because of this idiosyncratic practice. Recently one password had been Hobbes, the countersign Surrey. Apparently Hobbes was a famous cricketer who played for Surrey. Perhaps to British upper-classmen that sort of thing should be self-evident and easily remembered.

Richards continued moving through the 'A' Company perimeter, noticing a number of dead Germans scattered on the ground wherever they had fallen in the battle. One motorcyclist sprawled in a ditch next to his BMW. A few minutes later, he found a platoon sergeant who had been in Richards's platoon before his transfer to the mortar company. A Greek from Montreal, the soldier was using a ditch for cover. Richards lay down beside him and the two men stared out at the darkness beyond the edge of the village. Meanwhile, several privates came out of slit trenches and unloaded the ammunition from the mule. The sergeant looked desperately tired and was unimpressed by the ammunition delivery. "What we need is more men," he told Richards. "Sorry," Richards replied. "I wasn't authorized to bring more men up. I'd offer to stay myself but my orders are to take the wounded men back across the river, so I'll have to leave you."[9]

Regretfully, still feeling inadequate about his role, Richards returned to battalion HQ to find the wounded on stretchers and the party ready to set off. Some of the more lightly injured were helped up onto mules, and those who were ambulatory either fended for themselves or gave each other a hand. About a dozen men had to be carried out on stretchers, requiring forty-eight men to carry them all. Trying not to drop or unduly jostle the casualties, Richards and his party slithered off down the muddy slope toward the river. It was terribly hard work, especially as the heaviest man in the entire battalion was among the stretcher cases. Richards took his turn on the stretcher, trying to ensure that each stretcher-bearer had at least a few minutes' break along the way. It was raining heavily and everyone was soaked through. The wounded tried hard not to moan or cry out, which was particularly difficult for those clinging to the mules. Everyone knew that a party this large, making as much noise as they were, could easily attract German attention.

Just as they crossed the river the Germans must have heard them, for the party was bombarded by mortars. They pushed on to the road, where a small convoy of trucks waited. The mortaring continued. Richards's men hastily loaded the casualties into the trucks. Finally they had one more man to get into a truck. Bombs were going off at the side of the road and behind them, but the men were unable to crouch down because of the need to hold the stretcher high enough to get it in. Without ceremony, Richards and another man shoved the wounded soldier in as best they could and yelled for the trucks to get going. One man had to remain behind because the trucks were all full. Richards and a medical corporal remained with him, the two men lying nervously in a ditch next to the stretcher as bombs continued to fall all around.

When the mortaring eased somewhat, Richards thought he heard voices on the other side of the road. "Does that sound like German to you?" he asked the corporal. The man listened. "Can't tell, could be." Richards decided he had to find out and slipped the safety catch off his Thompson. "I'll go with you," the corporal whispered. The two men crawled on their stomachs across the road. On the other side, the corporal tapped Richards on the shoulder, pulled out his pistol, and handed it to Richards. "Will you carry this for me, sir? If they catch me with it, they'll kill me." According to the Geneva Convention, medical personnel were to be unarmed. Like almost every officer, Richards never used a pistol or wore one in a holster, to avoid being easily marked by German snipers as an officer. Mindful even in the darkness of this, he shoved the gun into his jacket so it was well out of sight. Crawling through a hedge, the two men discovered that the voices belonged to a section of Seaforth Highlanders digging in near the road adjacent to the riverbank — sent there to provide protection for the engineers scheduled to build a Bailey bridge in the morning.

Richards chatted with the men for a few minutes until the Germans started mortaring the area again. Richards and a Seaforth both dived into one of the slit trenches, Richards landing on top of the other man. The officer apologized. "It's all right, sir," the soldier countered. "I feel even safer with somebody above me." Finally the truck returned, the wounded man was loaded, and a relieved Richards left the blast-torn river bottom to the small party of Seaforths.[10] He had had enough war for one night.

◆ ◆ ◆

"After nearly sixty hours of fighting and 'Standing To' the troops are beginning to look tired, the strain and excitement has keyed them to a pitch higher than has ever been reached in any previous battle in the Italian campaign," wrote the Patricia's war diarist on the grey, warm morning of December 7.[11] Lieutenant Colonel Ware was thankful that the Germans had let the battle for Villa Rogatti slacken. There was no repetition of the previous day's counterattacks. Resistance was limited to light, but continuous, shelling and mortaring of the Canadian position. The PPCLI waited for the engineers to construct the bridge across the Moro below the village. It was expected that later in the day the Loyal Edmonton Regiment and a British tank squadron would cross the newly erected Bailey bridge, advance through Villa Rogatti, and jump off toward Villa Jubatti and Villa Caldari.

So Ware was astonished and dismayed to receive instructions at noon to expect relief by the British Royal West Kent Regiment in nine hours. First Canadian Infantry Division, he was told, was shortening its line west of San Leonardo by handing off Villa Rogatti to the 8th Indian Division. Ware protested to 2nd Canadian Infantry Brigade commander Brigadier Bert Hoffmeister. Once again, he argued that from the stronghold of Villa Rogatti the brigade could break through to the Ortona-Orsogna lateral highway and roll the German flank up to force Ortona's surrender. Hoffmeister agreed that Ware's plan was sound and the one both he and divisional commander Major General Chris Vokes favoured.[12] But it was a moot point because Royal Canadian Engineers commander Lieutenant Colonel Geoff Walsh claimed it was impossible to launch a Bailey bridge over the Moro below Villa Rogatti. No bridge, no offensive.

The engineers' failure was all the more frustrating because, in anticipation of the offensive, the entire brigade had realigned itself westward during the night. At least a day would be lost moving the battalions back toward San Leonardo and developing a new attack plan. The failed assault by the Seaforth Highlanders of Canada had proven that San Leonardo was heavily fortified. Instead of being able to outflank this fortress and advance "along the grain of the country," the Canadians would now have to attack the village head on. Such attacks always meant greater numbers of killed and wounded as the "advantages of topography lay with the defenders."[13] Reluctantly, Ware conceded defeat and told his men to prepare to withdraw from Villa Rogatti. His mood was sour as he saw the spirits of his soldiers crumble around him. Against the odds they had fought a battle and won. Where the other attacks had failed, the PPCLI had succeeded. But now it seemed to have been for nothing.

◆ ◆ ◆

On the ridgeline across the river from Villa Rogatti, Lieutenant Jerry Richards was still unaware of the PPCLI's orders to withdraw. Richards dodged from one three-inch mortar position to the other, checking on his men and searching the opposite ridgeline for possible enemy targets. Without fail, each time he went into the open, an enemy antitank gun hidden somewhere across the Moro snapped a shot in his direction. The shell would come in on a thrumming flat trajectory and strike with a crack that threw mud and vegetation flying. Other guns were shelling the area steadily, but it seemed this gun was deliberately sniping at the young officer.

Richards was running toward his slit trench when he heard the distinctive thump of the antitank gun firing. He dived into the trench just as the shell exploded on the hole's edge. Tremendous pain wracked him. Lying face down in the trench, unable to move, Richards was sure he was dying. Blood poured over his face. Because he couldn't move, Richards remembered the driver whose legs had been torn off in the jeep, when Richards had received his first wound.

The same medical orderly who had spent the night before with him in the river bottom turned Richards over. "Are my legs all right?" the lieutenant asked anxiously. The orderly told him they were okay. Richards asked after his men and learned some were wounded. "Go look after them," he said. "No, no, they're not too bad," the orderly responded, as he cut open Richards's shirt and started bandaging the six ragged holes in the officer's stomach. "Your left arm is fractured too, sir," the orderly reported, before injecting him with morphine. As he drifted off to sleep, Richards was aware of being carried on a stretcher toward an ambulance that had driven up. Then he fell into a deep darkness and escaped the pain.[14]

♦ ♦ ♦

Crouched in their shallow slit trenches on the ridgeline, the Hastings and Prince Edward Regiment had endured a terrible night that dawned into an equally dreadful day. Through the long hours of darkness buckets of rain had poured down, transforming the ground into a slimy quagmire. German shelling and mortaring of the small beachhead on the northern shore of the Moro continued without pause. Shell craters riddled the area. Olive trees and grape vines were torn and splintered, some ripped out by the roots, others blackened by fire. A large number of dead Germans lay scattered throughout the area. In the grey morning, the soldiers looked out of their holes at a landscape resembling historical photographs of the No Man's Lands of the Great War. The incessant noise of explosions; the foul blended odour of decaying flesh, blood, and cordite; the mud and filth covering the soldiers from head to foot, all combined to render this a place of unparalleled misery and fear. The fear grew with the sure knowledge that the Germans must try to throw the battalion back over the river. They would attack soon. To wait would only allow the Canadians more time to solidify the position.

As the day wore on, the Hasty P's did what they could to improve their odds of holding out. Lieutenant Stan Walker's antitank platoon, aided by men from 'C' Company, undertook the amazing feat of carrying two six-pounder antitank guns and ammunition across the Moro. They then dragged and pushed the wheeled weapons, which weighed about half a ton, through the deep mud to 'A' Company's forward position. Two three-inch mortars were also manhandled over and set up in a gravel pit just below the ridgeline. The men struggling with these heavy loads were inspired by the strength of 'C' Company's Sergeant Major George Ponsford. The bulky Ponsford carried burdens twice the weight of any of the others and always seemed to be there at the critical moment during the movement of the guns.[15]

While the infantrymen strengthened their defences, the battalion's pioneers ignored continual shelling from 105-millimetre German artillery and sporadic machine-gun fire as they tried to improve the diversion at the Moro. Several times the pioneers pulled back and Sherman tanks rolled down to attempt a crossing. Each time the tanks bogged down in the riverbed and were forced to withdraw or become hopelessly mired. Major Bert Kennedy's frustration mounted. Without tanks, the battalion was in great danger of being forced back or even overrun and destroyed.

At 1600 hours, Kennedy was called back across the Moro to attend a 1st Canadian Infantry Brigade Orders Group. Brigadier Howard Graham informed the battalion commanders that Kennedy's small Moro River salient was to be the starting point for a major brigade assault the following day toward San Leonardo. It was more vital than ever that Kennedy's battalion hold out. Indeed, he should attempt to get men up on the ridge itself and secure the San Donato road junction.[16]

As darkness fell over the battlefield, 'A' and 'B' companies each slipped a platoon onto the ridge and succeeded in extending the perimeter forward to encompass the road junction. The advancing soldiers met only light resistance that faded away at first contact.

Meanwhile, Quartermaster Sergeant Basil Smith laboured through much of the night to get rations up to the men on the other side of the river. Smith's provisioning party of men and food-laden mules found itself in an area of muddy flats near the riverbank. The mules sank into the muck to their knees, becoming unable to move either forward or backward. It took hours for Smith's party and some pioneers to build a rock and gravel track through the muddy section to provide secure footing for the mules. Obviously the Germans had earlier registered the mud flat as a likely bottleneck for forward movement of supplies, as it was subjected to regular mortaring. "Here however the mud proved helpful," Smith later wrote in his diary. "The danger from mortar fire is not the explosion, which is up and out and is confined to a very small area, at ground level. It is the fragmentation of the bomb which causes the damage and in this soft mud, they bury themselves quite deeply before meeting enough resistance to detonate the charge, which reduces fragmentation to a minimum."[17]

The mortar fire weighed less heavily on Smith's mind than the outcome of what should have proven a perfect afternoon spent foraging near battalion HQ. At loose ends while waiting for nightfall to come, Smith and two other quartermaster company personnel had gone exploring. They chanced upon Nicolo Annechini, a farmer who had spent half his life in Canada. Annechini had worked for the Canada Cement Company in Lakefield, Ontario. Having lived two years in Lakefield himself, Smith spent a pleasant hour with the farmer reminiscing about better times.

Annechini also showed the soldiers a German gun emplacement destroyed by a direct hit from a Royal Air Force bomb. Smith was grimly impressed by the gruesome sight. The bomb had literally torn the gunners to bits, "morsels of bone, flesh and field-gray cloth bespattered the landscape."[18] Sightseeing over, the soldiers bought a five-gallon wicker-covered glass bottle filled with red wine from the farmer. Carrying the bottle in turns, "tenderly as a babe in arms," they made the two-mile return through some rugged gullies to battalion HQ. Along the way, they spoke with anticipation of how fine and warming their booty would be. In front of their tents, the soldier carrying the bottle lowered it gently from his shoulder to the ground only to have the bottle inexplicably disintegrate in his hands. Smith and his comrades watched mournfully as "the beautiful, rose-tinted liquid soaked into the ground."[19]

There would be no wine upon the resupply party's return to battalion HQ. Instead, Smith's party managed to complete the task of taking rations up to the line companies shortly before midnight, distributed the food, and then trudged back to catch a quick sleep and begin preparations for the next evening's resupply.

◆ ◆ ◆

No sooner had Smith's party crossed the Moro River en route to battalion HQ than the expected German counterattack against the Hasty P's rolled in. It started with a short, intense artillery barrage by self-propelled guns firing at close range at the two platoons that held the forward San Donato junction position. The moment the barrage lifted, a Panzer Grenadier company stormed forward, showering the fifty-man strong force with rifle fire and stick grenades. The 'A' Company platoon was forced to abandon its position or be overrun. Withdrawing to a point somewhat behind and to the left of the 'B' Company platoon, the surviving soldiers set up in a loose semi-circle and prepared to meet a new attack.[20]

This came in minutes, with the Germans infiltrating the gap between the two platoons. 'B' Company's No. 12 Platoon, under the command of twenty-six-year-old Acting Company Sergeant Major Bill Nolan, was now effectively cut off from the rest of the battalion. But the infiltrating Panzer Grenadiers were unknowingly moving into a narrow salient between the two platoons. Nolan allowed the enemy to come within thirty yards of his position before opening up with a withering volley of fire, to which the 'A' Company platoon added its weight. Hit from both flanks, the German force was cut to pieces. About forty soldiers were killed and several surrendered, while the rest fled in disarray. That brought the Germans' night counterattack to a decisive end.[21]

In the first glimmer of daylight, Sergeant Nolan observed that a platoon or more of Panzer Grenadiers had occupied a small farmhouse. From the building, the Germans could bring the road junction under fire and break up the planned brigade assault toward San Leonardo before it even got started. Nolan realized the Canadians would have to force the enemy out of the building.[22] He had fewer than twenty men in his platoon and some of these had to remain where they were to secure the road junction. Taking only one section of ten men, Nolan launched a frontal assault on the heavily defended position. Charging through heavy machine-gun and small-arms fire, the little force broke through the defences, fought its way hand to hand into the building, and drove the German defenders out. Twenty-five soldiers and one officer surrendered to Nolan and his men. The brigade's planned rallying point for the afternoon's offensive was secure.[23]

◆ ◆ ◆

While the battalion's two forward platoons fought heroically to keep the road junction open, divisional headquarters staff worked through the night and into the morning to ensure that the assault against San Leonardo would not mirror the earlier failure. The urgency to move to the offensive before the Germans destroyed the tenuous bridgehead had to be tempered by the logistical complexity of organizing a major attack. Major General Chris Vokes hammered out a plan fitting to a man at home in a boxing ring — a front jab and right hook combination designed to push the Germans out of San Leonardo. It would be a 1st Canadian Infantry Brigade show.

The 48th Highlanders of Canada would provide the hard jab against the defences of the 361st Regiment in front of San Leonardo, while the Royal Canadian Regiment struck against the Germans' right. Success hinged on the RCR's right hook through the bridgehead held by the Hasty P's. From the road junction just south of San Donato's little chapel, the RCR would storm up a small, muddy, unnamed lane for one and a half miles to San Leonardo. The road followed a relatively level plain thickly overgrown by dense vineyards and olive groves. This vegetation provided ideal defensive cover for enemy positions, while the level terrain also offered good routes for German armoured counterattacks against the advancing battalion's open flank. The latter threat posed a grave risk to the regiment because it was apparent that the RCR would have to attack unsupported by 1st Canadian Armoured Brigade — still unable to get tanks over the river and unlikely to do so before the early afternoon attack got underway.[24]

Vokes's concern about German tanks was strengthened by intelligence reports on enemy strength. A summary written up by Major N.L.C. Mathers of divisional General Staff estimated that the Panzer

Grenadiers could immediately deploy two squadrons of Panzer Mark IVs and probably bring up another squadron with twenty-four hours' notice. The report further concluded that the Canadians probably faced five infantry battalions, with the whereabouts of two other battalions unknown. (Unlike the Canadian divisional structure where regiment and battalion were synonymous, German organization was broken down in ever decreasing unit size from division, to regiment, to battalion, to company, to platoon, to section.) Second Battalion of the 361st Regiment and 3rd Battalion of the 200th Regiment were believed to be in positions to the rear of the German front line and available to counterattack the RCR assault. Equally worrisome was the fact the Germans had an unprecedented availability of artillery support. Mathers estimated the enemy had a full divisional artillery regiment of forty-eight guns ranging from 75-millimetre to 150-millimetre, about ten 75-millimetre infantry regiment guns, and two or three of the massive 17,520-kilogram, 170-millimetre guns that fired a shell weighing sixty-eight kilograms. The Germans were also known to have many Nebelwerfer six-barrelled mortars in the area. These mortars, which fired six shells apiece at two-second intervals, were known to Allied troops as "Moaning Minnies." The name derived from the ear-piercing shriek the shells made as they descended on a target like a clutch of explosive eggs. Already "Moaning Minnie" casualties were mounting throughout the divisional area.

Mathers wrapped up his report with the optimistic prediction that "the enemy will fight his forces until it is clear that we have succeeded in seizing a bridgehead which allows the full deployment of all our arms and have support routes which wipe out the river as a tactical feature. When he judges that point has been reached he will begin withdrawal to a new line. It appears that the enemy does not think that point has as yet been reached."[25]

Given the known German strength that could be brought to bear against the RCR and 48th Highlander dual assault, and the lack of tank support, it was obvious the Canadians needed some major artillery and air power in their corner. This they were promised. In addition to the Canadian artillery formations of the 1st, 2nd, and 3rd Field regiments of the Royal Canadian Artillery, the British 57th Field, 4th and 70th Medium regiments of the Royal Artillery, the British 98th Army Field Regiment of 105-millimetre self-propelled guns, and the 8th Indian Division's artillery would participate in what was to be the war's heaviest barrage fired to date by a western Allied force. Three hundred and fifty guns would lay on a sixty-minute barrage. Additional firepower would be provided by 108 fighter bomber and 72 light bomber sorties. Even a couple of Royal Navy battle cruisers would be on hand to throw their guns into the pot. During the barrage's last thirty minutes, the Saskatoon Light Infantry would bring the full weight of its 4.2-inch mortars and Vickers medium machine guns to bear against the German forward positions across the river.[26]

It was hoped that the German Panzer Grenadier regiments defending the Moro would suffer devastating casualties. Those defenders lucky enough to survive the barrage were expected to be dazed and disoriented by the mass of explosives going off around them. Before the confused troops could emerge from their holes to organize a defence, the Canadian infantry should be rolling over their positions. The bombardment was scheduled to begin at 1530 hours on December 8. The infantry battalions would begin their assault precisely at 1630 hours, going "over the top" in what everyone involved recognized as dramatically similar to a World War I attack plan. Lacking immediate tank support, however, Vokes had no alternative. Stealth had already failed. The steel and explosive of artillery and the flesh of infantry must win the day.

Orders cascaded out of Vokes's HQ and from Eighth Army's HQ, which endorsed the overall plan and committed the British and Indian artillery, the aerial bombardments, and the involvement of the Royal Navy. Trucks laden with shells and powder charges lumbered up to the artillery gun pits. Gunners worked desperately to stack the crates of shells near their weapons. Eighteen-year-old Gunner Bill Strickland had never seen anything like it in the two years he had been in the army. One truck after another came forward and the men staggered through deep mud with the boxes to get the shells to the guns. The fields were too wet for trucks to leave the road. Manpower had to suffice. Four 25-pound shells to a box, a total weight of 110 pounds. Two men carried a box together, each holding a rope handle on the box's side in one hand. Often the boxes had to be carried 200 yards from the road to a gun.

Sweat poured off Strickland's body. Some of his comrades

stripped off their shirts and jackets despite the night's cold and the occasional icy shower. The work continued for hour after deadening hour through the night and well into the morning. The gunners had been told success depended on them. If they failed to shatter the German resistance, the infantry would die. Strickland hated that thought. He ignored the sweat, ignored the pain in his arms and back, ignored the quiver in his legs. There were still more shell cases to carry to the stack that was now shoulder high. Strickland and his comrades worked on.[27]

# THREE

## BREAKING THE MORO RIVER LINE

# 9

## INTO THE INFERNO

He began every radio broadcast the same way: "This is Matthew Halton speaking from Italy." The thirty-nine-year-old native of Pincher Creek, Alberta, was the most renowned Canadian war correspondent and the Canadian Broadcasting Corporation's senior European correspondent. A small, balding man possessed of a cultured and eloquent voice, Halton had followed the 1st Canadian Infantry Division from Sicily to the Moro River. Halton reported little of the grand strategies and tactics that directed the troops forward into battle. Instead, he attempted to enable Canadians at home to visualize the soldiers' day-to-day experience. His sympathies were always with the men in the front lines. To capture their stories meant getting up close to the fighting. Halton and his assistant, Arthur Holmes, were often to be seen in a jeep well inside the Germans' field of fire.

If Halton was war's narrator, Holmes was the means behind the voice. He was a recording engineer genius. Having spent ten years as a wireless operator on ocean-going ships before joining the newly founded CBC in 1933, Holmes was fascinated by the challenge of producing disc recordings in unstable conditions. At the time, all recording had to be carefully undertaken in an environment that ensured the 78-rpm disc recorder cutting the track was perfectly level. With the outbreak of war, Holmes recognized that radio's great advantage over newsprint was the ability to bring the sounds of war into the nation's living rooms. That would only be possible if the recording equipment could function on the battlefield. In January 1940, Holmes toured the French Maginot line and the British Expeditionary Force positions to acquaint himself with the conditions under which the recording equipment must operate. He then set to work designing what the CBC overseas unit required.

As the war progressed, Holmes designed and equipped the European correspondents with several mobile units that worked well enough while the Canadian army was based in relatively static camps in Britain. He knew, however, that once the army took the offensive the large civilian vans required to carry the heavy recording equipment would be too unwieldy and prone to breakdown. Holmes decided the gear had to be customized to fit into the army's Heavy Utility Personnel (HUP) carriers, which were basically four-wheel-drive station wagons. Inside the cramped space of a HUP, Holmes installed three turntables, amplifiers, a regular four-input sound mixer, sufficient batteries to run everything, and a battery charger. Having three turntables enabled Holmes to keep recording as long as there were discs and to simultaneously play back recordings already cut. This made it possible to dub from disc to disc, edit a finished broadcast, and then feed it through short-wave transmitters without the technician ever leaving the interior of the HUP.

The HUP recording studio was an amazing feat, but Holmes hadn't stopped there. Although the HUP could keep up with an advancing army, it was still too cumbersome to deploy on the front lines. What was needed was a more portable studio that could be installed on a jeep or even carried by hand. Holmes's solution was a small studio system that was contained in two large boxes weighing eighty pounds apiece. Mounted on the back of a jeep, and drawing power from the vehicle's battery, the mobile unit featured a twelve-inch recording turntable and vacuum-tube amplifier in one box, and a motor generator with leads to clip to a six-volt battery in the other. When the HUP and portable equipment followed 1st Canadian

Infantry Division into battle in Sicily and Italy it worked like a charm, enabling Holmes to record the voices of Halton and his alternate correspondent, Peter Stursberg, in every imaginable battlefield and weather condition.[1]

On December 8, the portable set was positioned inside an old building in San Vito Chietino. A hole blown in the wall during earlier fighting provided a perfect view of the entire Canadian front facing the northern ridgeline of the Moro River valley. Behind this position, the artillery regiments of the division were scattered in the fields and folds of ground, gunners hunched over their weapons, munitions at the ready. It was 1526 hours.

"In four minutes," Halton announced into the microphone, "there will be a tremendous artillery barrage on the enemy positions across the Moro from here. The barrage will continue intermittently for an hour or so and at half past four our infantry — I can't say which infantry — will move across the valley, across the little river, and up out of the valley to attack the enemy positions. It is incredible that one is watching the battle, and that one should have such a dramatic view of the battle, and that on such a gorgeous day — with the warm sun and the Adriatic dancing in the light. War on such a day seems particularly tragic and unreal. . . . It's so beautiful, I mean the view from here. The other side of the valley, an enchanting patchwork of vivid reds, greens, and yellows, like daubs of paint, like a painting by Cézanne, but the enemy is waiting there. Only two to three thousand yards away."[2]

◆ ◆ ◆

Not far from where Halton was recording his broadcast, another noncombatant observer lay in long grass on the skyline, mindful of how exposed this position rendered him and his companion to enemy eyes. Forty-three-year-old Captain Charles Comfort of the Historical Section of General Staff was a painter. His job was to capture the Canadian war with pencil and brush. Beside him lay another artist, Major William Ogilvie. The two painters were fast friends, both dedicated to the execution of their historical task. Together the artists waited for the guns.

Like Halton, it struck Comfort that this was not a day suited to war. The afternoon sun was warm. "Nearby a lizard basked on a stone, still, like ourselves, except for the rapid pulsing of his soft belly; a lark's song descended from the zenith. . . . To our right was the headland that marked the estuary of the river, now held by the Hastings and Prince Edward Regiment, beyond it, the empty Adriatic, shimmering in the late autumnal sunshine. The valley below was typical of the water courses that channel this coastal plain, two hundred feet perhaps to its floor, a thousand yards across. At the bottom, a muddy stream, high at this season, meandered through shrubs and vetches and occasional clumps of willow. . . . The reverse slope, with its burden of olive, rose in gentle folds to its crest, the highway snaking up its flank toward San Leonardo. The plain beyond undulated off to the horizon with its plotted fertility and cube-like white farm buildings. Ortona gleamed attractively in the distance, clustered about the cupola of San Tomasso.

". . . As the minutes ticked away, insects buzzed in the sunshine; a magpie, followed by its pendulous tail, flitted in deep swags across our line of vision. Five minutes to zero. . . . An idle shell whined across the valley; the horizon wavered in the cordial-like heat haze. . . . One minute."[3]

◆ ◆ ◆

Twenty-one-year-old Lance Sergeant Victor Bulger of Cobourg, Ontario, stuffed wads of cotton into his ears, knowing the scant protection this safety measure provided his eardrums. Bulger was second-in-command of one of the four twenty-five pounder guns belonging to 'D' Troop of the 1st Field Regiment's 'B' Battery. The battery's guns were dug into heavily mudded positions about half a mile south of San Vito Chietino.

As the second hand ticked down, the six-man gun team prepared the weapon. One shoved the gleaming brass shell into the gun breech, another rammed it into the barrel. Then the cartridge case was added. 1530 hours. Like a rippling wave running through the gun lines positioned around San Vito, the artillery fired.[4] The order was for "intense fire," so the gunners' pace was rushed. Five rounds a minute. Three hundred and fifty guns hurled more than 1,500 shells every sixty seconds toward the German lines in a barrage that crept across the landscape, leaving nothing in its path unscathed.

As the barrage started, Halton scrambled though the hole in the wall of the old building. He held the microphone aloft, enabling Holmes to clearly record the tremendous volleys of fire. It was impossible for Halton to speak, the noise of the firing was deafening. Inside the building, Holmes hunched over the recording equipment, capturing the massive din for posterity on his discs. The day was moving toward dusk and it seemed to Halton that the bombardment hastened the onset of approaching darkness.

◆ ◆ ◆

"Then inferno broke loose," Comfort wrote in his diary, "the earth trembled with cataclysmic shock. Instantly the pastoral valley became a valley of death. From its fertile groves sprang the instant and terrible orchids of death. The first impact was of sound, gigantic and preposterous sound. One was shuttled from warm sunlight into the roaring darkness of an endless tunnel. It battered and pounded the eardrums from all sides. We lay stunned and fearful, clawing the earth, as flights of frightened birds crossed the valley and passed over our heads to a relative safety. Before our eyes sprang the grey-blue flowers of death, withering instantly in the breeze, to form a concealing veil of sulphurous vapour, struggling to hide the agony of the clamorous garden. . . .

"No sound of speech or movement could be heard above the infernal dissonance; all was lost in the tumult of its fury. The target pattern soon became clear; neat rectangles were searched and scorched with fire, the finger pointing here and then there. Soon they all fitted together with diabolical accuracy, like the parts of a gigantic puzzle. When the assembly was complete, all that the eye could encompass had been burned with fire. The valley was gone, hidden in an opaque cloud of acrid cordite. One was possessed of a great fatigue, a throbbing of the temples. What a dreadful monotony it was, of key, of tempo, of colour, of purpose and effect."[5]

At 1600 hours, the Saskatoon Light Infantry support battalion opened up with its Vickers medium machine guns, "spraying the enemy positions with penetrating bursts like pneumatic drills. To our astonishment, the enemy replied with the even faster falsetto of the Schmeisser. How could humans survive such a barrage? Why were they not helpless inarticulate blobs of quivering jelly?"[6]

So intense was the rate of fire that Bulger and the other Canadian gunners, like Gunner Bill Strickland, were amazed to see the barrels of their guns glow translucent red. They could actually see the shells sliding up the barrel prior to blasting off toward the enemy lines. Strickland's cotton padding fell out of his ears and minutes later a dribble of blood ran from each eardrum down his cheeks. Around him gunners had torn off their coats and shirts to work the guns barechested, their bodies dripping with sweat. Strickland was reeling with exhaustion, passing shells forward at a manic pace. His sergeant's mouth opened and moved, but Strickland heard no sound.[7]

At 1630 hours the firing abruptly ceased. Bulger felt numb, his whole body oddly dislocated by the continuous concussion of the firing. The smell of cordite was choking and a light blue smoke fog cloaked the firing position. He could have dropped to the ground. But there was no time to rest. The gun required cleaning, the hundreds of spent cartridges needed piling up, and hundreds more shells waited to be carried from the roads through the mud to replenish the gun's ammunition supply. Any moment more firing plans could be announced, and the men would once again turn to the guns. During the long years of waiting in Britain, the artillerymen had been strictly rationed in the numbers of shells they could fire. It seemed at times that each shell had to be personally signed off by a regimental commander before it could be fired. Not so on December 8. The Canadian gunners had fired off thousands of rounds, rendering any accurate accounting of munitions spent impossible.[8]

◆ ◆ ◆

"So you could hear the barrage," said Halton, speaking into the microphone. "You must have heard it. You can hardly see the valley, it's very ghostly now. . . . God knows what's happening down there, our men are down there. The enemy must have been dazed and bewildered by our barrage."[9]

Comfort wrote: "Everywhere destruction and disintegration: shattered buildings, mutilated trees, a spectral landscape of heaped-up fleshless bones, jostled by concussion and blast in a hideous monotonous danse macabre. Such was the new tempestuous world of cataclysm and shock we had inherited. Jesus Christ! How long can it go on? How long can this frail human mechanism stand it?"[10]

Even as the Germans began to hammer the Canadian lines with a

The schoolhouse at San Vito Chietino that served as the Advanced Dressing Station throughout the battle.
— ALEXANDER STIRTON, NAC, PA-114037

Canadian tank recovery crew rescues two Shermans that ran off the road during the December 9 assault on San Leonardo.
— T. ROWE, NAC, PA-131644

A knocked-out Panzer Mark IV stands abandoned in the ruined farmland between the Moro River and The Gully.
— ALEXANDER STIRTON, NAC, PA-107937

'B' Company of The Seaforth Highlanders of Canada advances up a trail toward Ortona, visible in the far distance.
— FREDERICK WHITCOMBE, NAC, PA-152749

A Seaforth Highlander killed by a sniper while moving through a vineyard on the outskirts of Ortona, December 20, 1943.
— T. ROWE, NAC, PA-141302

'B' Company of the Loyal Edmonton Regiment advances into Ortona on December 21.
— T. ROWE, NAC, PA-116852

Loyal Edmonton riflemen fire on three Germans crouching in a slit trench one hundred yards away during the fight on Ortona's outskirts.
— T. ROWE, NAC, PA-163935

Two German paratroopers surrender to the Canadians at the edge of Ortona.
— T. ROWE, NAC, PA-107934

Loyal Edmonton Lance Corporal E.A. Harris fires at a German position in Ortona.
— T. ROWE, NAC, PA-114490

A Three Rivers Regiment tank prepares to fire another round up the Corso Vittorio Emanuele.
— T. ROWE, NAC, PA-163933

Loyal Edmonton troopers advance into Ortona. Lance Corporal W.D. Smith (far right) is carrying a #18 wireless set.
— T. ROWE, NAC, PA-163932

A six-pounder anti-tank gun in action on the edge of Ortona, December 21.
— T. ROWE, NAC, PA-141671

On December 23, Three Rivers Regiment tanks push up Corso Vittorio Emanuele toward the rubble pile at Piazza Municipali.
— T. ROWE, NAC, PA-114028

Cattedrale San Tommaso after its destruction.
— T. ROWE, NAC, PA-136308

Christmas Day at the front. It is not known whether this picture was taken during the Seaforth Highlanders of Canada dinner or farther back in the lines.
— FREDERICK WHITCOMBE, NAC, PA-163936

The war continues
unabated on
Christmas Day. A dead
paratrooper in his slit
trench. The weapon is an
MG-42 machine gun.
— FREDERICK WHITCOMBE, NAC,
PA-115190

Although often used as an
illustration of the dinner at
San Maria di Costantanopoli,
this photo was actually of the
Christmas dinner served at
divisional headquarters in
San Vito Chientino on
December 26, 1943.
— T. ROWE, NAC, PA-152839

Canadian soldiers take cover
in the Banco di Napoli on
Corso Vittorio Emanuele.
— T. ROWE, NAC, PA-107936

A truck and jeep burn in Ortona after being hit by German mortar fire. A Bren carrier stands in the foreground.
— T. ROWE, NAC, PA-170291

Men of the Loyal Edmonton Regiment rescue Lance Corporal Roy Boyd from the rubble of a destroyed building. Boyd was buried for three-and-a-half days.
— T. ROWE, NAC, PA-152748

Battle over, civilians and soldiers alike find walking through the streets of Ortona a difficult task.
— T. ROWE, NAC, PA-114032

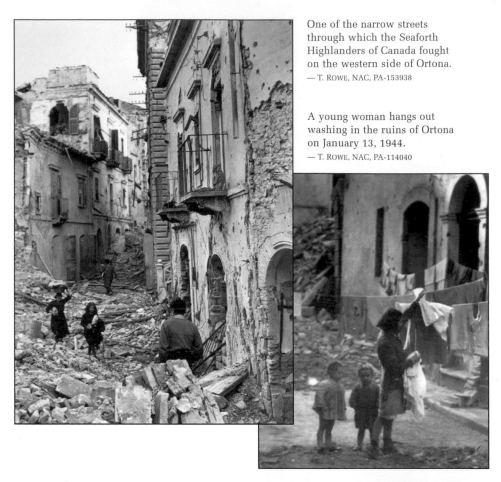

One of the narrow streets through which the Seaforth Highlanders of Canada fought on the western side of Ortona.
— T. ROWE, NAC, PA-153938

A young woman hangs out washing in the ruins of Ortona on January 13, 1944.
— T. ROWE, NAC, PA-114040

Graves of Loyal Edmonton Regiment soldiers who died in the Ortona street battle.
— ALEXANDER STIRTON, NAC, PA-115151

counter-barrage of artillery, Comfort imagined the infantry on both sides setting about their deadly purpose. "Men were emerging from deep hiding, like sullen beasts, shaken, baited, and desperate, crawling in cover in the vapour-filled valley, jockeying with death mid this fearful cacophony. What of those men? Were they battle-wise and again secure in cover? Nothing, it seemed to us, could survive that fire as it tossed earth and trees high in the air. Yet down there were Canadian Engineers, ready to sweep the fords and get the bridge across; on their start line were the 48th, waiting for the quiet, 'All right fellahs, let's go!'"[11]

◆ ◆ ◆

The moment the artillery bombardment lifted, the leading companies of the 48th Highlanders of Canada and the Royal Canadian Regiment scrambled out of their slit trenches and disappeared into the shell smoke blanketing the battlefield. The 48th Highlanders descended from the ridgeline on a two-company front, advancing on line to the left of the destroyed bridge and the road running up from the valley bottom into San Leonardo. They followed roughly the same route taken two days earlier by Captain W.H. Buchanan's 'B' Company of the Seaforth Highlanders of Canada. The Highlanders' orders were to occupy the same spur of land between San Leonardo and the hamlet of La Torre where, before being forced to retreat, Buchanan's men had destroyed many German positions. If successful, the Highlanders would control the western flank of San Leonardo. From this position, they would be able to blunt any attempt to use the road from La Torre as a path for reinforcing the San Leonardo garrison or for counterattacking the village once the RCR wrested it from German control.

It was customary for the Highlanders' company commanders to lead from the front, as officers had done in wars since time immemorial. On December 8, Captain Lloyd Smith of 'D' Company and Major F.G. McLaren of 'B' Company were consequently in the vanguard. Smith was so confident that he offered a five-pound bet to any taker that his company would cross the Moro without a single casualty.

Smith charged down a depression descending to the valley bottom, his men close on his heels. The company moved so quickly that it outran a sudden, heavy German mortar and 88-millimetre antitank gun bombardment that slammed down on the valley's southern slope and marched methodically down the slope toward the river. The Panzer Grenadiers obviously knew an infantry attack was underway and hoped to break it up by shredding the advancing troops with shrapnel. Smith's company burst out of the depression, splashed through the river, scrambled up the other slope, and overwhelmed two lightly defended German positions in mere minutes. Had there been any takers for Smith's bet he would have lost. There was one casualty. Crossing the river, Corporal N.K. Thompson sprained an ankle, but was able to keep up with the rest of his section despite the injury.

While 'D' Company went virtually unscathed, McLaren's 'B' Company was less fortunate. Just before the river, an 88-millimetre salvo caught the trailing sections of his company. Six men were killed outright, another mortally wounded, and Company Sergeant Major Nelson Merry had his leg torn off. Stretcher-bearer Joe Kendel was killed when he rushed forward to tend the wounded. His hand mangled by shrapnel, Private Charles Palmer staggered back to battalion HQ to summon help. A Regimental Aid Post jeep with medical orderlies and the battalion padre on board raced to the scene to recover the wounded and dead.[12]

Leaving the RAP men the task of sorting out dead from wounded, McLaren led the remainder of his company across the river and up a narrow gully running toward San Leonardo. Again there was virtually no infantry resistance offered by the Panzer Grenadiers. The defence seemed entirely dependent on concentrations of mortar and antitank gunfire. It was as if the Grenadiers, perhaps believing the Canadians would not attack the same point twice, had failed to reoccupy the defensive positions wiped out in Buchanan's earlier attack. The other possibility was a lack of communication between the two Panzer Grenadier regiments holding this section of the Moro River line. In the earlier attack Buchanan had discovered, and exploited, the fact that he had attacked the exact point where the 200th and 361st Panzer Grenadier regiments' defensive positions met. Such points always constitute weak links because of the difficulty of two regiments effectively communicating and coordinating defensive action. The Highlanders struck this same naturally weak point, already badly mauled by Buchanan's raid.

Trying to stay ahead of the enemy shelling, McLaren had no time to radio his situation to battalion HQ. This caused Highlanders commander Lieutenant Colonel Ian Johnston some anxiety as he waited anxiously for news that the initial objective was secure. Until his leading companies were both on their objectives, he could not risk taking the other two rifle companies forward.

At 1800 hours, just ninety minutes after going into the attack, McLaren's company reported that it was on the objective and had been contacted by a 'D' Company patrol.[13] Both companies were digging in and would have their areas secure within fifteen minutes. At 1830 hours, Johnston led the other two companies over the Moro, following 'D' Company's route and enjoying a similar lack of casualties. Once on the other side, Johnston located a deep cave that would serve adequately as a forward battalion HQ. He radioed 1st Canadian Infantry Brigade commander Brigadier Howard Graham at 2000 hours that his battalion controlled its objective.[14]

Believing from confused radio traffic between Graham's HQ and the RCR that all was well with the right hook attack, Johnston sent a patrol to San Leonardo. He expected the patrol would find the RCR entrenching itself inside the small village. Approaching the small grouping of buildings, which were badly battered by days of intense artillery bombardments, the patrol leader called out, identifying himself as a 48th Highlander. This was met with a hail of machine-gun and rifle fire. Despite the fact that the machine guns gave off the distinctive high-pitched shriek of German automatic weaponry, the patrol leader still assumed San Leonardo must be in RCR hands. Undoubtedly the gunfire was coming from jumpy Canadians availing themselves of the firepower of captured German weapons. He called out again, eliciting the same result. Incensed at the perceived stupidity of the RCR troops, he withdrew and reported his findings to Johnston.[15]

Unsure who occupied San Leonardo, Johnston could do little but wait for the morning. He conducted a tally of casualties and was relatively pleased to find that he had suffered only eleven dead and thirteen wounded in an always risky frontal assault against what had previously been a heavily defended position.[16] None of the casualties were officers, so command control in the morning should be excellent. One troubling factor about the casualties was the surprising number of dead compared to wounded. Usually artillery and mortar fire injured far more men than it killed. In that sense, the Highlanders had been anything but lucky.

◆ ◆ ◆

The 48th Highlanders' attack had been intended not only to secure a bridgehead on the western outskirts of San Leonardo but also to clear the river valley of enemy infantry. This would enable the Royal Canadian Engineers to build a bridge across the Moro River free of immediate enemy interference. It was imperative the RCE have a bridge ready by morning. If the engineers failed, the Highlanders' success would be for naught. Without tank support, the Highlanders and RCR would face the impossible task of holding ground against determined counterattacks by combined forces of armour and infantry.

The task of building the bridge fell on the shoulders of thirty-two-year-old Major Robin Bothwell Fraser. Born in Coaticook, Quebec, Fraser had moved to Toronto before the war and worked as a draughtsman. When war broke out in September 1939, he immediately enlisted as a lieutenant. Promotions had come steadily, and Fraser had earned a reputation as a resourceful and determined engineering officer.[17]

The engineers planned to confine the river to a culvert over which a corduroy-road causeway would be constructed. The corduroy road would consist of 800 twelve-foot-long round timbers of eight-inch diameter set side by side. Under this would be a culvert built out of several rows of connecting lines of forty-gallon drums, with the bottoms cut away so each allowed the river to flow through the next in line. A bulldozer would fill the streambed with dirt, forcing the river into the culverts, then grade a track from the bridge to the existing roadway. It required thirty-four three-ton trucks to carry the timbers, drums, and other construction supplies.[18] So many trucks in a small area would be extremely vulnerable to enemy fire if the opposing riverbank was not cleared of German machine-gunners.

Although the Highlanders had secured their objectives at 2000 hours, nobody thought to tell Fraser. This left Fraser waiting impatiently with his convoy of trucks and 120 men on the road leading down to the Moro. At 2200 hours, Fraser decided the engineers either got to work or failed in their task.[19] He took six sappers and a D-7 bulldozer, driven by Sapper Milton C. McNaughton, down to the river. Fraser later wrote in the company's war diary, "That D-7 seems to make as much noise as an entire tank brigade as it moves down to the job."[20] Deciding that no bulldozer work was required on the southern side of the river, Fraser told McNaughton to find a way to get his machine over to the other side and start grading the diversion needed there. McNaughton clanked eastward across the rough country until he found a possible crossing point. By this time, however, the sound of the bulldozer had attracted the attention of the Panzer Grenadiers. Shelling of the river valley intensified, and some machine-gun positions dug in on the valley in front of San Leonardo started searching for the bulldozer with bursts of fire. McNaughton paused, waiting for things to quiet down. When the Germans kept firing, he finally said, "Aw, the hell with this," and drove his D-7 into the riverbed.[21]

The bulldozer boiled up out of the river onto the other bank and rumbled back toward the planned bridge site. But the dense foliage and other obstructions along the shoreline forced him to detour away from the river and toward the enemy positions. A fretting Fraser saw the bulldozer moving across the skyline a good quarter mile inside what was still enemy territory. The Germans saw McNaughton, too, and raked his machine with heavy machine-gun fire. Miraculously, McNaughton and the bulldozer drove through the intense fire virtually unscathed and returned safely to the riverbank.

By now Fraser had four lorries, two loaded with barrels and the others with timbers, down at the river.[22] A team of sappers set about installing the culvert and then laying down the timber bridging, while McNaughton cut the diversion up to the roadway. The cut he graded varied from zero elevation to twelve feet over a distance of only eighty feet, requiring extensive shifting and shoring of natural terrain. It took McNaughton seven hours to complete the task.[23] Despite heavy enemy fire, the engineers suffered surprisingly few casualties during their night's work. Only three men required evacuation for wounds. Fraser and a few others received minor wounds, but stuck to their jobs.[24]

One thing was increasingly obvious. The Royal Canadian Regiment did not possess San Leonardo, nor was it anywhere near the eastern edge of the village. Fire from both positions never faltered. While Fraser had no idea what had happened to the RCR, he knew that their failure boded ill for his ability to keep the bridge open come morning. But he was determined the engineers would do their job regardless of enemy fire.[25]

◆ ◆ ◆

In fact, the RCR was still a good mile short of San Leonardo and engaged in a costly punching match with the 200th Regiment and supporting armour. The battalion's attack plan had been dashed within minutes of 'A' Company, under Captain Sam Liddell, crossing its start line at 1630 hours. The company had passed through the Hastings and Prince Edward Regiment's front-line positions into an orchard immediately south of the road running along the ridge from San Donato to San Leonardo. Major Strome Galloway's 'B' Company was scheduled to follow in five minutes. Once these lead companies secured a position on the road about halfway to San Leonardo, 'C' and 'D' companies would jump past to a point just outside the village. Leapfrogging through this new strongpoint, 'A' and 'B' companies would secure the community.

The entire movement required an advance laterally across the 200th Regiment's front line, and would depend on surprise and bold execution. Once the RCR left the lines of the Hasty P's, it would be dependent on its own resources. The four companies would move as an isolated island through enemy territory. If successful, the regiment would regain contact with other Canadian forces upon its occupation of San Leonardo. If the attack failed, the RCR would have to fight its way back to the Hasty P's or die trying.

The Panzer Grenadiers were not surprised by the RCR attack. Liddell's company advanced no more than fifty yards into the orchard before being caught in the open by a deadly accurate shower of mortar bombs. Every man in one platoon section led by Corporal L.F. Meister was killed. Casualties in all the other platoons were heavy.[26] 'A' Company pushed on despite its losses, moving forward in line at a steady pace. Waiting his turn to advance, Galloway saw Sam Liddell with his company HQ "striding through the smoke and dust as if he was going for a stroll. His coolness was most admirable, as was that of his whole company."[27]

Mortaring of the orchard continued unabated, so Galloway decided to lead his company over to the right where an open culvert offered some protection. The deviation worked — the company suffered no initial casualties. Galloway led his men out of the culvert into a vineyard. Darkness was lowering onto the battlefield with its usual December haste just as a German machine gun opened up on their right. Three men fell wounded before the enemy gun was knocked out.

In the darkness and tangled terrain, Galloway became confused. He led 'B' Company off into the thick of the German lines, eventually stumbling into a bridge on the coast highway to the north of San Donato.[28] Risking a furtive look at his map by flashlight, Galloway realized his position. He would have to stop the advance, turn around, and try sneaking back to the ridgeline road. All around them, 'B' Company heard Germans shouting and moving back and forth. Veering away from the concentrations of noise and sometimes slipping between groups yelling across to each other, Galloway's men returned to the road without incident.

By this time, the mortar barrage had lifted and an unearthly silence had settled upon the eerie landscape of twisted trees and torn vineyards through which the soldiers passed. But the silence was shattered when Galloway entered a farmyard and a dog began to bay. The major was so unnerved he yanked his pistol out and shot the animal. One of the men behind him riddled the dog with a Thompson submachine gun. Quiet returned.[29]

Minutes later Galloway reached his objective overlooking a bend in the road, and sent a runner to 'A' Company's position beside another bend slightly ahead of his own. Both positions were situated on a low hill. The runner returned with news that Liddell had reported being on his objective, code-named Halifax, some time earlier. Although 'B' Company was still engaged in its walkabout, RCR commander Lieutenant Colonel Daniel Charles Spry had decided to send Captain Lavoie's 'C' Company up to Halifax and accompany it with his forward battalion HQ. Galloway radioed back that he now occupied his objective, code-named Toronto. 'D' Company, commanded by Captain C.H. "Chuck" Lithgow, departed the Hastings and Prince Edward position and moved toward Toronto.[30]

When 'C' Company finished groping its way slowly through the darkness to Halifax, it immediately headed off for the next objective. Spry remained at Halifax, setting up a battalion HQ in a mud-floored ramshackle farmhouse. Lavoie's company advanced only a couple of hundred yards before Lieutenant Dave Bindman's platoon stumbled on eight German infantrymen hunkered down in a ditch beside the road. Bindman, experiencing his first day in combat, rushed forward waving his Tommy gun and the enemy soldiers surrendered without a shot being fired by either side. This promising start ended, however, when 500 yards out, 'C' Company walked directly into a strong Panzer Grenadier counterattack coming down the road from San Leonardo. At its head was an armoured car, followed immediately by a Panzer Mark IV tank.

A confused battle broke out between 'C' Company and the advancing Germans. In the face of the armoured car and tank support, the outgunned Canadians were soon beating a hasty, confused retreat to Halifax. Casualties were heavy. Although some of the wounded had to be abandoned, most were dragged or carried back by their comrades. When the survivors of 'C' Company stumbled into 'A' Company's line, they quickly reorganized and helped strengthen Halifax's front. Weapons pointed toward the darkness, the soldiers waited for the Germans to reach them. Against the armour they had little but the unreliable PIAT guns and the mortar platoon's three-inch tubes, which had been brought up by mules.

As 'C' Company pulled back to Halifax, 'D' Company closed on 'B' Company's objective, Toronto. In the lead was No. 16 Platoon, commanded by twenty-two-year-old Lieutenant Mitch Sterlin. The company's other two platoons were farther back, still negotiating a deep, narrow gully. Whether because Sterlin's platoon was observed emerging from the gully or by pure misfortune, a German artillery salvo crashed into the gully, transforming it into a cauldron of blood. Lieutenant Bill Darling was mortally hit, more than a dozen other men were seriously wounded. Unhurt, Captain Lithgow ordered the two platoons to retreat from the killing zone to the gully entrance.

His wireless set was ruined, the operator dead. One of the stretcher-bearers was also dead and the stretcher broken. Lithgow had no communication and little means to evacuate the many wounded. Realizing it would take the rest of the two platoons to carry the wounded back to the safety of the bridgehead, Lithgow sent them back and set off alone to report his actions to Spry. The two platoons managed to drag themselves back along the line of advance to safety. Meanwhile, Sterlin led the remaining platoon of 'D' Company up to Toronto and received instructions to occupy a house near 'A' Company's position. The two-storey farmhouse obviously belonged to a more prosperous family than most working the land around Ortona. It had a cream-coloured stucco exterior, with rooms generously lit by wide windows. A narrow front entrance door was set directly in the centre with a window on either side. The excellent firing ports provided by all the windows and its occupation of a slight rise in the ground put the house in an excellent defensive position.

From a gully to its right, Galloway's 'B' Company heard the distinctive whine and clanking of tanks forming north of the RCR defences. When a patrol crept a short distance up the road, it saw by the moonlight a large number of tanks lined up in a row on the muddy track, apparently waiting for the order to attack.[31]

Half surrounded by German tanks, Spry realized he had little option but to dig in and fight off the enemy counterattacks. His only hope of holding the Panzer Grenadiers at bay rested on the ability to call on artillery support. Luckily, Spry had excellent radio communication with his supporting artillery regiment. At midnight, with the sound of the German tanks closing, he laid down, around the entire RCR perimeter, a semi-circular wall of high-explosive and shrapnel shells.

Hunkering in a slit trench near the farmhouse occupied by Sterlin, twenty-year-old Lieutenant Jimmy Quayle could not believe the volume of fire descending in front of him. "Shell after shell after shell like an artillery conveyor belt. . . . Black plants bloomed everywhere in the field, spawned seeds of shrapnel and died."[32] Quayle tried to squirm deeper into the slit trench, but it had been dug to size by his batman Private Pierre Gauthier. The private was five-foot-four, Quayle six-foot-three. Shrapnel sprayed overhead. Fearing that any moment the barrage would enter the RCR lines and that the "artillery was making a stupid mistake," Quayle ran back to 'A' Company HQ.

Not realizing that Spry had brought battalion HQ forward with 'C' Company, he was surprised to find the battalion commander sitting calmly on the mud floor next to the RCR's assigned forward observation officer. The FOO was passing on firing coordinates that were almost exactly those held by the RCR to the on-call gun batteries. Quayle told Spry of the danger posed by the closeness of the shelling. "I know. It has to be that way," Spry responded. He then turned his attention back to interrogating a German officer who remained "very erect, very polite, and totally uncommunicative."[33] Realizing that Spry was right and that some rounds of the protective wall of fire would likely fall inside the Canadian position, Quayle returned to his platoon position.

Minutes later, rounds from one salvo did fall short, landing near the headquarters. Three soldiers were wounded and two Indian muleteers killed. Several mules, used to carry the FOO's radio equipment and the three-inch mortars, were torn to pieces. The German armour, apparently deterred by the heavy shelling, never appeared. Soon enemy shells started falling to the immediate south of 'A' Company's position. Spry realized that the Germans, seeing shells land in the area occupied by 'A' and 'C' companies, had assumed the RCR must be dug in farther to the south. They remained deceived throughout the night, continuing to bombard the wrong location. For his part, Spry kept calling salvoes down on the edge of his battalion's position whenever the Germans made the slightest move toward it.

As the night wore on, the RCR reorganized. The battalion HQ was full of wounded. When moonlight shone down through the rickety roof onto the mud floor, it was decided they had to be moved to a more solid location. The cream-coloured building occupied by Lieutenant Mitch Sterlin's 'D' Company platoon was sturdy and sound, so the wounded were transferred there.

Spry and his battalion command staff on the scene spent the remaining hours of darkness gathering an appreciation of their current position. One thing was clear. The Panzer Grenadier resistance was too strong and the casualties suffered so far too heavy to enable the RCR to continue its attack toward San Leonardo. Spry concluded that the flat little hilltop his battalion occupied was defensibly untenable due to an overlooking low ridge and the flat terrain, providing perfect ground for tank manoeuvre. Downhill from the house, already dubbed Sterlin's Castle, was a slight reverse slope.

Spry decided to shift everyone down the slope and to leave Sterlin and his platoon in the house to hold the right flank closest to the road. This meant again moving the wounded out of what would now become the RCR's forward defensive point. The move was completed without incident. The regiment concentrated in a tight little island with Liddell's 'A' Company holding the northern flank, Lavoie's 'C' Company the east, and Galloway's 'B' Company the remaining edges of the circle around battalion HQ, the three-inch mortars, the wounded, and the surviving muleteers. The lateral attack had failed. The RCR was cut off and possibly surrounded.

There remained one glimmer of hope. Shortly before daylight, Spry received word from Brigadier Howard Graham that 2nd Canadian Infantry Brigade supported by tanks would cross the river in the morning and smash its way into San Leonardo. Once San Leonardo fell, the RCR should be able to fight its way through to the village. Failing that, it was probable that the Panzer Grenadiers would at least have to divert their attention to containing the 2 CIB assault. That would enable the RCR to withdraw to the Hastings and Prince Edward bridgehead. Immediate orders for the RCR were to dig in and hold.

# 10

## You Take It Now

At 0430 hours, December 9, Brigadier Howard Graham signalled Major General Chris Vokes at 1st Canadian Infantry Division headquarters. Graham was plagued by a duodenal ulcer that was causing him increasing pain. Now that pain was accentuated by the admission of failure. "It appears," he reported, "that it is not possible for me to form the bridgehead as ordered by you, but at least the operation enabled the diversion to be prepared. . . . It would be of great assistance if tanks were pushed over as soon as possible. . . . It has been an exceedingly busy night."[1] Vokes had assumed as much from the night's 1st Brigade radio traffic and reports. He had accordingly reworked his offensive plan. Originally the Seaforth Highlanders of Canada battalion, supported by the 14th Canadian Armoured Regiment, more commonly called the Calgary Tanks, was to use San Leonardo as a jumping-off point to attack toward the Ortona-Orsogna lateral road. Now the combined force would have to first take the village.

At least Vokes finally had a bridge across the Moro. It had not helped his disposition to learn that during the night the 8th Indian

Division engineers had achieved what the Royal Canadian Engineers had deemed impossible. By manhandling all the parts of a Bailey bridge across to the northern bank of the Moro, the Indian sappers had succeeded in launching a stable crossing in the reverse direction over the river directly below Villa Rogatti. Lieutenant Colonel Geoff Walsh's "impossible bridge" had proven possible after all. The opportunity to have outflanked the defences around San Leonardo by moving armour and infantry out of Villa Rogatti, as advocated so fiercely by Princess Patricia's Canadian Light Infantry commander Lieutenant Colonel Cameron Ware, could have worked. That was nothing but fodder for speculation by historians now; the opportunity had been lost and the Canadians must continue with the more direct, undoubtedly bloodier, head-on attack. An added insult came when the Indians erected a sign over the new structure naming it "The Impossible Bridge."[2]

Vokes's bridge before San Leonardo was ready at 0600 hours, not a minute too soon. The tank attack was scheduled to begin in precisely one hour. German shelling of the bridge location intensified as dawn approached. Time and again, Major Robin Fraser's exhausted engineers rushed out on the bridge and frantically repaired damage caused by shell strikes. The engineers took heavy casualties. While only three engineers had been wounded during the bridge's construction, twenty-two were killed or wounded keeping it in repair for the duration of the attack.[3]

◆ ◆ ◆

Brigadier Robert Andrew Wyman, commander of 1st Canadian Armoured Brigade, listened soberly as Vokes changed the tasking for the Calgary Tanks. The new mission would be a desperate attempt to retrieve victory from failure. Carrying a company of Seaforth Highlanders of Canada on the outer hulls, a squadron of Sherman M-4 tanks would race across the bridge and gain entry into San Leonardo. Wyman personally carried the news to twenty-five-year-old Major Ned Amy, whose 'A' Squadron of the Calgary Tanks would undertake the risky mission. Amy and his tanks were already formed up astride the road on the southern ridgeline of the Moro River valley. With a false dawn only just penetrating the overhanging cloud, Wyman gave Amy the news. "They [1st Canadian Infantry Brigade] haven't taken the bridgehead. You take it now," he said simply.[4] Amy, a graduate of Royal Military College who had been born in Newcastle, New Brunswick, had only been promoted to the rank of major two months earlier. Given overall command of the combined infantry and armoured force, he now shouldered responsibility for the attack.

Amy got underway immediately. At 0730 hours, the tanks fired up their engines and the Seaforths' 'D' Company, commanded by Captain Alan Mercer, broke into sections and boarded the twelve tanks. Setting off in a single-file column, the tanks descended into the valley. The sound of the tank engines and tracks churning through the mud of the road immediately attracted German mortar and artillery fire.

With the valley slope exploding all around, Amy directed the leading tanks to speed up. Careering down the hill, two of the tanks failed to negotiate a tight corner and the thirty-two-ton machines both rolled down a thirty-foot embankment.[5] While most of the infantry jumped to safety as the tanks toppled over the edge, Private McConnell, 'D' Company's one-hundred-pound, five-foot-tall runner, was pinned under one of the tanks. It would take several hours for one of the tank crews to dig him out unhurt.[6] The two tanks had to be abandoned until tank recovery equipment was able to winch them back out of the ravine.[7] As the remaining ten tanks approached the valley bottom, the German mortar bombardment was joined by intensive machine-gun fire, forcing the Seaforths to abandon the tanks and make their way forward on foot through the limited protective cover of the vineyards and olive groves. The infantry refused to be driven to ground, advancing despite heavy casualties.

Grinding up the steep road toward San Leonardo, the lead tank triggered a pressure-activated Teller mine. Shaped like a covered cooking pan about two and a half inches deep and fifteen inches across, the Teller mine was loaded with high explosive. When the tank rolled over the plunger-style trigger buried just under the surface, the mine exploded. While a single mine lacked the force to destroy an armoured vehicle, it was sufficient to break a track and immobilize the tank. Amy's tank column lurched to a halt behind the damaged tank blocking the road. The infantry were moving off beyond the armour. There was only one way Amy could continue the tank attack. He ordered his driver to head cross-country toward the top of the ridgeline and radioed for the remaining eight tanks to follow. The combination of mud, devastated olive orchards, and tangles of wire and torn vines in the vineyards made the going next to impossible. Five of the tanks soon bogged down, but the other four bulled their way forward.[8]

Lieutenant John McLean's infantry platoon was first to scramble up to the ridgeline. It advanced with Amy's clutch of tanks following close behind. Cannon and machine-gun fire from the tanks helped McLean sweep aside strong concentrations of German defenders and gain entrance to San Leonardo. One hundred yards from the village, Amy's tanks were held up by a German antitank minefield. McLean, with only ten men left, stormed into the built-up area, setting off a deadly house-to-house battle. McLean himself killed eight Germans, took eighteen prisoners, and captured ten machine guns. Amy could do little more but wait impatiently for a team of Seaforth pioneers to come up and sweep a path for the tanks with mine detectors. The mine-detection team arrived on a tank, bolstering Amy's strength.[9]

Meanwhile, twenty-two-year-old Corporal Thomas James Price found himself relieved of command when an officer whose tank had become bogged down ordered him to turn over his tank to the officer's command. Price started trudging toward the rear, but he realized the need for tanks at San Leonardo was desperate. Spotting a tank that appeared to have suffered mechanical failure rather than becoming bogged down in the mud, Price ran over and got the demoralized tank crew to come out of the safety of their hull to effect repairs. As Price and two crewmen worked to fix the tank, they were subjected to heavy fire from nearby enemy machine guns. Soon the tank was operable and Price took over command, directing the tank up the slope toward San Leonardo. He arrived just as Amy led his tanks into the village.[10]

Of nearly one hundred men who had started off on Amy's tanks, only thirty-nine Seaforths remained. Among them was twenty-three-year-old Company Sergeant Major Jock Gibson, who had just been promoted to his new position and still wondered what exactly a CSM was supposed to do. Gibson figured one task he might perform was helping out his old unit, No. 18 Platoon. He headed toward San Leonardo with a runner and signalman in tow. As he led the way behind some buildings a shot rang out. Feeling a bullet clip his ear tip, he turned to see the young runner sagging toward the ground. The same round had struck the man in the side of the face and blown out the back of his skull. Gibson rolled into cover and continued working his way into the town, trying to find the remainder of No.18 Platoon.[11]

From his position on the outskirts of the village, Amy caught only occasional glimpses of the infantrymen "as they ducked from doorway to doorway or scurried from cover to cover."[12] He was paying scant attention to the firefight going on between German and Canadian infantry inside San Leonardo. His concern was to keep an eye on the approaches for enemy armour, which he expected to arrive imminently. This task was complicated when the Germans set a haystack in front of his position on fire, sending a thick screen of smoke drifting across the enemy's probable line of approach. Amy told his driver to shift the tank to one side of the burning haystack. When the move was completed, he looked northward and saw a German tank bearing down on him. Swivelling the turret, Amy engaged the tank at a range of 150 yards, quickly knocking it out. Moments later, one of his other tanks destroyed another advancing Panzer that came within forty yards of it. As the German tank started to burn, a Seaforth infantryman, who had been helplessly hiding in the grass just in front of the advancing enemy tracks, jumped up and rushed over to pat the Calgary tank on the side. "You big cast-iron son-of-a-bitch," the soldier cried, "I could kiss you."[13]

The German armour–led counterattack continued, a dozen tanks supported by infantry rolling in from several directions. Inside San Leonardo, Gibson poked his head around the corner of a shattered building and saw what looked to him to be a new Tiger tank coming down the lane with infantry riding on top. Gibson realized that the tank would have to come around the corner he was hiding behind and that the lane was so narrow the monstrous machine would be unable to make the turn. Looking over his shoulder, he was delighted to see a Sherman creeping down the street toward him. Gibson ran to the Calgary tank. Pointing the corner out to its commander he yelled up, "There's a big Tiger coming around that corner. He can't get around that corner. It's too narrow."

The Calgary tank commander ordered armour-piercing shells

readied and loaded, then waited until the German tank rolled around the corner and, as Gibson predicted, proved unable to complete the turn or rotate its turret. Seeing the Canadian tank, the infantry piled off and fled back down the lane. The Calgary gunner started punching rounds through the turret and the tank, in reality a common medium Panzer Mark IV, soon burst into flames.[14] Like most infantry, Gibson tended to think that all tanks were the behemoth Tigers, which were virtually invulnerable to Allied tanks and that all antitank guns were the equally feared 88-millimetres. Gibson joined his platoon and helped it in the vicious house-to-house fighting that followed.

By 1030 hours, Amy's tanks had broken the German counterattack and the enemy force started withdrawing toward the northeast. Strewn around San Leonardo and inside the town were the wrecks of eight German tanks.[15] Fifteen minutes later, Seaforth commander Lieutenant Colonel Doug Forin moved with the rest of the battalion over the Moro to consolidate the hold on the village won by 'D' Company and 'A' squadron of the Calgary Tanks. Soon two troops of the Calgary Tanks' 'B' squadron were rolling across the river to reinforce Amy. The first stage of the battle for San Leonardo was mostly over. Still, the fighting on the edge of the village continued with the Canadian reinforcements trying to expand the size of the battalion's holdings.

Seaforth scout Private A.K. Harris accompanied the leading elements of infantry reinforcing San Leonardo. He later wrote in his diary: "Most of the houses on the South side are blackened hulls and still burning. They smell as usual of H.E. [high explosive] fire and the dead. . . . We are to spend the night here, so our section takes over a house. It is not a bad house. It is dry and has an upstairs full of rubble to absorb the shells from above, with a room or two on the north side for protection. These are the principal qualifications of a first class residence. An unexploded twenty-five pounder shell is embedded in a wall. We make ourselves comfortable."[16]

As some of the Seaforths settled in, a Calgary tank was knocked out on San Leonardo's outskirts by a hidden antitank gun. The crew managed to escape from the burning tank but had to abandon its commander, who was badly wounded and suffering from severe burns. An attempt to reach the injured man with an ambulance jeep was driven off by enemy fire. Seeing the situation, twenty-one-year-old

Acting Sergeant John McDougall and medical orderly twenty-three-year-old Acting Corporal Gordon James Barss of the Royal Canadian Medical Corps crossed 200 yards of open ground under intense enemy fire, administered first aid to the wounded officer, and then carried him back to safety. Their action undoubtedly saved the officer's life.[17]

◆ ◆ ◆

The Calgary Tanks' successful crossing of the Moro River proved a mixed blessing for the 48th Highlanders of Canada, dug in on the western flank of San Leonardo. Because the Royal Canadian Regiment attack had failed to take San Leonardo during the night, the Highlanders had found themselves in the morning cut off from the rest of 1st Canadian Infantry Division. Until morning, it seemed the Germans had remained unaware of the presence of Lieutenant Colonel Ian Johnston's battalion. With the first glimmer of dawn, however, that happy situation abruptly ended.

During the night, Johnston had established the battalion HQ in a large cave overlooking San Leonardo with the idea that it would provide a good view of the village and the RCR's dispositions there. Now the Canadians in the cave found themselves looking down the barrel of a Spandau machine-gun position that enjoyed a perfect field of fire into the cave's large entrance. Both Germans and Canadians stared at each other in dazed surprise for a moment before the Highlanders dived for cover and the Panzer Grenadiers lunged to their weapon. Burst after burst flailed the cave entrance and minutes later six-round volleys of two-foot bombs fired by Nebelwerfers started exploding all through the Highlanders' positions. Soon 88-millimetre guns joined the chorus. Johnston was certain it would not be long before the Panzer Grenadiers launched a combined armour and infantry attack on his front.

The Highlanders were elated when they saw the Calgary Tanks roaring across the bridge and making their way up to San Leonardo. But as the tanks approached the village they started firing shells into the Highlanders' perimeter. One Canadian shell struck a metal barrel providing a roof over Major F.G. McLaren's slit trench, transforming it into a hail of fine splinters that caused multiple wounds to the officer's face. The concussion of the explosion also burst his eardrums.

Another soldier was killed by the tank fire before two soldiers could alert the tankers to the Highlanders' presence.

With the arrival of the Seaforths and tanks in San Leonardo, the Germans shifted their attention away from the Highlanders to a fierce attempt to regain the village. The Highlanders endured only continuing shelling throughout the day. As the morning wore on, Johnston received orders to move two companies to San Leonardo to reinforce the growing concentration of Canadian forces building there. The divisional plan was for the Loyal Edmonton Regiment to move up at day's end and occupy San Leonardo, while the Seaforths and Calgary Tanks took up positions beyond the town in preparation for a morning offensive toward the Ortona-Orsogna lateral highway.[18]

It was becoming increasingly apparent that the Seaforth assault on San Leonardo had not only caught the Germans by surprise, but also in the middle of executing a dual offensive against the bridgehead to the east held by the Hastings and Prince Edward Regiment and the isolated pocket held by the Royal Canadian Regiment. These attacks had left the Panzer Grenadiers with limited reserves to throw into the fighting at San Leonardo. With the RCR having narrowly escaped catastrophe and the Hasty P's ably holding their position, it seemed likely German attention would now shift entirely to the Canadian forces holding the village. Therefore Vokes wanted every man he could get close to San Leonardo to ensure that this key position — now the focal point of the Canadian effort to shatter the Moro River defensive line — was held.

# 11

## Sterlin Castle

In the early morning of December 9, the Royal Canadian Regiment's line resembled the circled wagons of a western movie. Although they were isolated on the northern edge of the Moro River valley between the Hastings and Prince Edward Regiment beachhead and San Leonardo, the men's morale remained high. At first light Lieutenant Dave Bindman, who had courageously bagged a group of prisoners during the night's fighting, encountered three enemy soldiers abandoning an undetected machine-gun post on the immediate flank of 'C' Company. Standing, Tommy gun to his shoulder, the officer exchanged shots with the Panzer Grenadiers before they broke and ran. Bindman ran after them, firing from the hip. Two privates surrendered, but the officer managed to escape. An elated Bindman marched his second set of prisoners back to the perimeter. Just as he entered the RCR lines, however, a mortar bomb struck directly in front of him. The officer fell, mortally wounded. Bindman had been in action for less than twenty-four hours.[1]

The mortar round that killed Bindman signalled the beginning of an intense German effort to destroy the RCR with the heaviest bombardment the regiment had so far endured. Shells blanketed their position, causing them to quickly dub the area "Slaughterhouse Hill" because of the heavy casualties suffered. Broken and torn bodies lay scattered throughout the perimeter, and the screams and moans of the wounded carried on the air. Two Sikh muleteers were killed, along with several of their animals.

Despite the intense shelling, the RCR was heartened to see Canadian tanks crossing the Moro River and moving up into San Leonardo. Soon Brigadier Howard Graham signalled Lieutenant Colonel Dan Spry that "one sub-unit Wyman's boys are across. They should be very close. . . ." At 0950 hours Graham added, "Brothers Number 2 [2nd Canadian Infantry Brigade] in town. . . . move over and contact."[2]

Spry issued orders to continue the lateral movement across the Panzer Grenadiers' front into San Leonardo. The attack on San Leonardo deflected the German artillery's attention from the RCR. As the shelling around Major Strome Galloway's position lessened, he was startled to see an Italian family emerge from a hidden cave. As they stepped into the open, a shell landed close by and one young man in the group appeared to faint. Closer examination revealed that he had died, presumably suffering a heart attack from fright. The women in the small group dropped to their knees. Apparently seeking God's mercy, they started calling lamentations toward heaven.[3]

♦ ♦ ♦

If God was present on the Moro River battlefield, the merciful side of his spirit was expressed through the efforts of the medical teams treating the many wounded. A complex operational network functioned under the most difficult of conditions to evacuate the wounded from the immediate battlefield along a chain of field dressing stations, surgeries, and hospitals located ever more distant from the embattled areas.

First Canadian Infantry Division's hurried entry into the battlefield at the beginning of the month had left the medical units scrambling to find suitable facilities for hospital operations close to the Moro River line. Many buildings in San Vito Chietino — the most logical base — were badly damaged, and the village was subject to near continual shelling. Matters had been further complicated when the Sangro River bridge washed out, effectively cutting the division off from an adequate transportation link until the British engineers replaced the bridge on December 9. Even then, it would be several more days before the wounded could be trucked across the bridge. A logjam of traffic flowed north as 3rd Canadian Infantry Brigade's battalions and other vitally needed forces moved to join the battle. Lacking priority status, the ambulances were unloaded and the wounded transferred across the river in the DUKW amphibious trucks, a slow process.

In response to these problems, the surgical teams moved closer than normal to the battlefield and conducted a large number of operations under enemy bombardment. Along with 1st Canadian Field Unit's surgery, No. 5 Field Ambulance Unit established a casualty collection post in San Vito Chietino. Other facilities were established at Rocca San Giovanni, a bit farther back than San Vito. When the Sangro bridge was restored, No. 1 Field Dressing Station, No. 4 Field Ambulance Unit, and No. 2 Field Surgical Unit also moved into San Vito. On December 9, the fierce fighting on the Moro River resulted in 230 casualties being evacuated through the Rocca treatment facilities to hospitals south of the Sangro River. Most of these were soldiers operated on earlier by the forward field surgery teams.

The most forward surgery was at San Vito in a school pitted with shell holes and lacking any glass in its windows. At any given time, this hospital housed one hundred or more patients either waiting for evacuation or in too unstable a condition to be moved.[4] Among those lying for days in this hospital was Princess Patricia's Canadian Light Infantry Lieutenant Jerry Richards, who had suffered shrapnel wounds to his stomach on the night of December 6–7. By the time Richards reached the surgery he was already developing peritonitis, a painful and dangerous inflammation of the transparent membrane lining the abdominal walls. The two surgeons, Dr. Frank Mills and Dr. Bruce Toby, had immediately cut away his bloody clothes and conducted emergency operations to contain the damage to Richards's abdominal organs and to sew up his external wounds. Richards awoke hours after the operation to find various intravenous tubes running into the veins of both legs. He was "surprised and pleased to be lying there alive in this bed," despite being naked except for the identity disks around his neck. Soon Richards learned that his clothes had

been either cut to pieces or so blood-stained that the medical orderlies had thrown them away. As he learned about the severity of his
wounds, Richards realized that his war against Germany was over.
He was facing a more personal war to recover from the wounds, and
would require several years of continued treatments.[5]

The surgical teams and medical orderlies in the San Vito operations depended on both the ambulance units, and the medical officers
and orderlies posted to the various battalions to clear the wounded
from the fighting lines. Geneva Convention rules required that these
men wear a red cross on a white armband for identification, be
unarmed, and not be fired upon while treating and collecting the
wounded. In reality, their job was as dangerous as any front-line
duty. Amid the confused, smoke-filled, and hazardous conditions
prevailing during a battle, soldiers rarely held fire when presented
with a target wearing an enemy uniform. Many stretcher-bearers,
orderlies, and medical officers died on the Moro River front trying to
rescue wounded soldiers. Some were shot by enemy soldiers. The
majority were killed by artillery and mortar fire, which exempted
nobody from its deadly rain.

As soon as a battalion established a new position, it set up a
Regimental Aid Post (RAP) in the safest and most comfortable location available. Usually this was a building with solid walls and a
sturdy roof that rendered it somewhat shellproof. If conditions were
too bad, as was the case on December 8–9 for the RCR dug in on the
reverse slope of the Moro River ridge, the RAP might merely be a
series of slit trenches close to the centre of the infantry's perimeter.
Once a wounded soldier reached the RAP he received basic, often
crude, first aid. Priority was placed on stopping external bleeding
and preventing the onset of shock, a major cause of battlefield death.
Wound cleaning to stave off gangrene was also a key task. Stabilization
of the patient was the focus, rather than extensive treatment of the
wound.

The medical orderlies forayed out from the RAP whenever a
wounded soldier was reported. Often the flow of battle required the
infantry to carry on the fight and abandon the wounded where they
fell. To do otherwise jeopardized everyone's safety, because a company
or platoon concentrating on tending wounded seldom could fulfill
assigned combat tasks. Leaving suffering friends was more easily

done if the soldiers knew that stretcher-bearers followed in their wake, determined to gather up the wounded and spirit them to safety.

The forward medical teams were assisted by the padres and chaplains assigned to each battalion. Men such as Roy Durnford, the Seaforth padre, Three Rivers Tank Regiment's chaplain Waldo E. Smith, and RCR chaplain Rusty Wilkes spent many hours under fire. Much of the time they helped man the jeeps fitted with stretcher racks to carry the wounded back from the RAP to rear-area hospital facilities. The clerics also oversaw the grim duty of burying the dead. This included the task of ensuring that grave sites were marked and coordinates recorded on maps so the bodies could later be recovered and moved to military cemeteries for permanent interment.

For many RCR soldiers killed on December 9, days passed before their bodies were recovered or buried. At 1430 hours, when the battalion moved off toward the safety of San Leonardo, it had no choice but to abandon its dead. Almost every man in 'C' Company was required just to assist the stretcher-bearers in carrying out the wounded who were incapable of walking on their own.

Providing a protective screen for the men assisting the wounded, Galloway's 'B' Company took the point position. The soldiers moved through a landscape transformed by war into a charred, mud-choked hellhole. Olive trees were shattered and stripped of leaves, vineyards were devastated tangles of wire and torn vegetation, most buildings had been reduced to rubble or had their roofs stove in by direct artillery hits, small fires burned across the plain clear to Ortona. Everywhere the men looked were shell craters. The mud underfoot was slippery and filthy. Forty-eight hours before, Matthew Halton had likened the Moro ridgeline to a painting by Paul Cézanne. Now it appeared colourless, a bleak world made even grimmer by the close slate-grey sky.

'B' and 'C' companies slipped clear of the RCR position without meeting any resistance. 'A' Company and the battalion HQ section were not so lucky. Just as they prepared to move off, the Panzer Grenadiers attacked, slicing between the two groups and isolating 'A' Company and Spry's HQ. Responsible for the wounded and under orders to get into San Leonardo, Galloway had no option but to leave the cutoff element to its fate. Upon reaching San Leonardo, 'C' Company immediately set off with the wounded down the road leading to the southern bank of the Moro River. 'B' Company took up position on the junction where the lateral ridgeline road intersected the main road entering San Leonardo.

Galloway was surprised by the reception Seaforth Highlanders of Canada commander Lieutenant Colonel Doug Forin gave him. "Thank God you have come," Forin said excitedly. He then proceeded to order Galloway to push his ravaged company forward of San Leonardo toward the enemy lines. Galloway's orders from Spry were to consolidate at the road junction inside the village, so he refused. Forin demanded to know what else Galloway would do to help him. Galloway told him his orders were to sit tight. If Forin failed to consider such action a help, that was too bad. He thought the lieutenant colonel left in a "huff."[6] Soon after, Galloway received a radio signal from Spry to withdraw from San Leonardo. He was to rejoin the RCR on the southern bank of the Moro, where the battalion was planning a reorganization for future operations. Because San Leonardo was taking heavy artillery fire, Galloway replied that he would link up with the rest of the battalion in the morning when it was safer to move.

◆ ◆ ◆

While 'A' Company and battalion HQ were left surrounded on three flanks with their backs to the Moro River valley, most of 'D' Company remained in the Hastings and Prince Edward battalion's perimeter, helping to fend off repeated counterattacks. The brunt of the German counterattacks fell on the front held by Hasty P's Acting Major Frank Joseph Hammond's Company 'B.' The twenty-nine-year-old had worked his way up from the rank of Lance Corporal and was known as a brave, stolid soldier. Seeing the advancing lines of Panzer Grenadiers, Hammond ordered his men to hold their fire. He let the Germans close to within 150 yards before unleashing a maelstrom of machine-gun and rifle fire, supported by the company's two-inch mortars and the battalion's three-inch mortars. The effect was devastating, throwing back the initial attack with heavy casualties.[7]

During this attack, Sergeant Gordon Pemberton was stunned by {a mortar bomb that landed near his slit trench. Head ringing from concussion, the twenty-seven-year-old from Port Hope, Ontario, still had the presence of mind to appreciate that one flank of his platoon section was hanging in the air, completely exposed to attack from a narrow ravine stretching back into the German lines. The Germans were raking the Canadian front with machine-gun and mortar fire, obviously trying to soften the position for a renewed assault. Pemberton realized the ravine approach had to be secured immediately. Unable to spare any men from his section's line, Pemberton decided to tackle the job himself. Snatching up a Bren light machine gun and a bag of magazines, he crawled across 350 yards of ground subjected to heavy enemy fire to occupy a position overlooking the ravine from the ridge opposite his section's trenches. As he set the Bren gun up on its bipod, assumed a prone position, and tucked the machine gun's butt into his shoulder, a knot of Germans turned a bend inside the ravine and started creeping toward his hiding spot. Pemberton let them come in close before opening fire. He burned off several magazines, sending the completely surprised Panzer Grenadiers fleeing. They left fifteen dead.[8]

As this attack was being repelled, more Germans dug in a machine-gun post right in front of Hammond's lines. From this position, the Panzer Grenadiers were able to lay down a screen of fire that forced 'B' Company to keep their heads down. Unless the post was destroyed, Hammond knew the next counterattack might well break through. Enlisting the help of thirty-two-year-old Company Sergeant Major Cecil Napoleon Yearwood, Hammond prepared a two-man attack against the German emplacement.

Both men armed themselves with Thompson submachine guns. While the rest of the company laid down supporting fire to force the Panzer Grenadiers to seek cover, Hammond and Yearwood charged the gun position, spraying the enemy with repeated bursts of fire. When they ceased firing, fourteen soldiers were dead or wounded, and the remaining eighteen in the position were standing with their hands up in surrender. This action broke the German offensive.[9] For the rest of the day, the battalion was subjected to little more than desultory shelling, mortaring, the occasional infantry probe, and a surprise aerial attack by a squadron of Messerschmitt 109s that screamed in off the Adriatic to bomb and strafe its positions.

◆ ◆ ◆

Similar counterattacks were also directed toward the isolated RCR element still trapped between the bridgehead held by the Hasty P's and San Leonardo. This small, battered group of soldiers was seriously threatened with being overrun. The Panzer Grenadiers sought to infiltrate behind 'A' Company and cut it off from the valley below. Were they to succeed, everyone in the encircled position would either be killed or forced to surrender. After about twenty minutes of fierce fighting, Spry decided a retreat into the valley and across the river by the nearest possible ford was the only way to avert destruction. He ordered Captain Sam Liddell's 'A' Company to hold until his battalion HQ group had successfully slipped away. Liddell's men would then follow by platoons.[10]

Breaking off a heavy action is a dangerous and difficult undertaking, usually requiring soldiers to relinquish good defensive positions and to cross open ground subject to fire from an alerted enemy. Heavy casualties are common. It is also common for some sections to get forgotten or cut off from the main body. The first two platoons of 'A' Company managed to extricate themselves and retreat to the river bottom. Casualties were light. At the river, Spry learned that 'A' Company's No. 8 Platoon was missing and Lieutenant Mitch Sterlin's No. 16 Platoon of 'D' Company, concentrated in the two-storey farmhouse dubbed Sterlin Castle, had similarly failed to join the retreat.

Unable to do anything for the lost units, Spry led his men across the Moro and ordered them to dig in on the river's bank. His concern was to set up a defensive line to prevent any attempt by the Germans to launch a major assault across the river to outflank and surround the Canadian units positioned on the north side of the valley. Soon Spry was reinforced by 'C' Company, which had completed its transfer of the wounded to safety.[11] The soldiers on the riverbank listened anxiously to the sounds of intense gunfire coming from the northern ridgeline, knowing the remnants of two RCR platoons were engaged in a bitter struggle to survive.

◆ ◆ ◆

Lieutenant Jimmy Quayle's No. 8 Platoon numbered only about fifteen men. They were dug in to the right of the house occupied by the ten men remaining in No. 16 Platoon. Quayle watched two young Panzer Grenadiers with haggard faces and empty-eyed, exhausted expressions creep toward the building. One held a Schmeisser 9-millimetre submachine gun, the second grasped the wooden handle of a stick grenade. As the Germans approached the front door, one of Quayle's corporals stood up in his slit trench and emptied a long burst of fire into the man with the submachine gun. Dropping his grenade, the other German fled.

Quayle yelled across the fifty yards separating the two platoons, repeatedly calling out "Mitch, Mitch." Finally Sterlin appeared in the doorway, waved almost cheerily, and disappeared back into the dark interior. Quayle started to rise, planning to go over and confer with his friend from officers training school, but a machine-gun burst showered him with splinters slashed off the trunk of a nearby olive tree. Quayle grovelled into his slit trench just as deadly accurate mortar fire bracketed the platoon.

While the tall and lean Quayle was the spitting image of a military recruiting poster, his friend Mitch Sterlin was the antithesis. Stocky, perpetually overweight, and renowned for his clumsiness, Sterlin was also easygoing to a fault. He seemed to retain platoon discipline through winning the men over as friends rather than by his leadership abilities. During officer training, Sterlin had always been the man who failed the obstacle course. He fell off the logs crossing rivers, was unable to climb over the walls, and was far to the rear during cross-country marches and runs.

But here was Sterlin, the unlikely officer, calmly leading his platoon in a terrific resistance against overwhelming odds. Quayle worried, however, that they were all going to die. Ammunition was running low. The lieutenant told Sergeant Albert Hocking to inform company commander Captain Sam Liddell of the situation. Repeatedly dashing forward and then dropping as machine gunners and mortarmen zeroed on him, Hocking disappeared from sight, heading in the direction of 'A' Company's HQ. He made an identically hazardous return trip only minutes later to report that everyone else had disappeared. "What do you mean they're gone? The whole company's gone?" Quayle shouted. "Not just the company," the grey-faced man panted between breaths, "but the whole bloody Regiment."[12] Sickened and angry, Quayle realized the two platoons had been abandoned; that somehow the rest of the regiment had withdrawn without his and Sterlin's platoons being advised.

There was precious little time to consider what should be done next, for the mortar bombardment lifted and a large German force charged the two platoons, guns blazing. The Germans were slowed by the deep mud, their run more of a clumsy stagger. Gunfire from Quayle's platoon cut down two of the enemy and the rest retreated.

Quayle shouted again to Sterlin, but received no reply. The door to the house stood open, and there seemed no sign of life. The mortaring resumed. Thinking Sterlin and his platoon were dead, Quayle reluctantly ordered his own unit to withdraw. Leapfrogging one section at a time through the others, Quayle's men made their way through the intense mortar fire. One man was killed on the way. As darkness closed in, Quayle's small force staggered through the river and joined the rest of the RCR.[13]

Unknown to Quayle, Sterlin's platoon was still alive inside the house. None of the men had heard Quayle's shouting. The intense racket of their guns firing in the small confines of the house had deafened them all. With six machine guns blasting the walls of Sterlin Castle, the Germans launched a frenzied final assault. A handful of Panzer Grenadiers fought their way right up to the building, seeking to direct fire through the windows and storm inside. Sterlin and his men cut them down with precisely aimed bullets. The bodies slumped against the wall, some remaining half standing. One oberleutnant tried shoving a stick grenade through the bars of a window. Sterlin's sergeant pushed his rifle barrel through the bars and shot the German at point-blank range. A soldier wearing an Iron Cross at his throat was also shot while trying to provide cover for his German officer. The enemy attack broke and the Germans withdrew. Their dead lay in knots surrounding the house. About fifty Germans had been wounded in the attack, rendering it impossible for them all to be evacuated by the small number of medical orderlies that came forward to help.[14] Sterlin's men held their fire while the orderlies tried to provide first aid to the badly wounded soldiers.

With this attack the battle of Sterlin Castle ended. The Germans made no further attempts to overrun the building. When night came, Sterlin and his men slipped away. They crossed into the Hastings and Prince Edward lines, then marched around to join Spry's forces facing the Moro River. Quayle was overjoyed to see his friend wander out of the dark night into the farmhouse serving as his company's headquarters. The two celebrated by drinking from a keg of bitter red wine found in the basement and eating a tin of sardines Sterlin had been saving for a special occasion.

"I guess today was it for us," Sterlin said. "Right," Quayle replied. "They say there's one time you get killed or you don't. And if you don't you're okay from then on." Sterlin finally said, "So maybe we'll be okay." Quayle offered him some more wine.[15]

# 12

## AT ALL COSTS

**A**s the fighting wound down for the night, the artillery and mortar units of both sides continued harassing their opponent's front- and rear-area positions. Under this fire, the forward infantry and armoured brigades licked their wounds as best they could. Both the 1st Canadian Infantry Division and the 90th Panzer Grenadiers knew the bloody contest of December 9 had ended in the Germans' Moro River line being irreparably breached. The Germans faded into the night, falling back to their next major defensive line. Where that line would be drawn, the Canadians had little idea. It might be immediately ahead. Or, come the morning advance, they might merely face delaying actions covering a German withdrawal to a line behind Ortona anchored on the Arielli River. For their part, the Canadians set about expanding their bridgehead around shell-torn San Leonardo in order to prepare a solid jumping-off point for the morning's hostilities.

Brigadier Bert Hoffmeister ordered the Loyal Edmonton Regiment to pass through the Seaforth Highlanders of Canada lines and take up a position immediately to the north of the village, while the Princess Patricia's Canadian Light Infantry settled in a short distance behind the Edmontons. Kept in reserve until now, the Edmontons were the only 2nd Canadian Infantry Brigade battalion still close to full strength. They would now take the point for a renewed offensive aimed at finally cutting the Ortona-Orsogna lateral road. The objective would be a junction where the road leading north from San Leonardo intersected the highway running from Ortona to Orsogna. The code name for this crossroads was Cider.[1]

While these plans were being drawn, Major General Chris Vokes's headquarters staff assessed the results of the past four days' bitter fighting. The divisional war diarist was jubilant. "This day will be remembered by the 1st Canadians for a long, long time," he wrote. "We had our first real battle on a divisional level with the Germans. The battle of the Moro River — the Germans counterattacked very heavily and were thrown back."[2] Not one given to praising Vokes, for whom he had little respect, Montgomery offered a laconic message: "Hearty congratulations on day's work and on throwing back counter-attack."[3]

The butcher's bill for that day's work was high. Casualties suffered by the two committed brigades exceeded anything the Canadians had previously faced. Among the 1st Canadian Infantry Brigade's battalions, the 48th Highlanders of Canada had taken the lightest losses: 16 dead and 22 wounded.[4] Unscathed prior to the fighting of December 8–9, the Royal Canadian Regiment had been hardest hit during these two days: 21 dead, 51 wounded or missing.[5] Locked in near continuous fighting in the hard-won coastal bridgehead since December 6, the Hastings and Prince Edward Regiment had lost fully one-third of its approximate strength of 400 as dead, wounded, or missing.[6]

Of 2 CIB's battalions, the Seaforths had suffered most. The December 9 attack on San Leonardo had cost more than 50 dead, wounded, and missing.[7] With the additional men lost during the earlier offensive against the village, no Seaforth company mustered more than 50 men on the night of December 9. The Princess Patricia's Canadian Light Infantry was in only slightly better condition. Yet it was falling on Hoffmeister's battalions to lead the way in the morning.

Because of the difficulty bringing the tanks of 1st Canadian Armoured Brigade across the Moro River, only the Calgary Tank Regiment had so far seen action. While that regiment's human toll had been surprisingly light — six dead, ten wounded — the cost in tanks had been heavy. Some tank crews had two or even three Shermans shot out from under them during the course of the two-day battle around San Leonardo. When a tank was lost to enemy fire, breakdown, or, as was all too common, bogging down in the ever worsening mud, the crew scrambled to the south shore of the Moro to pick up another one and roll back into the battle. Of the 51 battle-worthy tanks the regiment had put over the Moro during the fight for San Leonardo, only 24 were still operational at day's end.[8] Fortunately, most were either reparable or retrievable. Only 5 were written off as too badly damaged by enemy fire to be repaired.[9]

Although the effect of the massive weight of artillery fire brought to bear against the Panzer Grenadiers holding the Moro River line had been far less than hoped, by the standard of western Allied forces the sheer volume of fire had been daunting. In four days, the twenty-five pounders of 1st, 2nd, and 3rd Field regiments had blasted the narrow band of land stretching from the Moro River to Ortona with 65,000 rounds. Thousands more shells had been fired by main guns of the Eighth Army, naval ships, and the twenty-five pounders of the 8th Indian Division. Sustaining these rates of fire had placed a heavy burden on the supply network, which remained dependent on a single bridge spanning the Sangro River.[10] The artillery bombardments had been supplemented by intensive aerial strafing and bomber runs, mortaring by battalion and Saskatoon Light Infantry weapons, and the utilization of antitank weapons as close-up artillery. Responding German artillery and mortar fire had also been the heaviest directed at any Eighth Army division since the early battles in North Africa.

♦ ♦ ♦

Caught in the middle between the Germans and the Canadians, tiny San Donato had been devastated by this deadly rain. The small white chapel was reduced to burned rubble, most of the houses were destroyed or badly damaged. During the battle, fifteen-year-old Anna Tucci and her family lived a routine corresponding to the rhythm of the guns. By day they huddled in a cave cut into the escarpment facing the Adriatic; by night, when the shelling slackened, they crept back into their battered home to sleep in relative warmth. If the night's shelling unexpectedly shifted their way, the family cowered under the beds. Anna would try not to scream as the house shook from the concussion of nearby explosions and shrapnel spattered against its walls.

After days of hiding, the family's food supplies were mostly depleted. Yet the Tuccis counted themselves lucky. All were alive, nobody had been wounded. Not all the civilians of San Donato were so fortunate. Other families had seen both children and adults killed. For those who were wounded, there was neither the means nor the knowledge to treat their injuries. The people of San Donato desperately yearned for the battle to move past them. Frightened of the Germans, they believed when the Allies finally came they would receive much-needed succour.[11]

On the night of December 9, the last Panzer Grenadiers faded out of the San Donato area. As they left, they closed with mines all the paths that ran through the wide swaths of minefields they had previously sown through the vineyards and orchards, extending back to Ortona. Minefield warning signs were removed. Some empty houses were booby-trapped. Opening a front door might trigger a bomb leaned against it from the inside. An overturned kitchen pot on a table might conceal a stick grenade that would explode when the pot was moved or turned right side up.

Culverts running under roads were loaded with Teller mines, with detonators wired to be exploded by the weight of a vehicle passing overhead. Other mines were dug into the roadbeds. The German anti-vehicle mines, such as the Teller, and the anti-personnel S-mines were metallic and subject to detection by mine-clearing teams. Mines made by the Italian army, however, had wooden outer casings that eluded mine detection equipment. When the Italian army had surrendered, the German occupation forces had captured massive stockpiles of Italian armaments. The Panzer Grenadier engineers, like most other German engineers in Italy, were fond of the Italian mines. They randomly laced these deadly explosives among their own metal-cased ones — a deadly surprise for the Canadians and coincidentally for the Italian civilians.

Another hazard was presented by the hundreds of unexploded shells fired by both sides. Duds were common; others failed to explode because they landed on their sides or at some other angle that resulted in the failure of the detonating fuse in the nose cap to ignite when the shell struck. The German engineers were highly skilled at booby-trapping unexploded shells and mortar bombs. Even if left alone, the explosives presented a great danger to civilians and soldiers alike.

◆ ◆ ◆

Farther back from the immediate front at Villa Deo, Antonio Di Cesare, his mother, two uncles, and their families sought to live as best they could in a war zone. The men and teenage boys worked the fields when the artillery fell elsewhere. If a bombardment came their way, everyone fled houses and fields for a nearby grotto containing several natural caves. Sometimes the shelling caught them in the open or in their houses. Everyone then sought shelter wherever they could. In the houses they crawled under beds, in the fields they tried clawing holes in the muddy soil. Some failed to find safety. The number of dead and wounded rose with each passing day.

So far, because Villa Deo was to the west of the various approaches to Ortona, little of the shelling had been deliberately directed their way. Food was in short supply and all the homes were heavily over-crowded by Ortona refugees, but the civilians were coping. Antonio's family was wedged in with a total of twenty people living under one small roof.

The Panzer Grenadiers passing frequently through Villa Deo largely left the civilians alone. They neither demanded nor offered food. There was little looting or harassment, even of the younger women. Antonio thought the Germans were decent and were also victims of war. The whole family had grown fond of the young twenty-two-year-old engineering student turned soldier who often came to their home to chat during the evenings. When he failed to show up after the fierce fighting along the Moro River, Antonio became worried. Seeing a group of soldiers walking wearily past the house that night, he went outside to see if his friend was among them. Recognizing another soldier who had sometimes accompanied the engineering student during his visits, Antonio asked after his friend. Trudging on, the soldier said, "He is dead." His voice a monotone, the man did not look up as he spoke. He seemed exhausted or emotionally so numbed that he was beyond caring. Deeply upset,

Antonio told the rest of the family of the young man's fate. They prayed for him and for all the young men dying around them.[12]

◆ ◆ ◆

The 90th Panzer Grenadiers had taken a terrific beating during the fighting on the Moro River line. All regiments were seriously depleted. In the counterattacks against the Hastings and Prince Edward bridgehead on December 9 alone, German casualties totalled 170 dead and 30 captured.[13] The Panzer Grenadier strategy of determined and immediate counterattacks against every Canadian advance had cost them dearly. By the evening of December 9, Generalleutnant Karl Hans Lungershausen was forced to plug gaps in his defences with all available reserves because his four battalions of regular infantry and two squadrons of tanks were so reduced in strength. A company of infantry specialists equipped with half-tracks was brought forward, as were three engineering companies, two squadrons of light reconnaissance tanks from 65th Division, and the division's own reconnaissance squadron. In a bid to shore up the thinly stretched German defences, Lungershausen was given unprecedented access to artillery, boosting his weaponry from forty-eight to approximately seventy artillery guns. This excluded the usual artillery inherently linked to the division, and its assigned antitank gun battalion.[14]

Deeply concerned, German Tenth Army chief of staff General-major Fritz Wentzell reported by telephone to his superior, Generalfeldmarschall Albert Kesselring. Wentzell told Kesselring that their losses were such that the division would have to be reinforced and probably soon withdrawn. The Canadians, he said, were attacking "on the whole front from the coast to San Leonardo. Everything is being taken up there. 2nd Battalion 3rd Paratroop Regiment goes to Ortona."

"To Ortona?" Kesselring asked.

"Yes, so that he [the Canadians] will be prevented from getting there at all costs."[15]

The 3rd Paratroop Regiment was part of the elite 1st Parachute Division, considered one of the best divisions in the German army. Formed in Sicily in 1943 just prior to the Allied invasion, 1st Parachute Division was composed on paper of 16,000 men organized in three regiments, each divided into three battalions. The division had its own artillery regiment, antitank battalion, engineer battalion, and heavy mortar battalion, but no inherent tank regiment. Most of the paratroopers were veterans of many campaigns, including the invasion of Crete, and had seen extensive service on the Russian front. Newer recruits were superbly trained and selected from the fittest, most intelligent, and youngest enlistees.[16]

General Richard Heidrich commanded the division. Known as "Papa Heidrich" by the paratroopers, he bore a striking resemblance to Winston Churchill. Perhaps to enhance this similarity, Heidrich habitually smoked long, fat cigars. He had grey eyes that one captured British officer described as giving "an impression of ruthlessness that belied his corpulence."[17] Ruthless or not, the overweight general was highly respected by his men and by the German higher command. The soldiers thought he treated them "as if they were his sons." In return they were fiercely loyal.[18]

First Parachute Division was stationed in a relatively quiet corner of the Adriatic line on the upper reaches of the Sangro River. On the night of December 9, 3rd Paratroop Regiment began boarding trucks for a move to Pescara and from there south to Ortona. The following morning other elements of the division were scheduled to move to the coast.

Eighteen-year-old Obergefreiter Karl Bayerlein was second-in-command of a *gruppe* (twelve-man section) in the Fallschirmpionier (Parachute Engineer) Battalion. For the past two months, Bayerlein and the other engineers had been creating obstacles to enemy movement in the mountains by destroying roads and blowing up bridges.

Bayerlein had volunteered the year before for service. Approaching the recruiter's desk, Bayerlein noticed that his file lying before the recruiter bore a heavy stamp in black ink capital letters: "FIT TO SERVE IN THE SS." Only weeks earlier, Bayerlein had received a letter from his father, an infantry soldier serving on the Russian front. "Avoid the SS," his father warned. "You will be sent to the Russian front and if captured by the Russians you will be shot right away." Heeding his father's advice, Bayerlein told the recruiter that he did not want to join the SS, but rather wanted to be a parachutist. The recruiter, impressed by this martial ambition, approved his request.

At the Gardelegen and Wittstock airborne training centres, Bayerlein became an expert in the use of all standard German infantry weapons, as well as related Allied weapons. He was also trained to drive Allied military and civilian vehicles, including trams, in case he should be parachuted deep behind enemy lines. Although, since the heavy losses sustained during the airborne invasion of Crete, German military doctrine discouraged the aerial deployment of paratroopers, Bayerlein and all other paratroopers made six parachute jumps as part of their basic training.

When he joined the 1st Parachute Division, Bayerlein had been immediately impressed by the elite nature of the men with whom he served. The line officers were young, tough, and keenly intelligent. "They were always in the front and never claimed privileges for themselves." They ate the same food as the soldiers, slept when and where they slept, and led the way in battle.

Of small stature, Bayerlein was assigned to 3rd Gruppe, 3rd Platoon, 3rd Company. In parachute units, the third platoons were manned by the shortest men in the company and third companies received all the shortest men in the battalion. The tallest men went to the first companies, first platoons, and first gruppes. Bayerlein was given to understand the designation of men to units on the basis of height was a parachutist tradition. But it did have practical applications as well. Third Company was largely engaged in the task of building defensive bunkers and underground shelters, a task well suited to small men.[19]

On the morning of December 10, Bayerlein wrote in his diary: "A message arrives alerting us. . . . We must leave our quarters immediately and drive on SS 17 to Pescara."[20] The decision to send the 1st Paratroop Division to Ortona reflected a shift in intentions on the part of Tenth Army command. No longer was the intent to merely delay the Eighth Army advance. Now the purpose was to stop a formerly insignificant oceanside town from falling into Allied hands. The battle before Ortona was rapidly transforming into one of pride, where a German defeat would become a propaganda victory for the Allies, and vice versa, if Ortona were not to fall before the onset of winter prohibited further major offensive action on the Adriatic front.

# FOUR

## THE
## GULLY

# 13

## A Little Old
## Heart Starter

**M**AJOR General Chris Vokes's objective was to force the Germans
back beyond Ortona. As usual, Vokes's plan was simple and direct.
He planned to head straight up the closest road from San Leonardo.
It would be an Alberta show, with the Loyal Edmonton Regiment, in
concert with 'C' Squadron of the 14th Canadian Armoured Brigade
(Calgary Tanks), attacking along old Highway 16 to an initial objective designated Punch. This was a low ridge, nicknamed Vino Ridge
by the Canadians, that stood midway between San Leonardo and the
junction with the Ortona-Orsogna lateral road. The regiment would
then advance to the junction, code-named Cider.

When the Edmontons reached Cider Crossroads, the Princess
Patricia's Canadian Light Infantry would advance along the
Edmontons' right flank by seizing Vino Ridge, cross the narrow gully
behind it, and push 3,000 yards down the road to enter Ortona. As
the PPCLI made its move, the Seaforth Highlanders of Canada would
come up to support the Edmontons' left flank, meaning the entire
2nd Canadian Infantry Brigade would be positioned on the Ortona-
Orsogna lateral road. It was expected that once Cider Crossroads was

firmly under Canadian control, the Germans would cede Ortona. A short, sharp fight and Ortona should fall. Vokes's intelligence staff was certain "the next defensive stand would be made on the Arielli or the Foro Rivers several miles beyond."[1]

They were wrong. The Canadian intelligence analysts had missed the unique defensive opportunity presented by what they would all soon respectfully address as The Gully. Running parallel to, and south of, the Ortona-Orsogna road at a distance varying from 200 to 300 yards was a deep, narrow gully. Three miles in length, the gully was about 200 yards wide where it opened to the Adriatic shoreline and narrowed to about 80 yards' width where it levelled out just before meeting a secondary road linking San Leonardo to the Ortona-Orsogna highway. The Gully averaged a depth of about 200 feet, and along its U-shaped bottom the local farmers had developed rough, often intersecting, tracks backing their vineyards. Occasionally the narrow ditch in The Gully's precise centre ran with a shallow trickle of muddy water, but usually it was dry.

On Canadian tactical maps The Gully was indicated as a thin line, but its significance was little appreciated. Italy was riddled with gullies, ravines, and valleys descending from the eastern flanks of the Apennines to the Adriatic. To the Canadian high command, this small feature was just another of many minor obstacles. Outflanking The Gully was never considered.

What Vokes and his staff overlooked was the fact that this feature formed a natural trench, deeper and better designed by inherent topography than most major defensive fortifications constructed on the Western Front during World War I. Into its steep southern slope, the Panzer Grenadiers had dug deep gun pits and shelters that were impervious to Canadian artillery fire and difficult to hit with mortars. From these positions, the infantry could foray at will into the densely tangled vegetation covering Vino Ridge and fronting The Gully to engage the advancing Canadians. On the northern side of The Gully, the lateral road provided an excellent link for communications and the movement of German armour from one hot spot to another.

The Canadians had breached the Moro River line, but The Gully would render that victory hollow. As the Loyal Edmonton Regiment set off from San Leonardo toward Cider Crossroads at 0945 hours on December 10, it moved into the jaws of a superbly set ambush.

◆ ◆ ◆

At first the attack proceeded smoothly, infantry and tanks advancing into the smoke that drifted over the landscape following another softening barrage laid down by the Canadian twenty-five-pounder artillery. A cold steady rain fell, deepening the mud underfoot. Leading the advance was Lieutenant John Dougan's No. 16 Platoon of 'D' Company. Dougan's commander was Major Jim Stone, a six-foot-five bear of a man with a thick black moustache. Since Sicily, Stone had carved out a reputation for fearlessness on the battlefield. English born, the thirty-five-year-old Stone had been working in a northern Alberta forestry camp near Blueberry Mountain when Canada declared war. Four days later, he mounted his black mare Minnie, rode thirty miles to Spirit River, and hitched a ride to Grand Prairie where the Loyal Edmonton Regiment had opened a recruitment office. Having spent a couple of years as a school cadet in England, Stone knew his left foot from his right when it came to marching. This was sufficient in the poorly trained Canadian volunteer army to earmark him for promotion from private to lance corporal. Possessing a keen intelligence and great determination of will, Stone was soon fast-tracked into officers training.[2] By the time the Edmontons reached the Moro River, most every officer in the regiment recognized Stone as the natural heir to Lieutenant Colonel Jim Jefferson, the Edmonton commander.

Jefferson and Stone were polar opposites. Stone was a boisterous soldiers' soldier who mixed easily with the men from the ranks and could drink anyone under the table. Jefferson was a quiet, even shy, veteran of the prewar permanent force. Although Jefferson won the Distinguished Service Order for his regiment's determined stand in Sicily at a village called Leonforte, he was not a commander noted for directing his companies from close by.[3] On December 10, Jefferson and his battalion headquarters remained in San Leonardo. Also left behind was 'C' Company, kept in reserve to provide a solid footing for the Edmonton advance.

Dougan's platoon leading, the Edmontons made good progress and at 1000 hours the signal "Punch" reached Jefferson, who immediately radioed Brigadier Bert Hoffmeister at 2 CIB headquarters. "We are now proceeding to final objective," Jefferson said.[4] Brushing aside light sniper resistance that melted away as quickly as it materialized and enduring sporadic artillery and mortar fire, the Edmontons pressed on. At 1330 hours, Jefferson radioed Hoffmeister to report that three companies were on the objective and consolidating: "Exploitation not possible yet but will organize as soon as possible. Visibility poor, endeavouring to gain contact."[5]

According to the plan, the PPCLI was to now jump off from San Leonardo to cross Vino Ridge and dash for Ortona. Hoffmeister ordered PPCLI Lieutenant Colonel Cameron Ware to move out. Ware, who was at Jefferson's headquarters when the Edmonton commander reported receiving the "Punch" signal, was certain the message was wrong. "Christ," he said to Jefferson, "you haven't taken the crossroad yet."[6] Despite Ware's protests, Jefferson insisted the report was accurate and that his regiment now held Cider. Backing Jefferson, Hoffmeister ordered Ware to attack.

In fact, the Edmontons were far short of their final objective, still just approaching Punch — the point where the road crossed Vino Ridge. The signal reporting Punch as being taken had not originated from either Stone's 'D' Company or Dougan's forward platoon. Later investigations failed to resolve the mystery of where the erroneous report had originated, or if in fact Jefferson's headquarters had misunderstood some garbled message. One theory posed was that the messages actually originated from Germans having knowledge of the objective codes and using Canadian radios mounted in a captured jeep.[7] Whatever their source, the messages failed to justify Jefferson's more extensive report to Hoffmeister that assumed the capture of the vital crossroads.

Ware was convinced his battalion was in danger of being cut to pieces by an enemy heavily entrenched on Vino Ridge, but he had his orders. With Majors W. "Bucko" Watson and Donald Brain, who had just rejoined the battalion the previous day, Ware walked over to 'B' Squadron of the Calgary Tanks, the PPCLI's designated supporting armour. Just as the officers reached the tanks, a "stonk" — as the Canadians called heavy German artillery, mortar, or Nebelwerfer salvoes — pummelled San Leonardo. Ware ducked inside 'B' Squadron's command tank, while Brain and Watson could only shelter behind the tank. Both men were struck by shrapnel. Brain was killed instantly, Watson wounded in the foot.[8] Having lost two of four company commanders, the PPCLI attack was delayed for reorganization of its command structure.

◆ ◆ ◆

The sporadic shelling of San Leonardo created havoc among 2 CIB's battalion commands. All three battalion headquarters were squeezed into a village of fewer than fifty buildings, few of which were habitable because of battle damage. Saskatoon Light Infantry battalion commander Major Thomas de Faye spent much of December 10 darting from one HQ building to another, trying to maintain an accurate picture of the fighting. The mortars and medium machine guns of the SLI were supporting all three battalions. Everywhere he went enemy shells seemed to follow. One stonk falling around Jefferson's headquarters was so intense that the two men sought refuge inside a large fireplace as protection against the shrapnel singing through the house's windows.

Later, de Faye encountered PPCLI second-in-command Major R.P. "Slug" Clark, just a few minutes after Brain was killed. Clark was inside the PPCLI headquarters, a battered cement and stone house. Outside stood the tank behind which Brain and Watson had become casualties. As de Faye entered the house, another Moaning Minnie salvo plunked around the house. He and Clark dived under the cement stairwell for cover. Huddling there, washbasin-sized chunks of shrapnel banging against the walls, de Faye said, "This is a place that makes you very damned nervous." Clark tugged a jug of rum from inside his jacket, pulled the lid off, and handed it over to de Faye. The SLI major took a grateful, hearty pull. Clark followed suit. "A little old heart starter," Clark said, passing the rum back to de Faye, "a touch of the whip." The two men stayed in their shelter, drinking rum until the enemy bombs stopped falling.[9]

◆ ◆ ◆

The Seaforth Highlanders of Canada, in accordance with the battle plan, moved out of San Leonardo to form a line on the Edmonton left some 800 to 1,000 yards west of the village. Resistance was light to nonexistent, but enemy shelling continued to take its toll.

Following behind the lead companies came Lieutenant Colonel Doug Forin and his battalion headquarters. The battalion's scout platoon led, providing a protective screen for Forin and his staff. Several staff were encumbered with the heavy radio sets that were normally mounted in a jeep or Bren carrier, but today had to be carried on the men's backs because the mud was too deep for the vehicles. Seaforths scout Private A.K. Harris led the way across a small meadow to a house Forin planned to use as his forward headquarters. The door facing them was barred, so Harris battered it open, then turned to get help from another soldier in lifting the door off the hinges. Forin, increasingly weakened by jaundice and with nerves stretched close to the snapping point, came up behind him. At that moment, a German shell struck a tree just behind the small group. Shrapnel, wood splinters from the tree, and the blast of concussion ripped into the men.

Harris felt like someone hit him "in the back of the leg, hard, with a club." He rolled into a ditch, yelling with pain. When he sorted himself out in the bottom of the ditch, Harris saw only a tear in his trousers at calf level. Closer examination showed there was a hole in his leg and undoubtedly a shell fragment inside. His first clear thought was, "Hooray, Christmas in bed."[10]

Above Harris there were many groans of pain. He crawled out of the ditch and found Lieutenant D.S. McLaughlin, the intelligence officer who, like the PPCLI's Brain, had only returned to the battalion the previous day. McLaughlin was in considerable pain from shell fragment wounds to both legs. Harris thought because the officer had the energy to curse his wounds he should survive. Crawling on, he found Forin's runner, Acting Lance Corporal L.W. King, "going fast" from a stomach wound. A radio signaller, Private F.B. Beaton, lay dead a few feet away. Somebody said that Forin was also wounded by shrapnel, but Harris could get no idea of how badly. He lost track of Forin, who did not accompany the rest of the wounded to the advanced Regimental Aid Post — a house back on San Leonardo's outskirts.

As the RAP was under heavy shelling, Harris, King, and McLaughlin were loaded into an ambulance jeep for evacuation to the main RAP inside San Leonardo. King was unconscious and very pale, but still breathing. Harris wet his lips with water, knowing that he shouldn't give the man a full drink because of the stomach wound. The jeep, Harris later wrote, crept cautiously down "the shell pocked road to San Leonardo. . . . Shells blossom on the road on both sides. But the driver has critically wounded aboard. To hit a shell hole at high speed might kill them. He risks his life and takes his time."[11] The jeep arrived safely at the RAP.

Harris continued: "The RAP is a dark room in a battered house. Lights from car batteries hang over blood stained stretchers. Shells are still falling outside. Their crump is varied occasionally by the peculiar whir of slate shingles blown from nearby roofs. There are many wounded.

"The MO takes a quick look at King and he is carted through to the back room. He glances briefly at the field dressing on my leg. I suddenly realize I am also hit in the head and hand, scratches only. . . . The door opens to a weird noise. Two men come in. One is over six feet and heavy. He is only a boy. His eyes are glazed and from his open mouth comes a scream that rises and falls with the noise of shelling outside. Behind him is an RAP man. He has his hands over the youngster's ears and is talking to him in a soothing voice.

"The boy is an advanced case of 'shell shock.' The MO sends him into the back room to make way for the wounded. The company of the dead won't soothe his nerves much."[12]

Although Forin's wounds were not particularly severe, Hoffmeister moved quickly to relieve him of command and ordered Major Sydney W. Thomson, the battalion's second-in-command, to take over the Seaforth Highlanders of Canada. Like the boy, Forin had succumbed to battle exhaustion, which was starting to chalk up a heavy toll throughout the engaged Canadian regiments.[13]

◆ ◆ ◆

While the Seaforths were sorting themselves out after the loss of their commander and some of the battalion headquarters staff, including two officers wounded when a room in the rear battalion headquarters was riddled with shrapnel, the Loyal Edmonton Regiment was only now closing on the western flank of Vino Ridge. Lieutenant Dougan's No.16 Platoon still led, a couple of Calgary Sherman tanks rumbling along in support. Suddenly, from the thick vegetation blanketing the ridgeline, several German antitank guns opened up with deadly accuracy. The tanks supporting his platoon were struck and knocked out in seconds. Dougan watched in horror as the commander of one crawled out of the tank cupola, one leg blown off cleanly above the knee. Dougan's stretcher-bearer rushed over and dragged the man away from the burning tank. All the bearer could do to treat the wound was to dust the bleeding stump with sulpha and cinch a belt around it to serve as a tourniquet.[14]

Major Stone ran up and ordered the three Edmonton companies to immediately shift to the right and attack up the ridge toward the German antitank guns, now being protected by many hammering machine guns and rapidly firing mortars. The Edmontons headed directly into the face of this wall of fire.

No sooner had Dougan's platoon got underway than one of the worst personal battlefield calamities befell the young lieutenant. Wracked for weeks by dysentery, Dougan had to defecate — immediately. Seeing a small grove of olive trees he thought might provide a safe and somewhat private shelter, he rushed over, yanked his pants down, and crouched. From almost directly above him, Dougan heard a German officer start issuing commands that sounded like he was directing mortar fire toward a target. Seconds later, he heard the dreaded swish of a mortar shell falling and was horrified to see the bomb land tail first no more than four feet in front of him. Digging deep into the mud, the bomb sat there with its detonating fuse pointing harmlessly into the air. As he took flight from the grove, Dougan was unsure whether he had finished his business or not.[15] Rejoining his company just as the Edmontons' attack against the ridge fizzled, Dougan scrambled with his platoon down the ridge to regroup. They could see Cider Crossroads about 1,000 yards away, well beyond reach.

◆ ◆ ◆

PPCLI Lieutenant Colonel Ware remained certain the Edmontons were well short of the crossroads. His men faced a gauntlet of fire as they moved against the forward slopes of Vino Ridge. Deep mud rendered it almost impossible for the Shermans to keep abreast of the advancing infantry and the dense olive groves and vineyards reduced visibility to near zero. 'D' Company of the PPCLI, under Major P.L. Crofton, got up almost face to face with the hidden Panzer Grenadiers before the Germans opened up with devastating machine-gun fire. Crofton was struck in the leg, the third company commander lost that day.[16] The battle became virtually hand to hand. Germans and Canadians lay in the mud throwing grenades across the ridge at each other. Ware could see the effort was "abortive." When Ware heard on the radio that the Germans had opened a counterattack against the Edmontons' left flank, he ordered his men to break off, so they could move about a quarter mile west to directly support the Edmontons if necessary.[17]

While the Edmontons managed to beat off a series of successive counterattacks, the ferocity of these attacks showed that the Panzer Grenadiers were determined to continue the same tactics they had practised since the beginning of the Moro River battle. The Germans' growing desperation was also revealed by a repeat of an act of treachery that the Panzer Grenadiers had implemented earlier in San Leonardo. Following one failed counterattack, a group of Germans emerged from the brush with hands up to indicate surrender. As soldiers from one platoon walked out to meet the surrendering troops, the Germans dropped to the ground, as if on command, and a machine gun emplaced behind them ripped into the Canadians. Nobody was killed, but a good number of the Edmontons' wounded resulted from this incident. Edmonton casualties in the day's fighting totalled one soldier killed, twenty soldiers wounded, and one officer and nine of what Commonwealth armies called "other ranks" missing.[18] Vokes was so outraged when he learned of this ambush that he issued an advisory to the entire division informing the men of the event. His message ended erroneously with: "The Edmonton platoon was murdered in cold blood."[19]

As the battle wound down and darkness cloaked the ground, Edmonton patrols crept up to the very lip of The Gully. They stared down into its darkness, none daring to enter its depths to test the strength of the enemy forces hidden there.

◆ ◆ ◆

To the rear, Private A.K. Harris lay in the San Leonardo RAP watching ever more fresh casualties arrive. The runner named King had died earlier from his stomach wound. "The MO is desperately tired," Harris noted later, "but he never stops working or loses patience with the shock cases. He is talking to another of those, not as bad as the boy. This one is a friend of mine. He has had this trouble before and been evacuated before. But he is always sent back up. He is a bundle of nerves but never asks for a favour and gives everything until he snaps. The MO is asking him, 'Are you hit anywhere?' 'No.' 'Is there anything physically wrong with you?' 'No.' He probes his man but quickly comes to the conclusion that this one is genuine and has to be taken out. There is deep humiliation in my friend's face and he goes back to join the dead and the screaming case in the back room. He thinks he has let his friends down. He will be back again and again, shaking like a leaf every time we see action, going on to the breaking point."[20]

Later Harris, Lieutenant McLaughlin, and the boy with shell shock were put in a jeep with two RAP men and driven toward the south bank of the Moro River. The boy sprawled across Harris's sound leg. "With every shell burst or rattle of machine gun, he screams and twists convulsively. I have to hang on to him tightly to keep him in the jeep. We cross the repaired bridge and start up the other side. There is a hair-pin bend ahead that comes under fire regularly. The RAP men go this way often. There is tension in their voices. I hold my breath and wonder how I'll control the boy if we get a close one. We pass the turn safely. The RAP men and I suddenly feel talkative as the strain eases. We are over the bank on the south side. Ahead is rear RAP. It is night, and for me the battle is over."[21]

# 14

## ALL WE CAN DO

FIRST Canadian Infantry Division's orders for December 11 showed that Major General Chris Vokes and his staff still failed to appreciate how formidable a defensive obstacle The Gully presented. Vokes had two alternatives. He could try bulling his infantry and armoured regiments across The Gully in the area of Highway 16, or he could outflank The Gully by shifting westward to where this feature dwindled near the secondary road running from San Leonardo to the Ortona-Orsogna lateral. In this situation, once his forces were astride the lateral highway, they could attack Cider and then Ortona from the southwest and entirely avoid The Gully's defences.

Despite accurate reports by 2nd Canadian Infantry Brigade patrols that the enemy was so deeply entrenched in The Gully and along Vino Ridge that their positions were virtually impregnable, Vokes told Brigadier Bert Hoffmeister to renew the frontal attacks. He also directed the Hastings and Prince Edward Regiment to push out from its coastal bridgehead to find any German weakness that might exist directly in front of Ortona.[1] Vokes then ordered the divisional reserve of 3rd Canadian Infantry Brigade forward from its holding area north of the Sangro River to San Apollinare, a village on the southern ridge of the Moro River across from San Leonardo.[2]

During the night of December 10–11 the weather, relatively moderate by winter standards, deteriorated drastically. A heavy, cold rain poured down and the temperature plunged toward freezing. The already miserable conditions in which the troops fought worsened. By morning, tanks could barely move through the mud.

At first light, the Seaforth Highlanders of Canada, the Loyal Edmonton Regiment, and the Princess Patricia's Canadian Light Infantry prepared to attack the same positions that had stopped them cold the previous day. The Edmontons jumped off first, repeatedly battering directly at The Gully along the western edge of Vino Ridge. Each time, they were hurled back by devastatingly effective machine-gun and mortar fire. Radio reports on gains realized by this regiment continued to be confused and inaccurate. At 0950 hours, Hoffmeister's headquarters signalled Vokes that "two sub-units" of the Edmontons were apparently on Cider and that the PPCLI with a squadron of tanks would soon attack through the junction toward Ortona, "as soon as crossroads . . . firmly in our hands." At 1245 hours, this message was corrected with a terse signal referring to The Gully: "Loyal Edmonton Regiment have NOT crossed stream."[3]

The PPCLI, supported by a squadron of Calgary tanks, then moved off to create its own breach in the German line. This force attempted to cross Vino Ridge and establish a link between 2 CIB and the Hasty P's. Lieutenant Colonel Cameron Ware's men stumbled through tangled vineyards and olive groves heavily laced with booby traps, S-mines, and antitank Teller mines. By midafternoon, the battalion had bogged down near the edge of The Gully. As had been the case the previous day, PPCLI troopers engaged in a grenade-throwing exchange with soldiers of the Panzer Grenadiers 200th Regiment. The results were deadly for both sides. At one point, the PPCLI threw back one of the Germans' reckless counterattacks, taking forty prisoners. Despite breaking the enemy attack, the battalion was unable to renew its own advance.[4]

West of the Edmontons, the Seaforths' objective was a ridge overlooking The Gully and a three-storey, white stucco farm–manor house located on the opposite side, called Casa Berardi. 'A' Company, under the command of Captain Ernest Webb Thomas, was to seize the ridge and support the Edmontons' left flank. The twenty-nine-year-old, slightly built captain was a popular officer known to almost everyone as June, short for Junior. Supporting Thomas's company was 'C' Squadron of tanks from the 11th Canadian Armoured Regiment (Ontario Tanks), commanded by twenty-three-year-old tank commander Major Herschell Smith. Originally from Dauphin, Manitoba, Smith had been a university student before the war and a member of the Manitoba Horse militia. Nicknamed "Snuffy," he was regarded as one of the most competent tank commanders in the regiment. However, not even Smith could overcome the mud on the slopes, which made it impossible for the tanks to advance to the ridgeline.[5] Slipping and sliding a foot or more back for every three feet gained, and bracketed by enemy mortar fire, Thomas's men pushed on without the Shermans toward The Gully's lip. Despite heavy casualties, 'A' Company gained its objective at 1300 hours. As the company's remaining forty-five men started digging in, Thomas saw a large Panzer Grenadier group forming up for a counterattack against his position. Hopelessly outnumbered, Thomas withdrew his company's remnants down the ridge's reverse slope and called artillery fire onto the enemy formation.[6]

◆ ◆ ◆

By noon, as the 2 CIB attacks faltered before stiff opposition from The Gully, Vokes belatedly comprehended what he was up against. It was now clear even at divisional headquarters that the area fronting The Gully was "infested with anti-tank mines, the olive groves were booby trapped, [and] every house had been made a machine-gun post."[7] Vokes wrote: "Although a strong weight of artillery was used to support throughout, it was apparent that the defilade afforded by the steep reverse side of the gully, in which the enemy was well dug in, could not be adequately searched by the low trajectory field and medium guns. The only answer to the problem was provided by the 4.2- and 3-inch mortars."[8] Vokes failed to mention that even the mortars lacked sufficient punch or density of fire to rip a hole in the fabric of the German defences.

Remarkably, appreciating the toughness of The Gully as an obstacle did nothing to alter Vokes's tactics. Having mired 2 CIB in a hopeless face-to-face punch-up with the Panzer Grenadiers, and with 1 CIB strung out all along the Moro River's northern ridgeline, Vokes decided to commit his reserve brigade in further frontal assaults on

The Gully. Vokes ordered 3rd Canadian Infantry Brigade commander Brigadier Graeme Gibson to pass his West Nova Scotia Regiment through the tattered Seaforth lines and capture Casa Berardi.

The West Novas, under commander Lieutenant Colonel M. Pat Bogert, accordingly moved directly behind the Seaforths. Zero hour for the attack was 1800 hours. Because tanks had been of no value during the day, none were assigned to support the assault. Instead, close artillery support was promised by the 1st Field Regiment Artillery (Royal Canadian Horse Artillery), which assigned Captain John Ross Matheson the task of forward observation officer. The twenty-six-year-old son of a United Church minister from Arundel, Quebec, Matheson commanded 'B' Troop of 'A' Battery. Strapping his heavy #18 radio set on a mule, Matheson and his technical assistant Sergeant Gordon Denison linked up with the West Novas shortly before the attack.

What the Seaforths had failed to achieve in daylight, Vokes expected the West Novas to manage in darkness. The plan called for three West Nova companies to carry out the assault, while 'B' Company formed a mobile battle group and firm supporting base at San Leonardo with a squadron of Ontario Tanks. This group's task was to patrol to the west in hopes of finding a tank route that could be used to get armour onto the Ortona-Orsogna lateral.[9] As had been the case with breaching the Moro River line, any gains on the north side of The Gully would be hard to hold in the absence of tank backup. Finding a route that would enable the tanks to join up with the infantry was imperative if the Canadians were to repel the powerful combined armour and infantry counterattacks favoured by the Panzer Grenadiers.

Bogert met with his Seaforth counterpart Syd Thomson, who had only the previous day taken over battalion command. Thomson warned Bogert that the objective set by Vokes was unattainable. Bogert said he could and would seize Casa Berardi as ordered, opening the road to Ortona. Thomson was not impressed by this bit of braggadocio.[10]

The West Novas attack went in on a two-company front with 'A' Company to the left, 'C' Company on the right. In the centre, battalion HQ and 'D' Company followed close behind. Matheson, Denison, and their radio-carrying mule trailed Bogert's HQ group.

The Panzer Grenadiers expected the attack. As the West Novas crossed their starting line 500 yards northwest of San Leonardo, intensive artillery and mortar harassing fire tore into the soldiers. Three HQ soldiers were wounded, including the signals officer. The mule carrying the battalion's #22 wireless set fell, breaking the equipment, which provided the critical link to the artillery and brigade headquarters.[11] Matheson's #18 radio now provided the battalion's sole link to the rear.

Over the Adriatic a cold moon rose, and a wind off the sea swept aside the day's storm clouds. The night was frigid, frost glistening on the vegetation. With the moonlight providing only the faintest glimmer, the advancing infantry groped through the poles and overhead wires of the vineyards. The mud was often ankle deep, globbing onto boots to form a thick, heavy weight that made walking difficult.

To avoid these obstacles, battalion HQ kept to the road. This provided better footing for the mules, but it also channelled the unit over ground pre-targeted for artillery and mortar attention. The FOO unit approached one of the many curves in the road. Matheson led, Denison followed immediately behind, and a West Nova private trailed with the mule bearing the radio set. Behind this mule was another loaded with a Vickers medium machine gun. Matheson had just been issued a new improved helmet which, although still featuring the classic Commonwealth "piss-pot" design, was purportedly heavier and able to withstand shrapnel and bullet strikes.[12] As the group entered the curve, a solitary German shell landed directly on top of them. Six tiny steel fragments from the bursting round sliced through the new helmet and pierced Matheson's skull. He slumped to the ground unconscious. Both mules were killed. The infantryman leading the mule with Matheson's radio suffered a broken leg from shrapnel. Denison, caught between Matheson and the mule party, was amazingly untouched. As had been the fate of the West Novas' #22 set, the FOO radio was crushed by the dead mule.[13]

Denison could do little for his badly wounded comrade. He sat in the mud and held Matheson's head in his lap. Matheson was bleeding profusely, and appeared more dead than alive.

A short distance ahead of Matheson's party, an ambulance jeep driven by Chaplain Waldo E. Smith was coming back down the road. The chaplain and an orderly were returning from picking up a wounded Seaforth. They saw the shell strike on the opposite side of the approaching curve. "Good, that means we get by before the next one comes," Smith said and gunned the jeep through the gooey mud. Smith later wrote that as they turned the corner, the ambulance crew "found a shambles. . . . On the ground were men who twisted and cried out, and one who was still." Smith and his orderly jumped from the jeep and started tending the wounded. The private was in terrible pain from his broken leg, screaming in agony. Smith jabbed him with a morphine shot and bandaged the leg wound. He then turned to the soldier lying with his head on another man's lap. "There was a terrible gash in the top of it and two shell dressings were needed." As Smith worked, another ambulance jeep arrived. The wounded were loaded into the two vehicles and evacuated.[14]

Matheson's head wound left him in a coma for several weeks and rendered him permanently hemiplegic. Through the rest of December, he was moved ever further back down the Eighth Army's chain of hospitals, remaining on the "dangerously ill list." Initially, he was completely paralyzed due to damage to the brain's motor centres. He also suffered from traumatic epilepsy and amnesia. For months, the pain was excruciating. However, possessed of extraordinary determination and a belief in "God's grace," Matheson regained much of his mobility. Eventually he recovered the use of his arms and hands, and could walk with crutches.[15]

◆ ◆ ◆

The loss of its artillery FOO, and all the radio sets enabling communication with the supporting guns, left the West Novas to attack with what they carried: Bren guns, submachine guns, Lee Enfield rifles, and grenades. A plea was sent back for a new FOO to come up, but long before this unit arrived the West Novas were embroiled in an intense close-range firefight. At 2220 hours, the battalion approached The Gully's lip and the two forward companies walked into a storm of small-arms fire. With the rising moon at the Germans' back, the Canadians could barely see the flash of the enemy guns, let alone the firing soldiers. For the Germans' part, the moonlight starkly illuminated the West Novas, rendering them perfect targets. Men fell all along the front and the attack broke before it started. To the West Novas, it seemed as if the "Germans had popped up as if by magic out of the earth."[16] Pinned down, hopelessly outgunned, and suffering a devastating rate of casualties, Bogert ordered his men to dig in and keep their heads down until morning. By then he hoped to have a new FOO up and consequently break The Gully defences with well-directed artillery fire.

At brigade HQ in San Leonardo, Brigadier Graeme Gibson tried unsuccessfully to learn what was happening to the West Nova Scotias. With the battalion-to-brigade radio knocked out, only infrequent and jumbled reports were picked up by brigade's attempts to monitor the battalion radio net. At 0230 hours, a message reported the "enemy's unsparing use of shell and mortar." Gibson's anxiety increased. Lack of communication rendered him powerless, unable to provide artillery support. Confusing the picture further was the disquieting discovery that the military maps were riddled with topographical errors, especially in the area of The Gully. This meant it was difficult for FOOs and infantry commanders to determine their precise location and accurately direct artillery fire on nearby targets. The potential for artillery to hit its own side was increased exponentially.[17]

The map inaccuracies caused other problems. Shortly before midnight, Captain C.R. "Chuck" DePencier from the Royal Canadian Horse Artillery's 'A' Troop set off in a Bren carrier to find the West Novas and replace Matheson as their FOO. With him were technical assistant Gunner Bert Good, driver Gunner Bob Caughey, and radio signaller Gunner Rod Anderson. They followed two Sherman tanks along the north edge of the Moro River, and Anderson was surprised to suddenly lose sight of the big machines ahead of them. Turning a corner, Anderson looked down into the bordering ravine and saw that both tanks had run off the road. One had fallen on top of the other. Caughey kept going, leaving the tankers to sort themselves out from the accident. The West Novas needed the FOO team now, so stopping to help was out of the question.

Passing through San Leonardo, the artillerymen looked about for the West Nova guide who was to take them up to the battalion's headquarters. Nobody showed. They pressed on, winding past debris and shell holes that threatened to block the road. The carrier soon bumped into a road-blocking power pole. DePencier feared they were lost. The map and the surrounding lay of the land seemed at odds with each other. DePencier told the rest to stay with the carrier and set off alone on foot toward the front, hoping to find the West Novas.

Tensely, the artillerymen waited in the carrier for their officer's return. From about 200 yards ahead they started hearing sounds of armour and trucks heading toward Ortona. Then a firefight broke out behind them. The three men held a "war council" and decided Good and Caughey would walk back to contact the infantry engaged in the shooting. Anderson would remain with the carrier and radio sets. Breaking out a Bren gun he had retrieved from a dead 48th Highlander in Sicily and never used until now, Anderson prepared to defend the carrier. While he waited for his friends to return, a salvo of Canadian artillery crashed down around him, but caused no damage. Who directed this fire remained a mystery. Things were getting very hot and Anderson hoped the others would come back soon so they could clear this area.

Finally Good and Caughey returned. They had found a Canadian outpost and the infantry there confirmed the tanks heard earlier were Panzer Mark IVs. Anderson felt certain DePencier was either a prisoner or dead. Caughey turned the carrier around and the men fled back to San Leonardo, arriving just as day broke.[18]

Not long after DePencier wandered off into the night, he determined that the map reference for his scheduled rendezvous with the West Nova guide had been about half a mile too far north. DePencier realized he was well behind enemy lines. It was eerily quiet and he felt a gripping sense of danger. Suddenly he was surrounded by "some people in odd soldier suits and funny hats." The Panzer Grenadiers roughly led him away. Soon he was stripped of the Canadian division's secret codes for coordinating artillery fire, which he had had no time to destroy.

When Anderson reported from San Leonardo that DePencier was missing and presumed captured, divisional headquarters had to immediately issue new codes. The divisional staff angered Anderson by being far more concerned over the loss of the codes than DePencier's disappearance. A popular officer, DePencier was the second RCHA FOO to be lost that night.[19]

◆ ◆ ◆

In the predawn hours of December 12, the West Novas managed to re-establish radio contact with brigade headquarters. Lieutenant Colonel Bogert had made his headquarters in a half-demolished farmhouse near The Gully's edge. 'A' and 'C' companies were dug in to the building's front, 'D' Company behind. The next attack was set for 0800 hours. Bogert was worried about the problem of ensuring accurate artillery fire. The surrounding terrain was a confusing landscape that jibed poorly with the military map.

Shortly before 0730, he called for a "reference coordination" by the Royal Canadian Horse Artillery. This required firing several salvoes along a known line in front of the German position. From the explosions, his company commanders could orient themselves on the military map. They would then coordinate future fire requests to relevant map grids beyond their known position. In this way, Bogert hoped to ensure that the gunners back at RCHA headquarters could locate the correct targets on their maps and accurately execute the called-for barrages. Without dead-on artillery, there was little hope his attack could prevail against the Panzer Grenadiers' deep fortifications. Heightening Bogert's apprehension was the sound of one or more Panzer tanks prowling up and down inside The Gully, as if waiting for the Canadians to enter its depths. With no chance of Canadian tanks getting through the mud to support the West Novas, Bogert's regiment must attack an enemy that had it completely outgunned.[20]

The "reference coordination" barrage was at 0730 hours. Bizarre ill luck dropped the salvoes squarely on the West Novas' positions, especially in the battalion HQ area. There were many casualties. Among these was Lieutenant E.N. Doane of 'A' Company, who was killed instantly.[21] Sorting out the casualties inflicted by friendly fire was rendered impossible by the arrival seconds later of a German mortar and artillery bombardment. The West Novas' planned attack was cancelled. The men clawed deeper into their slit trenches, scrabbling for protection. When the fire eased up, Bogert scheduled a new attack for 1100 hours.

This attack, too, was scrapped before it started when the Panzer Grenadiers pre-empted it with a fierce counterattack at 1030 hours. Despite heavy covering fire from the lip of The Gully overlooking the Canadian positions, the West Novas easily repulsed the attack. As the German assault crumbled and the Panzer Grenadiers fell back toward The Gully, many West Nova infantrymen spontaneously decided to clean house. All along the front line, men from 'A' and 'C' companies jumped from their slit trenches and pursued the retreating Germans to The Gully's edge. The Panzer Grenadiers leapt down into the cover of The Gully and immediately the advancing line of West Novas was swept by fire from what seemed to be dozens of medium machine guns. The previously heard enemy Panzer Mark IVs also opened up with their main guns. Seventy-five-millimetre shells flew in at such a flat trajectory to The Gully rim that some actually ploughed forty- to fifty-foot-long furrows in the ground before exploding among the Canadians.

Washed back by the devastating German fire, the surviving West Novas retreated to their slit trenches. Bogert, dashing forward to call his men back before they were all slaughtered, took a bullet to the leg. He was carried back to the Regimental Aid Post located on the lower floor of the battalion HQ farmhouse. The RAP was clogged with wounded. Bogert refused to relinquish command, continuing to direct the fight from his position on the floor of the RAP until Major Ron Waterman could be brought up from the rear to relieve him at 1700 hours.[22]

After the chaos following the 1030 German attack, the West Novas could not possibly succeed in crossing The Gully. The battalion was so reduced in strength that the war diarist wrote, "all we can do is hope to hold until other plans are made."[23]

◆ ◆ ◆

The West Novas were not alone in achieving nothing but casualties in front of The Gully on December 12. The battalions of 2 CIB repeatedly tried to force their way forward against uncrackable resistance. For its part, the Loyal Edmonton Regiment could do little but hold its position in front of Vino Ridge. At first light, the PPCLI hit the ridge. Part of 'C' Company, Lieutenant George Garbutt's No. 13 Platoon, was on the far left, slightly behind the platoon to his right, which was slightly behind the platoon to its right. For the first 200 yards, the advance went undetected. But suddenly a shot rang out and a lance sergeant in Garbutt's platoon fell. Garbutt yelled to a corporal to swing his section left and provide covering fire, so the rest of the platoon could continue the advance. Before the section could respond, however, its Bren gunner, Private Jack Kennard, was killed instantly by a sniper bullet.

Garbutt and Lance Corporal Bill Talbot scrambled over to the cover of a small shed and peered around its corner, trying to spot the sniper. All they could see was a line of bushes running along a slight rise about seventy to eighty yards away. As they started to move away from the shed to rejoin the platoon, there was a terrific explosion. Talbot was blown off his feet but not hit. Garbutt's leg was broken by shrapnel and he suffered a number of serious cuts to other parts of his body, including one on his right wrist that immobilized the fingers of that hand. The lieutenant thought they had been struck by grenades thrown from inside the shed, but there was no sign of enemy movement there. The ground showed no indication of having been struck by a shell or mortar bomb, nor had there been any warning sound of one falling. Garbutt and Talbot crawled back to the platoon, with no idea what had caused the explosion. The PPCLI war diarist speculated at day's end that Garbutt had pulled a tripwire, setting off a booby trap.

Garbutt's men bandaged his wounds and splinted his leg. Then they tore a door off the shed which they used as a stretcher to carry him toward Vino Ridge's summit, where 'B' Company had managed to establish a position the night before around another old shed. They left him inside the building and returned to their company. Alone there for most of the day, Garbutt continued to lose blood. He was extremely weak by the time the PPCLI medical orderly arrived to do a better job of bandaging and splinting his injury. When night fell, Garbutt was evacuated by jeep, bouncing so badly in his stretcher on the rough road that several times he was thrown right off it. Garbutt would be hospitalized until May 1945 due to severe internal injuries.[24]

◆ ◆ ◆

Captain June Thomas's 'A' Company of the Seaforth Highlanders had gone up the west flank of Vino Ridge twice and been thrown back both times. Thomas had led the second attack himself on December 12 and personally determined that the Panzer Grenadiers had the entire hillside covered by well-set lines of overlapping fire. With only thirty-four men remaining in a company that had mustered nearly one hundred two days previously, Thomas knew he could never break through.

Nor did he think it necessary. Earlier in the day, a reconnaissance by Thomas to the left of his position had unearthed a route across The Gully over an earth-covered culvert. Thomas radioed in a report of the latest attack's failure to Major Syd Thomson. Thomson told him to try again. Looking at his men, Thomas thought it likely they might refuse to even try. He couldn't blame them. "No," he said, "I've been on a recce to the left and I can see a much better way of getting around and outflanking them on the left." "Go up and take the hill," Thomas was told. "No, I'm not going to go," he responded. Thomas then thought he heard Thomson say, "Okay, tomorrow at noon report back to battalion Headquarters. I'm sending Don Harley out to take over your command."[25]

It was a misunderstanding due to poor, static-plagued radio connections. Thomson heard Thomas say he could not and would not rouse his men for another attack. In response, the major said he would see what could be done to strengthen 'A' Company and was sending Harley up to be available if he needed support. Thomson was worried that, were Thomas to be wounded or killed, the company lacked sufficient internal leadership and cohesion to continue effective operation. Harley was to be Thomas's backup. Thomson was also worried that Thomas's refusal to execute another attack might indicate that the young officer was cracking under the mental and physical overextension that almost every man in the regiment was experiencing.[26]

Thomas, who had been in the Seaforth militia for four years prior to the war and was devoted to the regiment, settled down with his men at the foot of Vino Ridge. Expecting to be relieved of a command he was proud to have, he spent a mostly sleepless and depressed night.[27]

◆ ◆ ◆

Although the West Novas' main attack had failed dismally, the regiment did provide 1st Canadian Infantry Division's only ray of light since it had confronted The Gully. 'B' Company, under Captain F.H. Burns, had remained behind in San Leonardo as the other three companies and battalion HQ moved into The Gully debacle. Supported by a squadron of the 11th Canadian Armoured Regiment (Ontario Tanks), this company was to conduct reconnaissance missions aimed at finding a tank route across The Gully.

In the dark hours of the early morning of December 12, two patrols set out on this task. One was commanded by Lieutenant Gordon E. Romkey, the other by Lieutenant James Harvey Jones of Dartmouth. Romkey's patrol explored a route that it determined was impassable to tanks. In the course of its movement, the patrol was caught in a firefight with some Panzer Grenadiers and killed two of the Germans before breaking off and escaping with no casualties of its own.[28]

About the same time that Romkey's patrol was returning to San Leonardo, twenty-four-year-old Jones and his patrol were creeping deep into the enemy lines. They almost reached the Ortona-Orsogna lateral road by a route that seemed suitable for tanks. Jones heard German activity nearby, but was able to avoid alerting them to the patrol's presence. The section of gully Jones explored was near the westernmost end, where it faded away before a secondary road linking San Leonardo with the lateral road. It was also screened by natural bush and tree growth. Jones was puzzled as to why the Germans appeared to have posted no sentries to guard this natural crossing point. In the mud under the trees, Jones noted the distinctive track markings of Panzer Mark IVs, so it appeared the Panzer Grenadiers were also aware that it provided a good tank route for flanking The Gully. Sounds and voices coming from a small clearing nearby seemed to be made by a group of German tankers harbouring their machines there.

Jones led his patrol back to San Leonardo and reported to Captain Burns. After consulting with the tank squadron commander, Lieutenant F.P. Clarke of 'B' Squadron, it was decided that Jones's No. 10 Platoon and the tankers would attack along the discovered route at first light on December 13. Once across The Gully, the combined force would advance to Casa Berardi.[29]

# 15

## The Germans and the Mud

MAJOR General Chris Vokes was under terrific pressure from Eighth Army headquarters to break through The Gully and continue the advance to Pescara. General Montgomery had not yet abandoned his "colossal crack" strategy to open a road from the Adriatic to Rome. On December 12, he sent Canadian liaison officer Major Richard S. Malone to Vokes's HQ. "Old Monty wants to know what the problem is, why you are getting along so slowly," Malone told Vokes.[1]

Vokes could hardly believe what he was hearing. Didn't anyone at Eighth Army HQ read the situation reports that 1st Canadian Infantry Division filed every day? Livid, Vokes roared at Malone, "You tell Monty if he would get to hell up here and see the bloody mud he has stuck us in, he'd damn well know why we can't move faster."[2]

Monty's response was to have Malone take the Eighth Army Tactical HQ road sign and set it up a mile forward of Vokes's divisional HQ. When Vokes called Malone to find out what the sign was doing up ahead of him, Malone informed him that Monty was moving his headquarters forward to that position in the morning, so Vokes had best get his troops moving ahead.[3]

While this unsubtle harassment from the rear was going on, Vokes was also being pressured by the Canadian correspondents hanging about the HQ between their brief sorties closer to the front. Among these was CBC radio reporter Matthew Halton. Vokes considered Halton one of the more polite members of the press, but still a man capable of asking downright silly questions. "Sir," Halton said, "could you please tell me why you aren't getting on faster?" Gritting his teeth at hearing virtually the same question Monty had asked, Vokes replied in a steely voice, "For two very good reasons."

"Do you mind telling me what they are, General?"

"Not at all. The Germans and the mud."

An apparently bemused Halton said, "I never thought of that."[4]

Exchanges such as this reflected a growing problem, for which the Canadian regiments were paying the price in casualties. Vokes was being pressured to produce instant success against the German defences. Eighth Army wanted results. The press, realizing the battle was the hardest Canadians had so far fought in the Mediterranean theatre, were beginning to cast the struggle in terms of almost mythic proportions. "I don't know how to tell you about Canada's battle of the Moro River," Halton said in a broadcast. "The German is fighting us to the death and he opposes us for once in superior numbers of men."[5] In another broadcast, Halton said, "The time has come when the Germans have to stop the Eighth in its tracks or leave the road open to Rome. They are trying to stop us and are fighting hard."[6]

Halton was not alone. On December 8, Montreal's *Gazette* had rated the German defences at the Moro River as "makeshift." The *New York Telegram* on the same day afforded Ortona only scant attention, describing it as an Adriatic backwater port town of little importance. On December 11, however, the reports changed dramatically. *The New York Times* now declared Ortona the "chief obstacle facing the Canadians." Three days later, Associated Press in Algiers reported that the Canadians were "closing in on strategic road junction of Ortona." The *Ottawa Citizen* added: "The whole current Eighth Army thrust hinges on success of the Canadians in capturing Ortona.[7] The press, observed Major D.H. Cunningham in an analysis of the role of reporters in the December battle, "is a power for evil as well as good. . . . It played a large part in turning a tactical fight into a prestige battle with the consequent unnecessary loss of many lives."[8]

To what extent the growing press attention and Montgomery's insistence that Vokes hurry up the offensive influenced his decisions cannot be known. It seems probable, however, that the pressure contributed to Vokes's continuing to throw his battalions against The Gully in a piecemeal fashion apparently governed more by a desire for haste than any form of sound planning. On the night of December 12, Vokes issued yet another flurry of orders directing one of the only two battalions remaining in reserve to launch a frontal assault against the Panzer Grenadiers.

This time the futile task fell to the Carleton and York Regiment, composed primarily of men from New Brunswick. The 3rd Canadian Infantry Brigade battalion was to pass through the Loyal Edmonton Regiment's position on Vino Ridge and advance up the main axis of old Highway 16 toward Cider Crossroads. A creeping artillery barrage supplemented by the mortars of both 2nd Canadian Infantry Brigade and 3 CIB would closely precede the advancing troops. Fourteenth Canadian Armoured Regiment (Calgary Tanks) was "to give what support was possible in the deteriorating weather. On both flanks of the main thrust a coordinated effort to reach the lateral road was to be made with the West Nova Scotia Regiment on the left and the PPCLI on the right." The Hastings and Prince Edward Regiment was to continue pressing up the coast road. One company of the Royal 22e Regiment was to follow behind the Carleton and York Regiment to "mop up." Zero hour was set for 0600 December 13.[9]

While looking fairly impressive on paper, this coordinated plan failed to acknowledge the weakness of the supporting battalions. The West Novas, the PPCLI, and the Hasty P's could no longer function as regiments — casualties had reduced them to the size of mere companies. None of these regiments could offer much punch to support the fresh Carleton and York Regiment. The attack plan was basically a replay of those that had failed previously. One battalion was to go forward, virtually alone.

At 0600 hours, under an unexpectedly sunny sky, the attack kicked off with 'A' and 'D' companies leading and 'B' and 'C' companies following close behind to serve as a reserve. The Panzer Grenadier response was an immediate and violent opposition with medium machine guns, mortars, artillery, and tanks. The Canadians' creeping artillery barrage rolled on across The Gully, leaving the stalled infantry far behind. While managing to destroy three of the German machine-gun positions and taking twenty-one prisoners, the Carleton and Yorks were forced back from the ridgeline over-looking The Gully an hour after the attack began. Attempts to counter the German tanks with Shermans of the Calgary Tanks also proved fruitless, as one of the Canadian tanks was destroyed and most of the others bogged down in the deep mud.

Commander Lieutenant Colonel John E.C. Pangman tried repeat-edly to rally his troops and move them forward, but each assault crumbled before it could get underway. At 1600 hours things went from bad to worse when No. 16 Platoon of 'D' Company was cut off from the rest of the battalion by a German counterattack. Taking shelter in a house near Cider, the platoon was surrounded. Attempts by 'B' Company to break through to relieve them failed. The whole platoon was lost, twenty-eight of the men forced to surrender and the rest killed.[10] In all, the Carleton and Yorks lost eighty-one men, including four officers. Two were company commanders.

Among those taken prisoner was 'C' Company commander Major Graeme "Buck" Simms and the RCHA forward observation officer Captain Bob MacNeil. The two officers were part of a small unit overrun by a superior force of Germans. As MacNeil, the third RCHA FOO lost in as many days, walked into custody, a sergeant major said, "Come, Englander, for you the war is over."[11]

◆ ◆ ◆

Just as the Carleton and York attack faltered, so did the supporting assaults by the West Novas, the PPCLI, and the Hasty P's. The PPCLI attack saw 'B' Company use the artillery barrage to advance to the crest of Vino Ridge. As the barrage rolled on, the soldiers slugging their way through the mud saw a green flare come up out of The Gully. Seconds later, they were caught in a devastating counter-barrage that was obviously firing on a pre-targeted position in antici-pation of their advance. The company staggered back to its start line.[12]

The West Nova Scotia battalion really never got underway in the morning, being pinned down by heavy artillery, mortar, and small-arms fire throughout the day. At 1630 hours, 'A,' 'C,' and 'D' companies, with a strength of little more than one hundred men remaining, attacked what Major Ron Waterman thought to be a lightly held machine-gun position that had been harassing the battalion all day from about 300 yards to the right. The attack proved the position was anything but weak. Casualties were heavy. 'D' Company, with only one commander and ten men remaining, actually reached the objective but had to withdraw without succeeding in knocking it out.[13]

On the coast, the attempt by the Hasty P's to push two companies up the road was stopped dead on The Gully's forward slope by intense machine-gun and mortar fire. Their gain was measured in mere yards.[14] "Everywhere along the divisional front the enemy fought with that remarkable tenacity which he had displayed a few days before on the banks of the Moro; this morale factor, combined with his knowledgeable exploitation of the lateral gully as a tactical feature, made 90th Grenadier Division a formidable adversary," stated one after-action report.[15]

Finally, however, Vokes was recognizing that the only way of defeating The Gully was to outflank it. Urged by Brigadiers Graeme Gibson and Bert Hoffmeister to try combined tank and infantry sorties around the western flank of The Gully, Vokes had cut orders on the night of December 12 to mount two limited versions of such operations in the morning. Like someone who has burned his hand and is afraid of the heat, Vokes authorized both the Seaforth Highlanders of Canada and the West Nova Scotia Regiment to commit a company each in an attack at the separate potential crossings the two battalions had discovered the previous day. Each would be supported by a squadron of Ontario Tanks.[16]

◆ ◆ ◆

At 0700 hours, West Nova Scotia's 'B' Company platoon commander Lieutenant James Jones and Lieutenant F.P. Clarke of 'B' Squadron of Ontario Tanks set out to attack the clearing they had scouted the previous night. Clarke had three tanks and Jones's No. 10 Platoon spread itself in equal numbers on the outside hulls. The racket made by the advancing tanks was masked by the creeping artillery barrage supporting the Carleton and York attack. Clarke drove the tanks in fast. The lead tank tore past a small house containing one machine-gun position, startling the half-awake gunners. Before they could man their weapon, the second tank destroyed the position with a shot from its 75-millimetre main gun. The machine gunners were all killed. Farther along the trail an antitank gun was spotted. This, too, was knocked out by cannon fire before the dazed Panzer Grenadiers could get it into action. Infantry staggered out of their slit trenches with their hands up as No. 10 Platoon leapt off the tanks and rushed their positions.

Bursting through brush into a clearing, Jones's men and the tankers confronted a farmhouse and three Panzer Mark IVs in cover under some nearby trees. The house appeared to be a battalion head-quarters. Officers, orderlies, and other soldiers who were too clean and well dressed for front-line troops were clambering out of windows and doors and taking flight into the surrounding vineyards and olive groves. The head of a German popped up in the turret of one of the tanks. Jones threw himself prone, shoved the butt of the Bren gun he carried into his shoulder, and killed the man with a short burst. Clarke punched a tank shell into the enemy tank. Seconds later, another of the Canadian tankers dispatched one of the other tanks. The third German tank got off one round before being destroyed.

A splinter from that shell hit Jones in the shoulder, as he was mowing down the German staff fleeing the house. Despite serious pain, Jones continued to lead his platoon forward.[17] At 1030 hours the rest of 'B' Company, led by Captain F.H. Burns, arrived to reinforce the small raiding party. Jones "expressed the wish to carry on with the attack, but was ordered back for medical aid by his company commander," read his subsequent Military Cross citation.[18] Jones's platoon of about twenty-five men was credited with killing some thirty Germans and capturing a further fifty-two.

No. 10 Platoon remained to mop up enemy resistance around the tank harbour, while the rest of 'B' Company and 'B' tank squadron turned The Gully's flank and advanced northeast toward Casa Berardi. They followed a track running between the Ortona-Orsogna lateral highway and The Gully. When they were but 1,000 yards from Casa Berardi, with Cider Crossroads visible beyond, the combat team was barred from further advance by a narrow, deep ravine lying at right angles to The Gully. The tanks could not cross this obstacle, and when Burns tried leading his infantry across alone they were driven back by a now fully awake enemy. 'B' Company and the supporting tanks formed up on the western flank of the narrow ravine and refused to be budged by Panzer Grenadier counterattacks.[19]

◆ ◆ ◆

Captain June Thomas of the Seaforths' 'A' Company still expected to be relieved of command of the thirty-five men left in his unit. The wet, cold morning that dawned on December 13 did little to brighten his despondent mood. Neither did the arrival of Captain Don Harley, who was the battalion's mortar platoon commander and a capable rifle company leader. The two men talked little, both seemingly embarrassed by the other's presence. Thomas was sure Harley was just waiting for his watch hands to reach noon — the time that Thomas thought he was to report to Major Syd Thomson at battalion HQ.

About 1100 hours, Thomas's radio crackled with a message telling 'A' Company to go around the left flank along the track Thomas had discovered. A squadron of Ontario Tanks commanded by Major Herschell "Snuffy" Smith would provide support. The major was to have overall command of the combat force.

Thomas looked at his watch, then turned to Harley. "Look," he said, "you're not taking over until noon and it's only eleven o'clock. I'm still in command."[20] Harley didn't contradict Thomas. Neither did he assure Thomas that he was not supposed to assume command unless Thomas appeared unfit to continue leading his battle-weary and much reduced company.

The small unit set out, following a long, sweeping approach that crossed The Gully via the culvert Thomas had discovered the previous day. They met no resistance, but the mud caused two of the tanks to bog down. Only three remained operational as Thomas's platoon reached a low rise overlooking The Gully.

By now, the Germans were aware of the force's presence and sporadic sniper fire was picking away at them, but it seemed they all lived charmed lives — not a man was hit. Thomas could see that the gently rising terrain bordering the northern edge of The Gully before him was probably riddled with dug-in Panzer Grenadier positions. He broke his infantry into two sections that he and Harley would lead, and a third smaller section consisting of only three men. The two larger sections would take either flank, while the smaller provided some base of fire from the centre. Yelling up at Smith, he said,

"Light up what you can see. I'm going to just form open line and go over the top, because I think there's something down in the bottom of the valley."[21] He then told his men to fix bayonets and prepare to charge.

With a burst of cheers at Thomas's signal to advance, and screaming as they went, the thin line of infantrymen went over the top of the rise at a full run. The previous day Thomas had feared these men would rebel at another futile assault up Vino Ridge, but they didn't let him down today when there was a chance of success. The tanks rumbled along immediately behind. Thomas's section was on the left, Harley's on the right. The attack went in with such speed and force that the Panzer Grenadiers failed to realize the true size of the attacking force. Germans jumped up out of their holes and fled, others cast aside their guns and surrendered. Smith's Shermans knocked out two Mark IV tanks and their machine-gun and cannon fire prevented the Panzer Grenadiers from mustering effective resistance. As they closed on a small farmhouse, the door opened and an officer came out to surrender. Thomas discovered he had overrun 3rd Battalion's headquarters.

The infantry captain's biggest concern now was how to maintain control of all his prisoners, who must soon realize they outnumbered their captors. "Hell, how am I going to cope with all these people?" he muttered. He told his radio signaller to dump his set and take a couple of other men to round up the Germans before they started filtering back to their weapons. Thomas would retain communication with battalion HQ through Smith's tank radio. Leaving one tank to help with controlling the prisoners, Thomas and Smith pushed on toward Casa Berardi. They could hear heavy fighting in that direction, which they imagined was made by the Carleton and York Regiment breaking through The Gully and closing on their day's objective.

Another of the tanks got stuck, leaving them with only Smith's tank positioned in the centre of the advancing line. They overran another enemy trench system, taking more prisoners and sending many others scrambling toward Casa Berardi, which was little more than 500 yards away. A few minutes later, Smith's tank became mired in the muck. Frustrated, Smith and Thomas both knew they would have to halt the advance and withdraw. [22] They radioed the Ontario Tanks HQ and received permission to break off the action.

Having knocked out two German tanks, two antitank guns, and three self-propelled guns, and rounded up seventy-five prisoners, the small force had achieved miracles — especially as they had suffered not a single casualty.[23]

Smith's crew abandoned the tank. Rather than see the enemy capture it, Smith tossed a grenade inside to set off the ammunition and destroy it. The men then walked out to a position at the head of The Gully and dug in for the night. Thomas was surprised when Thomson congratulated him on the action and never raised the subject of his relief. Fearful of reopening the question, Thomas kept his own silence. He imagined that the success his company had enjoyed might have led Thomson to change his mind.[24]

◆ ◆ ◆

While the attack was recognized immediately by Vokes's intelligence staff as a "spectacular thrust on the left which almost loosened the whole front," it also revealed the foolishness of the previous strategy of trying to crack The Gully from the front.[25] A handful of men with a meagre number of tanks had achieved what several battalions, squadrons of tanks, thousands of artillery shells, and hundreds of aerial bombardment missions had failed to accomplish in three days of bitter fighting.

Adding to the frustration was the fact that the Canadians were unable to capitalize on either successful foray. Vokes had so scattered his three infantry brigades and the supporting tank brigades across the battlefront that he had nothing left in reserve. Moreover, his battalions were desperately weak from heavy casualties and losses to sickness, and the mounting toll that battle exhaustion was wreaking on the front-line troops. Most of his rifle companies had been in near continuous combat for over a week. The men were worn out from being able to catch only short naps between mounting assaults, conducting reconnaissance patrols, standing sentry duty, fighting off counterattacks, and enduring the endless concussive racket and danger posed by the night-and-day shelling and machine-gunning of forward positions. Nobody had changed his clothes. They were all unshaven, covered in filth, mud, and blood from their own minor cuts and scrapes and those of badly wounded or killed comrades. There was never enough food or an opportunity to eat it in any degree of comfort. At night they froze and during the day sweat and rain saturated their clothing, preparing them to endure yet another chilling night. Nerves were wire taut.[26]

Vokes now realized his error and in the late afternoon of December 13, he set about planning for a renewed offensive in the morning that would follow the path by which the Seaforths had achieved their spectacular success. The only battalion at close to full strength was 3rd Canadian Infantry Brigade's Royal 22e Regiment (Van Doos). With support from 'C' Squadron of Ontario Tanks, commanded by Major Herschell Smith, the Van Doos were ordered to advance at 0730 hours behind yet another creeping artillery barrage. This time, however, Vokes was certain the attack would finally open the door to the main lateral road.[27]

What Vokes didn't know was that the German defences in The Gully were never weaker than they were on the afternoon of December 13. The 90th Panzer Grenadiers were all but finished as a fighting force, and 1st Parachute Division had not yet managed to effect a complete relief. Some of its regiments were still only approaching Ortona from the north, others were in Ortona but still preparing to move toward The Gully. Had the reserves been ready to follow up the turning of the German western flank that day, the Canadians might have shattered the enemy line entirely before a defence of Ortona could be mounted by the paratroopers. Ortona might have fallen in the kind of short, sharp action that Vokes had originally envisioned once he won the north side of the Moro River. He was too late. As the Van Doos prepared, the Germans rebuilt and reinforced. The morning would see a bitter fight — one that would become a legend in the history of the French-Canadian regiment.

◆ ◆ ◆

Feldwebel Fritz Illi was a platoon commander of 6th Company, 2nd Battalion, 3rd Regiment of the 1st Parachute Division. He had been eighteen when Germany invaded Poland in September 1939. Hearing the news that Germany was at war, his entire high school class in Zuffenhausen had enlisted at nearby Stuttgart. Illi volunteered right away to be a paratrooper. Third Regiment was just forming, so Illi became one of its original members. His first action had been on May 10, 1940, when 2nd Battalion ghosted down from the sky onto the

Dutch airfield at Rotterdam. By December 1943, Illi had survived seven combat jumps: Rotterdam, Narvik, the Corinth Canal, Crete, Leningrad, Tobruk, the Caucasus Mountains, and finally Catania in Sicily. In Crete a mortar fragment had left his little finger dangling by some sinew. The medical officer sliced the finger off, slapped on a bandage, and sent him back into the action after yelling, "Germany needs every soldier to fight on!" Illi fought on for the fourteen days it took the parachutists to win Crete. At battle's end, 75 percent of Illi's company were casualties.

In June of 1942, twelve paratroopers, including Illi, were dropped deep in the Caucasus Mountains near a backwater called Mycoptoobasch. The entire team was heavily overloaded with weaponry. Illi went out of the Henckel 110's bomb-bay door armed with a Schmeisser, a pistol, plenty of ammunition, grenades, and forty kilograms of explosives. The team found its target, a railway bridge on the Tehran-Caucasus line, unguarded. They blew the bridge and, aided by a local anti-communist guide, walked for ninety-four days through Russian territory to reach the German lines.

By December 1943, the glory days of the German paratroopers were over. There would be no more combat jumps followed by intense fighting and then withdrawal to Germany to rebuild, retrain, and prepare for another airborne operation. First Parachute Division was in Italy to stay, serving in the front lines for the same extended stretches as the other divisions constituting the Tenth Army. Illi was now a twenty-three-year-old veteran of more than four years of military service on every German battlefront. One of the few remaining originals, he was a tough, battle-wise survivor. The paratroopers' heavy casualties during the years of airborne operations had thinned the ranks, and reinforcements had been steadily integrated. Illi had outlived most of the newer men.

The parachute divisions continued to accept only volunteer recruits. All were well trained. Airborne culture was hammered into the new recruits. "Cohesion was incredible," Illi would remember. "We would do anything for each other. Many were killed trying to save fallen comrades under enemy fire." Personal honour, regimental honour, national honour were everything. Surrender or cowardice in the face of the enemy was considered treasonous. If a man chose to dishonour the regiment by surrendering, he risked being shot by his friends. Few of the parachutists were members of the Nazi party; to a man, however, they were devoutly patriotic Germans. Dying for Germany was the ultimate expression of this patriotism. This is what the parachutist believed. This is what they taught the new men who came into their division.

As the Italian campaign ground on, the Parachute Division began to take in men from other divisions. They still ensured that these men were volunteers. And the old-timers who were jump-qualified or wore the ribbons of the earlier airborne operations and had "parachute qualified" annotated to their identity cards, thought of the non-parachutists as being a little less elite than themselves. Mostly they sought to hide this sentiment from the new men. To reveal it would have violated the regimental code of mutual devotion. They pushed the new men to rise to their level of training, physical fitness, and combat effectiveness. There was not a man in 1st Parachute Division who did not think he stood alongside Germany's finest soldiers.[28]

Among the new men was nineteen-year-old Willi Fretz from Karlsruhe. Responding to the call of national duty, Fretz had volunteered in December 1942, and after training was posted to the regular army's 305th Division. This was an Ost (east) division, so-called because many of its enlisted ranks were ethnic East Europeans or Asians rather than Germans. Most were conscripts pressed into German military service as an alternative to being sent to forced-labour camps. Fretz found that most of his comrades were Yugoslavians. The officers and non-commissioned officers were Germans, but often they were poor soldiers. Fretz's sergeant took an immediate dislike to him, accusing him of having "too many brains." The young man had hoped to attend medical school. From the age of fifteen until his military enlistment, Fretz had worked after school and on weekends as a volunteer *familus*, or helper, in the local hospital. While fighting on the Italian front through October and November of 1943, Fretz applied several times for permission to leave the army for medical school. The requests were denied: German losses were too heavy to spare a single fit man. Fretz realized his youthful dream was being lost to the war.

He saw his sergeant and commanding officer behave like cowards and then put their names forward for Iron Crosses. When the sergeant was too frightened to man a forward observation post, Fretz did the job alone. The sergeant received an Iron Cross First Class when he lied about the incident and cast himself in heroic terms. Then the man tried to buy Fretz's silence by offering him an Iron Cross Second Class. Insulted, Fretz refused the honour. His commander offered to send him to officers training. Fretz refused. He did not want to become what he no longer respected. The commander's response was to give him ever harder details, ever tougher assignments. On December 3, 1943, a call was put out for volunteers to the parachute division. Fretz put his hand up and left the 305th Division without a backward glance.

Already trained as an observer, Fretz was assigned to 13th Company of 3rd Regiment. The company was the regiment's heavy weapons unit, which comprised heavy machine guns, medium and heavy mortars, and some light artillery pieces. Fretz was given the job of controlling the mortar and machine-gun fire. He led a three-man detachment composed of himself as observer, a runner who carried messages, and a radio operator.[29]

Beginning the night of December 12 and continuing throughout December 13, the 1st Parachute Division moved into the Ortona area. The Canadians did not know it at the time, but on December 13 the Hastings and Prince Edward Regiment, Princess Patricia's Canadian Light Infantry Regiment, and the main body of the West Nova Scotia Regiment had been stopped in their tracks by parachutists rather than the Panzer Grenadiers they had been fighting since December 5. Fritz Illi's 2nd Battalion, 3rd Regiment went into the line and fought through the whole day. By day's end, 1st Battalion, 3rd Regiment was moving down from the upper Sangro River to the coast.

Illi was not in the lines at The Gully. His company was still in Ortona. Fretz's heavy-weapons company snapped its mortars onto base plates in a position next to Villa Grande, to the west of Ortona.[30] Obergefreiter Karl Bayerlein was working as a Fallschirmpionier, constructing positions above Francavilla about six miles north of Ortona.[31] Tenth Army command was planning to shift the entire division to Ortona, but it would take several days to effect the move because of transportation difficulties. There were not enough trucks to move all the regiments at once. Allied air superiority over all of Italy further exacerbated the transportation problem. Trucks or trains moving by day were likely to be destroyed by aerial bombardment or strafing. Rainy days were best. Although roads were transformed into quagmires, the Germans could at least move without fear of Allied planes.

Tenth Army urgently needed to replace the 90th Panzer Grenadiers. On December 13, a postscript added to the War Diary of 76th Korps, of which the 90th was a part, read: "A great fighting value can no longer be ascribed to 90th Panzer Grenadier Division. The units have become badly mixed and the troops are exhausted. The fighting value of at least two battalions has been used up. The present positions can only be held by bringing in new battalions."[32]

German Tenth Army high command was concerned that 1st Parachute Division was too weak to perform the task. It was still rebuilding after fierce fighting in Sicily and earlier in the Italian campaign. General der Panzertruppen and commander of the Tenth Army Joachim Lemelsen defended the decision to commit the division in a December 13 phone conversation with fellow Panzer General Traugott Herr. "The fighting strength of the paratroops is not as bad as it is always made out to be," he said. "It has been increased by the arrival of young reinforcements and can be considered as normal."[33] While it was true that the division's strength was relatively normal by the standards of the slowly crumbling German army, it was far from its designated strength. In the spring of 1943, 1st Parachute Division had been allocated a strength of 16,000 men.[34] By December, casualties had reduced the division to a total strength of 11,864, with almost 20 percent on a perpetually rotating furlough. This left the division with a real strength of only about 9,500, many of whom were not front-line infantry.[35]

Despite this weakness, the commitment of its 2nd battalion into the line on December 13 enabled the 90th Panzer Grenadiers to hold at The Gully. It also ensured that the planned Canadian attack on December 14 toward Casa Berardi would face fierce resistance.

# 16

## THE SAFEST PLACE
## FOR US

SOLDIERING ran in Captain Paul Triquet's blood. The thirty-three-year-old native of Cabano, Quebec, came from a French family with a long military lineage. His father, Georges, had served as a company sergeant major in the French army, was badly wounded in one of the battles of Champagne in 1915, and given an honorary discharge along with three medals for bravery. Paul's grandfather, Louis-Desire Triquet, had fought in the Franco-Prussian and South African wars, and a great-grandfather had seen service in Crimea. Georges had emigrated to Canada in 1905, met and married Helene Pelletier in a whirlwind Montreal romance, then settled in the small Quebec sawmill town of Cabano near the New Brunswick border. He earned a living as an accountant and insurance salesman. But when World War I broke out, he had immediately returned to France.

In the early 1920s, Cabano had a population of only 5,400, and there was little in the way of services for young boys. Georges Triquet decided the solution was to form a cadet corps that would promote martial discipline and spirit in a setting of organized sport and physical training. Paul, the oldest of seven children though not yet a teenager, was his first recruit. The two Triquets formed up on the school grounds. As father led son through the marching drill to the cadences of the French army, other boys looked on. Soon they joined in. Georges Triquet's cadets averaged a strength of fifty. Broomsticks were eventually exchanged for antiquated Ross rifles, which Georges Triquet secured through his connections as a militia reserve officer. Paul was promoted to cadet corporal. A superb athlete, he soon replaced his father as the physical training instructor.

Shortly before his sixteenth birthday, Triquet went to work in the local mill. He yearned, however, to join the army. He read every book available on the life and military career of Napoleon Bonaparte and other French generals and leaders. When he turned sixteen, Triquet immediately went to Quebec City and tried to enlist, claiming he was seventeen. The enlistment officer told him to go home and come back when he was nineteen. Triquet tried again a year later. This time he said he was nineteen and the enlistment officer believed him. When he returned to Cabano and told his parents that he had been accepted into the army, Helene expressed concern, but Georges hushed her. Paul's father was immensely proud.

Triquet entered the Royal 22e Regiment as a private. Other than two years out of the service for a brief experiment with a career in the Quebec provincial police, he remained in the army throughout the 1930s. He was a sergeant major when the war broke out. After the Van Doos deployed to Britain, he received an officer's commission.[1]

On December 14, Triquet commanded 'C' Company. Captain Ovila Garceau had 'D' Company. These two companies formed the vanguard of the Van Doos attack. Immediately behind were three Ontario Tanks, with four more a little farther back. 'A' and 'B' companies, plus Lieutenant Colonel Paul Bernatchez's battalion headquarters, provided a base of support. Also with the unit were two Royal Canadian Horse Artillery forward observation officers, Captain Bob Donald, just returned to the unit after a bout of jaundice, and Captain Harald Martin.

Although the advance was to progress on a two-company front, Triquet's company on the left was expected to face the toughest resistance. For this reason, one FOO would accompany Triquet, who also received priority call on Major Herschell Smith and his seven-tank-strong squadron. Shortly before dawn, RCHA Major George "Duff"

Mitchell met briefly with his two FOOs to decide who would accompany Triquet and who would stay with Bernatchez. The three men knew the FOO with Triquet would face the most danger. Mitchell fished out a coin. Martin said, "Heads I go with Triquet." It came up tails. "I'm glad it worked out that way because you have had more experience than Harald, Bob," Mitchell said.[2] Bob Donald was Mitchell's best friend. They had attended Royal Military College together and served their entire RCHA war careers in close proximity. Martin, at thirty-five one of the oldest men in the regiment, had been an insurance broker in Montreal before the war.

Artillery was considered vital to the attack's success. As with the failed attacks against The Gully's front, the Van Doos would advance behind a creeping barrage. Donald and Martin would also call in close supporting fire at specific targets.

As dawn crept closer, Bernatchez took his second-in-command Major Jean V. Allard aside. Of the attack, Bernatchez said, "It's a big risk, and if my command post is destroyed, you'll have to take over."[3] A sobered Allard returned to the rear echelon position and readied his jeep with radios. He also got a small truck organized with a wireless set aboard to provide a mobile link to 3rd Canadian Infantry Brigade's headquarters near San Leonardo. Accompanied by his driver, his batman, a radio operator, clerk, and a load of shovels, ammunition, a Bren gun, and boxes of rations, he drove up to a point near Triquet's company and established an alternative command post.

'C' and 'D' companies headed for the start line, at the culvert crossing that Captain June Thomas had discovered. Allard called out to Garceau, wishing him luck. Triquet walked up. "We're really going to get Jerry," he said.[4] Triquet's company numbered eighty-one men and Garceau's about the same. Morale was high. Royal 22e Regiment was a permanent force unit and many of the soldiers had extensive military service behind them. The regiment's long history and its place as the only exclusively French-Canadian regiment in the Canadian army meant the men had a unique tradition to uphold. Some of the soldiers came from Triquet's hometown. Since the war started, more than 250 men from Cabano had enlisted, most becoming Van Doos.[5]

At 0630 hours, the sixty-minute bombardment started. When the artillery lifted, the assault force was to strike down the route taken the previous day by the Seaforth Highlanders of Canada's 'A' Company and Smith's tanks. Once the Ortona-Orsogna road was gained, the Van Doos would advance east along it to Casa Berardi and Cider Crossroads. The plan was to repeat 'A' Company's exploits, but on a much larger scale that could not be repelled by the Germans. Major General Chris Vokes was certain that the 90th Panzer Grenadiers were finished as a combat unit. Intercepted German radio traffic had indicated the division was on its last legs. Vokes was unaware that during the night regiments of the 1st Parachute Division had stiffened the Panzer Grenadier line.[6]

◆ ◆ ◆

Triquet and Garceau expected to jump off at 0730 hours. No. 15 Platoon of 'C' Company was on point, Triquet's company HQ immediately behind, followed by No. 14 and No. 13 platoons. Once the infantry hit the road, the two companies would form an arrowhead-shaped two-company wide line for its advance on Casa Berardi. The point of the arrowhead would be the centre of the road.

At 0710, the two companies reached the start line and came immediately under intense German machine-gun and mortar fire. In the predawn briefing, they had been told the enemy was gone, that the advance to the lateral road should be largely uncontested.

The fight was on. 'C' Company crossed the culvert at a run. Machine-gun and mortar fire forced the leading platoon to hit the ground and crawl into the shallow shelter offered by some shell craters on the right of the muddy track. Triquet's HQ found cover in some shrubbery to the left. The other two platoons were sheltered from the German fire by a reverse slope. Seeing Triquet waving the two platoons forward, No. 14 Platoon's commander advanced to a position left and forward of Triquet. No. 13 Platoon's Lieutenant Marcel Richard missed Triquet's signal. On the other side of The Gully, a Panzer Mark IV poked out from behind a house about 500 yards south of the Ortona-Orsogna lateral highway and started blasting away. Smith's Shermans were wallowing through the mud well back of the platoons, trying to get forward. Richard realized that by the time the Shermans got up to engage the tank, the Van Doos might be slaughtered.

Antitank infantry doctrine called for a flanking movement. Richard initiated an independent action. He led his platoon to the left, leapfrogging by sections to the shelter presented by some olive trees and a vineyard. Although hidden from the tank's attention, the platoon was visible to German soldiers in The Gully itself. Richard's men were raked by machine-gun and rifle fire. Casualties were heavy, but the soldiers were committed now. They either advanced or died in place. At the end of the tree line they hit the dirt and wormed into whatever cover they could find. The tank was still out of the range of their PIAT gun. Richard and his two-man PIAT squad closed on the tank by crawling on elbows and knees down an even thinner line of brush and scattered trees paralleling the Ortona-Orsogna road. The tank was prowling in front of 'C' Company's main body, slashing it with machine-gun fire from a distance that kept it out of their PIAT range.

When Richard's PIAT squad tried loading the gun, it refused to cock. The weapon was useless. Richard knew that if the tank was not knocked out soon, it would form the base for a Panzer Grenadier counterattack right down 'C' Company's throat. He could see that the Germans were shaking off the effects of the artillery bombardment and returning to their fighting holes. Grey uniforms were crawling all over the landscape surrounding the road. Kneeling, so 'C' Company could see him, Richard waved the damaged PIAT over his head. When he had the attention of No. 14 Platoon's commander he hand-signalled his need for a new PIAT.

While he was communicating his plight to 'C' Company, the Mark IV rumbled back behind the house, remaining oblivious to the presence of Richard's three-man tank-killer team. The German infantry who had fired on No. 13 Platoon were more observant. Small-arms fire crackled around the three men. Snipers positioned in the upper storey of the house and across the highway added to the flurry of bullets. A slug caught Richard in the right collarbone. As his two comrades dragged him back to better cover, a soldier from No. 14 Platoon crawled into No. 13 Platoon's position with a new PIAT gun.

No. 13 Platoon Sergeant J.P. Rousseau grabbed the weapon and started following the same path Richard and the team had taken. The intense small-arms fire quickly drove him to ground. The tank rolled back and forth on the far side of the house, as if seeking the infantry's target. Rousseau lay still for fifteen long, terrifying minutes, waiting for a lull. Realizing Rousseau's plight, Triquet ordered No. 14 and No. 15 platoons to rush forward by sections. They set off in short, sharp bounds right into the teeth of the enemy fire. Triquet meant to create the illusion that the main force was intent on storming the house and tank in a frontal assault. Men from both platoons were killed and wounded in the deception, but it distracted attention from Rousseau. The sergeant jumped up and ran across open ground, the thirty-two-pound weapon cradled in his arms. When he was fifty yards away, the tankers suddenly saw him. They started turning the turret by its hand-driven cranking mechanism, trying to bring him under fire with the 75-millimetre main gun. Rousseau closed another fifteen yards on the tank, knelt on one knee to help steady the heavy PIAT, and fired a bomb. The bomb, read Rousseau's later citation for the Military Medal, struck "squarely between turret and traverse casing and the blast must have penetrated to the 75-mm ammunition stocked within the turret, for the Mark IV literally blew apart." The tank was torn into thirty pieces and the crew vaporized.[7]

The time was 0750, and the battle was only forty minutes old. By now Smith's tanks were approaching the lateral highway. One was knocked out by a Panzer Mark III, which the Ontario tankers destroyed in turn. Triquet's platoons married up and the company pressed on toward the highway, fighting through a network of well-dug-in German positions. Around them a tank battle erupted. Smith's squadron engaged several more Mark IVs and a 75-millimetre PAK antitank gun. Rousseau tried to help with his PIAT but the weapon jammed. This was an all-too-common occurrence, leading most infantrymen to hate the PIAT.[8] Smith's tanks, however, needed no help. They quickly knocked out two of the tanks and destroyed the antitank gun. The rest of the German armour retreated. Their own marksmanship had been deplorable. Had their fire been as accurate as that of Smith's squadron, the Ontario tankers would have been stopped in their tracks because the Germans were firing from protected positions, while the Canadian tanks were out in the open.[9]

The Germans, now identified by the Canadians as members of 1st Parachute Division, followed their tanks' lead and withdrew to the road. It appeared they were setting up for a last stand there.

◆ ◆ ◆

While 'C' Company and Smith's tanks pressed on, 'D' Company became lost in the confusing terrain. They wandered for a while, getting caught in small firefights, until finally the company blundered into the West Nova Scotia Regiment's lines on the south side of The Gully looking across to Casa Berardi. By the time the company realized its position, Triquet's company was far forward, engaged, as he later wrote, in "one long Calvary." Every foot forward was won in blood.[10]

As the Canadians closed on the road, a young woman gripping a small child in each hand popped out of the ground in the kill zone between them and the Germans. She ran toward the Canadian line, dragging the children with her. Every soldier suddenly held his fire until the trio passed through the Van Doos and scampered into cover behind their position. As if by pre-arranged signal, Germans and Canadians simultaneously went back to trying to kill each other.[11]

Triquet's men at last threw the Germans back and gained the Ortona-Orsogna lateral road. Fifteen men had fallen, including two platoon commanders. Lieutenant Marcel Richard, who had been shot in the collarbone, walked back to the Van Doos main lines on his own. He entered Allard's command post. Richard was as white as a ghost, and blood dribbled through the dressing over the bullet wound. Drawing himself stiffly to attention, Richard saluted with his left hand. Because of the wound, he was unable to lift his right. The young man asked in a steady voice for permission to be evacuated. Allard hurried to get the officer's dressing changed and had him taken to the aid post by jeep.

Allard soon went forward to personally assess the battle. On the track running across The Gully, he saw a thin line of khaki-clothed bodies stretching to the Ortona-Orsogna lateral. Triquet's dead served as route markers for tracking the line of attack.[12]

◆ ◆ ◆

At 0830, 'C' Company and Smith's tanks began a long, bloody advance toward the tall manor house of Casa Berardi. It stood 2,000 yards away. The small force fought its way through country devastated by more than a week of air and artillery bombardment. It was "a wasteland of trees with split limbs, burnt out vehicles, dead animals, and cracked shells of houses. Every tree and house was defended by machine-guns and tanks with the support of self-propelled guns; the stronger positions were attacked by Shermans while the infantry cleaned out what remained; two more Mark IV Specials were knocked out."[13]

The dwindling French-Canadian force was protected on either flank by a wall of explosives and shrapnel called down by the FOO, Captain Bob Donald. Smith's tanks were consequently freed to concentrate fire to the front. This was critical to breaking German resistance. Triquet's casualties continued to mount. His last platoon commander was wounded. He had to evacuate him with one soldier, who was also escorting two German prisoners. Before noon, Triquet reorganized his remaining thirty men into two platoons led by sergeants. They were still well short of Casa Berardi and now surrounded on all sides by a determined enemy. "The safest place for us is the objective," he told the men.[14]

Buttoned up inside his tank, Smith could not always see critical targets through the viewing slit. To get his attention, Triquet would jump up on the Sherman and drop gravel through the open turret hatch onto Smith's head. When the man poked his head out of the hatch, Triquet pointed out the target he wanted destroyed. Smith obliged with pleasure. When his men hesitated in the face of particularly stiff resistance, Triquet yelled, "They can't shoot. Never mind them! Come on!"[15] His men followed.

Triquet's headquarters group was cut to pieces. Only his orderly remained. The radio was smashed. He had to rely on Smith's tank radio to pass reports back to the battalion. Meanwhile the FOO, Donald, and his signaller, who was bent double under the weight of the heavy #18 radio strapped to his back, scrambled through the sparse roadside vegetation. Moving constantly, Donald continued to keep the shrinking force ringed by artillery fire. The "artillery," wrote Van Doos Lance Corporal E. Bluteau after the battle, "hammers without stop the German positions and I can say that the enemy doesn't like it, and that, if we get out of this impasse, the artillery will have a large share of the credit."[16]

Two hundred yards short of Casa Berardi, 'C' Company "was caught in a severe barrage" of fire from around the manor house. Only twenty-one Van Doos and five tanks were left. Ammunition was short, with no possibility of resupply. The enemy were engaging with tanks, numerous machine guns, and snipers. A Mark IV charged down the road. Smith blinded it with a smoke shell, while another Sherman fired down the roadway, using the road verge as a guiding line for its fire toward the target. When the tank's third shell struck the German tank, it burst into flames. At a range of 600 yards, a Mark IV Special was destroyed in an olive grove.[17] On the Canadian side, Lieutenant S.C. Campbell was fatally wounded when a mortar shell struck his tank turret, Lieutenant D. MacGregor received a scalp wound from a sniper's bullet that pierced his steel helmet. Another tank was immobilized when a track was shot out. The crew were out of ammunition and unable to escape. They would hide in the tank for the next three days because there were so many Germans around it was impossible to escape. Only two tank officers were still in action, Major Smith and Lieutenant Harrod. Four tanks remained.[18]

At about 1430 hours, the Canadians captured the manor house. Then they pushed on through a small scattering of buildings nearby, trying to reach the final objective of Cider Crossroads little more than 1,000 yards farther on. Although they came close, Triquet realized he could never hold the exposed ground. He wisely retreated to the manor house. With the tall, shell- and bullet-pocked structure forming the centre, the men established a circular perimeter that had the infantry on the outside and one tank pointing each direction. There were only fourteen Van Doos. Between them they had five Bren guns, five Thompson submachine guns, and a rapidly dwindling supply of ammunition. They were desperately thirsty. There was no water. The manor house's well was outside the perimeter and covered by snipers. Two men had died trying to refill their canteens there.[19] Drawing on his knowledge of French generalship, Triquet told his men, "Ils ne passeront pas." World War I General Henri Philippe Pétain had uttered this battle cry at Verdun, where the French army had made a determined, bloody stand credited with saving France from German conquest.

At dusk, Triquet, Donald, and Smith gathered near Smith's tank to discuss defensive plans. Triquet's orderly had just walked up with a tin of food and urged his commander to please eat something, when a shell came apparently out of nowhere and exploded nearby. Donald was cut almost in two. He died instantly.[20] The orderly, his stomach ripped open, also fell. He cried out, "I'm hit, Captain," and died seconds later.[21] Neither Smith nor Triquet was touched. The RCHA had just lost its fourth FOO in four days. Another FOO would be captured, killed, or wounded each day for three more days — the heaviest rate of FOO casualties the regiment suffered in the war.

As midnight approached, Triquet heard noise coming from The Gully. He yelled the password and demanded that whoever was coming out of the depths halt and give the countersign. "Don't worry, Paul," a voice called out. Triquet recognized it as Captain Oliva Garceau's. 'D' Company had managed to creep through the enemy lines from its position inside the West Nova Scotia Regiment's perimeter to reinforce Triquet.[22] Soon after, Captain Andre Arnoldi brought 'B' company along the highway by the same route Triquet and Smith had taken. Lieutenant Colonel Bernatchez moved up with the last company and his headquarters a short time later. The Van Doos dug in, creating a defensive island around Casa Berardi. The old building's cellar and stables had ceilings supported by massive gothic-style gables. Its upper storeys were also stoutly constructed, so that it was relatively immune to the effects of artillery or other German fire. Bernatchez made the stables and cellars the battalion's aid posts.

Shortly before Triquet's company was reinforced, a single Mark IV tank had roared out of the west, barrelled past the manor house before anybody could react, and disappeared into the gathering darkness heading hell-bent for leather toward Ortona. It was the last German vehicle to travel unmolested along the Ortona-Orsogna lateral road. After six days of fighting, The Gully was turned and the lateral highway closed.[23]

◆ ◆ ◆

The Germans recognized the import of failing to prevent Casa Berardi's capture. Generalfeldmarschall Albert Kesselring grumbled to Tenth Army commander General der Panzertruppen Joachim Lemelsen, "For two months now I have not been able to exercise proper command because everything evaporates between my fingers and runs down like water from the mountains." Lemelsen responded, "This whole thing must be blamed on the complete failure of 90th Panzer Grenadier Division." Kesselring agreed. "It is that outfit's own fault," he said. Drawing hope from the arrival of 1st Parachute

Division's General Richard Heidrich, Lemelsen said, "Wherever Heidrich is, everything goes all right. . . . The enemy advancing along the coast was flatly thrown back by Heidrich; others let themselves be simply overrun."[24]

The decision was made to relieve Generalleutnant Karl Hans Lungershausen as commander of the 90th Panzer Grenadiers, and replace him with the colourful cavalry officer Generalleutnant Ernst-Günther Baade. Independently wealthy, Baade was a brilliant if eccentric soldier. In the interwar years, he had been a renowned international horse rider. Rather than wear a proper military uniform, Baade preferred a Scottish khaki kilt, lacking a sporran, worn over his riding breeches. Suspended in a holster slung around his neck, he always carried a large pistol. Baade had overseen the masterful withdrawal of German troops from Sicily across the Strait of Messina. He was a commander who fought from a forward command post, where he would not be irritated by staff officers and clerks. Lemelsen's slight hope was that together, Baade and Heidrich could rescue the desperate situation around Ortona.

Tenth Army chief of staff Generalmajor Fritz Wentzell said in another phone conversation, "Intention of the Canadians will be to take Ortona. They could not get through on the coast and now they are trying further along the main road to Orsogna. When they have crossed it they will wheel around and press on towards Ortona. The Korps is trying to prevent this with the last available forces. New decisions cannot be made in this situation, one must try to throw in everything to prevent the Canadians from succeeding."[25]

In the 76th Panzer Korps' war diary, the December 14 notation read gloomily: "Enemy will bring up further forces and tanks and, in the exploitation of today's success, presumably will take Ortona."[26]

# 17

# A New Plan
# Is Needed

THE Royal 22e Regiment's capture of Casa Berardi was the only noteworthy progress made by 1st Canadian Infantry Division on December 14. The Hastings and Prince Edward Regiment, which had put two companies across The Gully on December 13, was unable to retain its grip in the face of a determined counterattack by the 1st Parachute Division. In the evening, the Hasty P's withdrew to the southern lip of The Gully and dug in.[1]

The Princess Patricia's Canadian Light Infantry sent one company to clear a house on the right flank being used by the Germans as an observation post. 'A' Company, commanded by Captain J.B. Hunt — an officer cross-posted from the Royal Canadian Regiment to the PPCLI when he returned to the division from a bout of jaundice and there was no spot in the RCR for him — was to receive covering fire from the mortar company. This fire, however, fell on the company instead of on the enemy. Despite heavy casualties, the attacking force pushed ahead until Hunt was killed when a bullet hit him between the eyes. Facing heavy fire from an estimated four machine guns positioned around the house, the surviving elements of the company withdrew.[2]

The Carleton and York Regiment spent the day on the defensive, finally throwing back another of the 90th Panzer Grenadiers' suicidal counterattacks in the late afternoon. As for the West Nova Scotia Regiment, it was too broken by casualties to do more than hold in place. The Gully remained a formidable barrier to any advance on Ortona. It was obvious that victory could be achieved only by capitalizing on the Van Doos' success at Casa Berardi.

Surprisingly, Major General Chris Vokes and his staff were less than jubilant over the Van Doos' achievement. Although Vokes quickly cited Captain Paul Triquet for the first Victoria Cross awarded to a Canadian in Italy and Major Herschell Smith for a Military Cross, he was hard-pressed to follow up the attack's success. Once again, Vokes had allowed himself to be caught with no available reinforcements to push through Casa Berardi in a race for Ortona. Only two of his nine regiments were unengaged. These were 1st Canadian Infantry Brigade's 48th Highlanders of Canada and the Royal Canadian Regiment. The RCR was still licking the wounds that had left the regiment in tatters after the battle to breach the Moro River line. The 48th Highlanders were in good shape, but were blocking the track that passed through La Torre to San Leonardo, far out on the division's left flank.

Vokes stared at his situation map, seeking a solution that would break the enemy line at The Gully once and for all. His decision-making was probably little enhanced by the arrival at his headquarters of General Montgomery and his entourage. Montgomery had come to receive a personal report from Vokes on the delay. When Montgomery left, Vokes decided he had to act. Trouble was that all he had immediately available was another squadron of Ontario Tanks. But maybe that would suffice. Vokes decided that a strong tank force inserted at Casa Berardi could dominate The Gully positions, enabling continued frontal attacks to shatter the German line at The Gully once and for all.[3]

Instead of shifting any of the regiments already engaged against the front of The Gully, then, Vokes opted to continue with piecemeal frontal assaults. The only difference this time was that the Van Doos and the tanks could bring pressure against the German right flank and slowly push it in to Cider Crossroads and perhaps beyond. Even if the Van Doos proved unable to advance against the Germans, the tanks might be able to direct fire down much of the length of the enemy positions dug in to the reverse slope of The Gully. The safe haven the Germans had enjoyed would no longer be secure from the devastating effect of 75-millimetre gunfire.

The task of carrying out the frontal assault was handed to the Carleton and York Regiment, which, of all the battalions facing The Gully, had so far suffered the lightest casualties. It was also one of the regiments closest to Casa Berardi. Vokes ordered the attack made at 0730 hours on December 15, following the usual pre-attack artillery barrage.[4] Ever workmanlike in his approach, Vokes perhaps failed to appreciate that mounting attacks in precisely the same manner and at the same time for several days running stripped away any chance of catching the Germans by surprise. The artillery bombardment would tell the paratroopers and Panzer Grenadiers precisely where to look for the attackers. Vokes still seemed not to appreciate that the weight of the artillery was largely nullified by both the mud, which soaked up much of the explosive force of the shells, and the safe haven The Gully's reverse slope provided. When the artillery lifted, the Germans would be there and waiting for the Carleton and York companies.

Vokes did realize the attack was likely to fail. If it did, he intended it to be his last frontal assault on The Gully. Instead, he would finally outflank the obstacle by a deep-penetration attack on the left flank that built upon the success of December 14. To prepare for this event, he ordered the 48th Highlanders and the RCR withdrawn from the forward lines so they could have a brief rest and resupply before embarking on a major engagement.

The battalions of 2nd Canadian Infantry Brigade moved to cover the points in the line vacated by 1 CIB. The Seaforth Highlanders of Canada moved to La Torre. The Loyal Edmonton Regiment shifted somewhat to the right and the PPCLI to the left, to cover their own front and that previously held by the RCR. This reorganization meant fully committing 2 CIB. Already seriously short of manpower, the battalions had to thin their lines so much that they would be hard-pressed to contain a major German attack. Vokes was gambling that the Germans had no intention of switching to the offensive from their defensive posture.[5]

To add more punch to the Canadian line, Vokes offered 2 CIB's battalion commanders barbed wire and mines. The Seaforths' commander, Syd Thomson, who had been promoted to acting lieutenant colonel, accepted the wire and erected a barrier with it along the front at La Torre. He refused the mines because of the physical difficulty of bringing them up with only mules as transport. The appearance of the wire in front of the Seaforth position made the battlefield bear an even more haunting resemblance to a World War I No Man's Land.

PPCLI commander Lieutenant Colonel Cameron Ware refused both mines and wire. He could see little use in the wire and told Vokes that "the enemy had already mined our area for us."[6] The Loyal Edmontons also declined the offer. Their front was teeming with mines and booby traps left behind by the Germans.

The RCR gladly withdrew from its position. The soldiers had been dug in at the northern edge of the Moro River valley, in front of the road that ran from San Donato to San Leonardo. This was the same area where the battalion had taken its mauling during the Moro River battle. This road was now known to the Canadians as Royal Canadian Avenue. Much of their time had been spent burying the dead left from the battle, both Canadian and German. Cleaning up around Sterlin Castle had proven the most difficult task. They found many of their comrades lying in slit trenches, rifles still gripped in their hands and pressed to their shoulders. The men looked eerily calm. Most had been killed by bullet wounds to the head, as had the dead Germans scattered throughout the surrounding groves and vineyards. On both sides, the rifle marksmanship displayed during the long day's fight at Sterlin Castle had been chillingly deadly.

RCR Major Strome Galloway was glad to hear that Vokes was finally realizing The Gully would never be breached directly. His diary notation for December 15 read, "A frontal attack across these vine-clad gullies just won't work. A new plan is needed."[7]

◆ ◆ ◆

Before Vokes would give the new plan a try, though, there would be one last attack. On December 15, the Carleton and York Regiment jumped off at 0730 hours in the wake of an hour-long artillery bombardment. 'B' and 'C' companies were in the vanguard, supported on the right flank by the Bren carrier platoon. As always, the artillery barrage had failed to neutralize the Germans, and the Carleton and Yorks had gone no more than 200 yards before the advance withered in the face of a hail of machine-gun fire. In little more than an hour, the attack was scrubbed. Twelve men were dead, including three officers. Another officer and twenty-seven other men were wounded.[8] One of the officers killed, Captain Elliott Maxwell, had earlier voiced a presentiment that he would die in the attack.[9]

Since 3 CIB entered the line, its West Nova Scotia and Carleton and York regiments had gained virtually nothing, but had suffered many casualties. The brigade intelligence officer wrote afterward that both battalions were "pretty shaken. . . . In general, reinforcements which were brought up were thoroughly scared by the stories they were told before they began the fight. Little care was displayed for the comfort of the troops. No rum or dry clothes were available and the men were unable to wash or shave. The forward companies bore the full brunt, and altogether battle administration had broken down."[10] Reinforcements were also insufficient to build the battalions back to effective fighting strength. The war diarist for 3 CIB noted on December 15 that "all units . . . were tired, under strength and nervous from the days [of] very heavy fighting and shelling they had been through. Reinforcements disappeared as rate of casualties was twice as high as number of reinforcements."[11]

The continued stand of the Royal 22e Regiment at Casa Berardi was an inspiration to the entire division. The deteriorating morale which the intelligence officer noted in his general assessment of 3 CIB's state on December 15 excluded the Van Doos. Although similarly shaken by casualties, the officer noted, they "had all the confidence in the world. They were now in a more favourable position for killing the enemy than ever before held."[12]

◆ ◆ ◆

While Royal 22e Regiment's morale remained high, they were far from possessing a favourable position for killing Germans. The regiment was under siege. In the morning of December 15, 'D' Company, commanded by Captain Garceau, took point on an assault toward Cider Crossroads. His company was butchered by mortar and machine guns. Casualties in the company hit 50 percent. Captain Triquet's 'C' Company, numbering only fourteen men, and Major

Smith's tanks tried next. They failed to get past the start line. The "strain and fatigue," Triquet wrote later, "were overpowering."[13]

Triquet spent the rest of the day running from one slit trench and shell hole to the next, trying to keep up the spirits of his boys. Round-faced, with a thin dark moustache and a genuine laughing twinkle in his eye, Triquet was an inspiration. What he didn't show his men was that spiritually he was being torn apart. Seeing all the dead men of his company and those of the other Van Doos companies scattered around Casa Berardi, Triquet was fighting to stave off despair. Burying the dead was impossible because of the raging battle. "I could only hang on by speaking to the few who did survive," Triquet said. At one point, Triquet heard someone mewling softly as he passed a slit trench. Going over, he discovered one of his young soldiers had been blinded hours before by a wound. Mortified that the boy had gone untreated for so long, Triquet asked why he had not called for help earlier. The wounded man said everybody was "too busy."[14]

Their thirst was agonizing. German snipers had the well completely covered, and all the Van Doos' canteens were empty. The wounded suffered the most. Ammunition was desperately short. Smith sent men back to loot the nearest knocked-out tank for shells, but there were still too few. If the Germans threw tanks against their position, there would only be a couple of minutes' worth of shells available to throw them back. After that, the four Shermans would be impotent chunks of steel. The Van Doos stripped the many wounded gathered in the stable and cellar of bullets and grenades. The harvest was pathetic. Even Triquet could hardly find words of inspiration around which the defenders could rally. "Ils ne passeront pas" was all he could offer. It was enough. The men grinned at him and stared over their gunsights. If the Germans came they would die.

At 1515 they did come. Two hundred infantry and several tanks drove directly up the road from Cider Crossroads toward the small island of defenders. Royal Canadian Horse Artillery Acting Captain Harald Martin was on high ground overlooking Casa Berardi. With Donald dead, Martin was the only remaining forward observation officer. His section came under heavy mortar and machine-gun fire. Snipers seemed to be hidden everywhere. In an action that would earn him the Military Cross, Martin ignored the enemy fire, ran up to an exposed outcrop where he could see the enemy advance, and brought accurate artillery fire down upon it. The maelstrom he called down shattered the German counterattack. But Martin had exposed himself. The Germans swung an antitank gun his way and let loose.[15] Martin was hit by shrapnel in both legs.[16] He refused to be relieved, lying on the overlook and continuing to direct accurate fire on the counterattack.

During the day, the RCHA fired 5,938 rounds in support of the Van Doos and the rest of 3 CIB. In a fifteen-minute period during the counterattack, the RCHA threw 1,500 rounds on the Germans in response to Martin's firing directions. Because of the difficulty moving the shells from the roads to the gun pits, most of these shells were carried on the run from the roadside for up to several hundred yards before being almost immediately shoved into the gun breeches and fired off. The gunners were staggering with exhaustion when the firing mission was over.

Looking out from his tank, Smith thought the shelling brought down on the Germans looked like "a large porridge pot bubbling."[17] With the help of the artillery, the Van Doos and the Ontario Tanks managed to stave off the counterattack. Casualties were heavy on both sides. When the attack broke, only seventy-nine infantry from all ranks manned the perimeter at Casa Berardi. Eighty-eight men were casualties. The aid posts in the cellar of the manor house and the stables overflowed with screaming and moaning men.[18] As darkness cloaked the battlefield, Smith could hear the Germans moving across the field and picking up their wounded. It sounded as if there were many of them.[19]

Major Jean Allard organized the rear headquarters into a rifle company. Cooks, typists, quartermasters, mechanics, and other rear-area personnel grabbed rifles, awkwardly fit themselves into combat webbing, and prepared to move out. A supply train of ammunition-laden mules and tanks carrying munitions for the tank squadrons at Casa Berardi formed up. Food, medical supplies, and replacement radios were jammed into the remaining spaces inside the tanks or lashed onto the outside hulls. Nobody knew whether the supply column could get through. Allard's small relief force set out well into the night and passed through to Casa Berardi without incident. The Germans slipped away from it, like so many ghosts. Allard organized the evacuation of the most badly wounded on the mules. He also delivered relief orders to Lieutenant Colonel Paul Bernatchez.[20] At first Bernatchez protested, but finally Allard convinced him that he should obey the ordered three weeks' leave in Cairo.[21] The Van Doos' commander was exhausted, probably suffering battle fatigue.[22] Allard took over. RCHA liaison to the Van Doos, Major "Duff" Mitchell, came up and established an observation post in the upper storey of the manor house.

Allard arrived at Casa Berardi with more than supplies and a means to evacuate the most badly wounded and the Van Doos commander. He brought orders directing the survivors to hold Casa Berardi at all costs for forty-eight hours.[23] It would take this long for 1 CIB to organize the flanking assault now understood to be the only means to crack The Gully. Hearing this news, Triquet stretched out on an old bed in the part of the manor house that served as battalion HQ. He slept in a comalike state for twenty hours.[24]

The defensive strength of Casa Berardi now rested on the supporting tanks, rather than the Van Doos. Although all four companies were present, their combined strength did not equal one full-strength company. Only seventy-nine men remained in the line. They took up defensive positions behind the tanks, instead of the normal procedure which would have seen them out front protecting the armour. Yet despite their exhaustion and reduced numbers, the soldiers in Royal 22e Regiment never doubted their ability to hold Casa Berardi against anything the Germans might throw their way.[25]

The forty-eight-hour pause was necessary. Unprecedented use of artillery had drained ammunition reserves. Every shell had to be brought thirty-five miles from the Sangro to the twenty-five-pounder gun positions. The daily requirement for the Canadian artillery regiments was 16,000 shells.[26] From the roads, the ammunition had to be carried through a deepening sea of mud. During the past few days, the recoil of the guns had embedded them so deeply in the muck that they had to be winched back to the surface. The gunners were exhausted and the delay gave them a necessary respite.

Not that the guns ceased firing. The thump of German and Canadian artillery continued to be heard across the entirety of the battlefield. Both sides were conducting aggressive patrolling; both sides continued to try and destroy known front-line strong points.

The rate of fire lessened, but the battlefield was never silent or free from danger.

◆ ◆ ◆

For fifteen-year-old Antonio Di Cesare, artillery was more of a danger than ever. Villa Deo, near Villa Grande, was being fired on more often by the Canadian guns. Some distance behind Villa Grande, the Germans had set up light artillery and heavy mortars. Their fire attracted counterfire. Enough of this fell short to make the fields surrounding Villa Deo dangerous, so the civilians no longer tried to work them. They stayed indoors most of the time. They waited for the Allies to come and liberate the village. They waited for the war to pass.[27]

To the immediate east of a ravine bordering Ortona, former navy gunner Antonio D'Intino refused to be driven from the fields. It was now more necessary than ever for him to tend the olives and vineyards. Explosions and shrapnel from artillery inflicted terrible damage on his plants. Pruning and staking were required to save them. The lines that held up the grape vines had to be constantly replaced. The family farm was pocked with shell holes. Then there were the dud rounds in the mud. Some disappeared entirely, forming deadly mines that he had to be careful not to unearth or trigger when tilling the soil. Others lay with detonators exposed. Having handled munitions for years in the navy, D'Intino was not scared by these shells. The twenty-eight-year-old would defuse them himself and render them harmless. If for some reason that appeared too dangerous, he would use some of the explosive from shells he had dismantled to blow the new one up.

When the shells fell on his farm and D'Intino was caught in the open, he took cover in the nearest of the many small holes he had dug for shelter from the German work crew roundups. The Germans who were now in Ortona had no further interest in D'Intino, as there were no more work crews. The soldiers were only interested in what vegetables he had in the garden that were ready to harvest. He could not stop them carrying off the food. D'Intino and his aged father frequently went hungry as a result. His father's health worried him. The old man grew weaker each day. He could not go outside, for he could not run fast enough to reach shelter if the shells came.

Across the ravine, Ortona was sometimes battered by shells or Allied bombers. Often smoke rose from the town. D'Intino also heard the sound of explosives going off throughout Ortona. He wondered if the Germans intended to destroy the entire town. Why else were there so many explosions?[28]

Americo Casanova had been sent to Tollo, a village to the north of Ortona and Villa Grande. His mother had thought the thirteen-year-old would be safe there from the fighting. Now the shelling of Tollo was increasing daily because of the nearby German artillery and mortar emplacements. Americo and about 150 other civilians took shelter in a large cave near the village. The cave had a big stone house in front of it. It had been the house's winery, and made an excellent shelter from the bombardments. There were no lights, however, only candles. And few of those. So the civilians lived in an almost perpetual nighttime. Food was scarce. There was little to eat other than grapes and apples. Everyone was hungry, all the time.

There were other young boys. Every day, a few of them would sneak from the cave to explore and watch the Germans who had occupied the village. They also foraged for food. Americo and two boys found some roasting corn and made a small fire to roast it on. They sat in a row before the fire, Americo in the centre. A shell fell nearby and a piece of shrapnel struck the boy on Americo's right. There had been no time to duck or flatten on the ground. Americo looked at his friend. He sat as before, still gazing into the fire at the corn. But the boy was dead.[29]

◆ ◆ ◆

The Germans used their two-day respite well. They dug deeper holes, set more minefields, and rigged more booby traps. They also started demolishing buildings in Ortona to create obstacles in the event that they must defend the town. Although this preliminary work was underway, the paratroopers still did not expect to seriously defend Ortona. Both Allied and Axis infantry doctrine did not support fighting in built-up areas, because it was difficult to control the flow of battle and the forces involved were often at risk of being encircled. When the Canadians came to Ortona they would probably bypass it. Such a manoeuvre would necessitate a German withdrawal from the town to avoid being encircled and trapped there, as the German army had previously been trapped in Stalingrad. If the Canadians breached The Gully for good, the expectation was that there would be a delaying action and then a retreat to the next natural defensive barrier — the Arielli River. That the Canadians would fight their way right into the town was almost unthinkable.

But it was well to be prepared. Since December 12, Feldwebel Fritz Illi and his platoon had been busy digging positions into the rubble created by knocking down buildings throughout Ortona. Sometimes the Allies helped by destroying buildings with their shelling. As Illi and his men worked on setting up positions that enjoyed good fields of fire down the streets, Fallschirmpioniers laid mines all over, especially where they would serve to protect the paratroopers' firing positions.

There were few veterans in Illi's platoon. Most of the men were new recruits and Illi thought their training substandard. The youngest man in the platoon was seventeen, the oldest twenty-eight. Few had seen combat before. Illi expected that many of them would die in Ortona. They had too little experience. The inexperienced soldier in battle was a danger to himself. He knew that those who survived for a week or two would have a better chance of surviving in the long term. It was the new soldiers who died most quickly. They made stupid mistakes and sometimes those mistakes got veterans killed as well. It made the veterans wary of the inexperienced soldiers. For now, however, the front was rather quiet. This would give the new soldiers a bit of time to get used to the sound of battle. It also meant they had time to prepare. When Tommy came, Illi's men would be able to give him a proper welcome.[30]

# 18

## MORNING GLORY

BEFORE the major offensive to seize Cider Crossroads got underway on December 18, Major General Chris Vokes decided to test the waters one last time at The Gully. Intelligence reported that the Germans were thinning out their lines, slowly withdrawing strength from their formerly uncrackable defensive positions around Cider. If this were true, it might still be possible to break through to Cider with a more limited, less complex, assault than the one being mounted.

The battered West Nova Scotia Regiment was ordered to probe the German defences with a strong attack. Three companies would participate: 'A,' 'B,' and 'C.' Their combined strength was only 160 men. At 1600 hours on December 17, the West Novas lunged at the German lines, supported by three Ontario tanks.[1]

They stumbled only a short distance through the mud before the Germans opened fire. The war diarist for 3rd Canadian Infantry Brigade wrote after the action that the West Novas walked into "very heavy enemy opposition . . . estimated enemy strength 500 with heavy covering fire from North of gulch. Enemy in area attacked appeared to have large number of MGs." The West Novas gave everything they had, bravely pushing head on into the gunfire despite mounting casualties. The tanks set a couple of houses on fire with shells and destroyed several haystacks that camouflaged German firing positions.[2] One tank was damaged when a Teller mine tore a track apart, but none of the tankers was wounded.[3] Around the armour, the West Novas were cut to bits. In only twenty minutes, the regiment was forced to retreat. A fifth of its remaining men had been killed or wounded.[4] Six officers were wounded, including Lieutenant G.F. Archibald, who had been mortally wounded and had to be abandoned on the field with a few other casualties. Rescued by the Germans, he died in their first aid post. Lieutenant Gordon Romkey narrowly escaped death on the very lip of The Gully. Rushing an enemy gun position, he was hit in the side of the head by a Schmeisser submachine gunburst fired at point-blank range. The unconscious officer was dragged to safety by his men.[5]

After the West Novas returned to their slit trenches, Major Ron Waterman wearily returned to brigade headquarters and reported to Brigadier Graeme Gibson. To date, he said, the West Novas had suffered 44 killed and 150 wounded in front of The Gully. Eighteen officers were dead or wounded, including former battalion commander Lieutenant Colonel Pat Bogert. These casualties, combined with losses due to sickness and battle exhaustion, rendered the regiment unfit for further offensive combat.[6] In ordering the attack, Vokes had brought about the near destruction of one of his nine infantry regiments.

♦ ♦ ♦

Vokes, however, still had eight other battalions. He had the close-to-normal fighting strength of the 48th Highlanders of Canada. And he had a combined arms two-stage offensive. The first stage was codenamed Morning Glory, the second Orange Blossom. Morning Glory was the 48th Highlanders' show. The regiment would cross the Ortona-Orsogna lateral road west of where the Royal 22e Regiment was isolated in Casa Berardi, advance north across open ground, and then swing right to cut into a road running from Cider Crossroads to Villa Grande. Once the 48th Highlanders had blocked this road, Orange Blossom would kick into action. This stage of the offensive called for the Royal Canadian Regiment to follow the Highlanders' path across the Ortona-Orsogna lateral but to swing right much earlier. The regiment would advance on a path bordered to the south by the Ortona-Orsogna lateral and to the north by a railroad track leading to Ortona. Once the RCR were astride the road from Cider Crossroads to Villa Grande, it would take a sharp right and, approaching from the north, overrun Cider. With Cider secure, the RCR would then advance up the Ortona-Orsogna lateral to Ortona's outskirts.

Both regiments were given tank support by 12th Canadian Armoured Regiment (Three Rivers Tanks). 'B' Squadron would attack with the 48th Highlanders, 'A' Squadron with the RCR. Held until now in reserve, this was the first involvement of the Three Rivers in the prolonged December battle.

Success for Morning Glory and Orange Blossom depended on overwhelming artillery support. The Germans were dug into defensive positions rivalling those of the Western Front in World War I. Just as it had required massive artillery barrages to blast the Germans out of their holes in that war, so the same force would be required to break the defences surrounding Cider Crossroads. The planned artillery operation dwarfed the earlier Moro River barrage, especially in terms of the concentration of fire. Fully 250 guns would participate.

Beginning at 0800 hours, the Morning Glory barrage would plaster a 1,000-yard-wide front and advance a distance of 2,200 yards. Every five minutes, the barrage would lift from the 300-yard-deep area it was concentrating on and move another 100 yards forward. The 48th Highlanders would follow behind this curtain of explosive at a distance never greater than 100 yards. The artillery officers promised the infantry that the trajectory of the shells would assure that the shrapnel and blast would be thrown into the faces of the Germans rather than back at the advancing soldiers.

Accurate fire was essential. If the barrage failed to hit where it was supposed to, and at the time it was supposed to, the attack would fail. In the worse case, misdirected or ill-timed artillery might slaughter the 48th Highlanders, who would be completely exposed to the exploding shells. Everybody knew the military maps that had been based on Italian sources were riddled with topographical and distance errors. To correct for this, observed artillery fire was carefully carried out along the planned line of advance throughout December 16 and 17. The firing was so spread out that to German eyes it would have appeared as nothing more than the normal random harassing fire both sides engaged in every day. New map references were then drawn up by artillery command. Forty-Eighth Highlander commander Lieutenant Colonel Ian Johnston was assured that, despite the fact that the new references bore little relation to coordinates on the previous maps, they would be accurate. The thirty-five-year-old officer from Toronto could only hope the gunners were right.

Due to the presence of the Royal 22e Regiment at Casa Berardi and increasingly deteriorating weather, observed artillery fire to correct the maps for Orange Blossom proved impossible. The gunners were forced to develop a firing plan based on the Italian maps. In the past, firing plans had sometimes been out by as much as 500 metres because of map inaccuracies. Everybody knew that basing a 250-gun barrage on the maps was extremely risky, but there was no alternative.[7]

It was estimated that each gun involved in Morning Glory and Orange Blossom would fire 600 rounds. During Morning Glory, the guns would be firing continually for 130 minutes — the time allotted for the 48th Highlanders to cross the start line and reach the objective.[8] The Royal Canadian Horse Artillery alone manhandled 8,880 twenty-five pounder shells and cartridges to its guns for the day's shoot — a total weight of 111 tons.[9] In addition to the artillery, every mortar in 1st Canadian Infantry Division, as well as the Saskatoon Light Infantry's anti-aircraft guns and Vickers medium machine guns, would rake the German positions in The Gully to force the defenders there to stay under cover while the attack went in behind them.[10]

The Canadians would not be attacking alone. Eighth Indian Division was to cross the Ortona-Orsogna lateral road and capture the village of Crecchio on the southern shore of the Arielli River. A feint, the attack would serve to prevent the Germans from moving reinforcements from this part of the line to engage the advancing Canadians. If successful, the attack would also give the 8th Indian Division a solid base from which to carry out a later advance on Villa Grande, an objective falling within its area of responsibility.[11]

On the night of December 17, Lieutenant Colonel Johnston held his final Orders Group conference in a small house near San Leonardo. The officers conducted the meeting by the flicker of candlelight. The degree of cooperation required to mount Morning Glory was evidenced by the number of officers in attendance. Thirty-five men crowded into the room. Only seven were 48th Highlanders. The rest represented the supporting units the infantry depended on. At the conclusion of the briefing, Johnston asked, "Any questions?" Normally there would be at least a few for even the most limited engagement. This night not a single question was asked.[12]

◆ ◆ ◆

The day before, the 48th Highlanders had been treated to a visit to a mobile bath station. At 0500 hours on December 18, the infantry were surprised to receive a hot breakfast, rather than the cold chow that had been the month's norm. The food helped warm them on this bitter morning. It was cold, with a nasty rain falling, and the ground underfoot was sloppy.[13]

Mud. They could never seem to escape it. As 0800 hours approached, Johnston was told by Three Rivers 'B' Squadron commander Major J.P.C. Mills that the night's heavy rain had rendered the ground too soft. If he took the tanks into the orchards and vineyards, they would only get stuck. The going would be greatly worsened when the artillery had finished churning up the fields.

Searching frantically for some solution, the two officers remembered there was a narrow donkey track to the right of the 48th Highlanders' line of attack. Mills agreed to take his twelve tanks single file up the track. The risk was great. In all probability, the Germans would have barred the use of the track with Teller antitank mines. If the first tank was blown up, the others, surrounded by a sea of mud, would be trapped.[14]

At 0700 hours, the 48th Highlanders moved to the assembly area and started a final equipment check. Nerves were taut. They were unfamiliar with the method of attack, and following the artillery barrage so closely was a frightening idea. Johnston would have to keep his men moving with the flow of the barrage. He could not afford to have the leading companies delayed in firefights with German strong points. So he decided to launch an uncommon Y-formation attack. This meant that Captain Lloyd Smith's 'D' Company would form the left upper point of a Y, Major John Clarke's 'A' Company the right point. Creating a base in the centre behind the two companies would be 'C' Company. Johnston's battalion HQ would follow 'C' Company, with 'B' Company serving as a reserve to the immediate rear. During the advance, 'A' and 'D' companies were to keep going no matter what. They were not to get locked into skirmishes to destroy pockets of resistance. This mopping up would be 'C' Company's job. The two leading companies were to reach the objective and secure it before the barrage ended. Nothing must be allowed to slow them.

Precisely at 0800 hours, the massed artillery fired as one. "The barrage opened," read an after-action report, "with a deafening roar, filling the air with the screams and sighing of passing shells and laying down a wall of bursting HE [high explosive] 1,000 yards long by over 300 yards deep." One observer called it "terrifying and effective."[15] In front of the 48th Highlanders, the ground erupted in geysers of earth quickly obscured by a thick fog of smoke. For twenty minutes, the barrage pounded down and the infantry and tanks waited. Then the officers moved forward and the 48th Highlanders crossed the starting line.

Orders came through hand signals and the commanding presence of the platoon leaders at the very front of the leading line. Everybody was partially deafened by the explosions, so verbal orders were useless. The two lead companies waded through mud, trying to keep up with the advancing artillery as it followed its schedule of a 100-yard lift every five minutes. Although described as open ground, the battlefield was a bewildering mess of shattered orchards and demolished vineyards. Wire for supporting the vines tried to tangle the men's feet and legs as they stumbled through the mud. Smoke lay so thick that visibility was cut to 200 yards. Platoon leaders used compasses to find their way.[16] Responding quickly to the surprise attack, the Germans brought light artillery and mortar fire down behind the advancing Canadian barrage. This failed to slow the 48th Highlanders' advance and casualties were light.[17]

Off to the right, the tanks struggled up the donkey track. The two lead tanks made relatively good progress, finding the path fairly firm under their tracks. Behind them, the next three tanks had a more difficult time because the first two had churned up the track. The other seven tanks were unable to make any progress up the muddy path and had to break off their advance. As they proceeded, the five remaining tanks fired on every building passed and blew apart haystacks that might hide German tanks or antitank guns.[18]

'A' and 'D' companies charged across the Ortona-Orsogna lateral road and started pushing through networks of enemy slit trenches. Many of the deeper trenches were collapsed. Dead and dying Germans lay everywhere. Few of the machine guns were manned. The Canadians rolled grenades onto the guns and, in compliance with their orders, kept going. Every wine cellar or deep hole in the ground had a grenade tossed into it. Behind 'A' and 'D' companies, the two following companies engaged in random, bitter exchanges of gunfire. While some of the Germans, now known to be paratroopers, stood and fought to the death, many others scattered to the right and left to escape the 48th Highlanders' advancing line.

The leading companies went so fast they were in danger of overrunning their own barrage. Johnston watched anxiously from his position at the rear of 'C' Company as the soldiers in the forward companies had to lie in the open "for long moments to wait for the shells to lift. In the open stretches, the boys were generally right up with our shells, and waiting for them to lift. Near the end, we had to check them or they'd have gone right into it."[19]

Major Clarke thought his men's discipline was "superb. The shell curtain carried us right to the objective."[20] At 1030, Clarke and Smith's companies reached the road running from Cider Crossroads to Villa Grande. A jubilant Clarke told his radioman to signal "Aster," the code for the final objective. The remainder of the battalion quickly arrived and consolidated the position.[21] The five tanks slogged into the perimeter shortly thereafter. As the first two approached, they mistook the Canadian infantrymen for Germans and fired a couple of shells before identities were clarified. A tanker, explaining the error to a 48th Highlander sergeant, said, "One of you muddied goofs looks exactly like those other muddied goofs."[22]

Considering the strength of the German defences, casualties were remarkably light. Four infantry were killed, twenty wounded. Half the casualties resulted either from short Canadian artillery rounds or the German artillery and mortar fire.[23]

It was a remarkable feat of arms.

◆ ◆ ◆

Morning Glory included a protective barrage delivered on the 48th Highlanders' left flank. Several salvoes of shells from this barrage fell directly on Villa Deo, where young Antonio Di Cesare and many civilians were caught inside the few houses or in small caves located in a nearby grotto. To Antonio, it seemed the shelling lasted for three to four hours. It was probably no more than fifteen to twenty minutes. Antonio and the twenty or so other people in his house cowered under the beds and kitchen table. The house was a side-by-side duplex, with a cement wall between the two units. Every time a shell exploded nearby, the entire building shook. Dust and plaster poured down from the ceiling. The windows shattered. Most of the shells were exploding on the other side of the duplex, spraying that unit with shrapnel.

Antonio heard a noise from the dividing wall. The thumping went on for minute after minute. Then suddenly a part of the wall fell away and hands reached into the room. Working with only a trowel and some kitchen utensils, the people in the adjoining home had breached the wall. They now widened the hole and started frantically squirming into the relative safety of the other unit. Five of them had been injured by shrapnel. Sheets and clothing were torn up to make bandages, but there was little else anyone could do for the wounded. There were no proper bandages or medicines to ease the pain.

The barrage ceased as suddenly as it had begun. A deep quiet descended. Huddled in the house, Antonio and the others found the silence as frightening as the bombardment's din. They had no idea what danger would come next. Antonio's uncle and another man crept to the front door and unbarred it. Opening it a crack, they peered into the lane and then, seeing nothing, stepped outside for a better look. Antonio followed. The air was choked with smoke and dust. Several figures were coming from the southeast toward the scattered houses. They moved carefully and furtively up the lane, darting forward in short dashes before ducking into cover. Antonio realized the helmets they wore were pan-shaped rather than the closer-fitting ones of the Germans. "The liberators are here," he told his uncle.

In truth, the liberators were just passing through. This was a 48th Highlander fighting patrol trying to make contact with the 8th Indian Division, and investigating the German strength positioned between the 48th Highlanders and Villa Grande. As he walked past, one mud-caked Canadian tossed Antonio a crumpled pack of cigarettes and said curtly, "Keep your head down, boy." Antonio ducked back into the house and the men barred the door.

◆ ◆ ◆

At 1145 hours, it was the Royal Canadian Regiment's turn. Orange Blossom opened with just as stupendous a barrage as Morning Glory. But where everything had proceeded like clockwork with Morning Glory, the inability to register the targets with observed fire the day before plunged Orange Blossom into immediate chaos.

The RCR's two leading companies, 'C' and 'D,' went forward on schedule. They were seriously understrength. In 'D' Company, Lieutenant Mitch Sterlin's No. 16 Platoon numbered just nine men. As the other two platoons had only sergeants for leaders, Sterlin's platoon took the company's point position. Throughout the Italian campaign, RCR attacks had almost always been led by 'A' and 'B' companies. The night before, the new battalion commander, Major Bill Mathers, had decided these companies needed a break.[24]

Mathers had taken over the battalion on December 16 when RCR commander Lieutenant Colonel Dan Spry assumed brigade command from Brigadier Howard Graham. The brigadier had to be evacuated because his ulcer had worsened. Mathers was a small, precise officer. On December 17, he made his command intentions clear during a battalion parade near San Leonardo. "Things are going to change in this regiment," he snapped. "No more slackness, no more slovenliness. Spit and polish smartness, and clean shaven daily, even if you have to shave in your own urine!"[25] He went on to berate the men to be more alert. A failure to be alert, declared the new commander, was the reason so many RCR had been killed and wounded during the battle for the Moro River crossing.

It was a poor start for an officer as yet untested by combat. In less than forty-eight hours as battalion commander, Mathers managed to earn the hostility of almost every officer and man in the regiment. In the mud and terrible conditions of the Ortona area battleground, being clean-shaven and maintaining a tidy uniform were clearly impossible. None of the men bothered shaving in urine. Quiet anger lurked in the ranks. Mathers told 'B' Company commander Major Strome Galloway that although he must remain with the reserve companies rather than marching at the head of the attacking companies, he did so with regret. Galloway, facing his fifteenth attack of the war, replied that he would happily remain with the reserves. Brimming with martial feistiness, Mathers ordered one platoon commander to conduct a fighting patrol into the very heart of Ortona the moment Cider Crossroads fell. "It is a job any subaltern would give his right arm to get," Mathers responded testily when the officer protested that the order was suicidal.[26]

If Mathers wanted to see the RCR perish in a bold and glorious charge against the enemy, he had no need to do so by throwing men into Ortona. Orange Blossom would come close to doing the job for him. As 'C' and 'D' companies crossed the start line, shells from the artillery barrage started falling on the Carleton and York Regiment overlooking The Gully and also on the 48th Highlanders. Both battalions radioed panicked calls for the artillery to be lifted.

The attack itself was going well at this point. Both companies were progressing against minimal resistance with 'A' Squadron of the Three Rivers Tanks following close behind. But the ever more wildly inaccurate artillery was killing and wounding soldiers in several Canadian positions. To stop what could turn into a friendly-fire slaughter, the gunners had to lift the barrage 400 yards ahead of the RCR and stop laying down protective fire on the battalion's exposed right-hand flank, which was bordered by the deeply entrenched German positions inside The Gully.

The moment the barrage was adjusted, the Germans returned to their guns. Both leading companies were decimated in minutes by a combined outpouring of machine-gun, mortar, and light artillery fire. 'D' Company commander Major Gerry Nelson, who had given Galloway a wink when he learned his company would lead the attack, was killed. Captain Chuck Lithgow, 'C' Company commander, was severely wounded. All the platoon leaders of both 'C' and 'D' companies were dead, wounded, or missing. Every man in Lieutenant Mitch Sterlin's No. 16 Platoon died. Sterlin was in the lead, with his men following behind in an arrowhead formation. The German paratroopers cut them down in a sustained volley of machine-gun fire.[27]

Acting Corporal Red Forrest was the senior man left in 'C' Company. He took over command of the remaining dozen men. Pinned in a couple of shell holes on the edge of The Gully, the small force held out for more than an hour against repeated counterattacks until a rescue party cut through to cover their withdrawal. When the rescue force arrived, they found Forrest fighting like a demon. He had been fighting almost maniacally for the entire time the unit was cut off, throwing grenade after grenade and loosing off furious bursts from his Thompson submachine gun. His actions probably saved the unit from capture or destruction. At one point, a sergeant lying in a nearby shell hole called out to him, "Who the hell do you think you are — Sergeant York?"[28] (Sergeant Alvin York was a World War I American who single-handedly captured 132 German soldiers on October 17, 1918.) Forrest's courage won him the Distinguished Conduct Medal.

But bravery was not enough. The RCR attack had been stopped cold. With the two forward companies both reduced to no more than fifteen men, Mathers ordered the battalion to consolidate in the shelter of a few buildings just 100 yards ahead of the start line. As he delivered the orders, Mathers was shot in the arm by a sniper. Galloway later found him looking "the heroic commander. His right arm rested in a black silk sling. He was smoking his pipe, and with his left arm was handing out instructions with dramatic gestures."[29] The seriously ill second-in-command, Major Ian Hodson, was brought up from the rear to replace Mathers. The RCR were happy to see Mathers go.

In the aftermath of Orange Blossom's failure, a new plan was improvised to seize Cider Crossroads the next day. Lieutenant Colonel Spry, seeing the battalion he loved in ruins, was forced to make a "terrible" decision. "The battalion," he wrote later, "was reduced to a strength of nineteen officers, one hundred and fifty-nine O.Rs [Other Ranks]. . . . I knew that as a battalion, the RCR would be worthless from the point of view of morale unless they got on their objective. . . . For morale and tactical reasons therefore it was vital for the RCR to return to the attack."[30]

During the night, Galloway approached Lieutenant Jimmy Quayle and offered him a revolver. "Where did you get it?" Quayle asked. "From Sterlin's body," Galloway replied. Quayle responded automatically, "No thanks, I don't really need it." He was in a state of shock. He prayed that a ghastly mistake had been made. Sterlin and he had survived so much together. "We were indestructible," he later wrote. All night Quayle waited for Sterlin to "come wandering in, dumb grin on his big, fat face, remnants of his platoon following, and saying, 'Hi fellows. Sorry we're late.' But he never came, that evening or ever."[31]

# 19

# THE DRIVE
# TO ORTONA

At dawn on December 19, the remaining officers of the Royal Canadian Regiment gathered in a small shack for an Orders Group. Major Ian Hodson told them that 'C' and 'D' companies, with a platoon from 'B' Company, were to amalgamate to form a single company numbering barely fifty men. 'A' and 'B' companies, each mustering about sixty-five men, would once again assume the lead, as they had done for every attack except the previous day's fiasco. Zero hour was noon. Lieutenant Jimmy Quayle shuddered as the attack plan developed: ". . . all expendable," he thought, "every single one of us."[1]

Even before the RCR Orders Group, offensive action was underway to ensure that Cider Crossroads fell at last. At 0600 hours, Captain L. Maraskas rolled up to December 18's RCR start line with tanks of 'A' Squadron's No. 2 Troop. Forming a line, the five tanks hammered two buildings housing machine-gun positions that had played a primary role in destroying 'D' Company. The tanks kept firing until the buildings were demolished. As No. 2 Troop returned from this mission, one tank lost a track to a Teller antitank mine.[2] It was believed the mine must have been planted by German sappers during the night, as the area had appeared free of mines the day before.

'A' Squadron joined up with the RCR just before noon. Major Strome Galloway climbed into the squadron commander's tank. Galloway would be the infantry force commander, as Hodson was too sick to perform the task. From the tank, he could direct the armoured support for the infantry, have constant radio communication with the supporting artillery, and still pass orders to the infantry platoons.[3]

Noon came and the orders to move were postponed. Fuel and ammunition for the tanks had failed to arrive. The road between San Leonardo and the front lines was awash with mud, hampering the movement of armoured supplies. Zero hour was set back to 1415 hours. The delay, noted an after-action report, "caused considerable mental agony to the waiting troops."[4]

Finally it was 1415. Supported by another intense creeping artillery barrage, the RCR moved out with the refuelled and re-armed tanks in tow. 'B' Company led, 'A' Company followed along in line with the tanks. It was a grisly advance. Quayle wrote that he "plodded despairingly over the shattered terrain past the bodies of 'C' and 'D' companies. I walked by Mitch. He lay flat on his back, ungainly as usual. Unseeing brown eyes stared at the sky and dark brown hair, neatly combed, stirred slightly in the wind. His steel helmet had fallen off and sat close by. His men lay in a ragged line on either side. . . . But something was missing. Madame Tussaud had done a good likeness but it was not quite Mitch. An astoundingly good effigy but that was all. Good waxworks."[5]

Shortly before dark, 'B' Company virtually strolled onto Cider Crossroads. They had met hardly any resistance and taken only two casualties. 'A' Company arrived and set up south of where the railway crossed the road running from Cider to Villa Grande. The tanks assumed supporting positions among the infantry.[6] Galloway hopped down from the tank he had been riding in and stared about at the objective over which so much blood had been spilled. It was "one complete mass of smoking shell craters and blasted trees." Selecting the largest nearby house as a command post, he moved a radio inside and then contacted battalion HQ. Major Hodson was now to bring up the amalgamated force built out of 'C' and 'D' companies and No. 4 Platoon (the Bren Carrier platoon) acting as straight infantry.[7]

Hodson's small group crossed the start line, expecting a virtual walk in the park after the easy time the lead companies had enjoyed. For 200 yards it was just that, but suddenly an intense barrage of well-directed German artillery caught both No. 4 Platoon in the lead and the battalion HQ section at the rear. Three men were killed, several others wounded. No. 4 Platoon started taking concentrated small-arms fire from a house on its flank. The small unit fell back "in disorder" to the rest of the force. Hodson decided to go to ground where they were until the German artillery eased.

Growing sicker by the minute, Hodson found it difficult to control his men and make firm decisions. He vacillated this way and that, but "eventually . . . decided to wait and move up after dark," the regimental war diarist recorded the next day. "When darkness came there was still much indecision until some of the junior Officers took the matter in hand and organized the move. . . . The group moved off, Sgt. Terry and Cpl. Davidson volunteering to lead. They led the composite [company] under Lt. [J.B.] Smith along the left of the [railway.]"[8]

Hodson's command group and what was left of No. 4 Platoon covered the rear. Things were so confused that some of the men failed to receive the order to advance and were left behind. They only joined the rest of the battalion in the morning. Not until 2100 hours did Hodson's group reach the forward companies of the RCR at the Cider Crossroads objective.[9] By this time, Galloway had organized a defensive firing plan with the supporting artillery. Plans had also been made to bring antitank guns, mortars, and Vickers medium machine guns into the position the following morning. Having finally seized Cider, the RCR was not going to be thrown back from it. If the Germans counterattacked, Galloway was determined the regiment would make the paratroopers suffer the same fate the RCR had endured the previous day.

♦ ♦ ♦

At 1st Canadian Infantry Division headquarters, Major General Chris Vokes wasted no time celebrating the capture of Cider Crossroads after two weeks of fighting. For the past few days, 2nd Canadian

Infantry Brigade had been kept largely out of the battle, giving it a chance to regroup, draw some reinforcements, and have a brief rest. On the evening of December 19, Vokes had the Seaforth Highlanders of Canada relieve the exhausted Hastings and Prince Edward Regiment from its long-held bridgehead on the coast road before The Gully. The Loyal Edmonton Regiment moved up to a position just behind Cider Crossroads. Meanwhile, the Carleton and York Regiment crossed The Gully and mopped up enemy positions on the north side of the lateral road to clear the way for the morning's assault on Ortona. Serving as a reserve battalion, the Princess Patricia's Canadian Light Infantry remained on Vino Ridge about a mile inland.[10] Another creeping barrage was planned that would precede an attack by the Loyal Edmontons up the Ortona-Orsogna lateral road into Ortona itself. As this attack went in, the Seaforths would break through The Gully directly in front of Ortona and fight their way into the town. Zero hour was set for noon on December 20.

Canadian intelligence officers advised Vokes that: "Having lost control of the [crossroads], the enemy is likely to fall back under pressure in the Northern sector, abandoning Ortona, and making his next stand on the line of the Arielli. . . . This is difficult country, well suited to delaying tactics and should provide a firm hinge for an eventual withdrawal in the Northern sector."[11] Vokes felt confident that once Brigadier Bert Hoffmeister got his two infantry regiments up to the Ortona outskirts, the 1st Parachute Division would withdraw to the north of Ortona.

Eighth Army headquarters staff were so convinced that the Germans would make no serious stand at Ortona that they were busily developing plans to turn the town into a maintenance and rest area. The high stone buildings of the town were thought ideal for providing comfortable winter quarters for a tired army. It was imagined that the port could soon be reopened and the damage caused there by the Germans easily repaired. For this reason, Ortona had been spared serious aerial or artillery bombardment. This contrasted starkly with the fate of Orsogna to the west, which had been reduced to rubble by almost daily aerial attacks by heavy bombers, light bombers, and fighter bombers flying out of bases in North Africa.[12] One British intelligence summary breezily predicted, "Eighth Army is going to reach the line of the Arielli by 24 Dec."[13] As so often in

European and North American wars, the promise of the end of battle for Christmas was being extended to the soldiers on the front lines. It was a promise that relied on the Germans putting up only a token act of defiance in Ortona.

◆ ◆ ◆

Unknown to the Canadians, 1st Parachute Division had accepted on the evening of December 18 that its defensive line based on The Gully and Cider Crossroads was lost. As the Carleton and York Regiment patrol discovered, the Germans started pulling men out of the deep fighting holes in The Gully soon after nightfall.

In Ortona, the Germans were preparing for far more than a token defence. Paratroop engineers and infantry worked frantically side by side to strengthen the defences. Obergefreiter Karl Bayerlein's Fallschirmpionier platoon had set up quarters near the old castle. Already the streets in the area were so full of debris from buildings shattered by Canadian artillery fire and the German demolitions that reaching his quarters entailed climbing over large rubble piles.

On December 18, Bayerlein and two comrades had gone back to Pescara to bring up more mines from the supply depot there. After loading up a truck with mines, the three men started driving back to Ortona. It was dark and they drove without headlights. Visibility was extremely poor. The driver failed to make a corner and the truck ploughed into a ditch on the right-hand side of the road. Unable to get the truck out of the mud, the three men spent the rest of the night in an abandoned nearby farmhouse. In the morning, the truck was spotted by the Canadians and artillery shells fell near it, but failed to score a direct hit. Bayerlein's companion Marcus, however, was badly wounded by shrapnel. He was evacuated to Pescara by motorcycle.

Bayerlein became separated during the day from his remaining comrade. Deciding nothing could be done to rescue the truck, he started walking back to Ortona. Near an abandoned German artillery piece, he found some captured British grenades and a revolver. He stuffed the booty into his pockets. Ortona was across a ravine. He could see it, but there appeared no easy way to get across the ravine and into the town. Endless salvoes of Canadian mortar shells flew overhead, many detonating harmlessly in the nearby sea. Coming across a large new home, Bayerlein entered it and found a group of men, women, and children in hiding. They offered him warm soup made from tomatoes and beans. He wolfed it down. It was the first food he had eaten since setting off for Pescara the day before. After leaving the house, Bayerlein came upon a railroad tunnel that passed under the ravine to the Ortona docks. Emerging from the far side of the tunnel, he saw for the first time the docks and fishing boats that had been destroyed by German engineers earlier in the month.

As he started following a track up the hill toward Ortona, Bayerlein came under friendly fire. Hitting the dirt, he saw that right ahead of him the path was sown with anti-personnel mines. He retreated, feeling very alone and frightened. Finally he found another route up the escarpment. Exhausted from the climb and his walk across the embattled terrain north of Ortona, Bayerlein flopped down not far from the body of a dead civilian. He slipped into an exhausted stupor.[14]

Soon after the 1st Parachute Division engineers started blowing up buildings, Americo Casanova's mother Angela, sister Maria, and brother Mario left Ortona. While she had sent Americo much earlier to Tollo, Angela had kept her nineteen-year-old daughter and twenty-one-year-old son with her. They had camped out in the countryside, maintaining a protective vigil over the four-unit apartment building that provided both home and livelihood. The decision to stay placed all three of them at great risk. Allied artillery fire often fell almost on top of them and the German soldiers were less predictable than before. Angela thought their behaviour seemed increasingly menacing.

When the soldiers entered the apartments, Angela would go down and try to keep the place from being ransacked. At about the same time that Cider Crossroads was falling into Canadian hands, she realized the futility of her mission when the Germans wired the entire apartment with explosives. Angela tried to reason with them, but was left with the impression that she was being punished for the many American furnishings and other goods that the family apartment contained. She tried to explain that these were from her husband, who worked in the chocolate factory in Hershey, New Jersey, and that she was neither pro-American nor anti-German. The soldiers ignored her. Finally realizing they intended to follow through with their plan, Angela fled. Minutes later, the Germans blew the apartment building in upon itself. Angela Casanova found her two eldest children and the three of them left Ortona, walking north toward Pescara.[15]

◆ ◆ ◆

Throughout the night of December 19 and well into the following morning, the sappers of 4th Field Company, Royal Canadian Engineers, worked frantically to repair the concrete bridge crossing The Gully adjacent to Cider Crossroads. Although the Germans had attempted to destroy it with explosives, the structure still stood. By 1000 hours on December 20, the engineers had laid a new deck and reinforced the minor structural weaknesses. The bridge could now support the massive weight of a Sherman tank or a Bren carrier pulling a six-pounder antitank gun. There would be no more need for the armour and other support weapons to slog across the muddy track curving around The Gully's westernmost extension. They could now come directly from San Leonardo to Cider Crossroads on the old coast highway. The new coast highway, following the Adriatic shoreline to Ortona, remained closed where The Gully widened to meet the sea. The Germans had succeeded in destroying the bridge there and ownership of the surrounding ground remained contested — something the Canadians were determined to change by day's end.

Precisely at noon, the Loyal Edmonton Regiment and the Seaforth Highlanders of Canada kicked off a joint attack toward Ortona. Their objective was to occupy a straggle of buildings bordering an escarpment a short distance from the town's southwestern flank. The Edmontons had farther to go — 3,000 yards, or almost two miles. However, their line of approach would be relatively flat, with the Ortona-Orsogna lateral road to the south and the raised bed of a railroad to the north. Sherman tanks from 'C' Squadron of the Three Rivers Tanks followed the two lead companies forward.

'D' and 'C' companies advanced, walking no more than seventy-five yards behind the forward creep of the artillery fire. 'D' Company's Lieutenant John Dougan and his platoon led that company's attack. Like all of the Edmonton platoons, No. 16 Platoon had only about twenty men instead of the thirty-five that constituted normal strength. The battalion's losses on Vino Ridge had not been completely replenished. Today, however, the low strength hardly mattered. The

Germans put up little resistance. Dougan's troops advanced through a system of zigzag slit trenches. They crossed one line of trenches after another. He caught only brief glimpses of the defending paratroopers through the smoke and explosions of the Canadians' creeping barrage.

"They'd pop up like bloody jackrabbits," he said later, "and you would have had to have a shotgun to get them before they scampered off down the trench. We pressed right on."[16]

As was typical of the man, 'D' Company commander Major Jim Stone had his HQ right up behind Dougan's platoon and the advancing tanks. The lead infantry need only look over their shoulders to see his towering six-foot-five form walking briskly along. For many it was a reassuring sight. Stone, meanwhile, was starting to doubt what he would later describe as the "efficacy of the barrage." Out in the middle of a field, over which the barrage crept with methodical devastation, five large white oxen grazed away in complete disregard of the deadly explosion of shells in their very midst. As the barrage moved on toward Ortona and Stone walked past the still grazing animals, it was apparent that not one had been touched.[17]

While the advance was proceeding well for the Edmontons, the Three Rivers tanks were having a tougher time of it, thanks to mud and Teller antitank mines. Shortly after crossing the start line at Cider Crossroads, Lieutenant T.E. Melvin radioed that his tank was finding it impossible to keep going along his assigned advance line to one side of the railroad. He requested permission to climb up on the road itself, where the traction would be assured. 'C' Squadron commander Captain F.W. Johnson, moving forward in his own tank, agreed.

A few minutes after Melvin's tank gained the road, there was a tremendous explosion. Fellow tankers and Edmonton infantrymen watched in horror as the tank blew apart. Tank parts, including the gear box and tracks, sailed in all directions as far as sixty and seventy yards away. The thirty-two-ton tank was lifted about twenty feet into the air by the blast. The crew — Lieutenant Melvin, and Troopers E. Kemp, J.B. Hughes, A.J. Rau, and G.B. Steenhoff — were all killed instantly.

Engineers, wrote the Three Rivers' war diarist at the end of the day, estimated that the explosion was caused by a remotely triggered charge of 200 pounds of TNT dug into the roadbed. A small group of

Germans, he added, had been left behind in a nearby house, "with instructions to set off the charge and retire if possible or give themselves up. The charge was set off at the opportune moment 'killing two birds with one stone,' and then [they] surrendered to the infantry who were some distance in front of the tank. The infantry took the Germans prisoner before the realization of what had happened dawned on them."[18]

The surviving tanks then became snarled in a heavily sown Teller antitank minefield. Despite a team of pioneers working with mine detection equipment and advancing ahead of the tankers, three tanks ran over mines and had tracks blown off. Another tank got mired in a mud hole just before entering the minefield. The remaining tanks lumbered on and, along with the infantry, arrived at the final objective just outside Ortona at 1426 hours. Stone radioed the signal "Crocus" back to Brigadier Bert Hoffmeister at 2nd Canadian Infantry Brigade HQ. There had been a short, sharp tussle with some paratroopers just in front of the objective. But the combination of the artillery fire, the direct gun support of the tanks, and excellent fire and manoeuvre tactics by the two lead companies had overwhelmed the paratroopers trying to hold the final trench line. Fourteen prisoners were taken.[19] The Edmontons started digging in and waited for the Seaforths to come up on their right-hand flank.

◆ ◆ ◆

The Seaforths' start line was on The Gully's southern crest. At noon, 'D' and 'C' companies would scramble over the lip of The Gully, down the muddy slope, and head for their objectives. 'D' Company commander Captain Alan W. Mercer's immediate objective was the peak of a long spur overlooking the mouth of The Gully. From this position, Mercer's men would provide covering fire for 'C' Company, which was to cross The Gully, scale a steep embankment, and establish a foothold on Ortona's outskirts around the Byzantine-era church, Santa Maria di Costantinopoli. Captain Don Harley, the mortar company commander who had accompanied Captain June Thomas's 'A' Company during its bold flanking attack a week before, had only assumed command of 'C' Company two hours before the attack started. He replaced Major David Blackburn, who had fallen sick and been evacuated.[20]

Harley had attended the morning's Orders Group thinking he would be in reserve. He was feeling quite content, not disappointed at missing the forthcoming fight. Then Lieutenant Colonel Syd Thomson turned to Harley and said, "Oh, by the way, Don, you're in command of 'C' Company. Davie is not well and he's going back." Harley would later recall that he "immediately got the jitters."[21] When the Orders Group broke up, however, he rushed to 'C' Company and got the men organized. Soon they were looking out over The Gully. Below them lay a brick factory, and on top of the facing escarpment Harley could see the church with Ortona behind. The day was clear and cold, visibility good.

'D' Company jumped off first, moving behind a light screen of artillery fire. Company Sergeant Major Jock Gibson stuck close to Mercer's side. Recently promoted to CSM, Gibson still had no real idea what his role was supposed to be. He figured it was safe to assume a CSM should be near the commander. As they approached the spur, some shells landed short, falling around the company HQ unit. Mercer was hit. Gibson took the runner's rifle, the runner grabbed Mercer, and the two men dragged the injured officer to cover.[22] 'D' Company started taking heavy small-arms fire from the area around 'C' Company's objective. At the peak of the spur, the men found what shelter they could and returned fire. As intended, this focused the German attention on themselves and away from 'C' Company.

Harley's eighty-six-man force got into the bowl of The Gully without incident. Sergeant J. Elaschuk's No. 13 Platoon was on point, the other two platoons following in an arrowhead formation with Harley's company HQ section in the centre. The men jogged forward, feeling very exposed. Because the Loyal Edmonton Regiment was closing on the outskirts, the supporting artillery had started to break off for fear of hitting the Edmontons. 'C' Company passed the brick factory. They had yet to be fired upon. The paratroopers were completely engaged in trading fire with 'D' Company.

Elaschuk suddenly yelled back to Harley that his platoon was inside a minefield. Mines were sown thickly all across the line of advance. 'C' Company started bunching up, slowing its pace to pick a path through the mines. They were out in the open, beginning to act like men fearful of trampling a field of daisies. Harley told everyone to pick up the pace, double time. There was no time for caution. If the Germans spotted them, they were going to get shot up. The men plunged into the minefield. Harley saw mangled bodies of Germans lying in the field among the mines. He also saw the mines. They had been poorly dug in. Each mine was clearly visible as a little hummock of soil. The Canadians leapt over and around them, like a group of prairie children running through a field riddled with gopher burrows. By the time they reached the other side, 'C' Company was going at a flat-out sprint.[23]

The men reached the embankment. It was fronted by a road and a waist-high stone retaining wall. The men crossed the road, vaulted to the top of the wall, and started climbing up the high bank. Harley, like every man around him, slung his rifle by its shoulder strap across his back, and went up on all fours.[24] Gasping from the exertion, fearing that any moment the Germans would see them, 'C' Company climbed desperately upward. So far they had suffered no casualties.

Just as they neared the crest of the cliff, the Germans awoke to their presence. A shower of grenades poured down. Several men were killed or wounded. The others paused, lying prone, feet dug into the steep slope. They fixed bayonets on their Lee Enfield rifles. Then Harley led them over the top. The men plunged into four machine-gun posts dug in on the cliff crest, killing some of the enemy soldiers and taking the rest prisoner. They gathered up about a dozen prisoners. Other paratroopers withdrew quickly, efficiently covering their departure with well-directed fire.

Harley realized that remaining at the cliff edge was dangerous. If the enemy counterattacked, his company was vulnerable to being thrown back down the slope. Across about 400 yards of vineyards, Harley could see the church belfry and roof. He decided to make for the church immediately. Sergeant Elaschuk's platoon was sent to the left to clear paratroopers out of several small huts. Lieutenant D.C. Hanbury took No. 14 Platoon to the right and made for the church.

Elaschuk's men cleared the huts, but as Hanbury closed on the church his platoon was subjected to heavy mortar and small-arms fire. Snipers in the church belfry joined in. Hanbury and five other men fell wounded, Sergeant J. Mottl and two privates were killed.

With the leaderless Seaforth platoon wavering, the Germans struck back with a counterattack. No. 14 Platoon's survivors fled in disarray. But Elaschuk's No. 13 Platoon dug in its heels and repelled the attack with well-placed rifle and light-machine-gun fire. Harley ordered Lieutenant L. Robinson to take No. 15 Platoon out to the right and continue the advance on the church. Robinson led two sections of the platoon forward in a bayonet charge. They knocked out two machine-gun posts and forced the soldiers to withdraw. Robinson and two enlisted men, however, were killed. Two other men were wounded.

'C' Company threw back repeated counterattacks by the 1st Parachute Division. As evening fell at about 1730 hours, Harley's men were still 300 yards short of the church and taking heavy fire from enemy positions around the building. Sniping from the belfry added to the casualties. Half the company was either dead or wounded. The only Regimental Aid Post man with the company was himself wounded. Once it was dark, Harley had the company dig in and sent the walking wounded to the rear. A couple of these men wandered into the minefield on their way back and were killed.[25]

By radio, Harley and Lieutenant Colonel Syd Thomson discussed the day's events. Thomson said he was putting Harley in for the Military Cross. Harley said, "I'd rather be at the Savoy, Syd, than sitting up here." Thomson replied, "You wouldn't see the fireworks at the Savoy that you're seeing here." Harley snorted. "Well, I sure could do with a drink, chum, would you send one over?" Thomson agreed to see what could be done about that.[26]

Harley's company came under temporary command of the Loyal Edmonton Regiment, which was well ensconced to 'C' Company's left. The Gully was now at the back of the Edmontons and of Harley's company. Its entire length was clear of the enemy. The obstacle that had caused so many casualties over so many days had again become nothing more than a geographical feature. Come morning, the job to take Ortona itself would begin.

◆ ◆ ◆

During the night of December 20, as part of the plan to fight a delaying action in Ortona until the Canadians threatened to turn the town's flank, German engineers laid charges at the base of a high watch-tower that rose up adjacent to Cattedrale San Tomasso. Precisely at 0700 hours the following morning, as Ortona rocked with explosions from demolitions being set off by the paratroop engineers along Corso Vittorio Emanuele, a terrific explosion rolled out of the northern end of the city. Smoke and dust obscured the plaza containing the old cathedral. When the smoke cleared, the watchtower and the southern half of the cathedral were gone. As if struck by a mighty cleaver, the grand dome of the cathedral had been sliced cleanly in half. Whether the cathedral was destroyed by explosives set inside it or by the watchtower toppling onto its dome remained a mystery. The Italian civilians near the cathedral could only gather briefly to stare at the damage before the continued demolitions and the artillery barrages hammering down on the town drove them back into the railroad tunnels and basements.

The magnificent and delicate frescoes that adorned the dome were half destroyed, the southern portion reduced to masonry fragments lying in a great pile below the undamaged half of the cupola. What remained was exposed to water and wind damage as the weather worsened. The Portale, a massive door designed by Nicollo Mancino, was completely destroyed. The ancient bas-relief, depicting the arrival at Ortona of the boat from Illyria which bore the casket of the apostle Thomas, was lost in the rubble.[27]

December 21 was a day the citizens of Ortona had celebrated for centuries. It was the Feast Day of Saint Thomas, the disciple said to be entombed in the town's great cathedral. On seeing the devastation wrought upon the cathedral that held the community's soul, the people of Ortona were convinced the German engineers had carried out the destruction purposefully. That they had done this act on the great holiday was considered an added dose of maliciousness.[28]

# FIVE

## LITTLE
## STALINGRAD

# 20

# A Bunch of
# Madmen

During the night of December 20, Major Jim Stone and Peter Carr
Harris, an officer in the Royal Canadian Engineers, walked up the
road from the Loyal Edmonton Regiment's front line to Ortona. Their
purpose was to determine if the road was mined. In the morning,
Stone hoped to take a combined infantry and tank force up the road
and roll from one end of Ortona to the other without stopping.
Everything was still. Stone and Harris moved cautiously, ready to
retreat at the first challenge or shot from a German sentry.

The two men paused when they reached the first buildings on
the south edge of Ortona. They waited. Listened. Still there was no
sound from the enemy. Before them stretched the wide, seemingly
arrow-straight Corso Vittorio Emanuele, the town's main street. Stone
signalled to Harris, and the two men advanced quietly up one side of
the Corso. They hugged the walls of the dark two-storey houses bordering the street. Stone and Harris went another eighty to ninety
yards without seeing a soul.

Neither man saw any immediate signs of mines or even gun

positions. The two returned to the Canadian line without incident. It seemed from their reconnaissance as if the Germans were not in Ortona at all. Stone knew this was false. They had to be there somewhere. But it appeared they did not plan to deny the Canadians a toehold in the town. He expected little resistance in the morning. Stone thought there was a good chance that the plan to push down the Corso to the other end of Ortona might succeed.[1]

◆ ◆ ◆

At dawn, under a grey, overcast sky, the Edmontons went into the attack. They advanced on a two-company wide front, with 'D' Company on the left and 'B' on the right. 'B' Company made good progress, quickly cutting through a cluster of small vineyards, olive groves, and vegetable gardens to establish a position inside some buildings on Ortona's edge.

'D' Company had no such luck. Stone's men advanced in a line across an open field. Seventy-five to one hundred yards away stood the houses of Ortona. The company was immediately taken under fire by machine gun–armed paratroopers hidden in slit trenches fronting the buildings. Snipers, firing out of upper-storey windows and from the roofs, added to what Stone later described as "murderous fire."[2] Men fell in droves, killed or badly wounded. 'D' Company was forced to withdraw, leaving many of the wounded on the field. They tried again a few minutes later with the same result. The company had gone into the first attack about one hundred strong. After the second failed attempt, only seventeen riflemen were still on their feet.[3]

Besides Stone, only one officer remained — Lieutenant John Dougan. Stone divided the company into three groups. He commanded one, Dougan another, and the third fell to Company Sergeant Major Ron Bowen. Stone was in a quandary. Attempting another attack seemed suicidal. But Edmonton commander Lieutenant Colonel Jim Jefferson was on the radio urging him to get his men forward. 'B' Company was on its objective. Jefferson told Stone, "You must push on."

Stone snapped back, "Reinforce success."[4] He wanted Jefferson to change the line of advance so that everyone followed 'B' Company's route into Ortona. Jefferson insisted Stone had to establish a position on the left side of the Corso. He needed part of the battalion on both sides of the street. Otherwise it would be unsafe for the tanks.

Stone, Dougan, and Bowen held a huddled conference. It was starting to drizzle lightly, but they were so used to the cold, wet weather that they paid no mind to their rapidly dampening clothes. Stone explained 'D' Company's task. He wanted one platoon to take the point. If it got through, the others would follow. The three men drew lots. Dougan, who considered himself little blessed with gambler's luck, predictably lost. "Can you lay down some smoke to cover us?" he asked Stone.[5] The major told Private Elwyn Springsteel, the company's two-inch mortarman, and his helper to lay on the smoke bombs.[6] Springsteel could see the German machine-gun positions on the edge of the town, so putting smoke where it was needed posed no problem.

Dougan considered his options. For six men to try striding across the machine gun–swept open ground was simple suicide. There was, however, a small ditch running directly from the Edmontons' forming-up position to where a large house stood on Ortona's edge. The building looked to be a *pensione*, or small apartment house. The ditch was narrow, and about three feet deep. It occurred to Dougan that if they hunched over and ran up the ditch in a single-file line, they might remain unnoticed by the German machine-gunners. Of course, a wise German officer would have set a machine gun right smack at the end of the ditch to prevent precisely this kind of infiltration.

In fighting the Germans, Dougan had previously found that often the tactic that seemed most unexpected because of its hazard was the one to take. The Germans tended to dismiss the possibility of their enemy taking bold, aggressive action. The proper way to mount an attack was to advance by sections over the open ground on a wide front. This was what the Canadians had already done. This was precisely what the Germans would again be expecting. Bunching up in a ditch was madness. "Hell, we're all going to die anyway," Dougan thought, "might as well give it a go."[7]

With Springsteel firing off smoke as quickly as his loader could drop bombs into the firing tube, Dougan and his men bolted down the ditch. As they neared the end, Dougan expected to hear the horrible ripping sound of a German MG42 machine gun. He kept expecting to die. But not a shot was fired. The ditch was unguarded. Dougan and his men piled out of it and up against the cover offered by the wall of the *pensione*.[8] He turned to look back, planning to wave Stone and the rest of the company over. They were already through. Stone came out of the ditch first, grinning fiercely. "Nobody but a bunch of madmen would have attempted that dash," Stone said.[9]

Behind them, still manning their slit trench positions in front of the *pensione* and other buildings, the paratroopers awaited the next Canadian attack. They appeared to have no inkling that the remaining fragment of 'D' Company was now to their rear. Dougan opened the door to the *pensione* and the men quickly secured the house. Stone led Dougan and several infantrymen up the stairs to the top storey. They found the rooms there empty. From the upstairs windows, they looked right down into the German slit trenches. Rifles, Bren guns, and Thompson submachine guns poked out of the windows and opened fire as one. The Germans died in place.[10] ·

With the paratroopers now alerted to the Edmontons' presence, the battle was on. Stone led his section out of the *pensione* and they proceeded to clear the buildings standing between it and 'B' Company's position to the right. Some prisoners were taken and held at the *pensione*, which Stone turned into his company headquarters. Shortly after the two companies linked up, Lieutenant Alon Johnson, the commander of the scout platoon, met Stone at the building. Johnson had been sent by Jefferson to confirm the precise location of Stone's company.

Stone told Johnson to take the prisoners back with him to battalion headquarters. As Johnson left with the prisoners, he heard Stone radio Jefferson. "Johnson's House is now in our hands," Stone said. "Johnson headed your way. He'll explain." When Johnson reported to Jefferson, he was able to point out the large building on Ortona's edge. For the rest of the day's fierce battle, the building was referred to by everyone in the Edmonton Regiment as Johnson's House.[11]

The fighting was chaotic. Germans and Canadians exchanged grenades by the dozens. 'C' Squadron of the Three Rivers Tanks rolled its Shermans up close to the edge of town and hammered German positions with the 75-millimetre main guns. No. 5 Troop of 'C' Squadron pushed 200 yards into the town itself, firing up numerous enemy positions as it advanced, but was unable to move up Corso Vittorio Emanuele due to lack of infantry cover. With 'D' Company too reduced by casualties to do more than widen its holdings of houses immediately around the *pensione*, the Edmontons' 'B' Company spearheaded the Canadian advance.[12] The tankers engaged two antitank guns, driving off their crews and capturing the guns.[13]

Forward movement of the tanks was seriously hampered by the many mines buried in the few streets paralleling Corso Vittorio Emanuele that were wide enough for the tanks. These streets were also choked with large piles of rubble the Germans had created by systematically blowing up buildings so their walls collapsed into the street. The tanks found it impossible to get over these mine-laden rubble piles. Even the infantry found moving in the streets difficult and dangerous. The paratroopers had snipers covering virtually every open space. 'B' Company took heavy casualties, but pressed on.

In 'D' Company's sector, Dougan was realizing that the German paratroopers were "tough babies."[14] He was in a street near the *pensione* when his section got tangled in a short grenade exchange with some of the enemy. The Canadians drove off the Germans. Dougan saw a wounded sergeant lying in clear view on the cobblestones. He shouted at the man to surrender. Slowly, calmly, the German raised his rifle and fired at Dougan. Dougan's men cut him down.[15]

◆ ◆ ◆

On the Edmontons' right flank, 'C' Company of the Seaforth Highlanders of Canada had pushed off at daybreak toward Santa Maria di Costantinopoli. They met with little resistance and soon had occupied the church. Things went so well on his front that Captain Don Harley initially figured the town would be cleared of German troops by nightfall.[16] 'C' Company started advancing up Via Costantinopoli, which arced from the eastern part of Ortona toward the southernmost square on Corso Vittorio Emanuele. Via Costantinopoli was bordered along much of its length by low stone walls protecting small gardens and olive groves. Interspersed among the gardens, and growing more numerous as the road advanced deeper into Ortona, were interlinked rows of two- and three-storey houses.

Harley's company got only a short distance up the street before meeting stiff German resistance. Several Three Rivers tanks followed a lane running off the Ortona-Orsogna lateral road east to the

Seaforth front and provided suppressing fire against German strong points. One tank from 'C' Squadron, named *Cobourg II*, parked square in the middle of the street and fired shell after shell down its length to knock out a number of targets. Soon spent brass cartridges lay in a ragged pile behind the tank, as the loader threw the empty shells out of a hatch.[17] With the tanks in support, Harley's men pressed on, making good progress until they reached the more densely built-up area.

It was soon clear that the paratroopers were not going to give Ortona up easily. It was impossible to flank enemy strong points by moving around them on the side streets. Every time Harley sent men off to check the flanking streets, they found them dangerously narrow and blocked by large piles of rubble from demolished buildings. Some of the piles were fifteen feet high, impossible to climb over without being completely exposed to sniper fire.

At 1100 hours, hearing matching reports from the two Edmonton companies in Ortona and from Harley's Seaforths, 2nd Canadian Infantry Brigade commander Brigadier Bert Hoffmeister decided that Ortona was going to be a tough nut to crack. He realized the entire brigade would have to be committed. Accordingly, he ordered all companies of the Seaforth and Loyal Edmonton battalions into the battle. The Princess Patricia's Canadian Light Infantry would remain in close reserve.[18]

By evening, the Seaforths were all in Ortona. 'D' Company was given the task of relieving the remnants of Stone's Edmonton company and protecting the Edmontons' left flank. This would allow the Edmontons, much reduced by casualties, to concentrate their strength on advancing up Corso Vittorio Emanuele.[19] The remaining Seaforth companies secured the area around Santa Maria di Costantinopoli. Lieutenant Colonel Syd Thomson moved his battalion HQ into the church.

The Seaforth war diarist noted that battalion HQ staff were shocked by the evidence of the stiff fight Harley's men had faced. He wrote that 'C' Company was "busy burying their own and enemy dead. The company's casualties being seven killed and many wounded. . . . Battalion strength . . . at that time 524, all ranks."[20]

◆ ◆ ◆

Knowing the Seaforths were protecting their flanks, the Edmontons pressed up the Corso on a two-company front. One company took each side of the main street. Buildings in this sector before the first square were scattered in closely packed little knots, with vegetable gardens between. Three Rivers' 'C' Squadron was able to provide good support against the paratroopers' sniper and machine-gun positions, which were usually located in second- and third-storey windows. The presence of Teller antitank mines, however, meant that mine-sweeping teams from the Royal Canadian Engineers often had to precede the tanks. It was a dangerous job, especially as the sniper fire was extremely accurate.

The Edmontons pushed on, reaching the first square, Piazza Vittoria, just before nightfall. Three Rivers' No. 5 Troop, which had been supporting the advance through the day, withdrew at 1400 hours and was replaced by No. 1 Troop. The new tank troop, commanded by Lieutenant F. Simard, had advanced to within one hundred yards of the square when Simard's tank lost its left track to a Teller mine. Working under fire, Simard and his crew managed to rig up a tow chain and hook it to the rear of another Sherman. The other tank then dragged Simard's machine out of the immediate battle zone where it could be safely repaired.[21]

When night fell on Ortona, the tanks withdrew to the town's outskirts. In the narrow streets, they were too vulnerable to being destroyed by paratrooper raiding parties. The lines between friend and foe were hopelessly blurred. Germans and Canadians sometimes were directly opposite each other or even shared the same house. In the darkness, movement was dangerous, the guards on both sides jumpy and firing at any sound.

The Seaforths' 'D' Company started taking over the area held through the day by Major Jim Stone's Loyal Edmonton company. As Captain Alan W. Mercer had been wounded the day before, the Seaforth company was now commanded by Lieutenant John McLean. Company strength was only forty-two men of all ranks. Both Canadian and German artillery and mortars were at work. The town rocked with explosions and the racket of collapsing walls and roofs. McLean's men hived off in small groups to replace the equally scattered Edmontons. Whispered passwords proved to Edmonton and Seaforth alike that they met Canadians. McLean left four men here, five men there, two men in another shattered building. 'D' Company was soon scattered in a thin semi-circle facing northwest toward the town's heart.[22]

Company Sergeant Major Jock Gibson and McLean spent the night circulating from section to section, ensuring the men were alert, and generally boosting morale. In the sections, the soldiers tried sleeping in shifts. The din of the shelling, however, made sleep nearly impossible. So, too, did the knowledge that mere feet away the Germans were also clustered inside houses. When the shelling eased, they could hear guttural voices talking in soft whispers. Sometimes the voices grew loud and boisterous, as if the paratroopers were in a beer hall back in Germany enjoying a fine evening of camaraderie.[23]

◆ ◆ ◆

Obergefreiter Karl Bayerlein was exhausted. The last two days had passed in a frenzied blur of demolition and mine-laying tasks. The twelve engineers in his section had sown innumerable Teller anti-tank mines into the forward rubble piles. If a tank tried bulling its way over the rubble, almost certainly one of its tracks would trip at least one mine's pressure detonator and be immobilized.

There were three detonators built into a Teller mine, one on top, one on the side, and another on the bottom. The paratroopers could position a mine against a building or inside a room, hook a length of wire to the side detonator, and reel it off to a secure position many yards away. When Canadian infantry came near the mine, a para-trooper would give the wire a yank and out popped the detonator pin. Seven and a half seconds later the mine would explode with an enormous blast. By attaching the third detonator to a stake buried underneath the mine, Bayerlein and the other engineers were able to create a deadly booby trap. Once the mine was discovered, the Canadians would think it could be safely picked up and disarmed. But when they lifted the mine, the detonating pin hooked to the stake would pull free, setting off the mine.

German mines were all steel-cased and vulnerable to detection by Canadian engineers using metal detectors. To heighten confusion and make every obstacle even more difficult to surmount, Bayerlein's team laced Italian wooden-box mines in among the Tellers and anti-personnel S-mines.

As they fell back in front of the Canadian attack, Bayerlein and his men packed Italian box mines or boxes of blasting powder into outside stairwells and behind doors. Tripwires were strung across the stairs or hooked to the doors. If a soldier tripped the wire by going up the stairs or by opening a door, the detonator immediately ignited and the explosive charge blew up. In the dark gloominess of hallways and stairwells, it was almost impossible for anyone to spot the tripwires. At times the booby traps were set with a macabre sense of humour. Quite a number of the homes in Ortona had been updated by the installation of water closets. Bayerlein and his men attached a bomb to the flush handle. When a soldier took advantage of the comfort of indoor plumbing and flushed, "boom."[24]

As the day wore on, Bayerlein and his team finished their mining work and took to the roofs of some of the higher buildings behind Piazza Vittoria. They lay just back from the edge of the roofline and sniped at the advancing Canadian infantry with rifles. Bayerlein wrote in his diary that evening: "As soon as we were spotted the enemy brought in tanks. These fired shells until the buildings fell. The only possibility of escape was to jump on the other roofs of adjacent buildings. The enemy artillery is constant and falls everywhere in the city. The visibility was limited because of the dust of the explosions and houses collapsing. . . . In the evening we move closer to the front line. Our quarters are in the basement of a chemist shop near one of the main crossroads."[25]

The paratroopers in Ortona ended the day pleased by the defence they had offered. Casualties had fallen within acceptable limits and they had made the Canadians pay in blood for every bit of ground given up. The channelling effect achieved by the creation of rubble piles on the narrow side streets served its purpose. The Canadians were forced to follow the path of least resistance up the main Corso, bringing them into one pre-selected killing ground after another. Generously equipped with Schmeisser submachine guns, light machine guns, and medium machine guns, the paratroopers were able to lay down vicious curtains of close-quarters gunfire that rendered the streets almost impossible for the Canadians to use. Scattering snipers throughout the buildings added to the hazard of any attempt to move along the street.[26]

While General Richard Heidrich's paratroopers were confident that they could hold out as long as required, the view at Generalfeldmarschall Albert Kesselring's headquarters was gloomier. His chief of staff, General der Kavallerie Siegfried Westphal, telephoned the Tenth Army chief of staff, Generalmajor Fritz Wentzell, in the early evening of December 21. Kesselring and Westphal had misinterpreted signals from the battlefront and believed that Ortona had fallen. These messages had also reached Berlin. "High Command called me on the phone," Westphal said. "Everybody was very sad about Ortona."

A puzzled Wentzell replied, "Why? Ortona is still in our hands." As far as Wentzell could see, the paratroopers were exacting such high casualties from the Eighth Army attackers that there was no reason to give up Ortona until the 1st Parachute Division's flank was turned and the soldiers in the town faced being surrounded.[27]

# 21

## THEY ALWAYS
## MESS THINGS UP

**A** bold dash. Another madman's gamble. Major Jim Stone believed he knew how to smash through 1st Parachute Division's defences along Corso Vittorio Emanuele. If the German intent was to funnel the Canadians down its length through one killing zone after another, and there was no way for the Loyal Edmonton Regiment to outflank these zones, then the solution was to do the unexpected. Running like wildmen up the ditch had allowed his mangled company to win entry to Ortona. So why not do the same thing on a grander, more daring scale? Was not the Corso itself rather like a ditch?

After the first day's dreadful fighting in the Ortona streets, Stone knew that the Germans would expect the Canadians to advance cautiously in the morning. But moving into the face of the enemy could only result in a prolonged and bloody house-to-house fight. Yesterday had proven how costly such an approach would be. Stone sought a way to prevent the regiment being decimated by the heavy casualties that a protracted battle in a town must entail. It was entirely likely that the paratroopers were not holding the town in great depth. They probably had a strong, well-manned defensive line. Behind that, there was unlikely to be any significant number of defenders. The paratroopers would be planning on withdrawing in staged steps from one prepared defensive position to another, bleeding the Canadians every step of the way. Stone was certain that the parachute division was implementing in Ortona a small-scale version of the strategy which Tenth Army had implemented so effectively to slow the Eighth Army's advance all the way up the boot of Italy.

If he could pierce the line and get behind the Germans, they would be unable to re-establish a blocking line in front of his advance. The paratroopers would have to abandon Ortona or be isolated inside the town and face destruction. Boldness was the key. What Stone needed was to hit the paratroopers with a miniature "colossal crack" that would send them reeling right out of Ortona.

Stone tracked down the Three Rivers Tanks commander and explained his plan. "Let's start at first light tomorrow morning," he said. "You put your tanks in low gear, get your sirens going, and fire your main armament at every building forward of you and your machine guns at the houses on the side of the road. I'll put my infantry alongside the tanks and let's try and go through."[1] It took some argument, because the commander started quoting chapter and verse from armoured tactical doctrine that stated tanks were not only of limited value in fighting within built-up areas but also extremely vulnerable to being destroyed by enemy action. Finally, however, Stone won the tank commander's somewhat reluctant agreement to give the gamble a try.

That Stone was developing the tactics for the Edmontons' December 22 attack reflected a shift in the regiment's lines of command. Lieutenant Colonel Jim Jefferson had established his battalion headquarters on Ortona's outskirts. This was unlike Seaforth Highlanders of Canada battalion commander Lieutenant Colonel Syd Thomson, who had set up shop right on the town's edge in Santa Maria di Costantinopoli. In fact, Jefferson's headquarters was almost as far back as 2nd Canadian Infantry Brigade commander Brigadier Bert Hoffmeister's. In a battle where troops were facing each other across distances of mere feet, trying to exercise effective control or to dictate strategy from such a distance to the rear was difficult, if not impossible.

Because of the distance between Jefferson's headquarters and the rifle companies in Ortona, command of the Edmonton Regiment effectively shifted to the senior commander on the immediate scene. That was Major Jim Stone. The officer was well suited to the role. He was resourceful, independent-minded, determined, brave to the point of near recklessness, and, because he had come up through the ranks, well versed in small-unit tactics.

◆ ◆ ◆

Stone's attack went forward as planned. Tanks of the Three Rivers' No. 2 Troop moved out in single file down the very centre of the Corso. Stone's 'D' Company led for the Edmontons, the other two companies following. Losses on December 21 had been so high that Jefferson had ordered the rifle companies reduced from their normal strength of four companies to three. Even so, each company, including a reinforced 'D' Company, barely mustered 60 men apiece instead of what should have been a total strength of more than 400. Stone found the noise made by the tanks' sirens and the thunder of their 75-millimetre guns in the narrow street "terrifying."

The distance from Piazza Vittoria to Piazza Municipali, where a small cathedral and the municipal hall stood, was 300 yards. The Corso descended from the Canadian-held square to the municipal square on a grade of about 3 percent. This meant that the Canadians would be well silhouetted for the German defenders during their advance. The buildings lining this section of street were relatively modern, built in the last two centuries. To the west of the Corso, for the entire length running from the Piazza Vittoria to Piazza Municipali, the streets and buildings dated back to the Renaissance. Beyond Piazza Municipali, past the shattered ruin of Cattedrale San Tomasso to the ancient castle overlooking the sea, the Corso narrowed and the surrounding buildings and streets became a warren of buildings dating back to the 1400s.

Stone was elated. The attack rolled forward against virtually no opposition. He figured the Germans were frozen by fear and confusion. Progress toward the main square was rapid. Ahead stood a massive rubble pile, perhaps twenty-five feet high. It appeared to have been constructed by blowing the better part of the cathedral on the edge of the square out into the street. Despite the height of the pile, Stone thought the tanks could get over it. If tanks and men kept going, they would get right through to the castle and the battle would be won.

But suddenly, little more than twenty-five yards short of the rubble pile, the lead tank paused. The other tanks ground to a halt, maintaining their preset intervals between each other. They also ceased firing their guns. The infantry milled about, unsure what was happening. By pausing, the tankers were hopelessly messing up the attack. As an infantryman, Stone believed it was an all-too-common experience. Stone jumped up on the lead tank. "What the hell's the matter?" he yelled.[2] The tank commander pointed at a scrap of sheet metal lying in the road. "It's probably concealing a mine," he said. Stone was incredulous. The entire street, from one end to the other, was littered with bricks, stones, chunks of metal, broken boxes, and other debris from the battered and destroyed buildings fronting it. What made this piece of metal special? Stone tried to convince the man to get going again. He could feel the attack's momentum slipping through his fingers, like so many grains of wheat. The tank commander said petulantly, "Don't you realize a tank is worth $20,000? I can't risk it."

"You armoured sissy," Stone snapped. "I've got twenty to thirty men here with no damned armour at all and they're worth a million dollars apiece. You're just a bunch of goddamned armoured sissies."[3]

But it was too late to save the plan. Whether the Germans had been in shock from the violent directness of the attack or had never intended to defend that stretch of the Corso, they were alert now. Small-arms fire started snapping around the Edmontons and the men dived for cover. The tanks would advance no farther. Suddenly a 57-millimetre PAK antitank gun started shooting at the lead tanks from a position on the corner next to the church. It was so placed that the Three Rivers tanks were unable to return its fire. Stone ordered his PIAT man to knock the gun out. The man fired from too far away, the round sailing harmlessly over the armoured shield that protected the crew manning the weapon, and exploding in a white flash of smoke inside the church.

Furious that his bold plan had failed because the tankers lacked sufficient courage, Stone yelled in frustration at the PIAT man, who was starting the unwieldy process of trying to reload the antitank weapon. Knowing that at any moment the Germans were likely to hit one of the tanks, Stone pulled a smoke grenade and chucked it in front of the antitank gun. He then charged the gun single-handedly, pulling a fragmentation grenade off his webbing belt as he went. Running up to the gun's armour shield, Stone pulled the pin on the grenade, tossed it over the shield at the gunners, and pressed himself against the shield's protective cover. The grenade exploded, killing the entire crew.[4]

The forward attack was faltering fast despite Stone's heroic attempts to get things moving again. He and Lieutenant John Dougan moved up to the rubble pile, trying to find a way for the tanks to get across it. On the way, Stone saw that the sheet metal scrap hid nothing but cobblestones. Knowing he had been right and the tanker wrong just made him all the madder.[5]

Dougan was more philosophical. He thought the great height of the rubble pile had scuttled Stone's plan, but in his friend and superior's current state of mind there was no way Dougan was going to make the man see this truth.[6] Dougan saw that a couple of men from 'D' Company had managed to crawl over the pile. They were moving cautiously up the street toward the municipal hall. One suddenly crumpled. Stone told Dougan that it looked as if the man might have been electrocuted because there were some live power lines lying on the street. However the man had died, there was no doubting that the other side of the rubble pile was a bad place to be. Dougan called the remaining soldier on the north side of the pile back. The officers then ordered the infantry to batter their way into the houses on either side of the street and get to work.[7]

The house-to-house battle that Stone had hoped to avoid now started in earnest. Within minutes, the fight ceased to be one he could effectively control. Sergeants, corporals, even privates operated on their own initiative. On the other side of the rubble pile, three machine guns were covering the Piazza Municipali from a nearby building on the left side of the street. Combined with the fire coming from at least two other machine guns, these guns meant that anyone moving around the rubble pile was likely to get killed. One of the other machine guns was firing out of a circular opening in the upper portion of the municipal hall's front wall. The paratroopers had developed this machine-gun position by removing the town clock and sandbagging the opening to create a stout fortification.

Private C.G. Rattray and two other soldiers set their sights on knocking out the three guns in the building on the left. Under fire, the men crawled over the rubble pile and forced their way through the front door. Rattray left it to the other men to clear the riflemen defending the lower floor. He stormed upstairs and surprised five paratroopers manning the three guns. The startled Germans surrendered. Rattray found himself in possession of five prisoners, three machine guns, four rifles, and three Luger pistols.[8]

Elsewhere the battle did not go so well. When a stick grenade came bouncing down the stairs at him, Private Melville McPhee ducked into an alcove off a stairwell. The twenty-one-year-old from Drumheller had been plagued since Sicily by stomach ulcers, and for the next hour at least his experience did little to ease the condition. Every time he tried to move from the alcove, the German above him tossed down another grenade, forcing McPhee to cower back until the shrapnel stopped flying around. It seemed the man had a limitless supply of grenades. Outside the walls of the house he was cornered in, McPhee could hear machine guns blazing, rifles cracking, and grenades exploding. But nobody came into the building and there was nothing he could do to get out. Finally he poked his head out of the alcove and no grenade came bouncing down the stairs. McPhee took off, leaving the grenade-throwing German in undisputed possession of the building.[9]

◆ ◆ ◆

At 1700 hours, with night falling, the tanks of 'C' Squadron withdrew from Ortona as they had the night before. The infantry spread out through the buildings on either side of the Corso and settled in as best they could for the night.

Just before dark, Brigadier Bert Hoffmeister visited both the Loyal Edmonton and Seaforth Highlanders of Canada forward companies. He decided that the following morning the Seaforths should move across the Edmontons' rear and come up on their left flank, both to protect it and force an advance through the older, western portion of the town to a square on Via Cavour. Via Cavour angled off Corso Vittorio Emanuele from the Piazza Municipali to the western edge of the town. If the Seaforths could reach Via Cavour and advance up it to Piazza Municipali, they would be able to break the German defence of the square by outflanking it.[10]

The Three Rivers' 'A' Squadron was brought up to the outskirts of the town. The squadron would reinforce 'C' Squadron in the operations inside Ortona. Among the tankers in the squadron were the three Turnbull brothers, Joe, Gord, and Bill. The movement of the tanks must have been observed by the Germans, for the tank harbour was heavily shelled during the night. Lance Corporal Bill Turnbull was wounded in the leg by shrapnel and evacuated.[11] The youngest, Bill was the first of the brothers to have been wounded. Although worried about his brother, Joe took comfort in the fact that the wound was not too serious. As a veteran of the Spanish Civil War, Joe knew they faced probably their toughest fight since landing in Sicily, and there was a good chance that if all the brothers went into the town at least one of them might die in its narrow streets.[12]

◆ ◆ ◆

Obergefreiter Karl Bayerlein had spent his day in the thick of the fight for the Piazza Municipali. He and some comrades had occupied a position on the roof of the small church. Two of the men had fired rifle grenades down on the Canadian tanks, but had caused no noticeable damage. They had, however, attracted the attention of the tankers and barely escaped from the position before it was blown up by repeated main-gun shell fire. Despite the vicious fighting, Bayerlein and the rest of his squad found time during part of the afternoon to have a nap in the basement of the chemist's shop that served as their billet. They were worn out from having spent the previous night laying more mines and carrying out numerous demolitions.[13] Bayerlein had wandered through the town like a mule, carrying Teller antitank mines on his back and shoulders. Always he was mindful that one enemy bullet could result in his being blown to pieces by his deadly burden.[14]

During the night, Bayerlein took up an assigned position on the roof of the chemist's shop. His duty was to keep watch and to snipe at any enemy he might see. The darkness hardly made for good sniping conditions. A few fires burned in Ortona, but no Tommies were highlighted in front of the flames. Soon after he got settled, Bayerlein heard strange voices speaking a language other than German. His first thought was that the enemy were on the floor immediately below him and he was about to be attacked. Then he realized he was hearing Italian and that the voices were coming from a distant source. He listened for a moment. They seemed to be coming from a nearby house, probably from the basement. The battle for Ortona was hellish enough for soldiers, he thought. Terrible that civilians should be caught in its midst.

Bayerlein knew that most of the people of Ortona were hiding in the railroad tunnels running under the town, rather than in basements of the houses over which the Canadians and the Germans were fighting. In the tunnels they were fairly safe, although there was little food or water. The Germans were also using the tunnels for shelter, and as a route for moving unmolested around the northern part of the town. The tunnels were where most of the paratroopers rested during the night, and where reinforcements waited to go forward to relieve the front-line troops so they too could rest.[15] Only one paratroop battalion, 2nd Battalion of 3rd Regiment, was actually deployed inside Ortona at this time, along with Bayerlein and a good number of other men from the engineering unit.[16] Because of the narrow nature of the Canadian penetration into Ortona, the paratroopers were able to hold the front with little more than about one hundred men committed to the battle at any given time. This enabled the remainder of the battalion to rest in the railroad tunnels.[17]

On paper the Canadian strength appeared greater than that of the Germans, but in the streets of Ortona the two forces were actually evenly matched. The two Canadian regiments engaged in the fighting within Ortona had entered the battle already weary and under-strength from casualties suffered in more than two weeks of virtually continuous fighting. By comparison, 1st Parachute Division was relatively fresh and its battalions were close to what passed for normal strength in the always depleted German army. The paratroopers enjoyed excellent morale, were well equipped for the task of street fighting, and were confident of controlling the flow of the battle from their strong defensive positions. Many of the veterans also had experience in fighting in urban areas on the Russian front. While every German, from mere infantryman to Generalfeldmarschall Kesselring, was convinced that the soldiers of the Eighth Army possessed both greater numbers and surpluses of war matériel, they also believed that the German was a superior soldier, equipped with a natural boldness and audacity no British or Commonwealth soldier could possibly emulate.[18]

The Canadians were so seriously understrength that their two battalions barely equalled in numbers the single parachute battalion. The Germans also enjoyed the defensive advantage. They were dug into well-designed defensive positions and it was up to the Canadians to root them out — always a costly proposition. Unlike the 90th Panzer Grenadiers, who had allowed themselves to be ground up in near-suicidal counterattacks, doctrine in 1st Parachute Division opposed anything but very limited counterattacking. Rather, the paratrooper approach was to do precisely what they were doing in Ortona: establish formidable defensive positions and hold them for as long as possible. The paratroopers were also trained to infiltrate small parties behind the facing enemy units. Acting independently, these groups could cause havoc among the enemy ranks with lightning-fast raids and by establishing machine-gun positions that could bring devastating fire on enemy positions from the rear.

A Canadian intelligence summary written by Major N.L.C. Mathers on December 22 cited the most noteworthy characteristics of 1st Parachute Division's tactics as exemplifying "dogged tenacity, extreme economy in manpower (evidenced by their reluctance to counterattack), skill in timing a withdrawal, and skill in concealment. . . . Often they are thrown in to help restore a critical situation. This manner of employment has largely governed the organization and equipment of parachute troops: they tend to be well supplied with machine guns, mortars and antitank guns, but generally operate without their own artillery. . . . The fact that these 'specialists' have appeared on our front to relieve the exhausted 90th Panzer Grenadier Division gives us a clue to the enemy's intentions and fears."[19] The fear, surmised the intelligence report, was an Eighth Army breakout and seizure of Pescara. The German intention was that 1st Parachute Division stem that breakout and hold the 1st Canadian Infantry Division in place until a strong defensive line could be constructed behind the Arielli River. This was, Mathers noted, the first time 1st Parachute Division had fought as a complete division. Usually it was sent into battle only on a regimental or even battalion scale.

Mathers's summary added that for purposes of interrogation any captured paratroopers "were the toughest we have had to face yet and, of course, the most security minded." Most of the veterans had served on the Russian front and had fought in Crete or Sicily, or both. When captured, they "knew what the score was and their discipline, morale and security are excellent. It is no wonder that they are the 'picked troops' and sent to whichever sector of the front needs strengthening. It is also interesting to note the condescending way in which the parachutists talk about the infantry, 'they always mess things up, and we, the parachutists, have to straighten them out.' And they too are the troops which have been put into the line to stem the advance of our Division."[20]

Canadian intelligence determined that by the evening of December 22, the 90th Panzer Grenadier Division, except for its inherent artillery unit, which remained behind to add to the German artillery presence, had withdrawn from the Ortona area. Generalleutnant Ernst-Günther Baade now faced the challenging task of rebuilding the devastated division he had inherited only a few days earlier. The 90th Panzer Grenadiers were broken as a combat division. It would require months to rebuild its manpower and develop a renewed unit integrity. The losses of veteran troops, however, could never be replaced. None of the division's battalions were believed to have more than one hundred men left. The 3rd Battalion of the 361st Regiment had been hardest hit. Even on December 15, Mathers reported this unit had only 12 men left out of a normal strength of about 300. The division's strategy of repeated counterattacks had virtually destroyed it. More than 400 Panzer Grenadiers had been taken prisoner, most when counterattacks had crumbled. Hundreds of others had been killed or wounded.[21] While the German division had succeeded in slowing the Canadian advance to a crawl through the mud and had blocked it for days in front of The Gully, the price paid robbed the achievement of both glory and strategic value.

# 22

# FIGHT FOR
# THE BULGE

HAVING committed 2nd Canadian Infantry Brigade to a slugging match against the 1st Parachute Division over ownership of the streets of Ortona, 1st Canadian Infantry Division commander Major General Chris Vokes now sought to speed conclusion of that battle by threatening the German defenders from the rear. During the battle for The Gully, the 48th Highlanders of Canada had inserted a narrow salient into the heart of the German defences northwest of Casa Berardi. This had enabled the Canadians to cut the road linking Cider Crossroads to Villa Grande. Since creating the salient on December 18, the Highlanders had been trying with little success to expand the depth of penetration into the German line.

In the afternoon of December 22, Vokes decided that the salient could serve as the jumping-off point for a major northeastern thrust by 1st Canadian Infantry Brigade. The ultimate goal of the attack would be to cut the roads running from Ortona to Tollo and the coast highway leading to Pescara. All supply and reinforcement of the paratroopers defending Ortona was confined to these roads. If he could break through and put blocking forces across the roads, the

Germans in Ortona would be surrounded. If successful, Vokes could transform Ortona into a miniature Stalingrad.

It was common knowledge among the Allies that a similar strategy had forced the February 2, 1943, surrender of the 91,000 remaining survivors of Generalfeldmarschall Friedrich Paulus's starving and exhausted Sixth Army to the Russians at Stalingrad. During an unparaleled, brutal six-month battle, more than 200,000 Germans had perished amidst the ruins of the city. For the last three months of the battle, the Sixth Army had found itself trapped in Stalingrad after the Russian army succeeded in surrounding the city with a two-pronged pincer-style offensive launched on November 19, 1942. Allied military analysts were declaring Stalingrad to be the turning point in the war on the Russian front. Where before the Germans had been on the offensive, they were now permanently thrown into a defensive stance, slowly and inevitably being forced to withdraw from Russia's heartland. Paulus had been given no choice but to allow himself to be surrounded. In one of his increasingly common, irrational directives, Hitler had ordered the Sixth Army to hold Stalingrad at all costs. Paulus had done so. The cost had ultimately been the destruction of an entire army. The chance that General Richard Heidrich would allow his paratroopers to suffer the same fate was comparatively remote.

Nevertheless, once the Canadians started to threaten its lifeline, the parachute division's options would be limited. Either stay and face destruction or flee Ortona.

Vokes issued his orders to Lieutenant Colonel Don Spry late that afternoon. The attack plan contained three phases. In the first phase, the Hastings and Prince Edward Regiment, which had just com-pleted a move from the coast to Casa Berardi, would attack through the 48th Highlanders' front line. Its objective was a bulging ridgeline one thousand yards to the north of the Tollo road. Bordering the southern flank of the Riccio River, the ridge followed a gradually rising course north to a position overlooking the road from Ortona to Tollo. Once the Hasty P's gained the edge of the ridge, the 48th Highlanders would kick off phase two by leapfrogging through the Hasty P's and capturing the ridge's highest point, which overlooked two hamlets, San Nicola and San Tomasso. Phase three would entail the Royal Canadian Regiment, which had just been bolstered by an influx of reinforcements, striking northeastward off the high ground to cut the main road north of Ortona.[1]

Staff at Spry's brigade headquarters believed that even if only the first two phases of the offensive succeeded, the Germans must still surrender Ortona. Once 1 CIB was on the heights overlooking the two hamlets, all the roads north of Ortona would be subject to directed artillery fire, and would face the immediate threat of being severed by further Canadian offensive action. General Heidrich would then have two choices. He could commit his paratroopers to counterattacks against a strong defensive position in hopes of forcing the Canadians back to Casa Berardi or cut his losses by retreating from Ortona.[2]

The offensive would follow the well-established pattern that had enjoyed greatest success during Morning Glory. First, a massed preliminary artillery bombardment involving four field and three medium artillery regiments. Second, a combined armoured and infantry force advancing behind a creeping artillery barrage to the objective.

That was the plan, but even on the evening of December 22 doubts about its prospects of success were being expressed. Once again, rain was wreaking havoc on the Canadian tactical plans. Preliminary reconnaissance by 48th Highlander patrols that afternoon had revealed that the ground over which the tanks were expected to travel was extremely muddy. During the night the rain intensified, and by morning the ground was a boggy soup. This boded ill for the armour's ability not only to keep up with the advancing infantry but to reach the objective at all.[3]

Dismissing this gloomy prognosis, Spry ordered Hastings and Prince Edward commander Bert Kennedy, who had been promoted to lieutenant colonel on December 11, to proceed with the attack. Kennedy had only just returned to the battalion after being evacuated on December 15 with jaundice. He was weak, but as feisty as ever.

The Hasty P's had seen little significant fighting since December 15. Along with the 48th Highlanders, they were one of only two battalions in the division fielding close to normal strength in the rifle companies. They had also been able to get a little more rest than most of the other battalions. Still, even after the fighting on their front had cooled down, the Hasty P's had continued to lose men during patrol actions, and German artillery fire had inflicted an

almost daily toll in casualties. The worst casualties the battalion had
suffered during their quiet duty had come on December 16. A platoon from each rifle company was withdrawn from the front lines
and sent into San Vito Chietino by truck.[4] Among the platoons was
No. 12 from 'B' Company. Once the men had bathed, changed, and
picked up their Christmas parcels, they started reloading into the
trucks. Suddenly a large shell struck near the No. 12 platoon's truck.
One man was killed, several others wounded. The survivors got out
of the truck, carrying the wounded toward the village square. Another
shell caught the unlucky platoon.[5] When the smoke cleared, four
more men were dead, another twenty-three wounded.[6] Only four
men in No. 12 platoon were left unscathed.[7] Hasty P's Quartermaster
Sergeant Basil Smith was horrified to see so many of the men he
thought of as "his" injured in what was supposed to be a safe rear
area. "This is a damned tough break," he wrote in his diary that
night, "to come through the toughest battle which has been fought in
Italy and then to get it here. It would seem there is no 'SAFE' area in
this corner of God's footstool."[8]

On the morning of December 22, just how dangerous the entire area
could be had again been impressed on the Hasty P's. The battalion
had started mounting up in trucks for the move from San Leonardo
to Casa Berardi. By 0830 hours, most of the men were on board.
Some of the battalion headquarters staff, Smith wrote, were "just
standing around awaiting the order. Without even a warning whistle,
a shell landed fairly in the midst of the group clustered around our
RAP [Regimental Aid Post] truck. . . . One moment they were chatting in a casual, carefree manner and one split second later, all three
were gone."[9] Dead were Medical Officer Dr. Charlie Krakauer, medical sergeant Charlie Reid, and medical orderly Clayton Young. The
three men were torn into unidentifiable fragments.[10] Grimly the survivors gathered up the body parts, buried them in one grave, and
drove toward their next battle.

◆ ◆ ◆

The Hasty P's moved into the attack at 0930 hours on December 23.
'A' Company led, with 'C' Company following close behind. In sup-
port was 'A' Squadron of the 11th Canadian Armoured Regiment
(Ontario Tanks). Because of the mud, the tanks were confined to a

narrow track running at a right angle from the road from Cider Crossroads to Villa Grande, toward the infantry battalion's objective. Sappers from the Royal Canadian Engineers, working with metal detection equipment, walked ahead of the tanks to clear the track of Teller antitank mines.

Even without the mud, the terrain over which the Hasty P's attacked was hopeless tank country. It was almost exclusively vineyards, which formed ideal antitank obstacles. In this area, the wire used to train the vines was strung between thin concrete posts rather than the lighter wooden stakes that the Canadians had encountered closer to the Moro River. When a tank pushed through the rows of vines, the wire rolled into tangles held taut by the concrete posts. Tank tracks fouled or were even torn loose by the wire. Meanwhile, the paratroopers enjoyed ideal cover in which to set up gun positions and ambush the tanks with remotely triggered mines. The mud was increased by the centuries-old cultivating practice of deeply tilling the soil between the vine rows. In soil of such loose consistency, the slightest bit of rain rendered the land a quagmire. By following the tracks, the tankers hoped to work their way to a position where they could then bushwhack just a short distance through the vineyards to reach the infantry positions.[11]

Despite these problems, tanks and infantry made good progress from the start line toward the objective one thousand yards away. Moving closely behind the creeping artillery barrage, the infantry suffered very light casualties, coming up on the base of the low hill at 1030 hours. At this point, the artillery had to lift to allow the Canadians to seize the high ground without being caught in their own artillery bombardment.

It became immediately clear how the tactics of 1st Parachute Division differed from those of the 90th Panzer Grenadiers. The paratroopers had made no attempt to stop the Canadian advance to the base of the hill. Instead, all their strength was concentrated in a network of fortifications dug into the side of the hill and along the ridgeline itself. The 3rd Battalion of the 3rd Regiment now tore into the Hasty P's with heavy machine guns, mortars, and light artillery. 'A' and 'C' companies were brought to an abrupt halt by the German fire within one hundred yards of the ridgeline.[12]

Never one to steer clear of a fight, Lieutenant Colonel Kennedy collared his assistant, Lieutenant Farley Mowat, marshalled up 'B' Company, which had been following behind the battalion HQ unit, and rushed forward to rally the faltering attackers. Mowat was impressed by Kennedy's refusal to surrender to the natural instinct to hunch one's shoulders when enemy bullets and shells whizzed close overhead. The commander strolled across the battlefield, issuing orders in an icily calm voice. By setting such a courageous example, Kennedy stiffened the determination of his regiment. The riflemen advanced again into the face of the enemy fire.[13]

While Kennedy was rallying his men, the tanks had ground up a gravel track to a point a few hundred yards to one side of the infantry. From here, the only route was through the vineyards. Lieutenant A.W. Hawkins led off with his Sherman to test the ground north of the track. Slogging through the mud, he soon found himself confronted by a shallow gully not indicated on his map. The sappers sweeping ahead of him for mines started descending into the gully, but were immediately forced back by machine-gun fire covering its entire length. Hawkins decided to proceed on his own. The tank rolled over the edge, and minutes later was disabled when an anti-tank mine tore off a track. It was 1100 hours. The tanks could go no farther toward the Hasty P's until darkness allowed the engineers to find a path for them through the heavily mined vineyards.[14]

Despite losing the tank support, Kennedy was able to keep his men advancing. By midday, the Hasty P's had fought through to the objective on the ridge. Kennedy then brought up 'D' Company and positioned it off to the battalion's right. Casualties during the day had been heavy, with thirteen men killed and at least twice that many wounded. But the paratroopers had also suffered heavily. Kennedy walked through the ranks, unmindful that he was pre-senting himself as a target for German snipers. "Take it easy, lads," he told his men. "No matter what happens we will look after you."[15] For their part, the soldiers had started calling the ridgeline over which they fought "the bulge," an accurate description of what their position inside the German lines looked like on a map. Officers soon picked up the term and the battalion's after-action reports each day referred to the ridgeline fight as the Battle of the Bulge.

Infantry and tanks remained separated and susceptible to being overrun by counterattack. Links to the Canadian main front line were fragile and could easily be severed by determined German action. In light of the situation, phase two was postponed until Kennedy's men could work their way forward from the regiment's main objective to a position that would serve as the 48th Highlanders' start line. Advancing 'B' Company forward the necessary 400 yards took several hours. Once this objective was taken, word was sent back to the Highlanders to come up to the extended perimeter.[16]

The Hasty P's were 1,000 yards ahead of the main Canadian lines and linked to the main line by an L-shaped thread running back to the Ortona-Orsogna lateral. This was an extremely tenuous position from which to continue an offensive, but Spry believed the risk had to be taken. He ordered the Highlanders to go forward at 1400 hours.

Meanwhile, Hasty P's Quartermaster Sergeant Basil Smith set to work getting rations up to the rifle companies. During the night, he led a ration party forward. The men in his party strapped food-laden dixie cans on their backs and carried the rations to the front-line soldiers. Several times along the way, Smith's party nearly blundered into the German lines. Once the food had been delivered, Smith volunteered the party as stretcher-bearers to bring out the half-dozen wounded men urgently requiring evacuation. He carried out a soldier named Jack Telford, who had enlisted on October 3, 1939, at the same time and place that Smith had joined up. Telford had been hit in the spine, thigh, and head by mortar fragments. Back at the RAP, Smith waited around until he learned of Telford's prognosis. The new medical officer, Dr. Homer Eshoo, told Smith that Telford would live and probably regain most of his health, but that his soldiering days were done.[17]

In the forward position, the rifle companies spent the night fending off small, determined infiltration parties. The paratroopers were employing another of their favoured tactics — slipping about ten men at a time through the extended Canadian formations to strike at them from the rear. Heavily armed with machine guns and Schmeisser submachine guns, these teams caused the battalion a largely sleepless, nerve-wracked night.[18]

# 23

## THE UNMUFFLED DRUMS OF HELL

WHILE the Hastings and Prince Edward Regiment fought its way along the ridgeline toward the Tollo road, the fighting inside Ortona continued unabated. The Seaforth Highlanders of Canada had, as planned, moved behind the Loyal Edmonton Regiment's rear during the night of December 22. In the morning, the Seaforths undertook a slow, costly advance through the narrow streets of the western part of the town's old quarter. The Edmontons, meanwhile, slogged their way through Piazza Municipali and started a crawling advance up Corso Umberto I, a wide esplanade along which summertime tourists had strolled in the prewar days. Progress for both battalions was measured in a house or two gained every hour.

With the tanks finding street movement hampered by mine-laden rubble piles, the Canadians manhandled the battalion six-pounder antitank guns into the town. They turned the guns into house-busting weapons, and also used them to blast gaps in the rubble piles. Two seventeen-pounders of the division's 90th Anti-Tank Battalion were deployed on the coast road just outside the town and started bombarding the old castle and other large buildings inside Ortona. It was discovered that the armour-piercing shells of the six-pounders, designed to penetrate a tank, would also punch good-sized holes in the walls of the old stone or brick buildings. Once a hole was opened, they switched to high-explosive shot and gutted the structure with shell after shell until the Germans inside were either killed or forced to retreat.[1] Sometimes the antitank gunners continued punching a building with armour-piercing and high-explosive shells until its outside walls or the roof collapsed. A slow, bloody task that exposed the antitank gunners to machine-gun and sniper fire, this house-clearing technique offered little hope of driving the paratroopers out of Ortona before the end of the year.

While most of their guns were deployed in Ortona itself, the Edmontons' antitank gun platoon managed to dig two six-pounder guns into firing pits located on the southernmost mole protecting the harbour. From this position, the gunners could direct fire up against Corso Umberto I. They started systematically knocking down build-ings facing the escarpment, blowing away every structure standing on the eastern edge of Ortona to a depth of one block. This reduced much of that part of the town to rubble, sparing the infantry the task of clearing it on a house-by-house basis.

These gunners were completely exposed to the enemy. As soon as they started firing, the Germans retaliated with a counter-barrage of mortar and light artillery. Antitank platoon commander Captain Ed Boyd was shocked to see that the loader manning the first gun on the mole was none other than Private Howard Mabley. Back in England, the thirty-year-old farmer from the Peace River District of Alberta had frustrated Boyd's determined efforts to turn him into a soldier. His campaign of sullen passive resistance against learning the art of war had ended in the man being shuffled off to work in the kitchens. This was despite the fact that Boyd had spent an entire week personally forcing Mabley to repeatedly go through the basics of gun drill. "Load. Aim. Fire. Load. Aim. Fire," he had yelled as Mabley fumbled with the gun. It had been hopeless. The farmer was never openly insolent or disrespectful. There was nothing he did to provide an officer with an excuse to bring him up on charges of dis-obedience. He simply would not, or could not, do the job well, no matter how long he was made to practise. Finally, Boyd gave up. Mabley went back to the kitchens.

There the man stayed until December 23, when Boyd unexpectedly found him loading the six-pounder. "What are you using for brains?" Boyd demanded of Sergeant Jim de Young, who commanded the gun. The sergeant defended himself, saying that Mabley had insisted on loading. And look at the result, de Young told Boyd. "Never before or after did I see loading like it," Boyd said later. "Eight hundred rounds went through that gun. . . . The crews would rush into the gun positions, fire fifteen to twenty rounds as quickly as possible, then rush back to safety before the counter fire started. . . . Every round through that gun was loaded by Mabley."[2] By the end of the day, Mabley was stone deaf, but he would man the gun for the rest of the battle despite the fact that his hearing would be permanently lost.

The second gun was better concealed than the first. It was positioned through a gap in a long brick wall. Behind its protective cover, the gunners were able to prepare themselves before lunging out to snap off a blaze of rounds. As soon as the German shells started to whine their way, they scampered back behind the wall. After leaving Mabley, Boyd stepped out from behind this wall as the men rushed once again to the gun, and heard a ping. A sniper bullet zipped between his spread legs, passing just slightly below his crotch. Boyd ran behind the wall before the sniper could chamber and snap off another, more accurate round.

◆ ◆ ◆

The paratrooper working the sniper rifle had fired across a distance of close to a mile. Yet he had come within inches of killing or wounding Boyd. Throughout the battle for Sicily and the long march up the boot of Italy, German snipers had plagued the Allied forces. The Germans made extensive use of these soldiers. A well-placed, competent sniper could force an entire battalion to deploy in reaction to the threat posed. German strategy was for snipers to move out at night and crawl deep into positions that the Allies would have trouble finding and destroying. At first light, they would start killing. German gunpowder released virtually no smoke, and the sniper rifles emitted little muzzle flash. This made it extremely difficult to locate the sniper.

German snipers sought victims worth killing. An infantry private was a poor target. His death would do little to destabilize an attacking platoon or company. Rather, the snipers were trained to focus on officers, non-commissioned officers, and radio signallers. After paying the price in the first days of Sicily, Canadian officers, from lieutenants to brigadiers, had ditched their holsters and pistols for rifles or Thompson submachine guns. Those who kept pistols stuck them inside their coats or shirts. Binoculars were similarly hidden. Some ripped the rank insignia off their uniforms. Every measure was taken to avoid looking like an officer, to blend with the soldiers around them. For an officer to stride about waving arms and yelling orders was to write a death warrant across his own forehead. The officers learned to give orders with a calmly spoken word or two that was passed along the line, or to exert control with a subtle movement of the hand or inclination of the head.

Even bold officers such as Major Jim Stone and Lieutenant Colonel Bert Kennedy took measures to make themselves appear less obviously in command. They did not shrink from enemy fire, but they did not seek through flamboyant demonstration of command to draw fire upon themselves. The truth was that Captain Paul Triquet of the Van Doos had been wrong during the attack on Casa Berardi. He had said, "Don't worry, they can't shoot." But the Germans shot very well. Canadian military analysts thought the German snipers were inferior to none. They were also considered immeasurably patient. It was nothing for a sniper to allow an entire company of infantry to pass by his line of fire without taking a shot at obvious targets. Instead, he would wait for the company headquarters or even the battalion headquarters to come forward, then shoot the radio signaller. Betrayed by the antenna waving above the radio on his back, so burdened he often walked bent over, and rendered deaf by the headphones, a signaller was virtually helpless to defend himself. He was also linked by the umbilical cord of the radio handset to the most desired sniping targets on the battlefield, either a company commander, an artillery forward observation officer, or, better still, a battalion commander or even a brigadier.

It took most of the march up the Italian boot for the Eighth Army and 1st Canadian Infantry Division to start meeting German snipers with their own. The British and Commonwealth command had no experience to draw upon. They responded to the slaughter of officers and radio signallers with hesitant, fretful steps. First, they issued six sniper rifles to each battalion with the idea that an equivalent number of soldiers would be transformed into deadly snipers. Designated the Lee Enfield No. 4 Sniper's Rifle, these rifles were just Mark 1 Lee Enfields mounted with a tangent rear sight and fitted for a telescopic sight. A thin cheek rest was also attached to the top of the rifle butt to allow the sniper to have some comfort during the long process of selecting targets, and to provide better gun stabilization against the effect of recoil.

German sniper rifles were equally crude. The standard German rifle was the Mauser Kar 98k, first constructed in 1935. It was little more than a shortened version of the rifle that the Germans had used in World War I. Rifles lacked the flair in weaponry that obsessed Adolf Hitler and the German high command. Their attention went to automatic weapons, tanks, jet-propelled aircraft, and self-propelled missiles, such as the V-1 and V-2 guided-missile bombs that would soon terrorize Great Britain. Because of this obsession with the sexier forms of weaponry, most German infantrymen carried a crude, inferior rifle into battle.

But the German snipers learned to use the rifle with masterly skill. They formed an elite of their own. They operated outside the confines of platoon, company, and battalion structures, normally reporting to regimental or battalion command. German snipers were as well trained in reconnaissance, observation, and unit identification as they were in shooting to kill. Every German division had a large number of snipers. First Parachute Division had more than most. In Ortona, the German snipers exacted a terrible price. And the designated snipers were supplemented by swarms of other parachutists who also took up sniping positions and were relatively capable marksmen.

Dug into heavily fortified positions, the German snipers and machine-gunners controlled movement on the streets of Ortona. To stay on the streets was to invite a bullet. To counter this threat, the Loyal Edmontons and Seaforths responded by deploying overwhelming superiority in firepower from the antitank guns and the Three Rivers tanks.

They had only a poor semblance of snipers themselves to deploy — six to a battalion. And these men were seldom left free to work independently from company-level operations. In Russia, Communist snipers had learned to counter German snipers through the development of patiently maintained hiding positions. They were also backed by a spotter equipped with binoculars or a spotting telescope. A Russian sniper and assistant would lie in a pile of rubble or in a basement, peering toward an area from which a German sniper was known to be firing. Sometimes the vigil took hours, other times days, even weeks. At last the German sniper would betray himself and the Russian would deliver a killing shot. Some of the best and most patient Russian snipers were women. Commonwealth troops seldom had such patience. They sniped as opportunity arose and only occasionally took the hours and days to counter the German snipers with stealth of their own. Most Canadian snipers were as likely to be drafted into working as riflemen as to be allowed to remain solely snipers. Seldom were they properly deployed. So the balance remained tipped in the favour of the German snipers.[3]

◆ ◆ ◆

In Ortona on the morning of December 23, the Germans seemed to retain the initiative no matter what actions the Canadians took. Paratroopers dominated the roofs with sniper fire. Machine guns controlled the streets. Mines made tank movement nearly impossible. Everything found inside a building was likely to be booby-trapped. At night, the paratroopers infiltrated back into positions from which they had been cleared during the day. The town seemed like some kind of evil maze, Germans sprouting up behind, beside, and in front of the Seaforths and Edmontons. Sheer endurance and dogged determination were about all the Canadians could offer up. They were still learning the ropes in the bloody world of street fighting. The parachutists were veterans. They had fought in Leningrad. Some had served in the streets of Stalingrad before the Sixth Army had been surrounded there. They had learned in the harshest training schools on earth. The veterans of the urban battles on the Russian front had passed their experience and knowledge to the newer recruits. In Ortona, they demonstrated their skill with deadly efficiency.

Feldwebel Fritz Illi and his platoon were constantly on the move. They believed themselves to be outnumbered and outgunned. Illi was exhausted — he had never seen such awful fighting. There seemed so few of them to hold an entire town against what he thought was an entire division of the Eighth Army. Since the British had burst into the town, the fighting had been continuous. (Illi had no idea the enemy were Canadians. To him they were just Tommies. British, Canadians, New Zealanders, and other Commonwealth troops all wore the same khaki uniforms, the same helmets, and carried the same weapons. So he thought he fought the British.) His platoon, slowly chipped away by casualties, moved every few hours from one position to another. Most of the positions were either firing pits dug into the rubble piles or small fortifications inside houses. To his veteran's eyes, Illi's men were substandard. He spent most of his time directing their fire, warning them about the hazards that could kill them. For the past three days, he and his men had slept hardly at all. They had not washed. From a distance, the Canadians seemed so clean, so well dressed, so strong and robust, and so very well armed.[4]

◆ ◆ ◆

Company Sergeant Major Jock Gibson and a small section of men from the Seaforths' 'D' Company worked their way up a narrow street leading toward a large square on Via Cavour. They kept to one side, pressed close to the walls of the buildings. One man would dash forward and duck into a doorway, then the next would leapfrog past him to the shelter of an alley. It was a frightening task, as they were very exposed to enemy ambush. Gibson was weary. His uniform was covered in what seemed to be several weeks' worth of mud, the blood of fallen comrades, the grime of gunpowder and sweat. He needed a shave and would have given just about anything for a bath.

Coming up on an intersection, he saw an officer and two Seaforth privates approaching the door to a nearby building. The officer raised his rifle, obviously intending to bash the door open with its butt. Gibson had a premonition. "Watch out!" he yelled. "Don't touch that door." The words had just left his mouth when the officer banged the door with the rifle butt, knocking it open. An explosion threw the man into the street. Forgetting about the danger of snipers, Gibson ran to him. The officer's ankle was hanging loose, connected to his leg by only a small scrap of flesh and muscle. Gibson strapped the ankle back to the rest of the leg as best he could with a bandage, and helped drag the man to the battalion HQ at Santa Maria di Costantinopoli. Then he returned to the never-ending battle.[5]

◆ ◆ ◆

Whether the Canadians used the streets or tried to advance by jumping from house to house by the second- or third-storey balconies, they were invariably exposed to fire. Trying to gain access to buildings through windows or doors made it easy for the paratroopers to ambush them with booby traps. A new strategy was needed. In the afternoon, Loyal Edmonton Captain Bill Longhurst thought he had the solution. He had set out to capture a stretch of rowhouses, but the street was totally enfiladed by machine-gun fire. Moving in the street would be suicide. Longhurst summoned two of the battalion's pioneers and got them to make a demolition charge with plastic explosives that could be moulded to whatever shape was required. This kind of charge was called a beehive, created by tying together whatever amount of plastic explosive was judged necessary to achieve the desired destructive effect. Sometimes the beehive would be wrapped around the end of a pole so that the charge could be put in place from a distance by extending the pole from a covered position to its destination.

Longhurst had the pioneers take the charge up to the top floor of the rowhouse his unit held. Germans were positioned in the building next door. Longhurst later wrote, "To get the right height they placed the 'Beehive' on a chair and leaned it against the wall. While the 'Beehive' was being set I gathered all my men on the ground floor. With the fuses set the pioneers tumbled down the stairs, and as they reached the ground floor, there was a loud explosion. We all tore up the stairs in order to get through the mouse-hole before the dust subsided, but there was no hole. What we thought was one wall was actually two walls. Again we set a 'Beehive,' went through the same routine as before, and this time found ourselves in the next house.

"The leading section into this house was the follow up section. It immediately cleared the floor and manned all windows covering the house on the opposite side of the street. The first section then came through, cleared the next floor up, then moved down and cleared the bottom floor."[6] The process of clearing floors was dangerous and bloody business. When a hole had been breached in the wall, the first section hurled a few grenades through. After these exploded, one or two men would jump into the smoke- and dust-filled room and rake it with Thompson submachine-gun fire. If there were paratroopers in the room, they usually died before they could react. The next section would move out. An upstairs floor would be cleared by spraying the stairwell with an automatic weapon and then charging up before the Germans could respond. Downstairs floors were subjected to showers of grenades thrown down the stairwell and then a mad rush by troops firing submachine guns and Bren guns.

Longhurst dubbed the wall-breaching technique mouse-holing, and word of its effectiveness spread like lightning through the two Canadian battalions. Although, as far as the Loyal Edmontons were concerned, Longhurst had invented a new method of street fighting, this was not exactly the case. British tactical doctrine for "Fighting in Built Up Areas" included a strategy known as the "vertical tactic." In 1941, a British Army training film showed troops employing a method of breaking into a house by cutting a hole in the roof, either with an axe or explosive charge. They then followed up by bursting through behind a screen of grenades.[7]

Commonwealth forces had had little expectation of actually having to fight in towns, so no attempt had been made to train either officers or common soldiers in the vertical technique, or even to make them aware of its existence. Loyal Edmonton Major Jim Stone had been to the British battle-drill schools, where the technique was supposed to be taught, and he had never been introduced to it. When Longhurst reported his success to Stone, the officer thought the tactic ingenious. "It was utterly new to me," he later said.[8]

Longhurst blew his way through one wall after another, managing to clear the entire block in a long afternoon of mayhem. To his surprise, each time his men occupied a house on one side of the street, the Germans withdrew from the house immediately opposite. This meant his men needed only to clear one side of the street to move the Canadian front forward.

The Seaforths added their own distinctive stamp to the mouse-holing method, and many of their pioneers denied that mouse-holing was an innovation they learned from the Edmontons. Sergeant Harry Rankin of the Seaforths' Pioneer Company argued that it was simply the logical thing to do, once the hazard of moving in the street was realized. Rankin's platoon was recovering hordes of Teller antitank mines, which were perfect for the task of mouse-holing. He would jam a bayonet in the wall, hang a Teller on it, slip a short time fuse to the built-in detonator, light it, and run like hell. Usually the result would be a nice hole in the wall through which the infantry could move. Sometimes the charge would fail to open a hole; other times it would bring the entire house crashing down. "We aren't exactly practising scientific demolitions here," Rankin would say, when an officer complained that the house he was planning to capture had instead been demolished.

Rankin never gave a thought to the destruction he was wreaking on Ortona with his explosives. There was a job to do, so he did it. If a tank was having trouble getting around a corner because the street was too narrow, he would set some plastic explosive charges and blow the obstructing walls out of the way. Destruction on demand, with nothing sophisticated about the methods. All a Seaforth had to do was send the word back, and Rankin and his team would appear to work their explosive magic.[9]

In this manner, the Canadians slowly bludgeoned their way through the streets of Ortona. Germans and Canadians alike laid waste to the town. The air was choked with smoke and dust. Fires burned in the wreckage of buildings. Hour after remorseless hour witnessed the constant din of explosions, machine guns rattling, rifles cracking, and masonry collapsing.

◆ ◆ ◆

Even from a distance, the savagery of the battle for Ortona was apparent. About two miles south of Ortona, war artist Captain Charles Comfort was based in a rear-area camp among the trees of a pretty orange grove located about a mile north of San Vito Chietino. "The very smell of death and destruction," he wrote in his diary, "reached us. . . . A holocaust of red glowed in the sky, revealing a ragged skyline as tongues of flames leapt into the night. We peered through the trembling darkness . . . overlooking the awesome scene. Downwind from the action the frightful intimate sounds of battle were all too clear, bursts of automatic fire, the Bren and the Schmeisser answering one another, each with its own distinctive accent. A dozen concurrent dialogues penetrated the blunter, duller, but more profound thunder of the gunning. From the intervening vineyards rose a ghostly vapour, like a shroud winding itself around the town. The most boisterous and profane among us became silent in face of what we witnessed. The morbid fascination of destruction held us in its grip as life and its monuments dissolved before our eyes. Over all, the deafening voice of guns beat a massive dirge like all the unmuffled drums of hell."[10]

The tent camp from which Comfort observed the battle was close to fifteen-year-old Anna Tucci's home in the ruins of what had been San Donato. So few buildings remained standing that it was hard to remember a tiny hamlet had existed here only weeks before. The pretty little white church where Anna and her neighbours had gone to pray and attend mass was demolished, just so many bits of rubble.

Although German artillery still occasionally searched for targets around the area, life was slowly returning to normal. Anna's father worked in the mud to repair the damage to the olive trees and vineyards. It would be a long process, he said, but eventually the farm would again prosper. Meanwhile, Anna washed clothes for the Canadians in exchange for rations. The food became a mainstay for the entire family. Anna's father spoke a small amount of English and this led to his befriending two Canadian soldiers. They came most evenings to the battered Tucci home for a visit. The men always brought food for the family and cigarettes for Anna's father. There was still much *vino rosso* in the family wine cellar, so the soldiers never left the house with empty hands.

The noise of the fighting in Ortona carried constantly on the wind, and Anna sometimes feared the war would never end. Her father had thought that when the Germans left their positions on the Moro River, the battle would soon be over and they would be free to rebuild and enjoy a life of peace. But the battle had not ended. The war continued to threaten their lives. For those civilians in Ortona, they thought, it must be like living in hell.[11]

◆ ◆ ◆

The Canadians saw little of the civilians hiding in Ortona. Most were in the tunnels in the northern sector of the town, an area soundly controlled by the Germans. There were a few, however, in the basements of the houses they captured. Captain June Thomas, commander of the Seaforths' 'A' Company, was on the ground floor of a house when an elderly woman dressed all in black, as was usual for Italian civilians, poked her head out of a cellar door and beckoned him to follow her into its depths. Somewhat warily, he descended the stairs and found himself in a dark, dank room lit only by candlelight. To his surprise and delight, the woman offered him a cup filled with steaming hot tea. In the shadows, he saw several children staring at him with big eyes. Thomas figured he must present a scary sight. There was something curiously restful about the whole scene in the cellar. The candles, the children, the warming tea, and the wrinkled smile of the old woman.

Outside, however, the war waited on him. Thomas forcibly gulped the scalding tea and handed the mug back to the woman. Then he ran back up the stairs, firmly closed the door to the cellar, and returned to his men.[12]

Nearby, journalist Christopher Buckley was also in a cellar. Buckley, along with Ross Munro and Matthew Halton, were the major war correspondents covering the battle. Their reports were drawing extraordinary attention. British, American, and Canadian newspapers carried headline stories comparing the battle in Ortona to that of Stalingrad, both in terms of ferocity and strategic significance. The *New York Times* ran two stories on consecutive days: "For some unknown reason the Germans are staging a miniature Stalingrad in Ortona," read the first day's report. The second described the fighting in Ortona as identical to "the fury of Stalingrad."[13]

In the cellar, Buckley was struck less by the fury of battle than by the stoic ability of humanity to survive all travails with some dignity and grace. "What a strange clutter of humanity it was," he wrote. "There were some five or six Canadian soldiers, there were old women and there were children innumerable. A painter of genius — Goya, perhaps — might have done justice to the scene. I felt no verbal description could do so. In the half-darkened room the pasta for the midday meal was simmering over the fire in the corner. Haggard, prematurely aged women kept emerging shyly one after another from some inner chamber where an old man, the grandfather of one of the numerous children, was dying. . . . Another old man was uttering maledictions against Mussolini. Then his wife surprisingly produced a jeroboam of Marsala and a half dozen glasses and moved among the soldiers, filling and re-filling glasses. . . . The children clambered around the Canadian soldiers and clutched at them convulsively every time one of our antitank guns, located only half a dozen paces from the door of the house, fired down the street in the direction of one of the remaining German machine-gun posts. Soon each one of us had a squirming, terrified child in his arms. And the old lady went on distributing Marsala."[14]

◆ ◆ ◆

After visiting the battalion headquarters of the Loyal Edmontons and the Seaforth Highlanders, Brigadier Bert Hoffmeister drove back to San Vito Chietino to check on the many wounded he knew had been evacuated from Ortona during the day. What he saw in the small hospital set up in the school there shocked him. The surgery was operating continuously, the two doctors seeming never to rest. German artillery was falling around the building. To protect one open-windowed wall from penetration by shrapnel, the medical staff had parked a hundredweight truck against the outside wall. The truck had suffered a direct hit and burned fiercely.

Wounded men lay everywhere inside the school. Most were on cots, but some were lying on blankets stretched out on the floor. The place was chock-full of wounded soldiers, many in critical condition. Hoffmeister was deeply disturbed to see that nobody had taken the time to even clean up the wounded men. "They still had the original blood from their wounds on their faces and their hands," he said later. Hoffmeister knew the male orderlies were doing the best they could for the men, but they were too few and were needed to perform basic first aid or to help out in the surgery. Yet in talking to the wounded, it was clear that the filth and blood covering them chipped away the last vestiges of their morale. Men could die if they lost the spirit to live. Hoffmeister was sure that unless conditions in the hospital were improved, there would be unnecessary deaths.

He managed to discuss the problem with surgeon Dr. Frank Mills. The doctor shared his concern. Hoffmeister suggested that a request be sent back down the medical service chain of command, calling for some of the nursing sisters stationed in a hospital south of the Sangro River to come forward and help out. Officially women were not allowed so close to the battlefield, but the need was urgent.

Mills agreed to forward the call for volunteers. On the morning of Christmas Eve, a small group of mostly British nursing sisters arrived at the hospital. The request had been presented to the women in a group meeting during the night. Every nurse present had volunteered to go forward into the battle zone to offer what succour she could to the wounded Canadians. Hearing the news, Hoffmeister felt overwhelmingly proud of "those girls and their willingness to risk their lives by working under shell fire and within range of long-range German mortars." They were, he thought, the angels of Ortona.[15]

# 24

# THE DARING
# GAMBLE

AT 1600 hours on December 23, the 48th Highlanders of Canada left the Hastings and Prince Edward Regiment's position on the ridgeline in a single file. About 400 men, they carried only rifles, Bren guns, Thompson submachine guns, ammunition, grenades, and a few rations. Left behind were the mortars, the antitank guns, and the Vickers medium machine-guns and mortars of the Saskatoon Light Infantry support battalion. They trudged past the forward platoons of the Hasty P's and disappeared one after the other into a night drenched by heavy rain.

A mostly friendly rivalry existed between these two regiments of 1st Canadian Infantry Brigade. Both were formed from militias in Ontario. The Hasty P's came out of the province's rural roots: the men were drawn from farms, mines, and small factory towns. The 48th Highlanders hailed from Toronto. To the Highlanders, the Hasty P's were the Plough Jockeys. That regiment retaliated by spurning the Highlanders as the Glamour Boys, soldiers who looked good in their kilts marching down Queen Street but were of little use in a fight.

Tonight the Highlanders wore no kilts. They moved quietly, each maintaining a space of only inches between himself and the back of the man in front of him. As they passed, one Hasty P muttered, "Good Christ! The Glamour Boys have gone crazy."[1]

The soldier was right. If successful, the Highlanders' plan would be hailed as a daring gamble. Failure would result in tragedy, perhaps the destruction of the regiment. The Highlanders had been ordered to take an incredible risk.

Lieutenant Colonel Ian Johnston had not wanted his regiment to make this attack. The evening before, he had warned 1st Canadian Infantry Brigade commander Lieutenant Colonel Dan Spry that a night attack along the ridgeline could not be undertaken unless the battalion could conduct a visual reconnaissance from the attack's start line prior to the onset of darkness. Because the Hasty P's had been delayed in capturing their objectives, such reconnaissance had proved impossible. The Highlanders reached the start line only after darkness had concealed all land features and the enemy positions undoubtedly lurking beyond the perimeter held by the Hasty P's. Johnston had argued that the attack should be cancelled. Spry passed Johnston's request up the line to divisional headquarters. Major General Chris Vokes and his staff had come back with an order to proceed with the fantastic plan. Vokes wanted to keep the momentum of the three-phase attack moving. To wait for morning would be to allow the 1st Parachute Division time to reorganize and possibly to block 1 CIB's plan to close the roads north of Ortona.[2]

Johnston and his company commanders were forced to plan a surprise attack in little more than an hour. Aerial photos of the area showed a meandering footpath that seemed to bear generally toward their objective — the ridge's highest point, which overlooked the hamlets of San Nicola and San Tomasso. Surrounding the path was a sea of mud and vineyards. Trying to move in any normal attack formation through the mud and vines in darkness would be impossible. The footpath, however, would offer firmer ground over which men could move in a more organized fashion. If the path was unguarded or only lightly guarded, the Highlanders might get through. There was a slim chance they could surprise the enemy. It was a dreadful night, the worst to date. Would the Germans not be keeping their heads down, trying to stay warm and dry? That was the faint hope.

It was a mile to the objective. If they ran into more than token opposition or were discovered while still too far from the objective, the attack would be a disaster. Entering a firefight from a single-file formation would inevitably end in mass confusion, with the companies all intermixed. A retreat would surely turn into a rout, with every man fending for himself. Casualties would be terrible, and the probability of the entire battalion ending up dead, wounded, or as prisoners was too awful to even contemplate.

Decision made and preparation complete, Johnston gave Major John Clarke a grin, shook the rain from his helmet, and said in a surprisingly cheery voice, "Lead on. Let's go!"[3] Clarke, commanding 'A' Company, was the first man in the line to leave the start position. Everything depended on him. The line of march was 'A' Company leading, 'C' Company immediately behind, then battalion HQ, 'D' Company, and finally 'B' Company.[4] When the last man in 'B' Company stepped off from the start line, the battalion was swallowed by the darkness.

◆ ◆ ◆

The column advanced at a slow, shuffling pace punctuated by sudden halts and long pauses. It was so dark that each soldier clutched the bayonet scabbard of the man before him. This meant the entire line was physically linked one man to the other from head to tail. In the lead, Clarke felt his way up the trail. Seeing the path itself was impossible; only the footing warned if he was losing the track. On either side was deep mud, while on the trail the mud was slightly firmer. To use a flashlight would instantly betray their position to the Germans. Not a single star glimmered through the overhanging cloud. The rain was a mixed blessing. It soaked and chilled them to the bone, but it also splashed down noisily on the surrounding vines and other foliage, concealing the small muffled noises that 400 men could not avoid making. A splash here when a man stepped into a puddle, the clink of metal when a grenade bumped a rifle barrel, a soft curse when a soldier stumbled and almost fell. Despite the cold that caused the men to shiver, sweat streamed down many faces.

From the aerial photos it had been impossible to develop a list of recognizable landmarks to mark their progress. Clarke could only follow the trail. He could only hope that no unknown path crossed the one they followed. To take a wrong turn and become lost would

mean disaster. To lose the trail and end up blundering in the vineyards would also spell disaster. All around him catastrophe lurked
in unknown, unseen ways. The pressure the officer was under was
almost unbearable.

Every few minutes, the surrounding countryside was softly illuminated by the glimmering light of a distant artillery burst or the
flash of a battery firing. Sometimes the light came from in front of
them, the fire of a German battery. Other times they were backlit by a
Canadian battery firing. Each time they froze, tried to become statues
who blended with their dark surroundings. Clarke used the brief seconds of dim light to try to orient himself.

They were about 700 yards out when the rattle of gunfire broke
out behind them. The Hasty P's were staving off the first paratrooper
infiltration party. At least some of the Germans were active. The
threat of the Highlanders bumping into a German patrol using the
trail heightened.

Out of the gloom, Clarke saw a house standing next to the path
before him. To get to their objective, the entire battalion would have
to walk past the structure. Clarke halted the column and advanced
on the house with the leading platoon. A German sentry hunkered
against the rain in front of a door. One of the Canadians crept
up, jumped the man, and knifed him to death. The other soldiers
moved quickly to cover every ground-floor door and window. Then a
section pushed the front door open and lunged into the house. In the
big central room, a group of fifteen paratroopers sat around a large
table. Their shirts were open, weapons leaning against walls or
hanging from pegs, Christmas parcels and bottles of wine crowding
the table top. The Germans stared blankly at the dripping, filthy
Canadians. Then two of the paratroopers awoke from their surprise
and sprang for their weapons. Clarke's men killed the two with bayonet thrusts. The surviving paratroopers quickly put their hands up
and surrendered.

The prisoners were bundled out of the house and sent back under
guard down the side of the long line. They had been warned that if
any of them tried to escape they would all immediately be killed.
They would meet the same fate if any noise or alarm was raised.
Clarke led the way again toward the objective. Soon another house
was encountered. This time it was unguarded. The Canadians burst

in and bagged six prisoners without a fight, rousting the dazed, sleeping Germans from their beds. They were passed back down the line and escorted from its tail through the night to the Hastings and Prince Edward Regiment's position.

The column pressed on, moving jerkily from one prolonged halt to another. There came a halt that was longer than any before. Then word came down the line from Clarke to Johnston. The major thought he was lost. Johnston and his intelligence officer hurried up the line to confer with Clarke. They found him in a small farmhouse. Two paratroopers sat in a corner of the main room. Both men were bleeding from minor bayonet wounds suffered in a short scuffle over possession of the house.

The three officers risked a flashlight inside the concealment of the house. They played the light back and forth from aerial photo to map. After a few minutes, Johnston and Clarke realized the Highlanders were not lost at all. Instead, they were standing precisely on the objective.[5] The time was 1940. It had taken the Highlanders three hours and forty minutes to cover a distance of one mile to their objective on the ridgeline summit overlooking San Tomasso and San Nicola.[6] Phase two of 1 CIB's offensive task had been achieved without a single shot fired. Remarkably, the 1st Parachute Division remained unaware of the presence of the Highlanders. Johnston set his men to work establishing a circular perimeter around the little farmhouse. The Highlanders' job was now to hold their position and wait for the Royal Canadian Regiment to carry out phase three. Midnight came and went. The Highlanders hunkered in their waterlogged, hastily dug slit trenches. It was Christmas Eve.

At 0300, Johnston ordered 'D' Company to send a thirty-man patrol back to the battalion's rear-area headquarters with the order for a party to bring the mortars, antitank guns, medium machine guns, and rations up to the forward position. The plan was for the patrol to follow a more direct, wider dirt track back to the Hasty P's and then to the rear-area HQ. The patrol set off, but returned only an hour and a half later with the report that the paratroopers had this route heavily covered. There was no way to get supporting arms up to the battalion, as the narrow trail used earlier was too poor to handle such heavy traffic. Luckily, the patrol had only briefly engaged in a firefight with the Germans, and had withdrawn without betraying the battalion's position or strength to the paratroopers. The battalion remained hidden, but Johnston knew this would change at daybreak.[7]

♦ ♦ ♦

At first light on Christmas Eve Day, the Royal Canadian Regiment moved into the Hastings and Prince Edward Regiment's perimeter. RCR commander Major Strome Galloway's orders were to advance through the Hasty P's to a position just south of where the 48th Highlanders were located. The RCR would then continue moving through the 48th Highlander ranks to cut the main coast highway north of Ortona. There would be no pre-artillery barrage, because the 48th Highlanders were positioned in front of the attacking force. However, the battalion would have four forward observation officers, one with Galloway and one accompanying each of the three leading company commanders. Their presence was intended to guarantee the ability of the artillery to bring immediate and well-targeted fire on any German strongpoints that might oppose the attack. The Ontario Tanks located near the Hasty P's were to try and lumber through the mud in support.[8]

From the outset, phase three of the 1st Canadian Infantry Brigade's offensive plan, aimed at encircling the paratroopers stationed in Ortona, was a cobbled-together and ill-planned effort. Even with reinforcements, the RCR was still seriously understrength from the mauling it had taken during the earlier fights at Royal Canadian Avenue and in front of The Gully. Galloway's men would be attempting to cross heavily contested ground. Throughout the night, the Hasty P's had fought off numerous attempted infiltrations by the paratroopers. Just before dawn, its right and front flanks had been struck by determined counterattacks. Both had been repelled, but the attacks showed that the Germans were lurking in the very terrain through which the RCR was expected to attack.[9] The mud would slow the attackers, while the vineyards sheltered the German defenders. Without the protection of a creeping barrage, the infantry would be exposed to enemy fire for the entire forward advance.

Galloway and Hasty P's commander Lieutenant Colonel Bert Kennedy climbed into a loft in the top of a tall house within the Canadian perimeter. From this perch, they were able to observe the ground over which the RCR would attack. The plan called for the battalion to push along the better-developed track that the Highlanders had found heavily covered by Germans during the previous night. Neither man liked the look of the terrain or the track. Galloway summoned the RCR company commanders into the loft and pointed out the route they were to follow in the attack. 'A' Company, commanded by Captain Dick Dillon, was to lead. Dillon, Galloway wrote in his diary, "was incredulous at the ground he had to cross."[10] Dillon's men were to move up a small gully for a short distance, then cross over its crest and follow the muddy, vineyard-bordered track to link up with the 48th Highlanders.

When 'A' Company emerged from the gully, it immediately came under heavy mortar and artillery fire. Within seconds, sixteen men had been killed or wounded. Captain Dillon, Lieutenant Buck Bowman, and Captain Fitzgerald, the FOO, were among the wounded. The company reeled back into the gully and took up a defensive position.

Galloway sent 'B' Company into the gully to strengthen 'A' Company's left flank. 'C' and 'D' companies closed up on the gully to the immediate rear of the two leading companies. 1st Canadian Infantry Brigade commander Lieutenant Colonel Dan Spry told Galloway to continue the attack when the timing seemed right.[11]

While these manoeuvres were going on, the battalion received a large draft of reinforcements, totalling eight officers and 144 other ranks. Five of the officers were RCR veterans: Captain Ted Littleford, Captain Ernie Jackson, and lieutenants Pete Hertzberg, Bill Powers, and Bill Bennett. The other three officers were newly minted lieutenants with little experience. Most of the infantrymen were "green" troops with no former combat experience. Galloway took the officers aside and gave them a short briefing on what to expect in this tough battlefield. He warned them not to "stick out their necks until they got battlewise."[12] The reinforcements were then divided into company lots and sent forward to bolster the depleted strengths of the four rifle companies. Captain Jackson took over command of 'A' Company.

Galloway saw no hope of fighting through to the Highlanders during the day. The Germans would see any attack coming and plaster it with the same deadly mortar and artillery fire that had shattered 'A' Company's attack. He would have to wait until night.

At 1830 hours, he sent 'B' Company under Captain Tony Burdett forward with instructions to creep through to the Highlanders. The company set off, advancing slowly and carefully through the impenetrable darkness of a night chilled by an icy drizzle. The mud sucked at the men's boots, turning the advance into an exhausting slog. Conditions soon worsened, as the lead platoon came into an area of vineyards where the vines were secured to training wires so low that the men were forced to drop prone and wriggle forward under the thick foliage. Soon the entire company was crawling under the low vines through the quagmire. Burdett's men wormed their way right into a trap. As they approached the other edge of the vineyard, they were raked by intense heavy-machine-gun fire. Several officers and men were wounded. Burdett, unable to direct his troops effectively in the morass of mud and the tangled vineyard, had to order a retreat.[13]

That was the end of the RCR's attempt to carry out phase three. Later that night, Spry told Galloway that the plan to cut the coast highway was scrapped. RCR would instead force open a corridor between the Hasty P's and the 48th Highlanders. This would enable a badly needed resupply and the supporting arms to be moved up to the now surrounded Highlanders. The RCR's new mission was to break the siege the Highlanders would surely face in the morning.[14]

For their part, the Highlanders had passed a surprisingly quiet day. Although Lieutenant Colonel Ian Johnston had sent out several patrols that discovered paratroopers digging in on all the regiment's flanks, only a few short firefights had ensued and just two Highlanders had been wounded. The battalion's position had been harassed throughout the day by snipers and some machine guns in a group of nearby houses, but their fire was largely ineffective. For some unknown reason, the Germans largely ignored the battalion for the entire day. With no supporting weapons of their own, it was impossible for the Highlanders to retaliate against the paratroopers. All they could do was dig in and carefully preserve their limited small-arms ammunition, so they could offer determined resistance to the counterattacks that must surely come.[15]

# 25

## IT'S CHRISTMAS EVE

Jock Gibson of the Seaforth Highlanders of Canada had finally found what he considered a worthwhile role for himself as 'D' Company's company sergeant major. He administered the resupplying with ammunition and grenades of the elements of his company scattered throughout Ortona. In the past two days, Gibson had built up a sizable stock of ammunition boxes and grenade cases in an apartment building just behind the company's main positions.

On Christmas Eve morning, however, Gibson realized that his effective system was jeopardized when several German mortar bombs landed close to the building. Gibson figured the paratroopers must have seen men coming and going from the ground floor and correctly surmised it served as a supply depot. If the mortars hit the building, all the ammunition stored there would be set off. He had to move the ammunition and move it fast.

Gibson rounded up some men and led them into the building. They started loading up with cans of ammo and grenades. Hearing voices in the top storey, Gibson checked upstairs and was surprised to find 2nd Canadian Infantry Brigade commander Brigadier Bert

Hoffmeister and a scout officer looking out a window at the German positions. Gibson knew "Hoffy" well. He had served as the officer's pipe sergeant in the Vancouver militia days. Gibson never even saluted. He just said, "You better get out of this building because they've got it spotted." Hoffmeister looked at Gibson with a mockingly stern expression. "You didn't shave this morning, eh, Jock?" Gibson laughed. "No, sir. I've been a bit busy." He warned Hoffmeister again that the building was likely to be hit by artillery any minute. Gibson then went back to moving ammunition. A few minutes later, as heavily laden as he could manage, he fled the apartment building with the last of the ammunition boxes.[1]

About the time Gibson entered the room, Hoffmeister had come to the same conclusion as the company sergeant major. The window he and the scout officer were looking out of had been blown apart by a shell, so it now formed a gaping hole. His view of the nearby enemy positions was excellent. So excellent that after Gibson left he turned to the other officer and said, "If I can see them, then they sure as hell can see me." The two men ducked into the hallway and not a second later a German shell exploded directly in the spot where they had been standing. Hoffmeister and the officer ran down the stairs and out of the building. A heavy salvo of shells rained down, blowing the structure to pieces.[2]

Hoffmeister was having a terrible time keeping abreast of the ebb and flow of the battle his Loyal Edmonton and Seaforth battalions fought inside Ortona. The men were scattered all over in small clumps numbering from one man to a dozen or more. Along the wider streets, various tanks from 'A' Squadron of the Three Rivers Tanks were adding their weight by serving as close-quarters mobile artillery. If there was a building the infantry wanted knocked apart, the tankers were only too happy to oblige.

The situation was frustrating for a brigade commander. He could hardly exert any control over the battle. Nor could his battalion commanders do much. They tried to focus attacks along streets that would enable the Canadians to continue forcing the paratroopers back toward the northern edge of the town. This still meant that men had to get into the adjacent side streets and clear the buildings there. Otherwise, the Germans infiltrated behind the companies advancing up the main streets. With half the infantry busily mouse-holing their way from building to building, even knowing where the Canadian soldiers were half the time proved next to impossible.

To make his presence felt — in order to bolster morale as much as anything — Hoffmeister insisted on going into the town a couple of times a day. He would visit the forward battalion headquarters of both units and then try to get up close to the actual fighting for a first-hand look at the battle's progress, and to be seen doing so by the men in the line companies. Hoffmeister entered Loyal Edmonton commander Lieutenant Colonel Jim Jefferson's HQ just as the officer was sending some reinforcements out to the rifle companies. Among them was a young officer Hoffmeister thought looked bewildered by the instructions Jefferson was giving — instructions intended to help keep the officers alive.[3]

◆ ◆ ◆

Ortona ate up reinforcements at a frightening rate. There was no leeway in the streets for inexperienced soldiers to learn the art of urban combat. Lieutenant John Dougan of the Loyal Edmontons' 'D' Company received word around mid-morning that a group of about twenty reinforcements was coming forward to join the company. Dougan set off to guide the men into forward positions. Dodging from building corner to building corner, ducking into doorways, crouching in holes in the rubble piles, Dougan moved a hundred yards to the rear and then peered around a corner to see if the reinforcements were coming up. They were. Twenty or so of them, marching right up the centre of the street as if on parade.

Dougan stepped around the corner and started waving the men off, calling to them to take cover. He was too late. A mortar bomb exploded directly in the midst of the marching column. Seventeen of the men were immediately killed or wounded. Dougan helped organize a stretcher party to evacuate the wounded. Then, blood smeared all over his legs, Dougan made his way back to the front line. He felt terribly tired, terribly old. The weariness seemed to extend throughout his body. For some reason his left leg didn't work properly. He had developed a limp.[4]

An hour after, he joined company commander Major Jim Stone in the company headquarters set up in a badly battered old building. Stone looked over at Dougan with a puzzled expression. "What's the matter with your leg?" "Nothing, sir," answered Dougan. "What the hell are you dragging it for, then?"

Dougan looked at his leg for the first time since he had started limping. The left knee of his pants was torn. Parting the material slightly, he saw welling blood. Stone called a stretcher-bearer over as Dougan pulled the pant leg up. There was a hole in his knee, blood dribbling from the wound. A fragment from the mortar bomb that had shredded the reinforcement party had hit him. Dougan thought he was simply too tired to have felt the pain that such a wound should have caused. Despite his protests, Stone ordered the lieutenant to lie down on a stretcher. Dougan was then evacuated to the Forward Aid Post at battalion headquarters.[5]

The medical officer there told Dougan he would be sent back to San Vito Chietino immediately. Dougan was dismayed. He didn't want to leave the battalion. They had all come through so much together in the past few weeks. "It's Christmas Eve," he said. "I want to stay here and be with the regiment on Christmas." The medical officer, a friend of Dougan's, finally agreed that he could stay at battalion headquarters until Christmas Day was over. After that, he would have to go to the rear for treatment.[6]

A short time after Dougan arrived at battalion HQ, second-in-command Major Ted Day came in and stood beside his cot. "I've got something for you," Day said. Without further ceremony, he handed over a Military Cross and told Dougan it was for his bravery at Hill 736 in Sicily. Day then went back to work. A bemused Dougan wondered if he had got the medal this way because Day expected him to die from the wound.[7]

◆ ◆ ◆

The rate of casualties had reduced most of the rifle companies in the two battalions engaged in Ortona to fewer than thirty men, instead of a normal strength of about one hundred. Effectively, the Edmontons and Seaforths were less battalions now than rifle companies, the companies mere platoons. Despite their weakened state, the regiments continued to shove the paratroopers back, gaining ground building by building, block by block.

At Piazza Municipali, Corso Vittorio Emanuele broke up into a warren of streets branching to the right or left of the municipal hall.

One ran to the right, passing the Piazza San Tomasso, where the cathedral stood, and terminated in front of the old castle. The left-hand street was short, barely fifty yards long. It led into Piazza Plebiscita. This square was the junction of three major Ortona streets: Via Monte Maiella, Via Roma, and Via Tripoli. Via Monte Maiella ran in a straight line southwest from here to Piazza San Francesco on the southwest side of the town. Three large buildings dominated that square: the San Francesco cathedral, and the town's school and hospital. Following a northwestern line from Piazza Plebiscita was Via Roma, which hooked into the coast highway to Pescara. Running almost directly north from the square was Via Tripoli, which angled to the left after about a quarter mile and met the coast highway. At that point, it was bordered on one side by an escarpment overlooking the Adriatic and on the other by Ortona's cemetery.

The Edmontons were now fighting their way toward Piazza Plebiscita and also advancing along Corso Matteotti toward Cattedrale San Tomasso. Directly behind the Piazza was the head of Fosso Ciavocco, a narrow ravine that trailed down to the Adriatic, creating a physical barrier between the two northern sections of Ortona. The part of the town dominated by the great cathedral and the ancient castle was effectively isolated from the coast highway by this ravine. For this reason, the Edmonton advance into this area was less determined than the fight to seize the piazza and follow Via Tripoli. Once the Edmontons reached the northern end of Via Tripoli, any Germans in the area of the cathedral and the castle would likely withdraw along the Adriatic shoreline across the base of the ravine. They would be under Canadian guns the entire way. The Canadians did not expect the Germans to seriously defend the castle. It could be easily isolated, and the thick sandstone walls offered little protection from modern artillery. Already the seventeen-pounder antitank guns had punched several large holes in the walls, and artillery fire falling inside the castle walls had caused considerable damage to the interior of the ancient structure.

West of the Edmontons, the Seaforths were concentrating on capturing Piazza San Francesco. Once in possession of the square, they could drive the paratroopers up Via Cavour and Via Monte Maiella toward Piazza Plebiscita, which was expected to soon be firmly in Edmonton hands. Again, the Germans would be faced with either abandoning the section of town lying between these two streets or being crushed between the two advancing pincers of the Seaforths and the Edmontons' blocking force at the Piazza Plebiscita. To escape this entrapment, the paratroopers would have to allow the Canadians possession of virtually all the built-up areas of Ortona. They would be left holding the cemetery and a small scattering of houses in the Via Roma area. There would be no advantage in trying to defend this ground, so a complete withdrawal from Ortona should follow.[8]

While this strategy seemed sound, its execution was anything but systematic. The Seaforths and Edmontons spent most of the day battering against fiercely defended German positions, in the most bitter fighting soldiers on either side had yet seen.

◆ ◆ ◆

It seemed inevitable to Seaforth Bren gunner Private Fred Mallett that whenever a German position was located and engaged, at least one man in 'B' Company was killed or wounded during the ensuing fight. It also seemed that the number of German positions the Seaforths had to face ultimately outnumbered the company's dwindling ranks.

Ahead, another German position was discovered. The riflemen started closing on it. Mallett's job was to provide covering fire for the riflemen. He climbed to the top of a two-storey building, so he could fire over the heads of his comrades. The building was badly shot up. Only a half wall remained to offer some protection. To his right, the wall had a great gaping hole in it. But that area had already been cleared, so he didn't worry about being exposed to the windows of the buildings on that side.

As he looked over the half wall, Mallett sensed a movement in a window of the building that the riflemen were attacking. He rose to a crouch, bringing up the Bren to fire a burst at the shadowy target. Blinding pain engulfed him before he could squeeze the trigger.

Mallett regained consciousness perhaps five or ten minutes later, although he had no real idea of how long he had been unconscious. The soldier discovered that his right side was paralyzed. He lay on his right side, his back to the gaping hole facing the houses that were supposed to have been cleared of snipers. His left side seemed to still function. He started crawling toward the stairs. The moment he did so, however, another burst of fire hit him in the back. The sniper, obviously occupying one of the upper storeys of the buildings that Mallett had believed clear, had been keeping an eye on him, waiting to see if the first burst had succeeded in killing him. Mallett lay still for a long time, knowing if he moved again the German would shoot him. It was unlikely he would survive being shot three times.

Eventually he started crawling again, clawing his way across the floor with his left arm and leg. The German sniper must have dismissed Mallet as dead, for no third burst came his way. Mallett reached the stairwell and slid painfully down two flights to the ground floor. The men in his rifle section were across the street. They saw him struggling to reach the doorway.

One of the soldiers, ignoring the sniper fire, ran across. The man bent down, picked Mallett's 190-pound body up in his arms as he would a baby, and raced back to the rest of the section. Mallett was vaguely aware of a first-aid man working on him, then of four comrades carrying him on a stretcher through the streets. Later he found himself in a jeep, lying on one of its three stretchers. By evening, he was in an operating theatre in the field dressing station in San Vito Chietino.

When he awoke from surgery, Mallett assumed he must be dead. He could hear angels singing — a heavenly choir welcoming him with Christmas carols. Then a gruff voice brought him back to earth. He stared up at the doctor, who said, "Would you like one of the bullets as a souvenir?" Mallett said yes. A bullet with a flattened tip was handed over. Mallett discovered the choir was a group of nurses and orderlies singing Christmas carols to the wounded. Outside the building, the roar of incoming mortar shells threatened to drown the sweetly singing voices.[9]

◆ ◆ ◆

In the signals area of the Seaforths' battalion headquarters, Lieutenant Wilf Gildersleeve was worried that the radio team in 'D' Company might have been wiped out by a German sniper or artillery shell. His repeated attempts to raise them produced no response. It was possible, he knew, that the team's batteries had failed or that for some other reason their radio was out of commission. Gildersleeve stuffed a couple of batteries in his haversack, picked up his Thompson submachine gun, and headed into the Ortona streets to find out what was going on.

The tall former invoice clerk who had won a scholarship to the Pitman Business College for his boy-soprano singing at a British Columbia Music Festival competition moved warily. Eventually he came to a building near Piazza San Francesco, where 'D' Company's headquarters were located. As he stepped into the doorway, a very nervous sentry shoved a Thompson into his stomach and snapped, "What's the password?" Gildersleeve fumbled a moment, remembered, and gave it to him. The man stepped aside. The officer went upstairs to the radio room. Inside, he found the two signallers hunched over the radio. Both men were dead asleep. The set was still operating, the chatter of the various companies passing back and forth.

Gildersleeve gently shook his men awake. He supposed he should be angry. But the officer knew that the men had probably not slept for three days and had finally just surrendered to exhaustion. They were both good soldiers, one the oldest and the other the youngest member of the Seaforths' signals section. Private Vic Warner was forty, and it had only recently been discovered that Private Howard Wiley was a mere seventeen. When this battle was over, he would be shipped back to Canada for being underage. Gildersleeve left the spare batteries with the two men and returned to battalion HQ. He then ordered a third signaller to go to each of the company radio teams. The men were to ensure they alternated sleeping schedules so nobody fell asleep again while on duty.[10]

◆ ◆ ◆

Lieutenant Colonel Syd Thomson held the right wrist of his good friend, Major Tom Vance. The young officer, temporarily blinded by an exploding artillery shell in the first Seaforth attempt to cross the Moro River, had returned to duty only two days earlier. Now he lay in the Forward Aid Post with a sniper's bullet lodged just below the collarbone in the left side of his neck. Dr. Anderson stood opposite Thomson, slowly feeding plasma into Vance's left arm.

Vance was the son of a well-known Vancouver criminologist and had just qualified to practise law when war broke out. He and Thomson had met in Calgary in early 1940 during an officers training course. They had been fast friends ever since. In Britain, Thomson had a steady girlfriend, whom he had asked to marry him. Vance and Thomson had often gone on double dates, Vance taking out Thomson's girlfriend's sister. If asked to describe Vance, Thomson would have said he was an intelligent, unassuming, possibly too trusting young man with a brilliant future ahead of him in the postwar world.

There would, however, be no future. Holding Vance's right wrist, urging the beat of life in his veins to keep throbbing, Thomson felt the young officer's pulse slow and then cease beating altogether. Dr. Anderson and Thomson stared sadly across the operating table at each other. Then Anderson turned, picked up two glasses, and filled each with precious Scotch whisky. He set the glasses on Vance's chest. Doctor and battalion commander raised the glasses in a silent toast.[11]

Many individual soldiers Thomson had known since the beginning of the war had died or been severely wounded in Ortona, and the Seaforth Highlanders of Canada itself seemed to be perishing. Thomson wondered how the regiment would ever rebuild after such loss of experienced personnel. The stream of wounded and dying flowing through the Forward Aid Post was staggering. In the streets, the bodies of Seaforths lay scattered through the buildings and on the cobblestones. Nobody had time to gather up those who died, so they were left where they fell.[12]

The new men coming in as reinforcements, although they had experienced extensive training in Canada and Britain, were usually chewed up and spit out by the meat grinder of Ortona in mere hours. Thomson had seen Tom Middleton, the brother of long-time Seaforth Lieutenant Fred Middleton, arrive as a reinforcement that morning. The Middletons were both from Thomson's hometown of Salmon Arm in the British Columbia interior. Thomson had sent Tom Middleton out to 'A' Company, which was badly understrength.[13] Two hours later, the young man came back on a stretcher severely wounded. He started the long evacuation down a line that would end back in Canada with a medical discharge from the army.[14]

◆ ◆ ◆

Captain June Thomas's 'A' Company reached the edge of Piazza San Francesco in the early afternoon. The Canadians were unaware of its proper name. Previously it had just been marked on the map as an open space surrounded by some large buildings. Sprawled in the street before the San Francesco cathedral was a dead horse. Accordingly, the Seaforth commanders reported to battalion HQ that they now faced Dead Horse Square.

Thomas and his men had come up on the square by a narrow lane. Looking around the corner into the square, he could see that Germans were firing from the cathedral. Its bell tower already had a gaping hole in the southern side and other shell holes had been blown in the roof and walls of the building. The school was similarly smashed up, but there seemed to be no enemy fire coming from it. That was odd. Still, the Germans had not consistently defended every large building.

He decided to secure the school with one section of his depleted company.[15] Lieutenant Stewart Lynch slipped over to the school with the six-man section and ordered the corporal in charge of the men to sweep the building and then hold it.[16] The section consisted of reinforcements, mostly veteran Seaforths, who were returned from bouts of illness or who had been on other duties in North Africa until being rushed to Ortona. Among them was a twenty-six-year-old private, Gordon Currie-Smith, who had been cooling his heels in the reinforcement camp in Philippeville, Algeria, since arriving in North Africa from Canada en route to returning to the Seaforth Regiment.

Currie-Smith was a very small man, barely five feet tall and weighing hardly more than one hundred pounds. Yet he had been a professional soldier since the mid-1930s, serving first in the Irish Fusiliers and then in the Seaforths. Currie-Smith had not gone overseas in 1940 with the Seaforths, being detailed instead to the training camp in Vernon, British Columbia, to serve as a sergeant-trainer. With the Sicily invasion, Currie-Smith decided he had had enough of being out of the action and applied, as he had several times before, for a return to his regiment overseas. Called into the camp commander's office, Currie-Smith was informed he could have his transfer, but only if he agreed to a demotion to private. Knowing in advance this was likely to be the condition, Currie-Smith had already loosened the stitches from his stripes. He yanked the stripes off and hurled them on the desk in front of the commander, telling him in no uncertain terms where he could put them. The officer curtly sent Currie-Smith on his way.[17]

Now, looking over at the schoolhouse, neither Currie-Smith nor the corporal commanding the section liked the situation. It seemed ridiculous that the Germans would just hand over a large three-storey building without exacting their normal pint of blood. The corporal and Currie-Smith had only been in Ortona for a day. But they had already heard enough about the German penchant for booby traps to think the Canadians were being deliberately lured into the building. Lynch ignored their protests and told the men to follow their orders.

The small section entered the school, swept it, and then scattered throughout the ground floor. There were so few of them that each man had to operate alone. Currie-Smith was frightened. He felt tremendously uneasy about being in this building.[18]

Currie-Smith's concerns were warranted. Within an hour of the section's occupation of the school, an enormous explosion shook the square. Thomas was down an alley and didn't see what happened. Company Sergeant Major W.C. Smith did. The entire building simply erupted in a vast shower of masonry. When the debris stopped falling, Smith ran over to the rubble pile, hoping to find some survivors. He scrabbled his way through the debris, but it seemed all the men had been completely buried or blown apart. As he started back to the Seaforth lines, a sniper fired a shot from the church bell tower and the round creased Smith's backside. The man ran for cover.[19]

At least one man was still alive. Currie-Smith was wedged tightly on all sides by concrete blocks. Rubble covered him from feet to neck. Miraculously, a small space was clear around his face and a trickle of air flowed down past the concrete block looming immediately over his head. He could not see the sky. His legs, hands, and arms were all pinned tightly. Currie-Smith was entombed inside the ruin of the school.[20]

◆ ◆ ◆

German Fallschirmpionier Karl Bayerlein heard the explosion. He wrote in his diary at day's end, "Close to us, during the day, a whole building on the enemy side exploded under a huge bang and parts of the building flew hundreds of metres away. We were able to get under cover before the debris came down on us."[21]

Bayerlein thought perhaps the explosion had resulted from the water-closet trap. Many buildings had been mined this way in recent days. The amount of explosives being packed inside some of the buildings was unbelievable. They packed as many boxes of explosives in as they possibly could, using up the great surpluses of Italian mines and dynamite they had brought into Ortona. All day long, Bayerlein and his comrades alternately destroyed or mined buildings. They blew most of them down into piles of rubble to serve as tank obstacles and to clear lanes of fire for the machine guns.

The work was terribly dangerous. Bayerlein was very afraid a bullet would hit him while he carried a heavy load of mines and explosives. He was also slowed by the fact that the boots he had retrieved recently from an abandoned Italian supply depot had lost their soles. His attempts to secure the soles to the boot tops with wire had not been entirely successful.

Finally, the officer in charge told Bayerlein's section to go back to their basement in the chemist's shop and get some rest. To Bayerlein's amazement, the unit had come through the day without a single casualty.[22]

◆ ◆ ◆

The Seaforths spent several hours trying to root the Germans out of the cathedral in Dead Horse Square with no success. Thomas was getting fed up. A paratroop machine-gun position in the broken bell tower made any attempt to get inside the church and clear the building impossible. The gun also blocked a proper search for survivors in the ruins of the school.

Finally, however, he had the means to destroy the enemy gun. A Three Rivers tank named *Agnes* had finally bulled its way up one of the narrow lanes and reached the square. Thomas ran over to the tank and pointed the target out to its commander. "As much as I hate blasting the tower of that church," Thomas said, "I want you to get him out of there."[23]

The 'A' Squadron tank commander was Gord Turnbull. Turnbull said, "It's Christmas Eve and that's God's house."[24] Thomas insisted and Turnbull knew the officer was right. Although he hated to do it, Turnbull sighted the main gun on the steeple and blasted it to oblivion with one well-placed round. The machine gun was destroyed.

Thomas's men rushed the church and fought their way inside. The Germans retreated to the far end of the church and dug in around the pulpit. The ensuing bitter exchange of grenades and small-arms fire carried on throughout the night.[25]

With the machine gun in the bell tower silenced, a perfunctory search of the rubble of the school was conducted. No sign of survivors could be discovered. The Seaforths quickly withdrew from the destroyed building, as it was too exposed to German sniper fire to allow a more thorough search to be conducted.[26]

◆ ◆ ◆

Back at the Seaforths' battalion HQ, Syd Thomson had given his blessing to an extraordinary notion in the midst of the worst battlefield the regiment had so far experienced. Shortly before noon, Quartermaster Captain Bordon Cameron had suggested organizing a real Christmas dinner that could be served to the rifle companies one at a time in Santa Maria di Costantinopoli. The moment Thomson gave his enthusiastic endorsement to the plan, Quartermaster Sergeant Stan Wellburn went to work. The company cooks were brought up to the church and a field kitchen was established behind the altar. The cooks gave Wellburn a shopping list for desired food.

Wellburn spent several hours roaring around the countryside between Ortona and San Vito in a jeep, buying fresh vegetables from farmers who still had some crops left. He and a few other men then scrounged through ruined buildings for tablecloths, candles, silverware, and anything else that would help with place settings. Tables were made of planks and erected in the centre of the large church.

Much of the work was done under fire, as the Germans heavily mortared all of Ortona throughout Christmas Eve. At 1500 hours, Padre Roy Durnford arrived at Santa Maria di Costantinopoli and smiled when he saw the battalion staff all busy either carrying out regular duties or organizing for the dinner. "Well, at last I've got you all in church," he said, and then helped out with the preparations.[27]

◆ ◆ ◆

For the Germans, the day had not gone well. Despite the commitment of another full battalion to the battle, 1st Parachute Division commander General Richard Heidrich had to report to Tenth Army headquarters that "in hard house to house fighting enemy advanced to the centre of Ortona. Heavy fighting continues."[28]

The 2nd Battalion of 3rd Regiment, which had been defending Ortona since December 20, had suffered too many casualties and been too overextended across the 500-yard width of the town to prevent the steady, remorseless advance of the two Canadian battalions and their tank support. Heidrich had also made a costly error. His reserve battalion, 2nd Battalion of the 4th Regiment, was located three miles north of Ortona at Torre Mucchia. When it became apparent that the reserve unit was required to bolster the German resistance in Ortona, it had taken most of the day just to get the battalion moved up from Torre Mucchia.[29]

With more than half the town now in Canadian hands, it was only a matter of time before the town had to be surrendered. Yet Tenth Army had received a troubling new directive from none other than Adolf Hitler. Hitler had always taken a close personal interest in battlefield developments on every German front. Ever since Stalingrad, he had also started issuing directives that routinely denied the commanders on the scene the right to make an essential tactical decision — the decision to retreat so that a unit could live to fight another day. On December 24, Hitler issued an order that Ortona should be held at all costs. Heidrich appears to have responded by simply ignoring the order. Instead, he accelerated the destruction of Ortona by engineering demolitions. It appeared he had decided that, if the paratroopers could not hold Ortona, they would leave the Canadians in final occupation of a ruin riddled with mines and booby traps. He would also continue to exact a costly toll for every yard of town surrendered.[30]

◆ ◆ ◆

Brigadier Bert Hoffmeister had spent the day getting a good sense of the high price the Canadians were paying. He had nearly become a casualty himself on three occasions. First, when the shell hit the building that Gibson had used as a supply depot. Second, when he was moving across a street and looked down just in time to see and avoid two tiny prongs that betrayed the presence of an S-mine where his foot was about to land. And third, when he was walking across an open square to confer with a tank commander and the tanker was shot by a sniper. Had the sniper shot the infantry officer instead, he would have bagged a brigadier rather than a lieutenant, but Hoffmeister took care to look like any other soldier.

He was understandably still a bit shaken from those close calls when he paid a final evening visit to the Edmonton battalion head-quarters. As he waited for Lieutenant Colonel Jim Jefferson to finish a radio conversation with one of the rifle company commanders, Hoffmeister was drawn to a line of bodies lying in one corner of the room. A blanket was draped over each body, the faces covered. For some reason he could never afterward explain, he bent down and pulled back one of the blankets. He found himself looking into the unseeing eyes of the young reinforcement officer who only that morning had appeared so bewildered by Ortona.[31]

# 26

## AS MERRY AS
## CIRCUMSTANCES PERMIT

SURROUNDED by paratroopers of the 1st Parachute Division, the 48th Highlanders of Canada endured a "most unhappy Christmas." The regiment's war diarist went on to note that its soldiers were "practically unable to move in battalion area owing to enemy snipers and MGs."[1] The diarist's summary of the battalion's Christmas accurately reflected the experience of all the Canadians fighting on the Ortona front. There was no day off from the war for festive celebration. German and Canadian spent the day doing their best to kill each other. For many, Christmas 1943 was the last day of their lives.

The position the Highlanders occupied on the summit of a low ridge overlooking the hamlets of San Tomasso and San Nicola was a mile inside the German lines. Throughout December 24, the battalion's presence had gone mostly ignored by the paratroopers. But, as of first light on Christmas Day, the Highlanders became the target of increasing enemy attention. By midafternoon, Lieutenant Colonel Ian Johnston feared that the paratroopers were massing in front of 'A' Company's positions for a major attack on the beleaguered battalion. The sniper and machine-gun fire was now supplemented by increasingly heavy mortar and artillery bombardment. Some self-propelled guns, mounted with 88-millimetre cannon, lurked near the Canadian perimeter, smashing it with shell after shell.

If the Germans struck the Highlanders with a concerted counter-attack and managed to penetrate the outer defences, it was entirely possible the battalion might be overrun and wiped out. All the Highlanders had were their light weapons and a very limited supply of ammunition. Attempts to bring supporting arms into the Highlander position during the night had been unsuccessful. The squadron of Ontario Tanks was still more than a mile away and hopelessly mired in mud. Although the weather was starting to cooperate by bringing colder temperatures and no rain, it would be at least another day before the ground firmed up sufficiently to support the weight of the tanks.

There is an old military precept that the best defence is a good offence. Johnston thought it time to implement this tactic. If 'A' Company forayed into the German forming-up positions it might disrupt the paratroopers' plan to stage an attack. About 300 yards from the Highlander front stood two fortified houses, jointly code-named The Rock. The largest of these houses was thought to be a German headquarters. It became the attack's objective.

Responsibility for carrying out the attack fell to Major John Clarke's 'A' Company. The officer who had led the Highlanders single file through the dark night of December 23 to their current position knew his men faced a tough challenge. He also agreed with Johnston that it had to be done. Clarke gave the task to Lieutenant Jack Pickering's No. 9 Platoon, saying, "Put the fear of God and the 48th Highlanders into them."[2]

As Pickering set about readying his understrength platoon, he was approached by Lieutenant Ian MacDonald, commander of No. 8 Platoon. "Look here, Jack," MacDonald said, "both platoons should go. One can't do it alone. Go ask John." Pickering did and Clarke immediately agreed to the two platoons attacking as one. He warned both officers to be cautious, not risking heavy casualties unless there would be obvious gains realized. They were to withdraw if German resistance proved too stiff.[3]

To soften the way for the attack, a heavy bombardment from the supporting artillery regiments was called in by the forward observa-

Field Marshal Bernard Montgomery (right) considered Major General Chris Vokes little more than a "plain cook" as a military tactician. — ALEXANDER STIRTON, NAC, PA 132783

Canadian infantry on the long, dusty march up the Italian boot in the late summer of 1943. — ALEXANDER STIRTON, NAC, PA-132878

Captain A.H. Oliphant of the 1st Canadian Infantry Division directs traffic past his halted convoy on the coast road north of the Sangro River during the Canadian advance to the Moro River. — FREDERICK WHITCOMBE, NAC, PA-167911

Saskatoon Light Infantry support battalion gunners Corporal L. Mason and Private D. Holstein man a Vickers medium machine gun.
— ALEXANDER STIRTON, NAC, PA-116851

Ortona's northern mole (background) after being breached by German demolitions. Sunken ships lie in the foreground.
— ALEXANDER STIRTON, NAC, PA-137441

West Nova Scotia Regiment Private Edmund Arsenault mans a PIAT in a slit trench near Ortona.
— ALEXANDER STIRTON, NAC, PA-153181

First Canadian Infantry Division commander Major General Chris Vokes (left), 2nd Canadian Infantry Brigade commander Brigadier Bert Hoffmeister, and 1st Canadian Armoured Brigade commander Brigadier Bob Wyman in conference during the Moro River crossing phase of the battle.
— T. ROWE, NAC, PA-131064

A mortar team of the 3rd Canadian Infantry Brigade in action on the south shore of the Moro River.
— FREDERICK WHITCOMBE, NAC, PA-153182

Posing for this photograph in southern Italy are the three Turnbull brothers, Joseph (left), William, and Gordon, who served in the same squadron of the Three Rivers Tank Regiment. In the background, tanks are hidden in the trees.
— PHOTO COURTESY OF PEGGY TURNBULL

Field artillery tractor towing a seventeen-pounder anti-tank gun on a road bordering the Moro River valley. Sergeant H. Dunn observes the effects of artillery fire from the observation port.
— FREDERICK WHITCOMBE, NAC, PA-107933

On the night of December 8–9, the Royal Canadian Engineers pushed this diversion across the Moro River below San Leonardo. They called it "Chit House Crossing."
— T. ROWE, NAC, PA-141393

"The pastoral valley became a valley of death," wrote artist Charles Comfort of the Moro River valley. Comfort's task was to capture with brush and paint the experience of the Canadians fighting in Italy. Here, he works amid the ruins of Ortona.
— C.E. NYE, NAC, PA-116592

Private L.N. Welbanks (left), Sergeant G.D. Adams, and Private L.G. Thompson of the 48th Highlanders of Canada scramble back to their weapons during a counterattack by the 90th Panzer Grenadiers on December 10 near San Leonardo.
— FREDERICK WHITCOMBE, NAC, PA-166566

A platoon of 48th Highlanders of Canada ready for an attack near San Leonardo. Lieutenant Ian Macdonald looks through binoculars. Squatting next to him is Sergeant J.T. Looney. Privates A.R. Downie, O.E. Bernier, and G.R. Young crouch in front of the sergeant, while Corporal T. Fereday stands with a Thompson submachine gun and Private S.L. Hart lies prone with a Bren gun.
— FREDERICK WHITCOMBE, NAC, PA-136332

The body of a German Panzer Grenadier killed during a counterattack on San Leonardo.
— FREDERICK WHITCOMBE, NAC, PA-120783

Two Loyal Edmonton soldiers help two wounded comrades reach the Regimental Aid Post at San Leonardo.
— FREDERICK WHITCOMBE, NAC, PA-114487

During a lull in the battle for San Leonardo, Privates J. Miller and W.H. Hall dig a slit trench.
— FREDERICK WHITCOMBE, NAC, PA-167658

Loyal Edmonton Private H.R. Hansen keeps watch in San Leonardo over a street covered by German snipers.
— FREDERICK WHITCOMBE, NAC, PA-166563

Padre Roy C.H. Durnford (centre with prayerbook) conducts a burial service at San Leonardo on December 10, 1943.
— FREDERICK WHITCOMBE, NAC, PA-167913

An Italian refugee returns to San Leonardo on December 13. She is walking past a destroyed German Panzer Mark IV tank.
— FREDERICK WHITCOMBE, NAC, PA-136196

V Corps commander Lieutenant General Charles Allfrey (front right) speaks to Royal 22e Regiment's Caaptain Paul Triquet (front left) near Casa Berardi on January 26, 1944, after Triquet was awarded the Victoria Cross.
— D. E. DOLAN, NAC, PA-130592

Stretcher-bearers carry a wounded soldier across ground under enemy fire.
— T.ROWE, NAC, PA-14166

A Canadian Sherman
tank rolls into action
near The Gully.
— T. ROWE, NAC, PA-167138

Canadian troops move past the
burned wreckage of a German
self-propelled gun toward the front
lines at The Gully.
— T. ROWE, NAC, PA-166562

Men of the Hastings and Prince
Edward Regiment advance at The
Gully. The ring in the foreground is
from the turret of a demolished
German tank.
— T. ROWE, NAC, PA-136215

tion officer, Major Hawker. The two platoons then moved forward, supported by several Bren gunners providing covering fire. Initially, the two platoons made good progress, sweeping German snipers and light machine-gunners out of slit trenches set up practically on the edge of the Canadian lines.

The Highlanders got within 200 yards of the target house and paused in a small gully to organize a rush on the objective from two directions. Pickering was about to give the order to advance when two heavy machine guns opened up from the right flank. The ground between the gully and the house was level, providing no viable cover. Had the platoons already moved forward, they would have been decimated by the German guns. Pickering and MacDonald realized they could not reach the objective without suffering heavy casualties. All they could hope was that their limited attack would dissuade the Germans from risking an all-out offensive against the Highlanders. The two platoons withdrew to the Canadian lines.[4]

To maintain the pressure on the Germans, FOO Major Hawker directed artillery throughout the day against targets identified by Highlander patrols. Luring the German gunners into betraying their presence was a dangerous task. Private Gerard Michaud, who because of casualties among non-commissioned officers found himself commanding a small section, discovered the simplest way to expose German machine-gun positions was to draw their fire by moving out into the open where the gunners could see him. Several machine guns were discovered this way and destroyed by Canadian artillery. Inevitably, perhaps, Michaud's luck finally ran out. He was hit by a burst of MG42 fire and died instantly.[5]

The artillerymen back at 226th Battery, which supplied most of the support, radioed back several times to verify Hawker's map references. The salvoes were forming a perfect circle around a very small position and the danger of shells landing within that circle was high. The gunners were not to worry, Hawker said. "Just keep shooting. Just imagine we're an island."[6]

◆ ◆ ◆

The analogy was apt. By December 25, it was apparent that the 48th Highlanders were seriously isolated. Acting Brigadier Dan Spry, commander of 1st Canadian Infantry Brigade, could see no way either to reinforce the lost battalion or to facilitate a withdrawal from its tenuous position. The brigade's other two battalions — the Royal Canadian Regiment and the Hastings and Prince Edward Regiment — were too depleted by casualties to break through the German defences standing between their positions and the Highlanders.

An attempt at first light by the RCR to push through had stalled mere minutes after it began. 'A' Company, which led the attack, had advanced only a short distance before coming under devastating artillery, mortar, and machine-gun fire. Almost twenty men in a company numbering barely fifty were killed or wounded.

Lieutenant Jimmy Quayle, commanding No. 8 Platoon of 'A' Company, could scarcely believe the orders he had been given prior to the attack. Two hours before dawn, RCR commander Major Strome Galloway told the men at the Orders Group to go up the track to a cluster of buildings close to the Highlanders' lines, and dig in. Quayle wondered aloud if artillery or tanks would be in support. He was told airily that neither was necessary, since patrols had found no presence of German units in the area. A disgruntled and skeptical Quayle returned to his unit in time to welcome four new replacements. The only thing he noted about the men, whose faces were obscured by darkness, was that their last names all started with B.

Quayle prowled the lines of his platoon. During these wanderings, he later wrote, he saw that "two white objects protruded from the ground like strange fungi. I had passed them a dozen times. As light improved the strange blooms became hands with gray sleeves attached. One of our tanks had run right up the centre of the German's body and pushed him back down flush with the mud. All that showed were two pale hands projecting in a supplicating gesture. The face and greatcoat were level with the soil and hard to distinguish."[7]

No. 8 Platoon led the assault as ordered, with No. 7 Platoon immediately behind, and proceeded up the track without any artillery or tank support. Quayle, suspecting that the reports upon which the attack was based were bogus, sent two scouts ahead of the column and ordered his men to advance up a ditch bordering the track rather than on the track itself. They had gone only a short distance when the two scouts came running back full tilt, narrowly escaping a barrage of stick grenades and submachine-gun fire.

Quayle, ordering his men to ground, wondered if the earlier patrol had dodged danger by going into the field and just hunkering down at the first sign of shelter. It was not uncommon for reconnaissance patrols to shirk their assignment, then file a false report.

Mortars started quartering the platoon's position with deadly accuracy. One of the new "B" men took some shrapnel that passed right through his chest. A veteran private named McDonald said quietly to the man, "You can quit moaning now, I've been hit too." Blood ran down McDonald's face from a scalp wound. The platoon started returning fire with their small arms and achieved a spectacular result. In front of them, a German half-track vehicle loaded with ammunition and hidden in a haystack exploded in a massive blast.

Quayle saw Corporal Davino, a fearless veteran — "blood and saliva dribbling from his mouth, his face a bloated pumpkin" — being led past by a stretcher-bearer. Then came another veteran, Max Engleberg, with a right arm rendered useless by a wound. One of the 'B' men lay off to Quayle's left, crying softly. Quayle asked what was wrong. The man whimpered that his legs were gone. Quayle said he would carry the man back. "Sir, we'll both be killed," the new reinforcement said. The two men argued while bullets and shells whined overhead. Then Quayle hefted the man onto his back and carried him to safety. Twenty-three men from No. 8 Platoon had gone into the attack. An hour later, only Quayle and three other men remained unwounded. No. 7 Platoon had been similarly hard hit. Its lieutenant, Jim Joice, had been severely wounded; only eight men were unhurt. Together the two platoons mustered eleven men.[8] Despite its losses, 'A' Company went to ground and held its position rather than withdrawing.[9]

Major Strome Galloway pushed 'B' Company up on 'A' Company's left with instructions to outflank the machine guns holding up 'A' Company. That attempt failed, but Galloway persisted in pressing the attack. By midafternoon, he had established the regiment several hundred yards forward of the Hastings and Prince Edward positions.[10] But he was still more than a thousand yards short of the Highlander lines. The RCR, which had been seriously understrength on the morning of December 24, had lost more than fifty men in two days of fighting. The battalion's rifle companies mustered between them only about 150 men as dusk fell on Christmas Day.

Galloway established his headquarters in a small house inside the RCR perimeter. The largest room was overflowing with Italian civilians. German machine-gun positions in two houses no more than 250 yards from the building hammered the walls with occasional bursts of gunfire.

A little festive spirit was needed, Galloway decided. Captain Sandy Mitchell had earlier found an old mandolin in the house. So Galloway and Mitchell proceeded to entertain the troops. Galloway would establish radio contact with one of his company commanders dug in on the front line. Then, while the commander held the mike close to the mandolin, Mitchell strummed a few bars of "Silent Nigh" or another Christmas carol. The two men worked their way through all the companies this way. One of the officers in the HQ had bartered some wine and bread from the Italians, to which the artillery forward observation officer contributed a batch of bully beef. Feeling blessed to have even this meagre ration, the men settled down to Christmas dinner.[11]

◆ ◆ ◆

At Santa Maria di Costantinopoli, the Seaforth Highlanders of Canada battalion headquarters staff were ready at 0900 hours to start rotating the forward rifle companies through for their Christmas dinner. The war diarist wrote: "The setting for the dinner was complete, long rows of tables with white table cloths, and a bottle of beer per man, candies, cigarettes, nuts, oranges and apples and chocolate bars providing the extras. The C.O. Lt.-Col. S.W. Thomson, laid on that the Companies would eat in relays in the order of C-A-B-D, as each company finished their dinner, they would then go forward and relieve the next company. The first company was to be in at 1100 hrs, 2 hours was to be allowed for each company for dinner. The menu for the dinner being: Soup, Pork with apple sauce, cauliflower mixed vegetables, mashed potatoes, gravy. Christmas pudding and minced pie."[12]

Promptly at 1100, the men of 'C' Company came into the church. The war diarist continued: "From 1100 hrs to 1900 hrs, when the last man of the Battalion reluctantly left the table to return to the grim realities of the day, there was an atmosphere of cheer and good fellowship in the church. A true Christmas spirit. The impossible had happened. No one had looked for a celebration this day, December

25th was to be another day of hardship, discomfort, fear and danger, another day of war. The expression on the faces of the dirty bearded men as they entered the building was a reward that those responsible are never likely to forget.

"When C Company had finished their dinner, they relieved A Company so that they might come back the 300 or 400 yards for the same, and so A Coy relieved B Coy and B, D Coy.

"The latter were to become reserve Company, but the situation had grown tense with C Company on the left flank.

"Capt. [Jack] McLean took his [D] Company back into the fight. Christmas day was no less quiet than the preceding ones, but it is one that this Regiment will never forget. Pipe Major Edmond Esson played his Pipes several times throughout the meals. During the dinner, the Signal officer, Lieut. [Wilf] Gildersleeve played the church organ, and, with the aid of an improvised choir, organized by the Padre, Carols rang throughout the church."[13]

As the dinner progressed, Padre Major Roy Durnford recorded in his diary that outside the church there was the "deathly chatter of machine guns. Rumbling of buildings falling, roar of guns. . . . Shells whine and explode." When 'A' Company came in for dinner, he noted that Captain June Thomas looked "weary, strained, dirty."[14]

The field kitchen was set up behind the altar. Soon dirty plates were piled across the altar, rattling noisily whenever German shells fell close by. Durnford noted on the faces of the men now to warfare a "reluctance, the far away look, the nervous strain, the slight inebriation in a few cases."[15] While each man only received one beer, wine circulated freely and some of the soldiers took greater liberty with it than others.

Throughout the course of the day, Gildersleeve played the organ. It was pump-operated, located in a loft overlooking the altar. Various officers and men took turns operating the pump to keep the music flowing. As was customary for regimental dinners, the enlisted men were served by officers. None of the men in the line rifle companies had to lift a finger. Many chose to join Durnford in the chapel for prayers.

A few men, boisterous from the beer and wine, called out for soldier songs. Gildersleeve cringed each time, silently thinking, "Shut up, will you. Carols are the things to sing at Christmas time." He wanted none of the crude songs favoured by soldiers on a march. Gildersleeve was poignantly aware that for many of the men gathering at this table the meal and this Christmas would be their last. He played for hours, even after his fingers started aching. Gildersleeve had been the organist in a small church in North Vancouver. For some reason he could not explain, he had carried to war a single music hymn book that contained all the popular carols.[16]

As dusk closed in, candles were lit. 'D' Company arrived for the last sitting. Padre Durnford stood next to the organ in the loft and sang several Christmas songs solo. Then in the "flickering and shadows" he strolled among the men, taking time to speak with all and to ask how they were feeling.[17]

Earlier in the day, one junior officer had received tragic news. His wife, a young war bride in England, had committed suicide. Lieutenant Colonel Syd Thomson and Durnford had broken the news to him together and then taken him aside to a private corner where they offered what little consolation they could.[18]

For some of the men attending the dinner, the scene seemed utterly surreal. Lieutenant Dave Fairweather had only rejoined the battalion on December 20. Having been attending various officers training courses, he had missed all the previous fighting from Sicily to Ortona. His baptism of fire was Ortona, a hellish introduction to war. On Christmas Day, he assumed command of 'D' Company's No. 18 Platoon. When he arrived at the church, Fairweather learned he was getting six reinforcements. That was good news, for earlier in the day he had lost five men. With the reinforcements, his platoon strength would be bolstered to nineteen, still far short of the normal complement of thirty-five.

In the midst of the Ortona slaughterhouse, Fairweather later wrote, he "found it very unrealistic to sit down to [Christmas dinner] and then leave the table to go back into the battle, about twenty blocks away. It was a very subdued affair, and, I would say, that most of the men found it hard to take in, and it would be difficult to say whether they appreciated it at the time. My only criticism was that there was too much beer and liquor available. The vast majority did not take more than one bottle of beer, however, inevitably there was the exception and this ended in disaster."[19] More than one slightly drunken Seaforth, Fairweather thought, died in the hours immediately after the Christmas dinner because of a foolish error the soldier would never have made sober.

Dinner over, Fairweather led his platoon back to the fighting lines. On the way, a German shell screamed down. In the aftermath of the explosion, Fairweather saw that three of his reinforcements were casualties. One was dead, the other two wounded. His platoon was down to sixteen men.

Not all the Seaforths attended Christmas dinner at Santa Maria di Costantinopoli. At least one section leader refused to let his men go. Twenty-nine-year-old Private Ernest Smith commanded a six-man section. When the time came for his company to rotate back to the church, Smith told his men he was not going. More to the point, he said, they were also going to stay right where they were. Nicknamed "Smoky," Smith was a rough-and-tough former construction worker. He had enlisted in 1940 with the idea that going to war would be one way to see Europe and maybe other parts of the world. "I don't know what goes through the minds of those people who are in charge of this," he said, "but people are going to get killed going to that dinner and others are going to die coming back from it. So you're all staying right here."[20]

The men were angry and disappointed, but nobody dared argue the order. Most of the men were new reinforcements and Smith was their lifeline. He was teaching them the craft of soldiering right in a battleground. Earlier they had come into the building and one of the men had seen a much-prized German knife sticking out of a jar full of loose grains of wheat. The jar was on a windowsill, in plain view. When the soldier started to reach out to pluck the souvenir knife from the jar, Smith snapped, "Don't touch it." Perhaps thinking Smith wanted the souvenir himself, the man scowled. "Why?"

"I'll show you," Smith replied. With his rifle butt, he shoved the jar holding the knife out the window. Before it hit the street, the jar exploded. A grenade had been hidden inside the wheat grains. "There you are," Smith said. Anything that looked like a good souvenir, he cautioned the men, was going to be booby-trapped. Smith's section respected the man's soldiering skill and judgement. So, angry they might have been to miss the Christmas dinner, but they stayed in their position. As far as Smith was concerned, his decision kept at least one of them from dying that Christmas Day.[21]

◆ ◆ ◆

For the soldiers in the Loyal Edmonton Regiment, there was no elegant Christmas dinner. Many ate nothing besides their usual cold rations, despite an effort by the quartermasters to get roast pork and other luxuries up to the soldiers on the line.[22] Major Jim Stone had his normal rations and a cold pork chop, hastily gobbled during an afternoon spent trying to get past Piazza Plebiscita.[23] A massive rubble pile blocking the entrance to the square was frustrating efforts to get tanks through. Without their support, the Edmontons had little luck destroying the German machine-gun positions subjecting the square to a deadly deluge of fire. As the day wore on, Lieutenant R. Heggie managed to get his tank into a position on the rubble pile that allowed him to bring fire on the German positions, but Stone's 'D' Company was unable to press forward despite this support. At dusk, both the tank and the infantry withdrew to their start line just outside the entrance to the square.[24]

Elsewhere on the Edmonton front, the advance was also stalling. Much of the problem was simply that the battalion had too few men left to do the job. There were also too few veterans to ensure the new reinforcements pressed on. Stone's company, for example, numbered barely thirty men of all ranks.[25] Still, the Edmontons were slowly gaining ground against determined resistance.

'B' Company Sergeant J.E.W. Dick's platoon was stalled in midafternoon by a combination of severe machine-gun fire, sniper fire, and searing blasts from a dug-in German flame-thrower. This was the first time the paratroopers had used flame-throwers against the Canadians. Spraying a jet of flame from a wand connected by a hose to fuel and pressurized air tanks worn on the operator's back, the weapon could reach across the width of a street. Although cumbersome and often dangerous to the operator, the weapons introduced a terrifying new hazard to the Ortona battlefield. If caught in the fire stream, a soldier was instantly burned to death.

Dick set out to find a way to outflank the enemy positions, including the flame-thrower operator. Crossing an exposed alley, he found a ten-foot-long water pipe that a section of men could climb to reach a small room overlooking the German position. From their perch in the room, the section was able to bring flanking fire against the paratroopers, forcing them to retreat or die. Dick won the Military Medal for this display of initiative and boldness in the face of enemy fire.[26]

As night brought the worst of the fighting on Christmas Day to an end, Private Melville McPhee and his section received a small Christmas surprise. A man from the quartermaster section passed by and handed each man two bottles of beer and a few slices of cold pork. The beer tasted wonderful. Each man drank his two bottles slowly, knowing it would probably be many days before such a treat came again.[27] Nobody expected the battle for Ortona to end soon.

◆ ◆ ◆

There had been a moment of cheer for the Highlanders in battalion headquarters. At dusk, Private John Cockford, intelligence officer Lieutenant John Clarkson's batman, marched in with a Christmas cake. He had planned the treat for weeks. It was made from cornmeal with chocolate ration melted down for icing. In Campobasso, Cockford had liberated some walnuts from an Italian home and these were mixed in with the chocolate and some powdered milk. With a blunt finger, he had drawn in the icing the words "Merry Christmas" in Gothic script.[28] Officers and men fell upon the cake with glee.

Shortly after nightfall, there came another turn of good fortune when a small patrol from the Royal Canadian Regiment slipped into the lines of the 48th Highlanders. The patrol leader told Lieutenant Colonel Ian Johnston that Highlander Captain George Beal, a former Toronto Argonaut football quarterback, was leading a party of about sixty Saskatchewan Light Infantry men up the narrow trail used earlier by the battalion to capture its objective. The SLI soldiers were bringing rations, some light mortars, ammunition, spare batteries for the radio sets, and stretchers to evacuate the most badly wounded.[29]

The news lifted the flagging spirits of the Highlanders. Their food was all but gone, ammunition was critically low. The batteries for the radio sets were either exhausted or so low that every minute of on-air time had to be carefully apportioned. Some of the wounded were likely to die if not soon evacuated to a Forward Aid Post.[30]

At 2100 hours, the SLI carrying party reached the Highlanders. As expected, they brought with them food, ammunition, fresh batteries, and stretchers. Johnston took Beal aside. "You forgot to bring a tank. Ask Colonel Spry at Brigade to send us tanks, for God's sake." Johnston smiled then. "Tell him to send us just one tank and we'll massacre them." Beal laughed and asked Johnston if he was sure that all he wanted for Christmas was a tank. "That's right," Johnston said. "One Sherman."[31]

The SLI and Beal then gathered up seven stretcher cases and slipped back into the night, making a hazardous return journey down the path that curiously remained undiscovered by the Germans.

◆ ◆ ◆

As far as Fallschirmpionier Obergefreiter Karl Bayerlein was concerned, Christmas Day brought a welcome decrease in the intensity of fighting in Ortona. Harassing fire from Canadian artillery and mortars remained continuous, but the engineers were not called upon to carry out further extensive demolitions. When not standing guard duty, they spent most of the day sleeping. The rest was welcome and the men slept heavily despite the noise of the Canadian shelling and the continuous small-arms fire coming from the front lines.

In the evening, Bayerlein was delighted to see warm food brought up from the rear in containers delivered by motorcycle. The men bringing in the food had run the gauntlet of the Coast Highway, now subject to almost continual mortar and artillery shelling.

"We had potatoes, oranges, vegetables, roast beef," Bayerlein wrote in his diary. "We also put up a small Christmas tree." Obviously, headquarters to the rear "had not forgotten us." Still, Bayerlein noted, "There is no place for Christmas sentiments here. We do not know how long we can hang onto Ortona."[32]

German high command was also deeply concerned about the events in Ortona. Tenth Army commander General der Panzertruppen Joachim Lemelsen and Generalfeldmarschall Albert Kesselring conferred by telephone on Christmas Day. Kesselring told Lemelsen, "It is clear that we do not want to defend Ortona decisively, but the English have made it appear as important as Rome. . . . You can do nothing when things develop in this manner; it is only too bad that Montgomery was right for once and the world press makes so much of it." Lemelsen replied, "It costs so much blood that it cannot be justified."

◆ ◆ ◆

For his part, 1st Canadian Infantry Division commander Major General Chris Vokes issued the following message intended to rally the troops and put fire in their hearts and bellies: "This, the fifth Christmas of the war, finds us in totally different and less pleasant circumstances than the last four. However, let us have no regrets. We are out to do a real 'job' on our enemies and there will be no let-up in our efforts until we have accomplished this. Then we will be in a position to enjoy our Post-War Christmas Days to the full. May this Christmas Day, therefore, be as Merry as circumstances . . . permit."[33]

# 27

## CARRY ON

IT was a morning ritual practised by every company of the Seaforth Highlanders of Canada and the Loyal Edmonton Regiment. As dawn touched the ruins of Ortona, the company commander and sergeant major divided the platoon sections between them and then visited their allotted groups. Dawn was the worst time of day for men in combat. Ended was a long, often frightening night, passed with too little sleep. It was cold and usually wet. Another long day of deadly battle loomed. The soldiers shivered and wanted nothing more than to curl up in their fighting positions and leave the war to play itself out on its own.

That was when Captain June Thomas, Company Sergeant Major Jock Gibson, or Major Jim Stone slipped in next to them. A kind word of encouragement. A shake of a shoulder to waken the soldier unable to rouse himself. The proffered canteens. One held water. The other dark rum. A swig from either or both was invited. The rum was a restorative, it warmed the men and helped chase away some of the fear that had grown during the night into a force that might completely unnerve a man.[1] Far too many were being sent to the rear with uncontrollable shakes or because they had simply said, "I can't take it," and refused to continue the fight.[2]

On December 26, none of the officers or sergeant majors needed long to circulate through the companies. Hardly any numbered more than thirty men. Despite this, before the rounds were finished the battlefield had awakened. Canadian and German artillery shells whistled down and Ortona erupted in fire and smoke. Then came the ripping sheet sound distinctive of German machine guns, punctuated by the slower, duller thudding of the Bren guns responding in kind. Grenades popped, rifles cracked, the guns of the Three Rivers' Shermans boomed, Moaning Minnies shrieked into the Canadian lines, the Canadian antitank guns thumped, mortar rounds ripped holes in roofs and sent cobblestones whirring through the streets, and the shattering blasts of explosives tore buildings to shreds. It was a new day and the battle of Ortona raged on.

Seaforth Captain June Thomas was in a building separated from another by only a few feet. Glancing around the corner of an upstairs window, he saw a German peering back from a corner of the facing building. The German saw Thomas. Both men simultaneously ducked back. Thomas flipped the pin of a grenade and lobbed it around the corner at the German. After it exploded he rushed over, thinking to finish the job if necessary with his rifle. The German was gone. There was no sign of blood.[3]

Lieutenant Alon Johnson, the Loyal Edmontons' scout commander, had a good view over the northern part of the town. Once he had conducted a first morning patrol of the Edmonton line, there was little else for his scouts to do in the way of patrolling. So he put the men and himself to work as snipers. The Germans seldom presented good targets, but this morning Johnson got lucky. A paratroop officer popped up from behind some rubble and peered at the Canadian lines through his binoculars. The range was long, almost to the maximum extent of the Lee Enfield, but Johnson took aim and fired. The German went down fast. It was impossible to tell if the shot had struck home or not. Johnson hoped he had killed the man.[4]

Sergeant Major Jock Gibson ran across a wide street. Bullets started chipping the cobblestones near him. Gibson saw the muzzle flash of a German machine gun in a nearby building. He raised a Bren gun to his hip and loosed a long burst of fire toward the building. The recoil from the big weapon, meant to be fired with the gun well braced, nearly tore the Bren from his hands. He dashed on and took cover inside a ruined building. Gibson thought he would have been lucky to have hit the building, let alone the men manning the machine gun, but at least he had temporarily suppressed their fire.[5]

Private Melville McPhee lay near the top of a pile of rubble facing the shattered remains of Cattedrale San Tomasso. In the massive ruin lying at the foot of the great gutted dome, the Loyal Edmonton saw what looked to be someone crawling about. McPhee fired his rifle at the target, lost sight of it, and saw no further movement.[6]

Lieutenant Colonel Syd Thomson watched an old woman wandering about yelling and screaming in Dead Horse Square. She appeared to have gone out of her mind. Before he could send someone to bring her in, a shot rang out. The woman fell. German fire prevented the Seaforths carrying her body out of the square. Then the Sherman tanks came forward. Her body lay in their path. The tanks rolled back and forth repeatedly over her body as the day wore on. Slowly, inexorably, her corpse was ground into the cobblestones.[7]

From a building near the great cathedral, the Germans started spraying Edmonton positions once again with the flame-thrower. A six-pounder antitank gun was dragged up by hand. It blew the building into an alley. The weapon was not seen again that day and the Edmontons presumed it destroyed.[8]

Feldwebel Fritz Illi enjoyed teasing the Canadians with his excellent high-school English. He engaged the enemy soldiers in conversation whenever possible. Mostly he yelled over for them to pitch him tins of their delectable corned beef ration or cigarettes. The less imaginative responded by telling him to "fuck off." It seemed to Illi that most of the Canadians possessed little imagination. Others called on him to surrender. Illi answered in kind. Once a Canadian turned the tables on Illi and told him in perfect German that he should give up. The man said he had emigrated to Canada years before and now fought Fascism. Illi told the man he could not surrender, that to do so would not be honourable. Illi did not tell the enemy soldier that there were times he wanted desperately to flee the hellhole of Ortona. Since the battle had started, Illi had hardly slept, seldom had food to eat, and had not washed. He tried persuading the Canadian-German to "come back to his own people, but he said he could not."[9]

Lieutenant Dave Fairweather was amazed how well prepared the paratroopers seemed. Every time his section mouse-holed its way into a room, they found that every windowsill or shelf contained meticulously lined-up rows of ammunition clips for the German Mauser rifles or for the Schmeisser submachine guns. In the corners were stacks of cans containing loose ammunition or stick grenades. If the Germans ran out of ammunition during a fight, they just had to fall back to the next position and all the munitions they required would be waiting there for them.[10]

Three Rivers tank commander Corporal Joe Turnbull directed his tank *Amazing* onto the rubble pile at Piazza Plebiscita. The going was tough, but finally he had the tank perched precariously on the summit. Its tracks clawed and chewed at the ruins, inching forward. Once the centre of balance shifted and the tank tipped over the edge, the Sherman would be able to descend into the hitherto impregnable square. *Amazing* never made it. A paratrooper threw a sticky bomb onto the rear-engine compartment. An improvised weapon, a sticky bomb was an explosive charge encased in thick grease or other sticky substance so that it would adhere to metal when dropped or pressed by hand into place. The explosion tore open the engine compartment and set the tank on fire. Turnbull and his crew bailed out.[11] Two of the men, driver Trooper Joe Gallagher and co-driver Trooper J. Morrison, were wounded.[12] Turnbull helped the two uninjured men climb over the rubble pile and then boosted the wounded men up to them. Just as the other four men got over the top of the pile, a German machine gun started spraying the area around Turnbull with heavy fire. Unable to make his way to the safety of the other side, Turnbull ran into the German-held area of the square and wriggled into the safety of a cellar. Before he reached the cellar, the enemy machine gun stopped firing at him.

Across the square, Corporal Gord Turnbull saw his older brother being shot at by a German machine gun. He cranked the turret of his Sherman around and fired the main gun at the enemy position. When he ceased fire, his brother was gone. He had no way of knowing whether Joe was alive or not.[13]

The Seaforths' 'D' Company had only twenty-two men left when it received a small clutch of reinforcements sent up from battalion HQ. The men arrived at the company front with rifles, but hardly any ammunition and no grenades. Company Sergeant Major Gibson got them into the latest building he was using as a supply dump and started handing out the ubiquitous Type 36 grenade that was standard for all Commonwealth forces. "What's this?" one of the men said. Gibson gaped at him. "What do you mean, what's this?" The man looked puzzled, embarrassed even. "Well, I've never had one of these before." Gibson demanded to know what training the man had received. Not much, it appeared. The soldiers were equally unaware how to clean a Lee Enfield, and confessed to never having fired a Bren gun. "Lambs to the slaughter," Gibson thought. "They're sending us bloody lambs, who will just get butchered here." He turned to face the men and assumed his best parade-ground voice from the militia days. Holding the grenade aloft so they could all see it, he began, "This is a Type 36 grenade. It has a fuse length of . . ."[14]

Shortly after these men were sent to the forward platoons, Gibson entered an old shack on the edge of Ortona with several other men from 'D' Company. What seemed like an entire salvo of German shells shrieked down and struck directly outside. Gibson threw himself under a table. Everything in the room seemed to blow apart as shrapnel flew everywhere. He and two other men were the only ones to crawl out of the ruin. Gibson was unhurt. He was amazed to still be alive. The sergeant major was shaking, and every noise made him incredibly jumpy. Gibson realized he was a nervous wreck. It seemed impossible any of them would ever get out of Ortona alive.[15]

◆ ◆ ◆

Major General Chris Vokes came up to 2nd Canadian Infantry Brigade's headquarters to meet with Brigadier Bert Hoffmeister. Vokes got directly to the point. "Would you like to quit, Bert? Would you like to pull out of Ortona?"

Hoffmeister's response was immediate. "Chris, when this job was given to us it was represented to be a highly important objective. We have had a lot of casualties, we've put a tremendous amount into it up to now; given it everything we had. To tell the Seaforths and Edmontons now that they could pull out and that it wasn't all that important would have the most shocking effect, in my opinion, on the morale of these battalions, having paid the price they have paid up to that point. I think, furthermore, we're getting the upper hand slowly. In other words we're winning. I think we should end it."

Vokes looked long and hard at his brigadier. "Okay, carry on," he said.

It was a decision that Hoffmeister hated to make. A hell of a decision for any officer to have to assume responsibility for. But Hoffmeister believed in his heart and mind that it was the correct decision. The Edmontons and Seaforths had to see the fight through. They had to win it. If they failed to do so, they would never again be effective regiments. Their spirit would be irretrievably broken.[16]

Hoffmeister believed that Vokes would have accepted whatever decision he had made about the battle. If he had said, "Yes, we want to quit," Hoffmeister thought Vokes would have gone back to his superiors and requested permission to break off the battle inside Ortona. He thought Vokes's motive was entirely humanitarian. Vokes well knew how tired 2 CIB was and how many casualties it had suffered. But there could be no quitting. The Seaforths and Edmontons would have to soldier on and continue paying in blood for the "important objective" of Ortona.[17]

◆ ◆ ◆

As night closed in on Ortona, Private Melville McPhee stood guard duty in a doorway while his section ate and tried to sleep. The young man from Drumheller was exhausted, barely able to stay on his feet or to keep his eyes open. But he knew that were he to give in to sleep he and his comrades might well die. The Germans constantly infiltrated the Canadian lines at night. Earlier in the day, the Edmontons had discovered several tunnels running under the streets and realized the paratroopers had been using these tunnels to get in behind the Canadians. This explained how the Germans had seemed so easily able to come and go as they pleased from one section of the town to another. The Edmonton pioneers quickly blew the tunnel entrances closed with dynamite.[18]

McPhee was startled out of his reverie by the sound of movement in some rubble about fifteen feet away. As far as he knew, the rubble was on the German side of the line. He cocked his Thompson submachine gun and waited. A few seconds passed and then a German officer was suddenly framed directly in the doorway. He was looking straight toward McPhee. The young private pointed the gun at the officer's stomach and squeezed the trigger. He was sickened to hear only a loud click. McPhee waited for the German to gun him down. Instead the man disappeared. McPhee ran back into the room and grabbed a rifle. Then he returned to his position. Glancing out into the street, he saw no sign of the German. McPhee let the enemy officer go about his business and returned to guarding the doorway. He was not going to get himself killed trying to track the German through the streets of Ortona.[19]

◆ ◆ ◆

Obergefreiter Karl Bayerlein wrote in his diary that during the day the paratroopers had learned the Führer had issued an order that Ortona be "kept under all circumstances." There was no way the order could be fulfilled. "The enemy," he wrote, "has the major part of the city in his hands. With a tremendous barrage the enemy increased his fire. Everywhere there is destruction. The sounds of the engines of the tanks are very close. They advance with the infantry behind. They seized the hospital and the Via Cavour is in the enemy's hands despite our mines and booby traps. We could delay the enemy advance but we were not able to stop him. Our forces are too weak. The enemy power in personnel and matériel is in ratio of eight to one. The outcome is foreseeable."[20]

◆ ◆ ◆

Meanwhile, the fate of the 48th Highlanders of Canada remained very much in doubt. Well before dawn on December 26, Major John Clarke, commander of 'A' Company, heard extensive movement of German forces in front of his position. The previous day such noise had presaged a counterattack by the 1st Parachute Division battalions surrounding the Highlanders on a ridge overlooking the hamlets of San Tomasso and San Nicola. That counterattack had been broken before it got underway when Clarke had launched a two-platoon raid on the Germans' probable forming-up point. In the growing light, Clarke saw that the paratroopers were forming up in greater numbers along his front than they had the day before. Any counterstrike he might attempt with his thinly manned platoons would be decimated.

All 'A' Company and the rest of the Highlanders could do was wait for the Germans to attack and hope to beat them back.

Shortly after Clarke alerted Lieutenant Colonel Ian Johnston to the German force massing on his front, Lieutenant George Fraser, commanding 'C' Company, reported that the paratroopers were forming up on his front as well. Both German concentrations were subjected to heavy bombardments by the Canadian artillery, but the fire seemed to little deter the preparations that were visible from the Highlander lines.

The morning was cold, but dry. This gave Johnston some cause for hope. He had received word first thing in the morning that the Ontario Tanks were able to move again. The muddy ground had hardened overnight. Already tanks were working their way toward the front positions of the Royal Canadian Regiment. If a guide was sent back, the tanks would try to break through to the Highlanders. Intelligence officer Lieutenant John Clarkson was given the dangerous mission. He would have to make his way across one thousand yards of enemy-held terrain in broad daylight. Clarkson went alone, setting off at 0930 hours.

Shortly after he left the Highlander lines, the German artillery and mortar fire that had been harassing the lines since daylight rushed toward a fiery crescendo. Shells hammered down throughout the small island of the Highlanders' position. 'A' Company's headquarters took several direct hits. Clarke suffered back injuries when debris inside the house fell on him. He refused to relinquish command of the company, and was installed on a mattress under the stairs leading to the building's second storey.[21]

At 1000 hours, the German counterattack came in directly against 'A' Company's front. The Highlanders let the paratroopers advance almost to the front line before ripping into them with their Brens, Thompsons, rifles, and grenades. The intense fire broke the German wave, but some of the paratroopers managed to breach the defending line in several places. A fierce melee of hand-to-hand fighting broke out. The Highlanders fought with the desperation of men who knew there was no retreating. The battalion was cut off and surrounded; it either won or died. Eight Germans were killed trying to break through the back door of the company headquarters.[22] Most of these men were killed by Company Sergeant Major Gordon Keeler, who first showered

them with grenades from an upstairs window and then charged outside with his rifle and a fixed bayonet to stab the survivors to death.

From the battalion headquarters, artillery forward observation
officer Major Hawker directed a single artillery gun's fire into the
actual lines of 'A' Company. He could only trust that the Highlanders
would stay down in their slit trenches, so that the shrapnel and blast
would just kill exposed Germans.

One section of 'A' Company was cut off, pinned down by
machine-gun fire coming from two directions. Private Robert Crane
saw the section's plight. He grabbed a Bren gun, ran into the open to
draw the enemy fire, then returned fire while the section slithered
out of its holes and escaped to safety. The men in the small section
then turned their weapons on one of the machine guns and knocked
it out. Just as this gun was silenced, Crane's Bren gun jammed. He
threw down the useless weapon, snatched up a rifle with a fixed bayonet, and charged the remaining machine gun. Jumping into the
German position, Crane bayoneted the two men crewing the gun.

The German attack broke completely and the paratroopers fell
back. Although two more attempts were made to penetrate 'A'
Company's lines, these attacks, half-hearted compared to the first,
were easily driven off by decisive and accurate small-arms fire.[23]

◆ ◆ ◆

Lieutenant Colonel Johnston knew that the Highlanders could expect
only a temporary period of grace. The paratroopers were again
massing, determined to wipe the battalion off the face of the earth.
As long as the Highlanders held their position overlooking the coast
highway and the hamlets to the west of Ortona, they hampered the
ability of the 1st Parachute Division to resupply Ortona. Ever since
they had occupied their position, it was possible for FOO Hawker to
direct long-ranging fire against German targets on the coast highway.
Although surrounded, the Highlanders possessed the key to finally
unravel the German defence of Ortona. If the battalion could not be
shoved back, the paratroopers would be hard-pressed to continue
holding the port town.

Johnston knew he had little strength left to stave off another
major assault. His companies were badly depleted. Despite the
resupply of ammunition the night before, the earlier fighting during

the day had reduced the Highlanders to again counting bullets and grenades. The previous day he had unbalanced the methodical Germans with a spontaneous and undergunned attack by two 'A' Company platoons. Perhaps 'D' Company could accomplish similar magic. Johnston was laying his plans for 'D' Company to try drawing German strength away from 'A' Company's front through a diversionary attack when a cheer rose up from the ranks of 'B' Company, dug in on the southern perimeter.

Running outside his headquarters, Johnston saw three Sherman tanks rolling into the perimeter. At their head was Lieutenant John Clarkson, the intelligence officer. The officer had guided the tanks up the same narrow dirt trail that the Highlanders had followed to establish their position. The Germans still had unaccountably neglected to establish a blocking force on this obvious route into the heart of their lines.[24] It was a day late, but Johnston had his Christmas present in triplicate. Another, the last in the line of four Shermans, had bogged down in the still problematic ground that the first three had churned back into deep mud. Johnston hardly cared. He possessed what was needed to begin the massacre he had promised to deliver with even one tank.

Half an hour after the tanks arrived, Johnston moved to the offence with a major attack. It was now 1330 hours. With the infantry following, the tanks slammed out from the front line of the beleaguered 'A' Company. They hit so hard and with such concentrated firepower that the paratroopers broke immediately. The Germans fled the formerly impenetrable houses facing the Canadian front and in doing so ran into the flanking fire of 'C' and 'B' companies. As the 48th Highlanders war diarist described it, "quite a slaughter ensued."[25]

The tanks circled back, linking up with 'D' Company and driving again out of the perimeter on a hundred-yard front, to suppress the paratroopers in the houses from which they had harassed the infantry during their three days of isolation. The Highlanders again followed the tanks into the fray, and as the Shermans broke away the men plunged into the houses, clearing them in minutes. "This was," the war diarist noted laconically at the end of the day, "the most effective use of tanks this unit has made. Total at end of day was 40 enemy killed and 20 taken prisoner. Estimate of enemy casualties for the day in battalion area 100 to 120."

The Highlanders quickly set about burying the German dead in mass graves to prevent contagion and stench. The battalion's padre was so stricken by the spectacle that he dubbed the spot on which the slaughter had taken place "Cemetery Hill." Remarkably, the Highlander casualties during the day were slight by comparison. Major Clarke was injured, but continued to refuse evacuation. Lieutenant Ken Arrell, who had led the 'D' Company attack, was mortally wounded and would receive a Mention in Despatches for his work. Two other infantrymen had been killed and four wounded.[26]

At 2200 hours, another ration and stretcher-bearer party arrived. The isolation of the Highlanders was essentially finished, as the paratroopers lacked the resources to maintain a significant blocking force between the battalion and the rest of 1st Canadian Infantry Brigade. In its daily report to Tenth Army headquarters, 76th Korps, of which the 1st Parachute Division was a part, reported that "all reserves on the left wing of the Korps had been committed."[27]

The German leadership on the Ortona front was breaking down as well. For some unknown reason, 1st Parachute Division commander General Richard Heidrich departed from the Ortona area for a furlough in Berlin on the morning of December 26, at the very moment when his leadership was most critically required. He would later defend this decision, saying he believed the situation around Ortona was "more or less stabilized."[28] Yet the Germans were wildly overestimating the Canadian strength around the Highlander perimeter. The 1st Parachute Division report on the fighting for the day stated with regard to the Highlander battlefront: "In the centre of the divisional front the enemy attacked at about 1530 hrs with one reinforced battalion supported by 16 tanks in the direction of point 100 (1 km N.E. Villa San Tomasso) and succeeded in advancing to this point."[29]

Three tanks became sixteen, the shattered remnant that was the 48th Highlanders was inflated to a reinforced battalion. The Germans draped themselves in a cloak of delusion as to the strength of enemy force they faced, thereby mitigating their own failure to contain the 1st Canadian Infantry Division. Just as Fallschirmpionier Obergefreiter Karl Bayerlein noted in his diary on December 26 that the Germans in Ortona were fighting a superior enemy which outnumbered the paratroopers eight to one, so the German high command made the same kinds of overestimates. In reality, the Loyal Edmonton Regiment and the Seaforth Highlanders of Canada fielded between them in Ortona on December 26 barely more than 300 men and a dozen tanks of the Three Rivers Tanks. The Germans had equivalent strength and were fighting from defensive positions.

In the case of the 48th Highlanders, the Germans undoubtedly had enjoyed a numerical superiority at the beginning of the day. The tanks proved the equalizer. They combined with the determination of the Highlanders to transform the battalion's isolated island into a bastion of strength and then a jumping-off point for a devastating counterattack against the paratroopers. By the end of the day, there was no question of the Highlanders being thrown out of their position. The Germans simply did not have the remaining strength required to regain the offensive anywhere along the Ortona front.

Despite these major setbacks, the paratroopers were far from finished. Had they been, the Royal Canadian Regiment would have ceased being plagued by harassment from their guns. Yet throughout the day the RCR had its lines infiltrated by Germans. Worse, perhaps, it was impossible to draw water from the local well to brew up a good pot of tea. Every time one of Major Strome Galloway's men went out for water, he had to scurry for cover because of a machine gun that had the well covered. To his amazement, Galloway watched several of the fifteen or more civilians crammed into the battalion headquarters' building wander out to the well in an almost casual manner without drawing fire. "I guess they figure that because they are neutral God will protect them!" he wrote in his diary. Noting their imperviousness to enemy fire, however, he employed them to bring water back for his tea.[30]

The most amazing event, to Galloway's mind, was the news that General Bernard Montgomery had ceded command of the Eighth Army and was heading for Britain to assume a role in the forthcoming invasion of northern Europe. Only the day before, Montgomery had issued a Christmas message extolling the way the strength of this "great army" lay "in its team spirit, in the firm determination of every man to do his duty, and in its high morale. This army is a great family, with an ARMY 'Esprit de corps' and spirit the like of which can seldom have been seen before. . . . The Christmas message will be our battle cry, not only now, but also in the years to come." The somewhat inappropriate message was contained in his own missive:

"GLORY TO GOD IN THE HIGHEST AND ON EARTH PEACE, GOODWILL TOWARDS MEN."[31]

Montgomery left behind him an Eighth Army that was in tatters, bludgeoned to a standstill along the Ortona-Orsogna line. Things were so bad for the 2nd New Zealand Division, broken from repeated attacks thrown against the stout German defences dug in around Orsogna, that some of its troops mutinied. One eighteen-man-strong New Zealand platoon ordered to make a predawn attack balked. Fourteen of the men refused to go. The platoon was placed under close arrest and each man was sentenced to up to two years' imprisonment for refusing a direct order. The non-commissioned officers, unable to exert their authority over the dispirited men, were demoted back to the ranks. The New Zealanders had a reputation as tough, determined soldiers. But in the face of the relentless mud, cold, near constant rain, and determined resistance by the Germans manning their strong defensive bastions, the New Zealanders broke. For its part, the 8th Indian Division on the immediate left of the Canadians was faring little better. It had finally captured Villa Grande on December 25, but the division's advance had been sluggish. The Canadians had accomplished the most, and it was becoming apparent that they were close to done in as a result. Little more could be asked of the 1st Canadian Infantry Division. There were too few soldiers remaining to throw into the cauldron.[32]

Galloway, aware of much of this, gloomily made his way back to the RCR battalion rear headquarters. Things were so stalemated between his battalion and the Germans that no immediate offensive action would be possible in the morning. His presence would not be urgently required. He had not bathed since November 30. Nor had his men, but rank possessed certain privileges. Galloway peeled off his grubby and torn uniform for the first time in twenty-six days and luxuriated in a bath in a small foot tub set beside a roaring fire.[33]

# 28

## THERE IS NO TOWN LEFT

EDMONTON antitank gun commander Captain Ed Boyd faced an impossible task on December 27. Acting on orders from Lieutenant Colonel Jim Jefferson, who was chafing more and more over the slow progress the regiment was making through Ortona, Boyd sought an upper-storey position suitable to bring plunging fire from a six-pounder antitank gun down on German machine-gun positions in neighbouring buildings. Boyd knew the notion was mad, but orders were orders. There was no such thing as a suitable firing position in the upper floor of a building for a six-pounder. The gun was never intended to fire *down*. Logistic practicalities were boggling. The gun would have to be dismantled, the parts carried upstairs, and then reassembled. Sandbags would have to prop up the gun trails to angle the weapon down. In the confined space, the recoil and gun blast might well kill the gun crew. Setting up each shot would take a ridiculously long time because the entire sandbag-propping system would have to be realigned. Hardly likely the Germans would sit about chatting and sipping schnapps while the gunners laboured away between shots.

Boyd wandered from building to building with his team. He felt increasingly dispirited by his orders, as each room failed to yield a large enough hole in a wall to warrant implementing the bizarre scheme. Finally he found a sufficiently wide gap, looked out to see what targets might exist, and then saw nothing but stars.

Seconds later, Boyd regained consciousness and realized a German shell had punched directly through the gap. All three men in the room were wounded. A chunk of Leo Coty's calf was torn away. Edmontons' mortar officer, Lieutenant Tim Armstrong, was missing part of his buttock. A fragment of shrapnel was lodged in Boyd's skull just one-sixteenth of an inch from his spinal cord.

Ron Bowen, Company Sergeant Major of 'D' Company, organized the evacuation of the wounded men. While they waited for a Regimental Aid Post jeep to come up, Bowen gave Boyd a strong drink of vermouth laced with army-issue rum. Later Boyd learned that alcohol is a deadly mixture for head wounds, but at the time he was grateful for the drink's dulling sensation because administering morphine was prohibited for such wounds. As Boyd was being loaded into the jeep, he directed Bowen to tell Jefferson, "that his goddamned idea was no goddamned good."[1] The jeep Boyd was loaded aboard contained two other wounded men. They had been dug from the rubble of another building the Germans had blown in on the Canadians.

◆ ◆ ◆

Shortly after dawn on December 27, a platoon bolstered by reinforcements received during the night took possession of a large building near Cattedrale San Tomasso. Unknown to the Edmontons, the building had been heavily mined by the paratroopers. Soon after Lieutenant E.D. "Bunny" Allan and his twenty-three men occupied the building, it was demolished by a massive explosion. The Edmontons' pioneers immediately rushed to the rescue and started digging through the wreckage. From an adjacent building, a small group of paratroopers sought to drive the pioneers off by showering the rubble with stick grenades. Private G.E. O'Neill launched a single-handed counterattack against the German position and drove them back from the building. The pioneers recovered four injured men and one body. All the other soldiers were believed to have been killed and entombed inside the rubble.[2] But the pioneers kept digging in search of bodies and with the faint hope of finding survivors.

News of the demolition flashed through the ranks of the Edmontons and the other battalions of 2nd Canadian Infantry Brigade. Until now, the battle for Ortona had been fierce and bitter, but not vindictive. Now, however, the Canadians were looking for blood. They viewed the destruction of Allan's platoon as a form of base treachery and bloodthirstiness on the part of the paratroopers. The Edmontons sought vengeance in kind.

Captain Bill Longhurst, who had introduced the Canadians to mouse-holing, took the lead in organizing what the Edmontons considered just retaliation. He led 'A' Company in a hard-fought attack on a large building in the German sector. The men battled their way through the building room by room until they had cleared the Germans out. The regimental interpreter then crawled up to a window facing the adjoining building. He could hear an officer across the way berating his men for having surrendered the other building so easily. Longhurst sent a runner to round up some sappers and explosives. Half an hour later, the sappers crawled out from under the other building, where they had positioned a large quantity of explosives. Longhurst then blew up the building. The Edmontons claimed to have killed between forty and fifty paratroopers in this attack.[3] Later in the day, Longhurst and his men destroyed a second building that also contained some Germans.[4]

Increasingly, the weapon of choice on December 27 was high explosives. In the northwestern section of Ortona, the Seaforth Highlanders of Canada were held up before a factory that had been heavily fortified by the paratroopers. Lieutenant Colonel Syd Thomson told Captain June Thomas to delay further attacks on the factory until the morning. That would allow Thomas's 'A' Company to arm itself with a variety of four- to twenty-five pound explosive charges. Thomson instructed that the Seaforths should, rather than trying to capture the building, demolish it with the explosives.[5]

For their part, the German engineers spent the day engaged in a frenzy of demolition. Obergefreiter Karl Bayerlein's team carried out extensive demolitions in the vicinity of Via Tripoli, in front of the Edmontons. They were down to their last explosives and had orders to use up everything. Sometimes they demolished buildings one at a time. Other times they ran all the wires leading to explosives set in a row of buildings to a single detonator and brought the entire section crashing down. Around them, the Canadian shelling fell in tremendous salvoes that ripped other buildings apart.[6]

Both Canadians and Germans sensed that the terrible battle inside Ortona was reaching a climactic point. The paratroopers' hold on the town was tenuous. They retained control over little other than a small section of the old quarter of town fronting the indefensible castle, the relatively scattered buildings north of Via Monte Maiella and Via Tripoli, a large communal vegetable-garden plot, and the cemetery. The Canadians had the advantage now of artillery and tanks, which were able to operate more efficiently in the wider streets of the town's extreme northern sections. Three Rivers tanks formed up at the head of Corso Matteotti and hammered the castle with ninety to a hundred shells.[7]

Dead Horse Square was at last secured by the Seaforths. From the ruin of the hospital, which had been under almost continous shelling for three days, poured one hundred civilians. Throughout the battle, they had been sheltering underground in a large basement complex. Formed up in a column, they were hastily escorted out of town by the Seaforths.[8]

◆ ◆ ◆

Deep in the rubble of the school, which had stood next to the hospital, Private Gordon Currie-Smith lay as he had since Christmas Eve. For three days he had been buried in the rubble. He could breathe with difficulty and move his head slightly; otherwise the small man was completely immobilized by the concrete and masonry crushing down on him. Strangely, he was no longer thirsty or hungry. Currie-Smith was reconciled to the fact that the rubble pile would become his tomb.

Yet now, he heard voices, seemingly from far away. Voices speaking English. Currie-Smith let out a soft croaking sound, meant to be a cry for help. He paused, forced himself to breathe deeply, to try and find some saliva to lubricate his voice box. Then he yelled. He yelled as loud as he possibly could and then he yelled again.

The voices were suddenly above him. He heard the men's exclamations, their shouts to others, their delighted surprise. Currie-Smith told them who he was. One man stayed with him, while the others ran for shovels and other equipment. Then there were Seaforths everywhere digging and casting rubble aside to liberate him from his tomb. Soon the weight of the large concrete slab that had been wedged on top of him, but which had also given him the headroom necessary to survive, was lifted away. Currie-Smith was gently raised from the rubble by two men and put on a stretcher. Later he would say only that he felt "very, very happy." He also felt it was a "shame all those fine fellows had to die because an officer couldn't be told anything."9 Currie-Smith would spend the rest of the war in hospitals being treated for his injuries.

◆ ◆ ◆

As the Edmontons pushed past Piazza Plebiscita and moved into the Via Tripoli area, Three Rivers Tanks Corporal Joe Turnbull crawled out of the cellar where he had been hiding. The previous night had been long and harrowing. The Germans had seen him run away from the burning hulk of his tank *Amazing*, and he had spent a few nervous hours creeping around in the shadows of the cellar while paratroopers armed with submachine guns searched the area for him.

It was a frightening moment when he revealed himself to the advancing Edmonton infantrymen, because Turnbull had no idea what the day's passwords might be. Luckily, the jumpy soldiers recognized his filthy tanker's uniform as Canadian and held their fire. Turnbull returned to his tank squadron to report.

◆ ◆ ◆

Brigadier Bert Hoffmeister, commander of the 2nd Canadian Infantry Brigade, thought one more hard push might end the battle in Ortona. He also knew that the Edmontons and the Seaforths were too weak to deliver that final knockout punch. His only possible course of action was to commit the Princess Patricia's Canadian Light Infantry to the fray. Throughout the past week, the PPCLI had been in reserve on the edge of Vino Ridge. They had endured fairly continuous shelling, had lost men as a result, and were more than ready to do something productive that would get them away from the ridge position.

Hoffmeister had another reason for wanting to bring the PPCLI into Ortona. There were troubling intelligence reports that another paratrooper battalion was being moved into what the Germans appeared to be calling "Operation Ortona." If the Germans were actually planning to launch a counterattack against the Canadian forces in Ortona, Hoffmeister wanted to have sufficient strength in the town to meet that threat and repel it.[10] There were other reasons to suspect the Germans were up to something. Throughout the day, German aircraft swept in repeatedly to strafe and bomb portions of the town. Meanwhile, their artillery and mortar bombardments seemed to have lessened. Something was up, but its nature eluded the Canadian intelligence officers.[11]

The increasing pressure being applied to the German position in Ortona should have forced a withdrawal rather than the kind of retrenchment that a counterattack would require. To the west, 1st Canadian Infantry Brigade's three battalions had managed during the day to stabilize their front. The 48th Highlanders of Canada were no longer isolated, as the Royal Canadian Regiment had extended its front to join the Highlanders' position. Together, these two battalions and the Hastings and Prince Edward Regiment had opened the way for the Canadians to start breaking out from 1 CIB's position to cut the coast highway and encircle the paratroopers inside Ortona.[12]

Unsure what the Germans were planning, Hoffmeister could only draft plans to either end the battle in a renewed offensive borne by the PPCLI, or to repulse a counterattack with the same battalion. He went into Ortona to carry out his daily visits to the two battalion headquarters there, and spoke with an obviously exhausted Lieutenant Colonel Syd Thomson. The Seaforth commander weighed only about 140 pounds in his boots and wanted nothing more than a chance to rest.[13] Thomson thought the only thing keeping him going was rum. Hoffmeister patted him on the back and said, "Great show, Syd, terrific show, you are doing great." Thomson smiled wanly, bit back the desire to plead for a rest, and soldiered on.[14]

◆ ◆ ◆

As another day of fierce bloodletting drew to a close in Ortona, Canadian Broadcasting Corporation war correspondent Matthew Halton lifted his microphone and gave one of the updates that, since the Moro River battle, had transfixed Canadians across the nation. "An epic thing is happening amid the crumbling and burning walls of the compact town. . . . For seven days and seven nights the Canadians have been trying to clear the town and the action is as fierce as perhaps modern man has ever fought. For seven days and seven nights the Canadians have been attacking in Ortona, yard by yard, building by building, window by window. And for seven days and seven nights the sullen young zealots of a crack German parachute division have been defending like demons. Canadian and German seem to be both beyond exhaustion and beyond fear. The battle has the quality of a nightmare. It has a special quality of its own, like . . . the fight at Stalingrad. . . . the same apocalyptic pall of smoke and fire and maniacal determination. . . . The splitting steel storm never stops and the men in there are as if possessed. Wounded men refuse to leave and the men don't want to be relieved after seven days and seven nights. That is the report of effect of the Canadians in Ortona, that they have asked not to be relieved and deeds that have been done there will add records of selfless courage on the heritage of all men. . . . For us at least there is nothing but Ortona today. The infantry and the tanks fight from yard to yard with all the more stubbornness after the seven days and seven nights. And the Germans now know all too well the identity of the troops on the right."[15]

◆ ◆ ◆

Unknown to the Canadians, the seven-day nightmare of the battle of Ortona was ending. There would be no last-ditch desperate counterattack. No fresh battalion was being embarked on "Operation Ortona." Canadian intelligence had misinterpreted the intercepted German communiqué. General der Panzertruppen Traugott Herr, commander of 76th Korps, had in fact requested authority to withdraw the paratroops from Ortona. After consulting with Tenth Army commander General der Panzertruppen Joachim Lemelsen, Tenth Army chief of staff Generalmajor Fritz Wentzell responded to Herr's request at 1100 hours on December 27. "Army Commander gives consent to immediate beginning of preparations for withdrawal. The movement may be carried out during the night."[16]

The paratroopers disappeared like ghosts moving into the darkness. Feldwebel Fritz Illi and his platoon gathered up their weapons and other gear. Then they simply walked away from their positions in the front lines with hardly a backward glance. They marched past the cemetery and up the coast highway. At no time during the withdrawal was Illi's platoon fired on. And Illi had no sense that the Canadians knew the Germans were leaving.[17]

Obergefreiter Karl Bayerlein received word in the early evening that a withdrawal was underway. He wrote in his diary, "There is no town left. Only the ruins. In the evening at 2200 hours we left without making noise. The enemy did not realize this. We left with all our weapons. I had only five rounds of ammunition. The enemy gained a destroyed city. We left undefeated."[18]

◆ ◆ ◆

On the morning of December 28, Ortona did not waken to the rage of battle. Instead an eerie calm lay over the ruins. With two other men, Lieutenant Alon Johnson conducted a dawn patrol of the front lines. He later wrote that, "coming through a battered building near a well-known and very dangerous doorway, I heard something unfamiliar — the sound of excited voices somewhere in the distance. The significance of this babble seemed to escape the tired company rifleman guarding the doorway, but to me it suggested a sudden and radical change in the situation. Important enough to risk being shot at by showing myself in the doorway. Nothing happened, so I stepped into the street, once again drawing no enemy fire. Immediately the scouts and I moved forward through the rubble and battered buildings, taking what cover we could as we searched for the source of the ever-louder sound of chatter."

Johnson saw a group of civilians, who beckoned the Canadians forward. Seeing people coming out of cellars up and down the street, Johnson reckoned it safe to show himself. A young Italian who spoke English came up and proceeded to show Johnson the location of the German headquarters in town, warning him that it was probably mined. He then gave Johnson that curiously disdainful, haughty expression that Italians master so well. "I can't understand what took you so long. There weren't many Germans here." Johnson curbed a sharp retort. The young man guided Johnson through the rubble all the way to the shell-torn castle. It was empty. The paratroopers were gone. The Battle of Ortona was over.[19]

# 29

# AFTERMATHS

$A$T 0800 hours on December 28, CBC Radio war correspondent Matthew Halton bumped his jeep through the deep ruts that Three Rivers tanks had gouged into the road leading into Ortona. The town seemed strangely silent. Only a few machine guns could be heard chattering, and hardly any German shells were falling on the town. Canadian guns were quiet. In front of the battalion headquarters of the Loyal Edmonton Regiment, a group of bearded soldiers "who hadn't had their shoes off for thirty days were laughing." Halton jumped out of his jeep and went into the headquarters. As he came in, Lieutenant Colonel Jim Jefferson gave him a wide grin.

Halton said, "Don't tell me."

"Yes, I think we have Ortona," Jefferson said. "There's a patrol going through the fort now and if they find no Germans there, we'll know the thing is over."

A few minutes later Corporal Bill Clover, the radio operator, removed his earphones and reported, "Sir, the Germans are gone or else they are all dead."[1]

Halton wandered through the ruins of Ortona. His guide was

Edmonton Captain Vic Soley. He fed Halton a steady stream of stories, but Halton hardly heard him. The correspondent was horrified by the destruction he was seeing for the first time. "I went slowly down another main street and came to another square," he later reported. "The buildings were either empty shells or piles of brick and rubble, some covered with German dead and blood. And this havoc caused by shells, not bombs. On one pile of rubble, precariously balanced . . . was a Canadian tank. I see it now as I speak, as I will always see it — not static and dead, but dynamic in that minute when gallantly it climbed the mine-filled pile of rubble only yesterday and was struck down."[2] The tank was Corporal Joe Turnbull's *Amazing*.

Only one of Soley's stories imprinted itself onto Halton's consciousness. Last evening, Soley said, amid a final heavy German artillery bombardment, a young Italian woman was discovered buried alive in the rubble of a building. Edmontons and Seaforth Highlanders of Canada worked together to rescue her. The woman, they discovered as they pulled her out of the ruin, was not only pregnant but in the middle of labour. A sergeant from Vancouver got to work and helped with the delivery. Both mother and child were healthy and well. The woman had promised the men her son's middle name would be Canadese.[3]

◆ ◆ ◆

Throughout Ortona, Canadian soldiers wandered in a bewildered daze. Some sat down, kicked off their broken boots, leaned back, and slept like the dead. Others looted the buildings that had been left relatively unscathed. Major Jim Stone hated to see this. Posted throughout the town were German notices warning the paratroopers that looting was punishable by death. In many rooms, trinkets and various valuables sat untouched. Soon after the fighting stopped, however, Stone and the rest of the regiment learned that a couple of soldiers had discovered some silver hidden behind a wall. From then on, the plundering became rampant and there was a lack of will on the part of commanders to bring it to a halt. Stone tried speaking to some of the men, hoping to convince them that the looting was wrong. In no mood for lectures, they ignored him. Short of arresting a large number of his best soldiers, Stone saw that nothing could be done. So, like the other officers, he turned a blind eye. Soon a stream of packages containing everything from gold sovereigns to fine lace linens was making its way back by military post to Canada.[4]

Not all the soldiers were engaged in looting, of course. Many respected Italian property, taking only what was considered fair game for soldiers at war — food, liquor, and clothing. And meanwhile, the Edmonton pioneers set to work digging through the rubble of the building in which Lieutenant E.D. Allan's platoon had been buried, hoping that some of the nineteen men lost might still be alive. On December 30, Corporal J.H. Johnman and Private R.J. Williams heard sounds coming from the rubble. A frantic recovery mission ensued, and in minutes Lance Corporal Roy Boyd of Wembley, Alberta, was rescued from the ruins. He was the only one of the nineteen men to be dug out alive.[5]

During the days following the fall of Ortona, Seaforth and Edmonton officers made a token effort to extend and consolidate the hold the two battalions had on the town. Patrols were sent out to investigate all areas that had formerly been in German hands. In the rail tunnels, a patrol found a nicely decorated Christmas tree bearing a handwritten sign that read: "Sorry we can't stay to put mistletoe on, but we'll make it hot for you in the hills."[6]

It was still fairly hot in Ortona. Since December 28, the Germans had hammered the town repeatedly with artillery and mortars.[7] Throughout the last days of 1943, about three daily bombardments were usually directed against Ortona. The concentrations of artillery caused little damage to the already mangled town. The enemy shells also did nothing to deter the Princess Patricia's Canadian Light Infantry from moving through Ortona and advancing up the Coast Highway toward the Riccio River and Torre Mucchia, an ancient, tall tower standing atop a seaside promontory. On December 28, the battalion passed through Ortona and reached its objective about halfway between the town and Torre Mucchia without firing a shot.

◆ ◆ ◆

Although the battle for Ortona was over, some Canadians were still fighting. Major General Chris Vokes, commander of 1st Canadian Infantry Division, was not in a position to halt all offensive action now that Ortona had fallen. The country to the immediate south of the Riccio River was still contested. If the Germans were to be forced north of the Arielli River, the paratroopers must first be pushed back over the Riccio. To the west, the hamlets of San Tomasso and San Nicola remained important objectives, as did the crossroads to the north of these hamlets that joined the road from the coast to Tollo. On the coast, Torre Mucchia was essential to Canadian control of the countryside south of the Arielli River. The tower was not the necessary objective, although its commanding heights might serve well as a forward observation post. What mattered more was the actual headland upon which the tower stood. A triangular promontory protected on two sides by steep seaward cliffs, the relatively flat, bare summit provided a position that controlled the Coast Highway. Once the Canadians were in possession of the summit, they would be able to bring effective artillery fire against any targets using the highway south of the Arielli. On both German and Canadian military maps, the promontory was designated Point 59. Its capture became the final primary objective of 1st Canadian Infantry Division for December.

Frustrating Vokes's ability to fulfill this task was the same problem that had plagued him for most of the December fighting. He had too few strong battalions to easily achieve the mission. There was no question of any battalion from 2nd Canadian Infantry Brigade participating, other than the already engaged PPCLI. The Seaforths and Edmontons were no longer effective. On the western flank, 1st Canadian Infantry Brigade was nearly worn out. He believed the 48th Highlanders of Canada had it in them still to capture San Tomasso and San Nicola, but the other two battalions were only capable of supporting this effort. That left 3rd Canadian Infantry Brigade. The West Nova Scotia Regiment was still too weakened to be of immediate use. At best, Vokes thought the West Novas would be able to advance from Point 59 across the Riccio and reach the Arielli River. The Royal 22e Regiment was also very weak, but Vokes thought it strong enough to advance along the right flank of the Highlanders to seize the crossroads of the Tollo road. The Carleton and York Regiment was his last resource. So, once again, he was forced to ask one battalion to do the work with virtually no support from any other infantry unit. The PPCLI could take off some of the pressure by driving up the coast highway, but it was unlikely to get all the way to Torre Mucchia in time to significantly reinforce the Carleton and York companies.

Vokes faced another problem. The attacks had to happen immediately. Although the weather had improved for a few days, that trend was now reversing itself. Long-range forecasts predicted that by early January repeated storms bringing heavy rain and even snow would force movement on the Adriatic coast to grind to a halt. If Point 59 were not taken in the next few days, the chances of tanks supporting any infantry attack would be remote. The result could be that the 1st Canadian Infantry Division might spend the rest of the winter locked into a salient jutting into the German line. Such a position would be costly to defend. What was needed was a solid line dug in behind a river. The Canadians needed to own all the ground south of the Riccio, in the same way that the Germans were known to be planning to dig in north of the Arielli. Such positions provided a secure bastion behind which a division could rest, rebuild, and prepare for renewed fighting in the spring.

There was no way Vokes could afford to have 1st Canadian Infantry Division engaged in continued, long-term combat in more than the most limited manner. The division's fighting edge was gone. Its casualties had been so high that none of the battalions were truly combat effective. "Without a pause for reorganization," Vokes wrote, ". . . the offensive power of an infantry division is bound to become spent, not for lack of offensive spirit, but simply because the quality of the offensive team play within the rifle companies had deteriorated."[8]

◆ ◆ ◆

This need for reorganization was not just limited to the infantry. Tankers, artillery gunners, medical personnel, and supply service units had all been badly cut up in the month-long battle. The many separate cogs that kept the division functioning were worn down and depleted, including the equipment. Most of the gun barrels on the twenty-five pounders of the Canadian artillery required immediate replacement. The gunners were themselves ragged with exhaustion.[9]

First Canadian Armoured Brigade was greatly reduced in effectiveness. While actual numbers of tanks destroyed and crew casualties were far less than those suffered by the infantry, the brigade's three regiments had taken their heaviest combined losses to date in the Mediterranean theatre. More significantly, the battle weariness that affected the infantry also rested heavily upon the tankers.

On the evening of December 28, Joe Turnbull prowled the Ortona battlefield in search of his brother Gord. He had been told by other Three Rivers tankers that Gord had come through the battle unscathed. But Joe knew, too, that his brother might still be unaware that he had survived the destruction of *Amazing* and his subsequent escape into the German-held buildings of the Piazza Plebiscita.

He found Gord sitting in a shell hole, staring off into space, softly singing "Happy Birthday" to himself. Joe went down into the crater and joined him. Gord stopped singing. The two brothers sat together in silent companionship.

◆ ◆ ◆

On the morning of December 29, the 48th Highlanders of Canada swept across the Riccio River and took San Nicola without meeting significant resistance. The battalion's lead companies then wheeled to the right and advanced up the road toward San Tomasso. Resistance was expected to be heavier at this hamlet, so an artillery barrage was scheduled to precede the Canadian advance. 'A' Company moved off astride the road with 'C' Company guarding the left flank. The right flank was protected by a ravine. 'A' Company's No. 9 Platoon, which was in the lead, had been reinforced earlier to a strength of thirty-three. Its commander was Lieutenant Jack Pickering.

The artillery fire plan called for a barrage by two British field regiments against an area suspected of holding the main concentrations of German resistance. The blanket barrage screamed down as the Highlanders moved up the road toward the hamlet. Forty-eight guns fired short. The number of rounds that crashed down over the next few minutes were in the hundreds.

Pickering's platoon was caught squarely inside the maelstrom. Men were thrown every which way, like rag dolls. Some, bleeding from shrapnel wounds and dazed by concussion, staggered to their feet only to be ripped repeatedly by the shrapnel of more exploding shells.

In the midst of the carnage, Pickering screamed, "To the road! To the road!" The road was bordered by a small ditch. If the men could reach it, they would have some scant protection from the incoming shells. Two platoon section leaders, Corporal George Tomasik and Corporal Carl Harley, were killed trying to get the men headed toward the ditch. Pickering stood in the open, directing the remnants of his platoon to safety, while another corporal desperately dragged at his arm in an attempt to force the officer to take cover. Finally Pickering relented and the two men ran to the ditch. Pickering made it safely, but the corporal was severely wounded.

The moment the shells started to fall, 'A' Company commander Captain Hamish Macintosh realized the artillery was coming from friendly fire. The forward observation officer for the British guns was up front with Pickering's platoon. Macintosh waded into the middle of the strike zone. He screamed at the FOO to call off the guns. The man yelled back, "German shells! German shells!" Macintosh brushed the shocked officer aside, grabbed the radio handset, and ordered the fire plan stopped immediately.

As the smoke hung heavy over the road, No. 9 Platoon's nine unscathed survivors slowly rose from the ditch. Twenty-four men lay on the ground, but amazingly only three were dead. The cries and moans of the wounded were pitiful to hear. All the uninjured survivors in the platoon were seasoned veterans. Every reinforcement was a casualty. Caught in an unexpected circumstance, their battlefield inexperience had taken its tragic toll.[10]

Despite its casualties, 'A' Company quickly renewed the attack on San Tomasso. Lieutenant Pickering and his eight men joined the assault. Captain Macintosh, sickened by the tragedy that had struck the platoon, issued curt instructions to the officers before they set off. "Shoot anything you see," he said. The Highlanders went into the hamlet and did precisely that, sweeping the Germans out in fierce house-to-house fighting. Three more of the survivors of No. 9 Platoon died, including the sergeant, Bill Taylor. By nightfall, the Highlanders held both hamlets but were subjected to German artillery, mortar, and long-range machine-gun fire.[11]

◆ ◆ ◆

On the Highlanders' right flank, the Royal 22e Regiment attack on December 29 soon stalled in the face of heavy machine-gunning by Germans dug in on the opposite bank of the Riccio River. Two assaults were put in and both were repulsed. Faced by such heavy resistance, the attack stalled. Lieutenant Colonel Jean Allard, now commanding the Van Doos, ordered a halt until he could lay on an artillery fire plan for the morning.[12]

To the right of the Van Doos, the Carleton and York Regiment had begun a drive toward Point 59. Companies 'A' and 'D' led. The two companies were within 600 yards of the promontory when they were struck by withering artillery and mortar fire. The men pressed on through the shrapnel flaying the air, but soon came under intense small-arms and heavy-machine-gun fire. Major Winston Johnson was killed and Major Glen Foster and seven infantrymen wounded.[13] At the morning 3 CIB Orders Group, Carleton and York commander Lieutenant Colonel John Pangman had been told that intelligence staff expected the German defence of Point 59 to be relatively half-hearted. The paratroopers were believed to have insufficient strength in the battalions based on the Adriatic coast to mount serious resistance. This intelligence was wrong.[14] The paratroopers the battalion faced were members of the fresh 1st Battalion of the 1st Regiment, which had been shifted the previous night from a quiet point in the line near Orsogna. They were heavily entrenched and obviously determined to prevent the fall of Point 59 for as long as possible. The attack ground to a halt. Resistance was so intense that 3 CIB commander Brigadier Graeme Gibson ordered the Carleton and York Regiment to close into a defensive position and await the morning.

During the night, the paratroopers blew up the coastal highway bridge crossing the mouth of the Riccio just west of Torre Mucchia.[15] Although the paratroopers seemed determined to defend the headland, it was apparent that they also recognized the inevitable outcome of the battle. They would delay, but Torre Mucchia would eventually fall to the Allies. The only question was how many soldiers on both sides must die in the transaction.

◆ ◆ ◆

About two miles southwest of the crossroads leading to Tollo from the coast, Americo Casanova and some of the men who had been hiding in the cave behind the stone house had decided the fighting around the area was light enough for them to risk an outside fire. They had a little mutton and were roasting it over the small flame. A pot leaning against the fire contained a thin, watery soup. Americo was almost drooling with anticipation, his eternally empty stomach growling up a storm.

Everyone was so focused on the fire and the food that they only realized they were not alone when one of the men looked up and saw what they thought were British soldiers surrounding them, rifles aimed their way. Then one of the Tommies spoke, and to the surprise of the Italians told them in rough French to get back in the cave. The men and Americo quickly gathered up the scraps of half-cooked mutton and the pot of simmering broth, kicked mud over the fire, and fled into the dark shelter of the cave.

The French-speaking British soldiers moved off. Americo could hear them continuing to talk French back and forth as they departed. He looked at his uncle, who shrugged, as if to say "Who can make sense of this war?"

Several days later, Americo and the other civilians would leave the cave for good and return to Ortona. He would find his family's apartment building destroyed, his mother and siblings gone. Caught as they were on opposite sides of the front, the fate of his family remained a mystery. Not until June 4, 1944, would he be reunited with them.[16]

◆ ◆ ◆

Antonio D'Intino's family owned one of the poor houses in the fishermen's quarters on the northeastern flank of Ortona, as well as the farm across the ravine west of the town. On December 29, D'Intino left his ailing father and ventured into the town to check on the property. He made his way down Corso Vittorio Emanuele and Corso Matteotti, climbing over the massive rubble piles and passing the shattered Cattedrale San Tomasso. Ortona seemed like an alien landscape to him. It took him several minutes to realize that the family's house had been shelled and was nothing more than a ruin. He picked through the wreckage, but could find nothing of value.

As D'Intino searched the ruins, a young Canadian approached. He asked in perfect Italian if D'Intino might know a family that had lived in Ortona. D'Intino recognized the name. They were neighbours who lived just down the street. D'Intino said, "I'll show you." He led the soldier down the street to a badly battered structure and banged on the door. After a few minutes, the door opened a crack and an elderly man looked out warily. "Grandpapa," the young man said and embraced his grandfather, whom he had never met. As the two men were joined by the old man's frail wife, D'Intino walked quietly away, leaving the family to its reunion.[17]

Antonio Di Cesare's family also returned to Ortona a few days after the fighting ceased. His parents had taken precautions against looting by stashing all the family valuables in the ceiling of the house. They had not counted on the house itself being reduced to a burned-out shell. Nothing of value remained. Like many other civilians, they found a place in one of the battered buildings that was semi-habitable and unclaimed by its previous owners. Antonio helped the Canadian tankers clean the cakes of mud off the tracks each day in exchange for food. In this manner, he was able to help his family survive the long winter.[18]

◆ ◆ ◆

On the morning of December 30, the Tollo Road crossroads fell to the Royal 22e Regiment. As the paratroopers yielded the ground without offering any real fight, the Van Doos took the position without losing a single man. It was a mixed blessing, however, as the moment the Canadians occupied the new position they were hammered by intensely accurate artillery. An officer and sixteen infantrymen were wounded.[19]

Meanwhile, the Carleton and York Regiment continued toward Point 59 with 'A' and 'C' companies. Again, the paratroopers were waiting with machine guns and mortars. The attack crumbled 200 yards from the tower. Lieutenant D.A.S. Black and four other men were killed. Captain D.H. Andrew and lieutenants W.N. Laughlin and H.G. "Cubby" Morgan were wounded, along with twenty-one other men. Most of the casualties were from 'A' Company, which had also lost men the previous day.

Lieutenant Colonel John Pangman was deeply shaken by these losses. It seemed as if the New Brunswick regiment was being left out on its own with insufficient resources and support. Brigadier Graeme Gibson appeared uninterested in leaving 3 CIB headquarters to visit the battlefield to gain a first-hand appreciation of the difficulties the battalion faced. Pangman expressed his disgruntlement. Gibson's response was to order Carleton and York second-in-command Major Dick Danby to take over. Pangman was bundled away for a rest. He would never return to the regiment.[20]

◆ ◆ ◆

Increasing frustration was the order of the day for the Carleton and York Regiment. The fight for Point 59 seemed hopelessly bogged down in the mud, with an absence of determined backing from supporting arms, either artillery or tanks. The tanks, of course, faced the same problems that had plagued them throughout the past month — mud and mines. On December 31, tanks from the Ontario Tanks tried to push up the promontory in support of 'A' and 'C' companies.[21]

The tanks became mired in the deep mud of a minefield. Two tanks lost tracks to mines. A third bellied out on a Teller antitank mine and had its bottom escape hatch blown in. The tank's co-driver died instantly. A fourth tank got out ahead of the infantry, tripped a mine and, when the infantry attack again failed, had to be abandoned.[22] The infantry went into the minefield and formed a defensive ring around the other three tanks, ensuring the paratroopers were unable to move up and destroy the machines during the night.

While this attack was stalling, 'B' Company's No. 11 Platoon commander, Lieutenant Don Smith, set off on a reconnaissance patrol. He had only one man with him, a lance corporal armed with a Bren gun. Smith carried a Thompson. The two men were in a vineyard, struggling through the broken concrete support poles and fallen wires. Crossing some jumbled ground, Smith suddenly came under fire from a German MG42 machine gun. Smith hit the dirt, landing on top of a small pack. The lance corporal dropped a couple of feet behind him, letting off four rounds from the Bren as he did so. The bullets scythed right over Smith's back. When Smith looked over his shoulder, he saw the man perspiring and looking as if he was in shock. "I'm sorry, sir. I left the safety catch off." Smith realized he had just about been shot in the back by his own man.

Pressing closer to the ground, Smith noticed the small pack, lying abandoned in the mud. It was a Canadian pack. Printed in black paint on the upturned side was Lieut. H.G. Morgan. Smith and "Cubby" Morgan had been friends since meeting in Britain, and he knew the young officer had been wounded the day before. A few hours later, Morgan succumbed to his wounds while being operated on at the field dressing station in San Vito Chietino.

Smith and the still shocked lance corporal slowly extricated themselves from their pinned-down position and returned to 'B' Company headquarters. Smith told company commander Major

Burton Kennedy about the gun position, and the three-inch mortar was set up to knock the machine gun out. Smith pointed the German position out to the mortarmen, who popped a shot out that fell a bit short. Their next round was dead on the money and the German gun was knocked out.[23]

This successful destruction of a German position corresponded with an order from brigade headquarters for the Carleton and York Regiment and the Ontario Tanks to cease further direct assaults. Instead, the Canadians were to engage the Germans with concentrated mortar and artillery fire. When the German defensive positions were considered suitably softened up, another attack would be sent in.

The infantry battalion dug in for a miserable New Year's Eve. Lieutenant Smith found a small brick shack he thought might have once housed geese and established his platoon headquarters there. There was room in the shack for only Smith and two other men from the platoon. Outside, a vicious gale had blown in off the Adriatic and was lashing the men in their slit trenches with mixed freezing rain and snow. Inside the shack, Smith felt a bit guilty at his comparative comfort.

As he was starting to settle down on the floor for a brief rest, however, a German armour-piercing shell slammed into one end of the shack. Smith's runner was killed. The other two men were unharmed. Smith's platoon sergeant was badly shaken by the incident. Had the shell been high-explosive instead of armour-piercing, everybody in the shack would have died. When the sergeant failed to snap out of it, Smith escorted him back to company headquarters. Major Kennedy sent him to the rear as Left Out of Battle, consequently avoiding turning the man in as a battle-exhaustion case.

Smith went back to his platoon. The platoons were conducting hourly patrols, seeking enemy targets and watching for German counterattacks. With the sergeant gone, the only platoon leader left was Smith. He took out every patrol, finally conducting the last two alone. Stupid, he knew, but his headquarters troopers had done their turns. The rain and snow kept falling. Every man in the regiment was intensely miserable.[24]

◆ ◆ ◆

Seaforth Highlanders of Canada Company Sergeant Major Jock Gibson was feeling particularly good about life. On New Year's Eve, he was showered, shaved, dressed in a clean uniform, and well fed. And now this. In the basement of an Ortona house, Gibson had discovered a vast wine cellar. Wooden casks lined one entire wall. Where to begin? That was the only question. It looked as if this would be a good New Year's Eve after all.

Outside he heard some German shells banging down nearby, but figured the cellar should be secure. He started into the cellar heading for the wine barrels, when suddenly they began coming away from the wall in a massive landslide. Barrels blew open, wine gushed out. Gibson stared in horror as a tidal wave of wine rolled toward him. As he turned to run, the wine enveloped him and swept him right out of the cellar and into the street. He lay on the cobblestones, gasping and choking, grateful to be alive.

For the next two days, the Company Sergeant Major of 'D' Company shivered inside his soggy, stinking clothes until finally the quartermaster took pity on him and issued him a new uniform.[25]

# 30

## POINT 59

ON New Year's Day morning, 1944, the rain stopped. Carleton and York Regiment Padre Ernie McQuarrie led a small burial party to a point directly behind 'B' Company's No. 11 Platoon. Besides the padre, there were four men carrying the stretcher bearing the body of Major Winston Johnson. Lieutenant Don Smith knew Johnson by the nickname of Wink. He was the son of Smith's family doctor and was, at thirty-two, ten years his senior. Just before the war, Johnson had completed a law degree at Dalhousie University. He had been recently married when the war broke out. Smith remembered Johnson strolling with his fiancée down the streets of St. John, pausing to joke with Smith and his teenage friends.

Now he was to be buried in Italian mud, his grave marked by nothing more than a crude cross made from the wood of an apple crate. Johnson had been wearing one of the thin horsehide jerkins the Canadians wore over their uniforms for a little added warmth. The jerkin was riddled across the chest and stomach with bullet holes from a German machine gun.

"Why on earth are you burying him here behind my position?"

Smith wanted to ask the padre. It was hardly a quiet spot. Smith and his men tried forming up around the grave to pay last respects to the popular officer. Within a few minutes, however, German mortar and artillery rounds began falling and they all had to run for cover. But the padre was determined, a man Smith thought was a perfectionist in all he did — including the burial of the dead. This burial was started and the padre would finish the task regardless of the physical danger posed.[1]

◆ ◆ ◆

Burial parties and larger ceremonies honouring those lost to the regiments during December marked the first few days of January 1944. The surviving Seaforth Highlanders of Canada gathered on a point of land overlooking the Adriatic Sea. Here, the regiment's dead were interred in a small cemetery. There were, thought Lieutenant Wilf Gildersleeve, far too many crosses set there in tidy rows.[2] While Padre Roy Durnford led the men in prayers, Pipe Major Edmond Esson, described by Matthew Halton as "a handsome man with a silky black beard," played "Skye Boat Song" and "Piper of Drummond."[3] The mournful drone of the pipes lifted on the breeze blowing in from the sea.

The Seaforths and all the regiments of 1st Canadian Infantry Division buried more than comrades on these chill days in January. They had gone to war in the manner that regiments of the Commonwealth nations had always marched toward the sound of the guns. Each regiment was formed on a regional basis. Many of the men had long served together in the prewar militia units upon which the regiments drew when the call to arms was heard. Most of the Seaforths were from Vancouver, Victoria, Kamloops, Salmon Arm, Vernon, and the other southern interior towns of British Columbia. The Carleton and York Regiment hailed from New Brunswick; the 48th Highlanders of Canada called Toronto home. Brothers served side by side. Men from the same street formed platoons. Officers and men had been friends, relatives, and acquaintances in the civilian world. All of this served to build a cohesion that was lacking in armies which paid scant attention to regional affiliations, such as those of the United States and Germany.

The Battle of Ortona broke that cohesion. During the height of the fighting in Ortona, the Loyal Edmonton Regiment had received a draft of reinforcements on December 27. Most of the men sent to 'C' Company had been soldiers pulled in from the Cape Breton Highlanders Regiment, which had just recently arrived in Italy. The Edmonton war diarist joked that 'C' Company could now be "called the Bluenose Company."[4] What the Cape Bretoners thought of laying their lives on the line as part of a western regiment and a western brigade went unrecorded. It is doubtful, however, that they willingly left their own regiment.

After December 1943, the regiments of 1st Canadian Infantry Division would be divided internally. On one side stood the ever-shrinking ranks of old veterans who had marched to war together, landed on the shores of Sicily, slogged their way up the boot of Italy, and then fought through the mud and fire of the Moro River, The Gully, and Ortona. On the other side were the replacements, many of whom came from parts of Canada that were foreign to the regiments' veterans. Too many of these reinforcements survived only a short time before leaving on stretchers or being buried under Italian earth. Many a veteran made a studied effort to develop little or no relationship with these men, who were likely to fall by the wayside soon after arriving. The self-imposed isolation made all the more poignant the loss of each member of the old regimental guard.

◆ ◆ ◆

The losses that 1st Canadian Infantry Division suffered during December 1943 were staggering, especially in the line rifle companies. Total casualties from December 1 to December 31 were estimated at 2,339 men. Of these, 502 were killed. The officer ranks were devastated. Thirty-five officers died, 127 were wounded, and 14 were missing. Casualties in the other ranks were also heavy, totalling 467 dead, 1,544 wounded, and 152 missing. Many of those declared missing were dead, their bodies lost, sometimes forever, in the quagmire of the battlefield or the rubble of Ortona. Sickness had further depleted the ranks. Seventy-seven officers had been evacuated with sickness, 1,540 other ranks. Taken together, the regiments lost 253 officers and 3,703 other ranks to battle as casualties or to sickness.[5]

Against these losses, reinforcements received approximated only 150 officers and 2,258 other ranks. This left the division, according to a 1st Canadian Infantry Division report written at the end of December, short 60 officers and 990 men.[6]

The problem, however, went far beyond numbers. Most of the reinforcements arrived during the last days of the battle. This, Major General Chris Vokes wrote, meant that the men filling the gaps torn in the regimental lines "arrived at a rate which prohibited a normal and gradual absorption." They were also undertrained troops, who required intensive training even as the regiments reorganized to adjust for their battlefield losses.[7]

"It is most notable," Vokes added, "that the standard of minor tactics and unit tactics has deteriorated, and opposition which at one period would have been brushed aside in their stride, now causes untold delay and stickiness. The troops are tired and the team play within units is lacking. The men and officers are cheerful enough and in good spirits and morale is high, but units are not fighting fit." Vokes recommended that the division be given a long break from combat, so it could concentrate on once again attaining that "fighting edge."[8]

Another problem that plagued the division in a manner never before encountered was the heavy losses of men to battle exhaustion. Roughly 20 percent of all men evacuated as sick were battle-exhaustion cases. Divisional psychiatrists would return only between 20 to 25 percent of these to front-line rifle company duty.[9] It was now recognized that battle-exhaustion cases were seldom able to function effectively when returned to direct combat duty. These men might serve with perfect competence in rear-area units, but the regiments, like all rifle units in wars, faced shortages in front-line troops. The rate of battle exhaustion critically weakened the division, both during the December fighting and after.

◆ ◆ ◆

The casualties suffered by the Germans during December 1943 would remain shrouded in mystery and conflicting report. The war diaries of the 90th Panzer Grenadier Division would be lost later in the war, so no approximations of its casualties exist. Canadian intelligence estimates prior to its withdrawal, however, indicated that the Panzer Grenadiers had been effectively destroyed as a fighting unit. This was primarily due to the division's ill-conceived strategy of launching fierce counterattacks. Vokes would boast: "We smashed

90th Panzer Grenadier Division and we gave 1st German Parachute Division a mauling which it will long remember."[10]

Vokes had it right. The Panzer Grenadiers would be out of the line rebuilding their regiments until the division was sent scrambling from its rest position near Rome on January 22 to attempt to stem an Eighth Army offensive across the Garigliano River. This attack was aimed at distracting the Tenth Army from the joint Anglo-American invasion at Anzio, thirty-five miles south of Rome. The division's performance on this front would reflect its diminished fighting prowess, itself a reflection of the loss of veteran troops suffered at the Moro River and The Gully.

What of 1st Parachute Division? After the battle, Fallschirmpionier Karl Bayerlein and Feldwebel Fritz Illi both boasted that the paratroopers left the field undefeated and according to their own timing. Certainly the division was not mangled in the manner of the 90th Panzer Grenadier Division or even the 1st Canadian Infantry Division. Their defensive action was wisely executed, with few costly counterattacks. Yet the record shows that the paratroopers, too, suffered heavy casualties during the two weeks of their fight in December. Most battalions of the German division started entering the line on December 20. By December 29, Tenth Army chief of staff Generalmajor Fritz Wentzell stated during a phone conversation: "All the battalions of Heidrich [commander of 1st Parachute Division] have now a strength of merely one company [120 to 150 men]. The necessary steps to obtain reinforcements will be taken."[11] Total casualties officially reported for the nine days of fighting from December 20 to December 28 were 455. Of those, 68 were listed as dead, 159 as wounded, 205 as missing, and only 23 sick.[12] Yet there is little doubt that 1st Parachute Division entered the battle relatively fresh and not seriously understrength.

The figures don't add up, even assuming that most of the 205 missing were actually paratroopers who were killed. Unlike their Panzer Grenadier counterparts, the paratroopers did not surrender en masse at any point in the battle. Those few captured were usually isolated or overrun and faced the option of either giving up or dying. A surprisingly high number opted for the latter. In Ortona, the Canadians rounded up more than one hundred paratrooper corpses for mass burial. This reflected the unusual intensity of the battle and the pressure placed on the Germans. The parachutists seldom abandoned their dead to the enemy.

What remains clear is that, in the same way that 1st Canadian Infantry Division would rebuild itself to once again be considered one of the crack units of the Allied forces, so, too, would 1st Parachute Division remain an elite German force throughout the continued fighting in Italy. The Canadians would meet both the paratroopers and the Panzer Grenadiers several more times during their long march through Italy.

◆ ◆ ◆

The casualty figures tallied by Vokes's staff on December 31 did not take into account those men of 1st Canadian Infantry Division killed or wounded after January 1. It appears that Vokes and his staff considered the battle over once Ortona fell. There were the small actions along the Riccio River, but these were considered of little import once the Germans withdrew from Ortona. Vokes turned his attention to writing after action-reports. Yet the dying was not done.

On the forward slopes of the promontory known as Point 59, the Carleton and York Regiment and 'B' Squadron of Ontario Tanks continued a bitter, almost forgotten battle. 'B' Company platoon commander Lieutenant Don Smith saw a corporal in an adjoining platoon take a bullet in the chest. The man was out in the open between the Canadian and German lines. He fell into a muddy pool of water almost a foot deep. Smith marked the man's fall and turned his attention back to his platoon's efforts. Soon, however, Tommy, his batman, came over looking agitated. "Mr. Smith," he said, "are you going to let that man lie out there and die alone? Those bastards are ignoring the Red Cross when the stretcher-bearers try to get to him. I've been out, but I can't go back."

A track separated the company from the wounded man, and a German machine gun was firing down its length. Smith thought about it, and when the firing eased for a moment, dashed across the track to the wounded soldier. The man was unconscious, blood gurgling from his mouth and from holes in his lungs. Smith stood up, trying to throw the man in a fireman's carry over his back. Bullets from the MG42 machine gun whined around him, throwing up splashes from the water. His feet sank deeply into the muck. He struggled toward the Canadian lines. Then the paratroopers started using a rifle launcher to drop stick grenades around him. The little bombs seemed so close that Smith imagined he could reach out and catch one as it fell. Fortunately, the mud and water suppressed their explosions.

After ten minutes spent futilely trying to get the wounded man out, Smith had to give up. He lowered him into the mud and fled across the track to cover. His batman was sobbing hysterically, "Are you going to let him die out there alone?" Smith checked his platoon. It was holding out fine. No excuse there. Once again, he ran to the wounded man. Again the muck, again the rifle grenades, again the machine gun, again another ten minutes of futility before his nerve broke. As Smith dropped the man again he saw that blood no longer gurgled from the soldier's lungs or lips. He fled for safety.

That night, Smith crawled out to check the soldier. He was dead.[13]

◆ ◆ ◆

On January 4, after repeated and costly failures to capture Point 59, the Carleton and York attack finally was properly supported by a complexly planned and heavily delivered artillery barrage. 'B' Company led the assault. No. 11 Platoon, which numbered fifteen men, including Smith, was in front. The other platoons had even fewer soldiers. Smith formed his men up in a line. Five on each side of him, with the last in line at either end a corporal. The acting platoon sergeant and four platoon headquarters personnel were immediately behind Smith. They had no idea how many Germans were up on the promontory. The shelling lifted at 1600 hours and the company commander blew his whistle. "Mr. Smith, get moving." Smith blew his own whistle, knowing that the men probably couldn't hear it. Then, rather dramatically, he pointed at the objective some 140 yards away and started to run. Much to Smith's relief, his platoon followed. After the casualties the regiment had suffered, it was foolhardy not to assume the men might balk at yet another dangerous charge.

The mud formed like giant snowshoes on the soldiers' boots. But they were in the open and could only keep going. Smith gasped for breath. Everyone was slogging forward with tortured difficulty, the mud dragging on their legs. Small-arms fire started snapping at the line. On his immediate right, a formerly unreliable soldier sped up. Smith was impressed until he realized that the man was merely pitching forward in response to a mortal wound.

The platoon reached a row of barbed wire. Smith fought his way over it to find a slit trench immediately behind. It contained three paratroopers working an MG42. Smith brought up his rifle and emptied the clip into them. Then he threw a Type 36 grenade on top of the middle man in the position to guarantee the kill.

From the tower of Torre Mucchia, standing only yards away, a shot rang out. Smith saw a German soldier firing from its doorway. He charged the man and shot him in the chest at point-blank range. He then threw grenades through the doorway and a nearby window. Several of his men then rushed into the tower and swept through it, finding no other Germans inside.

Lying in a small defile running down to the Adriatic from the tower, a German cried, "Tommy, Tommy, help me. I'm wounded." Smith's first thought was, "We aren't Tommies. We don't want to be called Tommies." He also wondered, he later said, "how the bastard who was killing us for days now had the gall to call for help." Despite this, Smith sent a stretcher-bearer down to care for the wounded German.

Smith set the platoon to digging in, with no time to spare. No sooner had the paratroopers retreated from Point 59 than the Germans started to pound the promontory with artillery. One of Smith's men suddenly threw down his rifle and shouted, "I can't take it any more. I'm leaving." Smith walked over, shells exploding around the two men. Shrapnel sang through the air and cordite-reeking smoke rolled over the battlefield. Smith picked up the soldier's rifle and said, "Look, Junior, you hold onto your bloody rifle, get into that slit trench, and don't go anywhere unless I tell you to." Worried that the man's panic might spread and that the Germans might counterattack any moment, Smith could ill afford to lose even one more of his men.[14]

Minutes later, the other platoons of 'B' Company captured their supporting objectives. Point 59 was secure. 'B' Company had taken eighteen prisoners. The Canadian walking wounded marched them back. As the last rifle fell silent at Torre Mucchia, the great Canadian battle fought from the Moro River through Ortona to the Arielli River drew to a close.

# EPILOGUE

# ORTONA
# IN MEMORY

**D**ECEMBER 1998. I stand before the tombstones of the Moro River Canadian Cemetery. It is one of those crisp, clear, early winter days that CBC war correspondent Matthew Halton likened to a Cézanne painting. Sea purplish gray, sky azure, grass deep green, tombstones soft white marble. This Canadian cemetery is the largest of its kind in Italy. Of 1,613 graves, 1,375 hold Canadian soldiers. Not all died during December 1943. Some were moved here from other battle-fields nearby. All too many others perished in an ill-conceived January 1944 offensive launched against the Arielli Line by the newly arrived 5th Canadian Armoured Division.

Canadian Forces Major Michael Boire and I have come to this cemetery, as must all pilgrims drawn to Abruzzo province by the Battle of Ortona. Michael walks slowly from one tombstone to another. A name read, date of death noted, regiment identified, a moment of silent remembrance passed. He has a slight limp, the result of an airborne drop gone wrong. Michael, a keen military historian in his spare time, is stationed in Germany at Heidelberg. Once he heard I was coming to Ortona on a research trip, luring him down from Germany was easy.

We have spent several days going methodically over the December battlefield. Michael has offered me his soldier's eye and understanding of how ground affects a military operation. Today we measure the costs. Michael's parent regiment is the Three Rivers — the tankers who fought in Ortona's streets alongside the Loyal Edmonton Regiment and the Seaforth Highlanders of Canada. He carries a ring-binder version of his regiment's unpublished history. Many names cited in its pages correspond to those etched in marble.

There are also names that I will come to know well as I write this book. Mitch Sterlin, the unlikely hero. Tom Vance, a gentle and trusting soul. Bob Donald, the too-often-forgotten RCHA forward observation officer, who was part of the triad of officers who made Casa Berardi's capture possible during the gallant dash of Captain Paul Triquet's Van Doos. Sometimes on paper their short lives and the manner of their deaths can seem remote, distant. Today, I look at the ground on which they died, then the tombstones under which they lie, and they are cast in a clearer, sorrowful light.

Later, Michael drops me on the Moro River's southern ridge across from Villa Rogatti. He is returning to Germany. I plan to retrace part of the physical journey of the 1st Canadian Infantry Division regiments. I will walk my own short road to Ortona.

Fittingly, clouds have blown in from the Adriatic and drizzle is falling as I set off alone. The Canadian soldiers had only rough wool uniforms to repel the water. I wear Gore-Tex. Where they were heavily burdened by the tools of war, my pack holds featherlight 7x21 binoculars, a camera and lenses, a Swiss Army knife, a bottle of mineral water, and a thick wad of *lire*.

The Moro is now spanned by a stout concrete bridge on the road to Villa Rogatti. Once across it, I veer off the road and follow the river to a point that seems roughly in line with my understanding of the route the Princess Patricia's Canadian Light Infantry took during their night assault on Villa Rogatti. Behind me the river runs high. It is narrow, barely twenty feet across. Deeper this December than it was for the Canadians. A stick shoved in sinks to thigh-depth.

I climb through olive groves and vineyards. Moro River mud sucks at my boots, glues on, and forms the wide globular snowshoes the soldiers cursed. I add my own curses to the historic litany. But I can stop now and then to bang away some of the accumulation. Under fire, such fussiness would have been foolhardy. The vineyards offer difficult terrain. Overhanging wires force me to hunker down. It's hard to look up the slope bent over. Everywhere I see endless terrain features that even to an unpractised eye appear perfect for defensive gun positions. The same is true in the olive groves. There I stand straight, but the mud is deeper.

Eventually I circle up and into Villa Rogatti from the right flank, just as the PPCLI did. The town was rebuilt out of the battle's ruins. Stone and brick walls are deeply pocked by bullets and shrapnel. From Villa Rogatti, I walk winding country lanes toward San Leonardo. Farmers work the fields. They spread nets under the olive trees and then shake the fruit down to be harvested like fish swept from the sea by seiners. They are intent on their work. I pass unnoticed.

In San Leonardo, I pause for food at a small grocery. A woman prepares a sandwich. In my poor Italian I explain my purpose in tramping across country seldom visited by foreigners on foot. *Il Guerra*. As matter-of-factly as she cuts prosciutto and cheese, the woman says her parents died in the bombardment of San Leonardo. Sisters, brothers, all killed. The village ruined. She left an orphan.

Near her store is the monument to civilian dead. Such monuments are to be found in every village and hamlet near Ortona. This one is an abstracted image of a person with arms extended toward heaven, lips open, beseechingly. A plea for mercy? A cry to the heavens for a reason for their suffering?

Estimates of the number of civilians killed during the Battle of Ortona vary. Many Canadians question the accuracy of Italian figures. Statistics are numerous, contradictory. The most accurately detailed figure appears to be 1,314. A toll that links each numerical casualty to a name. But even this is complicated by a question of timelines. Canadians see the battle as spanning a time frame of December 5 to January 4. In the Italian mind, the battle lasted until the Allies left Ortona in the late spring of 1944. Not until the Allies were far enough north that the town and countryside were no longer subject to artillery fire or aerial bombardment did the battle end for them. Then there are the civilians killed even later by exploding shells and mines. Have they been counted?

Antonio D'Intino buried several close friends and relatives in the months after the battle. He also eventually married Anna Tucci, the young woman from San Donato. They live today much as Antonio lived in 1943, on the land across the ravine from Ortona. Their house is the same as the one in which his father died of pneumonia in the spring of 1944. It is still heated by nothing more than a small wood-burning brazier in the corner of the kitchen. When I visit them one late afternoon, they are in bed to keep warm from the unexpectedly chill December weather. They rise, wrap themselves in sweaters and scarves, and put blankets over their laps, open wine, and light a small fire. We sit for hours at the kitchen table, while they tell their stories. My hands grow numb taking notes in a cold the wine and the meagre fire do little to abate.

Antonio tells me of a time in the early spring of 1944 when seven teenage boys tilled a nearby field. They moved in line, working shoulder to shoulder. One boy struck the detonating pin of a Teller antitank mine. All seven were killed. Casualties of the battle? Or victims of the larger frame that was World War II?

Armies sweep into a landscape and fight their battles. Then they leave. The civilians are left to clean up the detritus. Between San Leonardo and The Gully to the south of Cider Crossroads, I see few signs of war's passage. Only the occasional stone building with its roof collapsed in a manner I now know is caused by the impact of an artillery shell. Those same buildings are usually deeply pocked by the strike of small-arms fire. As I walk along, I finger a fragment of shrapnel given to me the day before by a member of the Berardi family. Michael thinks, because of the width of its curving arc, it is a piece of casing from a 105-millimetre artillery round.

Casa Berardi still stands, little changed from when the battle raged around it. The Royal 22e Regiment erected a small memorial next to the building in honour of the heroism of Captain Paul Triquet and the other Van Doos who succeeded in capturing this objective against great odds and at the loss of many lives. There is also a plaque, installed by the Royal Canadian Regiment, on the side of Sterlin Castle, where Mitch Sterlin's small platoon held off successive waves of Panzer Grenadiers.

Walking through the Ortona countryside, lulled by the softly repetitive scenery of olive groves, vineyards, and farmhouses, I ponder the point of the battle. Historians and veterans alike remain conflicted. Should the battle have been fought? Michael and I worried this question at length while standing on ridges or sharing *vino rosso* and *grappa* at Ortona's Ristorante Miramere. At one point, we stood on a promontory looking north up the coastal highway. It may or may not have been Point 59, where the battle ended. We were unsure and there was no tower in sight.

Michael said, "Your job is to help defeat Germany by diverting divisions from northern Europe and from the Russian front. You are confined to a narrow band of ground between the Apennines and the Adriatic. There is no operational ground in the mountains. This road hugs the coast all the way to northern Italy, and from there you might get into Austria and even beyond that to Germany. There are the rivers, of course. Always another after the last one. To advance, you have to win the rivers. One at a time. Delay a month because of the weather and you achieve nothing. The Germans can move divisions freely while you sit and do nothing. So you cross the Sangro River and that brings you to the Moro River. The weather is closing in. But you have a fresh division. So you go one river farther. It would have been difficult to predict the cost."

Following a one-lane road passing under the massive concrete spans near the crossroads that today allow vehicles travelling on the coastal autostrada to whisk effortlessly over the width of The Gully, I decide that Michael's soldierly explanation is the clearest. There are Canadian historians who vie to saddle 1st Canadian Infantry Division Major General Chris Vokes with the blame for an ill-considered battle. Hardly fair. Vokes marched to orders, just as each private did. Bernard Montgomery gave the orders. His "colossal crack" turned out to be a colossal conceit. Michael's assessment regarding the coast highway and the unavoidable strategy of advancing up it to Italy's northern border was only part of Montgomery's reason. Pushing the commander to reckless haste was the desire to beat the Americans to Rome.

A fool's errand. Travelling to Ortona by train through the valley extending from Rome to Pescara was a sobering journey for me. It seemed inconceivable that Montgomery seriously thought the

Eighth Army could win Rome via this route of advance in winter. Defensible positions abound. Hilltop fortress towns provide virtually impregnable bastions upon which to anchor a defensive line. The terrain in that valley is far more hostile to an attacker than any I encounter between the Moro River and The Gully.

Whatever the individual verdict about the larger issue of the battle's purpose, there is another question historians and veterans push around when the subject of Ortona comes up. Was the battle well fought? Nobody questions the accomplishment of the regiments or of individual soldiers. They did their duty and did it well, absorbing casualties that might well have sent many armies fleeing the field. But there is the lingering question of whether Vokes mishandled the battle's execution.

Most veterans who offer an opinion seem to agree that he did. First, there was the opportunity frittered away at Villa Rogatti. An exploitation from there would have bypassed both The Gully and Ortona. But, of course, Vokes was presented with the "impossible bridge." So perhaps he is not entirely to fault on that miscalculation.

Then there is the issue of whether he should have taken the battle into the streets of Ortona. Certainly this ran against standard military doctrine of the day. Generally, you were to avoid fighting in built-up areas. Of course, nobody in either Vokes's or Eighth Army's intelligence sections expected the Germans to make a stand in Ortona. The same military doctrine argued that they would withdraw the moment the Canadians broke into the outer edge of the town. Once the Canadians and Germans started fighting in the streets of Ortona, it would be impractical for the Canadians to break off the action.

And then, as Albert Kesselring noted, the world press transformed the battle into a matter of Allied versus German prestige. More important to their respective commands, Canadian versus German prestige. It is significant that when the battle was finished, Allied public relations officers were cautioned about their dealings with reporters: "DON'T before Rome is captured claim it as a great military objective. Show that Rome as a town has no military significance." I think it is armchair hindsight that leads us to fault Vokes for getting drawn into the Ortona street battle.

Where Vokes was in error, where he came close to destroying the division he commanded, was in his overall execution. Specifically, his insistence on feeding the regiments into individual battles against well-defended objectives. It seems Vokes could not think on a divisional scale or implement a divisional-level offensive. He committed his regiments piecemeal, allowing each to be chewed up before withdrawing it and sending another into the fray. Several opportunities to achieve a breakthrough, particularly at The Gully, were thrown away through this approach simply because there was no regiment in reserve that remained capable of capitalizing on an advantage gained. Had he outflanked The Gully early on, rather than waiting until several regiments had been mauled in head-on attacks, the battle undoubtedly would have been decided sooner. It is also possible that he then would have seen the wisdom of abandoning the direct drive up the Ortona-Orsogna lateral into Ortona in favour of the hook he eventually had 1st Canadian Infantry Brigade and the 3rd brigade's Royal 22e Regiment and Carleton and York Regiment throw toward Torre Mucchia.

Standing on the southern edge of The Gully, it is unthinkable to me that Vokes failed to see the folly of frontal assaults. I wonder if he ever came up to the actual front to see where his regiments were dying? There is no record that he did. The Gully is a daunting land feature, readymade for defence. Too many Canadians died there needlessly. I am less convinced they died for no purpose in Ortona itself.

Generals, of course, make plans; soldiers pay the price of execution. It is their voices that murmur in my ear as I join the Ortona-Orsogna lateral road and walk along its verge through the industrial park that stands now on the ground across which the Loyal Edmonton Regiment made its assault on December 20. For every veteran's voice I can hear, there are many more who remain silent. Five out of six declined to be interviewed. Ortona has left its imprint on the hearts and minds of many soldiers in a way other battles perhaps did not. How often I heard, "It's not something to talk about. It should just be forgotten." These veterans were not talking of the war itself, or of their overall experience. They were speaking of December 1943.

Yet the veterans who were there seem unable themselves to forget. Many who declined an interview remarked that they had gone back to Ortona once, twice, sometimes repeatedly. In December

1998, a few days after I left Ortona for Canada, a group of about fifty veterans arrived. Their visit was a significant affair, but one organized and paid for by a private Canadian benefactor rather than the Canadian government. For the first time, Canadian veterans and German veterans sat down together in the church of Santa Maria di Costantinopoli for a Christmas dinner reminiscent of the one taken by the Seaforth Highlanders of Canada on Christmas Day, 1943. A group of Ortona citizens provided the meal. The dinner was accompanied once again by organ music played by Wilf Gildersleeve. Former enemies emerged as somewhat wary comrades. Many spoke of a healing being achieved.

Ortona itself is physically healed from the battle's destruction. Entering Ortona, as the Edmontons did, along Corso Vittorio Emanuele, I see a town that has risen anew from the rubble. The great dome on Cattedrale San Tomasso has been restored. Holes in the walls of Santa Maria di Costantinopoli were repaired. Many of the old buildings were reconstructed, so parts of the town retain its old-world charm. Elsewhere, the buildings are modern. Ortona has grown, sprawling over to the other side of the western ravine and extending to the edge of The Gully. But today few outsiders think of it as the "Pearl of the Adriatic." Ortona is a poor town, its economy fragile. There are many government-subsidized housing complexes. Most tourists are Germans, who are more willing than most people to swim in the heavily polluted Adriatic. The old castle is buttressed by a complex steel-scaffolding system. A sign declares that this is part of a restoration project. But the sign is a decade old and the work does not progress.

While Ortona is not prosperous, the countryside always amazes the veterans who return. When they marched over the Moro River, they entered a landscape ravaged by artillery bombardment. Their memories of it are stark. The farmers seemed desperately poor, simple peasants. It was a land remembered in black and white — rather like the old war photos and documentary footage that recorded the two great wars of the twentieth century.

The farms today are relatively thriving. Houses are well cared for. Country folk drive expensive Italian cars and chatter on cell phones in the same way as their city cousins.

In winter, the countryside is a lush collage of colours and thick vegetation. It is more reminiscent of the Quebec townships in early fall than of a land burdened by winter. Temperatures are erratic. In the course of one day, it can be so warm you strip to shirtsleeves, only to be shivering an hour later when a chill wind blows off the Adriatic. One hour more and a heavy, icy squall races over you. The night after my trek from the Moro to Ortona, I strolled after dinner through soft moonlight back to my hotel. The evening was warm. I wore only a blazer, unbuttoned. In the night, I woke to a hush reminiscent of Canada. Sure enough, it was snowing. In the morning, olive trees bowed under the heavy weight and some branches broke.

While Ortona and the surrounding countryside have recovered physically, the battle remains etched in the memory of the people. Remembrance is often paid. The stories of the suffering a family endured are nurtured and kept alive from generation to generation. So inculcated into the community psyche is the battle that merely mentioning that I am *Canadiense* and writing about the battle gains me entry to virtually any home. Despite the fact that the Canadians brought upon Ortona a great deal of destruction and death, there is a great sense of respect for the sacrifice made by the Canadians, who are viewed by all people of this area as liberators.

This stands powerfully at odds with the way Canada remembers Ortona. An unnamed CBC commentator broadcasting from London on December 28, 1943, said that Ortona would figure in the battle lore of Canada. Yet today few Canadians recall ever hearing the name. Even those who recognize the battles of Dieppe, Hong Kong, and the Canadian landing at Juno Beach during the Normandy invasion seldom know anything about Ortona. For some reason, the battle slipped quietly and decisively from the nation's consciousness. True, Canadians are not much given to remembrance of the battles in which fathers, grandfathers, and great-grandfathers fought. But the blind spot of memory with regard to Ortona seems inexplicable.

Two factors may be at work here. First, there is a tendency in Canada to wallow in military failure or perceived controversy rather than to explore and celebrate battles won. Book after book refights Dieppe and retackles the defeat at Hong Kong. In the Normandy invasion, Canadians were part of one of the climactic battles of the war. This has rendered it a good topic for anniversary tributes. But the Battle of Ortona was neither obviously timely nor possessed of any momentous controversy. So historians have turned their backs on it. Added to this is the reticence of the veterans themselves to describe their experience at Ortona. The psychic scar is still prevalent. In Edmonton, during the annual reunion of the Loyal Edmonton Regiment, one old soldier said to me, "I don't see what your interest in Ortona is. There were other battles. It was just one of them." Later the same man sat down and said, "I lost my best friends in Ortona. I never made friends like those again. Never." There were tears in his eyes. He brushed them away hard with an angry hand. Then he went to the bar, and ordered another double rye and water.

One veteran of the PPCLI, radio signaller Jack Haley, said he never felt free to discuss the reality of war with his family. Humorous events, sure — but not the horror of a battlefield. He said, "This is the first time I've ever talked about most of this. I'm glad to do so." In the slaughterhouse that was Ortona, there was little laughter. What humour the soldiers did see in unfolding events was usually macabre, the kind of thing only men in war could find funny. One veteran told how a man, returning to a house where his squad rested, played a joke by bursting through the doorway and yelling in German for them to surrender. One of his friends, startled awake, let him have a full burst in the stomach with a Thompson submachine gun. The man lived. At the time, the rest of his regiment thought the story of how he got wounded was hilarious. Try explaining the humour of this event to a sixteen-year-old granddaughter.

At Ortona, Canadians endured a terrible test of arms. Every battle can be ultimately viewed as tragedy. So there is a particularly Canadian tendency to reshape such events into tragicomedy, or an intellectual debate about a battle's causes or the reasons for its failures. This is impossible with Ortona.

As I walk the cobblestone streets and talk to some of those who were young civilians caught in the battle, I am struck by a difference in their perspective on the conflict. The people of Ortona pay it tribute, both by remembering the survivors and by absorbing it into the collective memory of the community. They have taken the battle into their hearts and emerged the stronger for doing so. The storekeeper in San Leonardo spoke openly and without great emotion about being orphaned by an artillery bombardment, I think, because hers was part of an experience that had been shared and spoken of through the generations. They did not skirt around the edges of what people endured. Rather, they confronted it directly and then were able to go on, to rebuild their homes and lives.

We could do worse than to follow their example.

# APPENDIX A
# THE CANADIANS AT ORTONA*

## 1st Canadian Infantry Division

**Canadian Armoured Corps:**
  **4th Reconnaissance Regiment**
    (4th Princess Louise Dragoon Guards)

**The Royal Canadian Artillery:**
  **1st Field Regiment**
    (Royal Canadian Horse Artillery)
  **2nd Field Regiment**
  **3rd Field Regiment**
  **1st Anti-tank Regiment**
  **2nd Light Anti-Aircraft Regiment**

**Canadian Infantry Corps:**
  **The Saskatoon Light Infantry**
    (brigade support group)
  **1st Canadian Infantry Brigade:**
    The Royal Canadian Regiment
      (permanent force)
    The Hastings and Prince Edward
      Regiment
    48th Highlanders of Canada Regiment
  **2nd Canadian Infantry Brigade:**
    Princess Patricia's Canadian Light
      Infantry Regiment
      (permanent force)
    The Seaforth Highlanders of Canada
      Regiment
    The Loyal Edmonton Regiment

**3rd Canadian Infantry Brigade:**
  Royal 22e Regiment
    (permanent force)
  The Carleton and York Regiment
  The West Nova Scotia Regiment

## 1st Canadian Armoured Brigade

**11th Canadian Armoured Regiment**
  (Ontario Tanks)
**12th Canadian Armoured Regiment**
  (Three Rivers Tanks)
**14th Canadian Armoured Regiment**
  (Calgary Tanks)

## Corps of Royal Canadian Engineers

**2nd Field Park Company**
**1st Field Company**
**3rd Field Company**
**4th Field Company**

## Royal Canadian Army Medical Corps

**1st Infantry Division:**
  No. 4 Field Ambulance
  No. 5 Field Ambulance
  No. 9 Field Ambulance
**1st Armoured Brigade:**
  No. 2 Light Field Ambulance

*Not all supporting units included.*

# Appendix B
# Canadian Infantry Battalion
## (Typical Organization)

**HQ Company**
No. 1: Signals Platoon
No. 2: Administrative Platoon

**Support Company**
No. 3: Mortar Platoon (3 inch)
No. 4: Bren Carrier Platoon
No. 5: Assault Pioneer Platoon
No. 6: Antitank Platoon (6 pounder)

**A Company**
No. 7 Platoon
No. 8 Platoon
No. 9 Platoon

**B Company**
No. 10 Platoon
No. 11 Platoon
No. 12 Platoon

**C Company**
No. 13 Platoon
No. 14 Platoon
No. 15 Platoon

**D Company**
No. 16 Platoon
No. 17 Platoon
No. 18 Platoon

# APPENDIX C
# CANADIAN MILITARY ORDER OF RANK

Private (Pte.)

Gunner (artillery equivalent of private)

Trooper (armoured equivalent of private)

Lance Corporal (L/Cpl.)

Corporal (Cpl.)

Lance Sergeant (L/Sgt.)

Sergeant (Sgt.)

Company Sergeant Major (CSM)

Regimental Sergeant Major (RSM)

Lieutenant (Lt. or Lieut.)

Captain (Capt.)

Major (Maj.)

Lieutenant Colonel (Lt. Col.)

Colonel (Col.)

Brigadier (Brig.)

Major General (Maj. Gen.)

Lieutenant General (Lt. Gen.)

General (Gen.)

# APPENDIX D
# GERMAN MILITARY ORDER OF RANK

Because the German army and the Luftwaffe ground forces had a ranking system where rank also usually indicated the specific type of unit in which one served, only basic ranks are given here. The translations are roughly based on the Canadian ranking system, although there is no Canadian equivalent for many German ranks.

| | |
|---|---|
| Schütze | Private, infantry |
| Grenadier | Private, infantry |
| Kanonier | Gunner |
| Panzerschütze | Tank crew member |
| Pionier | Sapper |
| Funker | Signaller |
| Gefreiter | Lance Corporal |
| Obergefreiter | Corporal |
| Unteroffizier | Lance Sergeant |
| Unterfeldwebel | Sergeant |
| Feldwebel | Company Sergeant Major |
| Oberfeldwebel | Battalion Sergeant Major |
| Leutnant | Second Lieutenant |
| Oberleutnant | Lieutenant |
| Hauptmann | Captain |
| Major | Major |
| Oberstleutnant | Lieutenant Colonel |
| Oberst | Colonel |
| Generalleutnant | Lieutenant General |
| Generalmajor | Major General |
| General der Artillerie | General of Artillery |
| General der Infanterie | General of Infantry |
| General der Kavallerie | General of Cavalry |
| General der Pioniere | General of Engineers |
| General der Panzertruppen | General of Armoured Troops |
| Generaloberst | Colonel General |
| Generalfeldmarschall | General Field Marshal |
| Oberbefehshaber Süd | Commander-in-Chief South |

# APPENDIX E
# THE DECORATIONS

Many military decorations were won by soldiers at Ortona. The decoration system that Canada used in World War II, like most other aspects of its military organization and tradition, derived from Britain. A class-based system, most military decorations can be awarded either to officers or to "other ranks," but not both. The exception is the highest award, the Victoria Cross, which can be won by a soldier of any rank.

The decorations and qualifying ranks are:

## VICTORIA CROSS (VC)
Awarded for gallantry in the presence of the enemy. Instituted in 1856 and open to all ranks. The only award that can be granted for action in which the recipient was killed, other than Mentioned in Despatches — a less formal honour whereby an act of bravery was given specific credit in an official report.

## DISTINGUISHED SERVICE ORDER (DSO)
Officers of all ranks, but more commonly awarded to officers with ranks of major or higher.

## MILITARY CROSS (MC)
Officers with a rank below major and, rarely, warrant officers.

## DISTINGUISHED CONDUCT MEDAL
Warrant officers and all lower ranks.

## MILITARY MEDAL
Warrant officers and all lower ranks.

# Glossary of Common Canadian Military Terms and Weaponry

### Antitank Guns

Canadian forces used two antitank guns at Ortona. The six-pounder was the main antitank gun attached directly to infantry battalions. Each battalion had its own antitank platoon. This gun had a range of one thousand yards and fired a six-pound shell. It proved invaluable as a close support weapon during the house-to-house fighting inside Ortona. Also available to 1st Canadian Infantry Division were the seventeen-pounder antitank guns of 1st Anti-tank Regiment. This was basically an up-gunned version of the six-pounder. It had greater range and greater hitting power because of the seventeen-pound shell.

### Bren Carrier

Also known as the universal carrier. A lightly armoured tracked vehicle capable of carrying four to six soldiers and their weapons. Provided no overhead protection, but was walled on all sides by armour. It had a top speed of thirty-five miles an hour. This was the Commonwealth forces battlefield workhorse. Its open design enabled it to be used for carrying just about any kind of military gear used by infantry. Some were converted into weapons carriers and played a combat role by being fitted with Vickers .303 medium machine guns, Bren light machine guns, or two-inch mortars, or were used as the towing vehicle for six-pounder antitank guns.

### Bren Gun

Standard light machine gun of Commonwealth forces. Fired .303 rifle ammunition held in thirty-round magazines. An excellent, although slow-firing, weapon. It had a range of about 500 hundred yards and weighed twenty-two pounds.

### Browning 9-Millimetre Automatic

The standard pistol used by Canadian forces. Officers in the line rifle companies generally kept their pistols hidden or even threw them away to avoid being easily identified as officers by German snipers.

### CIB

Canadian Infantry Brigade.

## CO
Any commanding officer, regardless of unit size.

## COTC
Canadian Officers Training Corps.

## COY
Abbreviation for company.

## DUKW
Abbreviation for the two-and-a-half-ton amphibious truck. American-made, six-wheeled truck, capable of six knots in water.

## EDDIES
Loyal Edmonton Regiment.

## FORMING-UP POINT (FUP)
A geographical point where a unit of any size gathers in preparation for an attack or other form of movement.

## FORWARD AID POST (FAP)
Most advanced aid post to which casualties could be withdrawn for treatment.

## FORWARD OBSERVATION OFFICER (FOO)
Artillery batteries had two officers, usually captains. During a battle, one officer remained with the guns to oversee their operation. The other, the FOO, accompanied the infantry regiment being supported. He usually was part of a three-man team that included the FOO, a radio signaller, and a Bren carrier driver. The FOO was in charge of calling for artillery support and directing the fire toward enemy targets that were threatening or holding up the infantry.

## GERRY
Common term for Germans. Also spelled Jerry. Canadians seldom if ever used the harsher term Kraut, which was favoured by American soldiers. *Tedeschi*, the Italian word for German, was also popular. As an alternative to Gerry, Canadians occasionally used Hun or Boche.

## GLAMOUR BOYS

Nickname for 48th Highlanders of Canada.

## GUNNER
The artillery regiment equivalent to a private.

## HASTY P'S
Hastings and Prince Edward Regiment.

## HE
High explosive.

## HMG
Heavy machine gun.

## HQ
Any headquarters.

## LEE ENFIELD RIFLE, NO. 4, MARK 1
Standard rifle of Commonwealth forces. The Mark 1 was made in Canada for Canadian personnel. It fired .303 ammunition contained in five-round clips. Effective range was 900 yards, but most accurate when fired at ranges under 600 yards. A highly reliable, rugged weapon. Capable of being mounted with an 8-inch spike bayonet.

## LMG
Light machine gun.

## LOYAL EDDIES
Loyal Edmonton Regiment.

## MG
Machine gun.

## MO
Medical Officer.

## MORTARS
The Canadians at Ortona had three weights of mortars: 2-inch, 3-inch, and 4.2-inch. The latter was a heavy mortar and operated by the Saskatoon Light Infantry in support of the infantry regiments. The three-inch was operated by a mortar platoon attached to each battalion, while two-inch mortars were carried directly into battle by a section attached to each company. A mortar effectively lobs a bomb on what is usually a high trajectory toward a target. The bombs can be high-explosive, shrapnel, or phosphorous (smoke). Range and firepower varied according to the size of the gun. The bigger the mortar, the greater its range and firepower. The three-inch, for example, could engage targets as close as 125 yards and as far away as 2,800 yards. Its bomb weighed ten pounds. The 4.2-inch fired bombs of twenty pounds and had a much greater range. The small two-inch put out only a 2.5-pound bomb, but was extremely useful for laying smoke screens.

## NCO
Non-Commissioned Officer. All warrant officers, sergeants, and corporals are considered non-commissioned officers. NCOs provide the leadership backbone of infantry platoons and armoured troops.

## ORDERS GROUP (O GROUP)
An Orders Group is a session at which the orders setting out the tactics to be

used in a forthcoming action are given to the participating commanders. Most actions entail multiple O Groups starting at the highest level and descending downward. A brigade planning an attack, for example, will have its first O Group called by the Brigadier. He and brigade HQ staff will brief battalion commanders and the commanders of included supporting arms (artillery, heavy mortars, etc.). Battalion commanders then brief the company commanders, who in turn brief platoon commanders, who pass the information down to the individual sections. What will start as a broad-stroke tactical plan at the brigade level will, by the time it hits platoon and section stages, become a set of intensely specified tasks that must be accomplished for the overall attack to succeed. A process of filtering out non-essential detail occurs all down the line until the section leader will have little idea of the purpose of his assigned tasks.

## PIAT
Projector Infantry Anti-tank. The hand-held antitank weapon of Commonwealth forces, weighing thirty-two pounds and firing two-and-a-half-pound hollow-charge explosive bomb. Difficult to load, prone to mechanical failure, and complicated to operate, the PIAT was an unpopular weapon. Effective against German tanks only if fired against thinner side and rear armour plate, or against the tracks.

## PIONEERS
Engineering personnel who were members of an infantry battalion's pioneer company. Pioneers had a higher level of expertise with regard to handling explosive, laying charges, carrying out demolitions, and defusing enemy mines and booby traps than the average soldier.

## PLOUGH JOCKEYS
Nickname for Hastings and Prince Edward Regiment.

## PPCLI
Acronym for Princess Patricia's Canadian Light Infantry, also known as Patricias.

## RAP
Regimental Aid Post. This first aid post was usually located near the forward regimental HQ.

## RCE
Royal Canadian Engineers.

## RCHA
Royal Canadian Horse Artillery. This regiment was also designated the 1st Field Regiment.

## RCR
Royal Canadian Regiment.

## SAPPER
A term used to describe explosive and engineering personnel in the Royal Canadian Engineers, equivalent to private in the infantry.

## SHERMAN TANK
The standard tank used by Canadian forces at Ortona was the Sherman M-4A2, usually called the M-4. It weighed just under thirty-five tons. The Sherman had a five-man crew, consisting of commander, gunner, loader, driver, and assistant driver. Its main armament was a 75-millimetre gun. Fixed into the front of the tank was also a .30-calibre machine gun and a .50-calibre machine gun that could quickly be mounted on top of the turret for use as an anti-aircraft weapon. The Sherman had a top speed of about twenty-nine miles per hour and a maximum range without refuelling of 150 miles. Although the Sherman would undergo only slight modifications over the course of the war, it was generally considered inferior to most German tanks in terms of both firepower and armour. It also had a higher profile, which made it harder to get into a hull-down (protected) stance than German tanks.

## SLI
Saskatoon Light Infantry Regiment. The more official, but less commonly used, abbreviation was Sask LI.

## START POINT (SP)
Also called the Start Line (SL) or Jumping Off Point. This was where a unit of any size formed up immediately before going into an attack.

## THOMPSON SUBMACHINE GUN
Fondly referred to as the Tommy gun by those who carried it, the Thompson was a .45-calibre submachine gun. The favoured submachine gun of Canadian forces and the only American weapon they respected. The Thompson could fit either a box or drum-shaped magazine. The use of .45-calibre ammunition gave the gun tremendous stopping power.

## TNT
Trinitrotoluene (explosive).

## TROOPER
The armoured corps equivalent to a private. Trooper harkens back to the armour's cavalry heritage.

## TWENTY-FIVE POUNDER
The workhorse artillery gun of Commonwealth forces. Incredibly durable

and reliable, the twenty-five pounder was manned by a crew of six. It was generally used as a howitzer — firing high-explosive shells at a high angle — but could also fire armour-piercing shot at flat trajectories. Effective range of 12,500 yards. Weighed four tons.

## TYPE 36 GRENADE

The standard grenade of Commonwealth forces. Metal case was ribbed, leading to its being called the "pineapple." Each of the eighty ribs broke into a separate shrapnel piece upon exploding. This type of grenade was usually thrown overhand in a lobbing manner. In Ortona, the grenade proved excellent for house fighting because it could be bounced down stairwells or rolled like a bowling ball down the length of hallways.

## VAN DOOS

Semi-official nickname for Royal 22e Regiment. Derived from *vingt-deux*.

## VICKERS .303 MACHINE GUN, MARK 1

Remarkably, the medium machine gun that the Canadians used throughout World War II was virtually the same gun Canadian forces had used in World War I. With a simple gas-assisted recoil system, the gun was water-cooled and fired belts of .303 ammunition. Its accurate range was 1,100 yards, but it could fling bursts much farther. At full automatic, the Vickers put out bursts of ten to twenty rounds. Rate of fire varied from 60 rounds a minute to 250 rounds, depending on whether the gunner was using slow or rapid fire. The Vickers weighed in at forty pounds. It had amazing endurance, seldom failing to operate in even the most adverse conditions. In 1st Canadian Infantry Division, the Vickers were manned by members of the Saskatoon Light Infantry Regiment.

Although an adequate weapon, the Vickers was outclassed in performance by its German counterpart. The MG42 was rated the best gun of its type in the world for years after the war. Introduced in 1942, it had a remarkable firing rate of 1,200 rounds a minute. The MG42 had another advantage over the Vickers. It was actually a light machine gun, weighing only 25.35 pounds. When fired using a bipod, the gun had a light-machine gun range of about 600 yards. On a tripod, the range more than doubled and the weapon proved effective as an anti-aircraft gun.

## WEST NOVAS

West Nova Scotia Regiment.

# NOTES

CHAPTER 1 / A COLOSSAL CRACK

1. Dr. Jerry Richards, interview by author, Victoria, B.C., 6 Nov. 1998.
2. Appendix 46 to War Diary, General Staff, Headquarters, 1st Canadian Infantry Division, Nov. 1943, National Archives of Canada.
3. Richards's replacement was killed at Ortona while acting as liaison officer for the PPCLI at 2 CIB HQ. Richards felt terrible when he heard the news, sure that he was responsible for his friend's death after convincing him to switch roles.
4. Eric Morris, *Circles of Hell: The War in Italy, 1943–1945* (New York: Crown Publishers, 1993), 222.
5. Nigel Hamilton, *Master of the Battlefield* (London: Hamish Hamilton, 1983), 449.
6. Morris, *Circles of Hell*, 223.
7. G.R. Stevens, *Princess Patricia's Canadian Light Infantry: 1919–1957* (Griesbach, Alta: Historical Committee of the Regiment, n.d.), 121.
8. Bert Hoffmeister, interview by author, West Vancouver, B.C., 23 Nov. 1998.
9. Bert Hoffmeister, interview by B. Greenhous and W. McAndrew, Directorate of History, Department of National Defence, n.d.
10. Thomas de Faye, interview by author, Victoria, B.C., 3 Nov. 1998.
11. Ibid.
12. Elwyn R. Springsteel, correspondence with author, Sept. 1998.
13. Don Smith, correspondence with author, Aug. 1998.
14. John Alpine Dougan, interview by author, Victoria, B.C., 23 Oct. 1998.
15. Chris Vokes, *Vokes: My Story* (Ottawa: Gallery, 1985), 140.
16. Princess Patricia's Canadian Light Infantry War Diary, 1 Dec. 1943, sheet 1, National Archives of Canada.
17. Basil Smith, "Memoirs of a Quarterbloke" (Ottawa: Directorate of History, Department of National Defence, n.d.), 34.

CHAPTER 2 / WAITING, WAITING, ALWAYS BLOODY WAITING

1. *The Tools of War: 1939/45, and a chronology of important events* (Montreal: Reader's Digest Association (Canada), 1969), 26.

2. Ian V. Hogg and John Weeks, *Military Small Arms of the 20th Century*, 6th ed. (Northbrook, Ill: DBI Books, Inc., n.d.), 104.

3. Ibid., 288–89.

4. Ibid., 243.

5. Harry Rankin, interview by author, Vancouver, B.C., 15 Oct. 1998.

6. Alon Johnson, interview by author, Victoria, B.C., 25 Sept. 1998.

7. Thomas de Faye, interview by author, Victoria, B.C., 3 Nov. 1998.

8. Ibid.

9. West Nova Scotia Regiment War Diary, Dec. 1943, 42-N-2, National Archives of Canada.

10. Jerry Richards, interview by author, Victoria, B.C., 6 Nov. 1998.

11. Nigel Hamilton, *Master of the Battlefield* (London: Hamish Hamilton, 1983), 449–50.

12. Ibid., 450–51.

13. Bernard Law Montgomery, *El Alamein to the River Sangro* (New York: St. Martin's Press, 1948), 132.

14. G.W.L. Nicholson, *The Canadians in Italy: 1939–1945*, vol. 2 (Ottawa: Queen's Printer, 1956), 291.

15. On Canadian maps this village was mistakenly identified as Villa Roatti, while German maps identified it as Villa Ruatti. In later years, this would cause some confusion among veterans and historians alike.

16. Jerry Richards, interview.

17. 3rd Canadian Infantry Brigade Headquarters War Diary, 5 Dec. 1943, p. 3, National Archives of Canada.

18. Nicholson, *The Canadians in Italy,* 291–92.

19. Alon Johnson, interview.

**CHAPTER 3 / PEARL OF THE ADRIATIC**

1. Fabio Dell'Osa, interview by author, Ortona, 9 Dec. 1998.

2. Americo Casanova, interview by author, Ortona, 8 Dec. 1998.

3. Antonio Di Cesare, interview by author, Ortona, 9 Dec. 1998.

4. Eric Morris, *Circles of Hell: The War in Italy, 1943–1945* (New York: Crown Publishers, 1993), 131.

5. Associazone Archeologica Frentana, *Immagini: Ottobre 1943 – Giugno 1944, Nove mesi di martiro* (Ortona: Soc. Coop. Iniziativa Cristiana, 1993), n.p.

6. Antonio D'Intino, interview by author, Ortona, 8 Dec. 1998.

7. Ibid.

8. Associazione Archeologica Frentana, *Immagini*, n.p.

9. Antonio Di Cesare, interview.

10. Americo Casanova, interview.

11. Antonio D'Intino, interview.

12. Casanova, interview.

13. D'Intino, interview.

14. Di Cesare, interview.

15. D'Intino, interview.

16. Stephen E. Ambrose, *D-Day June 6, 1944: The Climactic Battle of World War II* (New York: Simon & Schuster, 1994), 35.

17. Ibid., 34.
18. Di Cesare, interview.
19. G.W.L. Nicholson, *The Canadians in Italy: 1939–1945,* vol. 2 (Ottawa: Queen's Printer, 1956), 291.

## CHAPTER 4 / THE SHARP END

1. Farley Mowat, *And No Birds Sang* (Toronto: McClelland & Stewart, 1979), 228.
2. Terry Copp, *Battle Exhaustion* (Montreal: McGill-Queen's University Press, 1990), 54.
3. Thomas de Faye, interview by author, Victoria, B.C., 3 Nov. 1998.
4. W.R. Freasby (ed.), *Official History of the Canadian Medical Services, 1939–1945, Volume Two: Clinical Subjects* (Ottawa: Queen's Printer, 1953), 48-52.
5. Ibid., 52–53.
6. Alon Johnson, interview by author, Victoria, B.C., 25 Sept. 1998.
7. Freasby, *Official History,* 53.
8. Eric Bergerud, *Touched With Fire: The Land War in the South Pacific* (New York: Penguin Books, 1996), 92–93.
9. Dr. John Haley, interview by author, Victoria, B.C., 30 Oct. 1998.
10. Johnson, interview.
11. John Alpine Dougan, interview by author, Victoria, B.C., 23 Oct. 1998.
12. Peggy Turnbull and family, correspondence with author, Feb. 1999.
13. John F. Wallace, *Dragons of Steel: Canadian Armour in Two World Wars* (Burnstown, Ont.: General Store Publishing House, 1995), 181–82.
14. Joseph Turnbull, letter, 21 Oct. 1943, 2. Copy provided to author by Peggy Turnbull.
15. Ibid., 3.
16. Ibid., 7.

## CHAPTER 5 / RUSH JOBS

1. Farley Mowat, *And No Birds Sang* (Toronto: McClelland & Stewart, 1979), 219–20.
2. G.R. Stevens, *Princess Patricia's Canadian Light Infantry: 1919–1957,* vol. 3 (Griesbach, Alta: Historical Committee of the Regiment, n.d.), 122; Princess Patricia's Canadian Light Infantry War Diary, Dec. 1943, sheet 2, National Archives of Canada.
3. Hastings and Prince Edward Regiment War Diary, Dec. 1943, 33-N-4, National Archives of Canada.
4. N.a. "Battle of the Moro River: Hastings & Prince Edward Regiment," Directorate of History, Department of National Defence, n.p.
5. Hasty P's War Diary, 33-N-4.
6. Farley Mowat, *The Regiment,* 2nd ed. (Toronto: McClelland & Stewart Limited, 1973), 139.
7. Hasty P's War Diary, 33-N-4.
8. Mowat, *And No Birds Sang,* 221.
9. Daniel Dancocks, *The D-Day Dodgers: The Canadians in Italy, 1943–1945* (Toronto: McClelland & Stewart, 1991), 157.

10. Basil Smith, "Memoirs of a Quarterbloke" (Directorate of History, Department of National Defence, n.d.), 35.
11. Hasty P's War Diary, 33-N-4.
12. J.D. Forin, "Baranello to San Leonardo: The Seaforth Highlanders of Canada, December 1943" (Directorate of History, Department of National Defence, n.d.), 3.
13. J.D. Forin, correspondence with Dr. R.H. Roy, 19 Jan. 1968, University of Victoria Special Collections, 4–10.
14. Forin, correspondence with Roy, 1; Bert Hoffmeister, interview by author, West Vancouver, B.C., 23 Nov. 1998. It is a matter of speculation that, had it not been for the shortage of commanders in the Seaforths ranks at the time, Hoffmeister would have removed Forin prior to the battle due to his illness.
15. Major S.J. Simons, "2 Canadian Field Park Company RCE Unit History, Italian Campaign Campobasso to Ortona, Dec. 43/Jan. 44" (Directorate of History, Department of National Defence, 10 Feb. 1944), 4.
16. Forin correspondence with Roy, 10.
17. A.K. Harris, "Account at Ortona," n.p., University of Victoria Special Collections, 3.
18. Ibid., 3.
19. Reginald H. Roy, *The Seaforth Highlanders of Canada, 1919–1965* (Vancouver: Evergreen Press, 1969), 240–41.
20. Harris, "Account at Ortona," footnotes, n.p.
21. Seaforth Highlanders of Canada War Diary, Dec. 1943, sheet 4, National Archives of Canada.
22. Harris, "Account at Ortona," 4.
23. Forin, correspondence with Roy, 11.
24. Forin, "Baranello to San Leonardo," 3.
25. Ibid.

## CHAPTER 6 / NO GOOD, JOHNNY

1. G.R. Stevens, *Princess Patricia's Canadian Light Infantry, 1919–1957,* vol. 3 (Griesbach, Alta: Historical Committee of the Regiment, n.d.), 123–24.
2. Princess Patricia's Canadian Light Infantry War Diary, Dec. 1943, sheet 36-N-4, National Archives of Canada.
3. Stevens, *Princess Patricia's,* 124-26.
4. Dr. George Garbutt, correspondence with author, 30 Nov. 1998. In the PPCLI's War Diary and the regimental history by Stevens, which drew from the diaries, it is stated that Garbutt was with 'B' Company and single-handedly destroyed several machine-gun positions before running out of ammunition. This is false. Garbutt's exploits before Villa Rogatti are as given here. The destruction of the machine guns by 'B' Company appears to have been the result of the combined operations of numerous soldiers of that unit, not any one individual.
5. Cameron Ware, interview by Dr. Reginald Roy, 23, 25 June, and 10 July 1979, University of Victoria Special Collections.
6. Dr. John Haley, interview by author, Victoria, B.C., 30 Oct. 1998.
7. Garbutt, correspondence. The prisoners Garbutt's platoon took probably were

Poles. By 1943 many foreign nationals from occupied nations were being forcibly conscripted into the German army. Although these were usually assigned only to regular infantry units, rather than to more elite formations such as the 90th Panzer Grenadiers, a few cropped up in almost every division. In the main, these troops were nearly worthless to the Germans, fighting only so long as German officers and non-commissioned officers were at their backs, ready to shoot any who flagged in their devotion to duty. Once the officers were gone, the foreign conscripts usually threw down their guns and surrendered. Surrendered Poles became the primary source of new recruits for the Allied Polish II Corps in Italy, possibly history's only example of an army unit reinforced from the front.

8. Stevens, *Princess Patricia's*, 123.
9. Ware, interview.
10. Stevens, *Princess Patricia's*, 126.
11. Haley, interview.
12. PPCLI War Diary, sheet 4.
13. Garbutt, correspondence.
14. Ware, interview.
15. Haley, interview.
16. Stevens, *Princess Patricia's*, 126.
17. n.a., "Miscellaneous Biographies Army Personnel: Lieut.-Col. C.B. Ware, D.S.O.," Directorate of History, Department of National Defence, n.d., 10–11.
18. Haley, interview.
19 PPCLI War Diary, sheet 5.
20. Haley, interview.
21. *The Tools of War: 1939/45, and a chronology of important events* (Montreal: Reader's Digest Association (Canada), 1969), 39.
22. PPCLI War Diary, sheet 5.
23. Ware, interview.
24. Stevens, *Princess Patricia's*, 127.
25. Haley, interview.
26. "Miscellaneous Biographies: Ware," 10–11. For his courage at Villa Rogatti throughout December 6, 1943, Ware would be awarded the Distinguished Service Order.
27. Lieutenant Ruckdeschel, "Combat Report of the attack on Ruatti on 6 Dec. 1943. Appendix 'O'" of "Report #18 Historical Section Army Headquarters: The Campaign in Southern Italy (Sept.–Dec. 1943), Information from German Military Documents regarding Allied operations in general and Canadian operations in particular," Directorate of History, Department of National Defence, n.d., n.p.
28. Ibid.
29. G.W.L. Nicholson, *The Canadians in Italy: 1939–1945*, vol. 2 (Ottawa: Queen's Printer, 1956), 295.
30. Ibid.
31. Captain A.G. Steiger, "Report #18 Historical Section Army Headquarters: The Campaign in Southern Italy (Sept.–Dec. 1943), Information from German Military Documents regarding Allied operations in general and Canadian

operations in particular," Directorate of History, Department of National
Defence, n.d., 51.

32. Nicholson, *Canadians in Italy*, 295.
33. Both sides routinely overestimated the dead suffered by the enemy.
Ruckdeschel, for example, believed that most of the thirty men fired on by
tank 712 were killed or wounded. While German casualties at Villa Rogatti
during the Dec. 5–6 battle were undoubtedly high, it is unlikely that the
equivalent of one and a half companies was killed or captured, not factoring
in wounded, which usually outnumbered dead and captured by at least
about three to one.
34. PPCLI War Diary, sheet 5.
35. Ibid.

## CHAPTER 7 / MIXED RESULTS

1. J.D. Forin, correspondence with Dr. R.H. Roy, 19 Jan. 1968, University of
Victoria Special Collections, 11–13.
2. J.D. Forin, "Baranello to San Leonardo: The Seaforth Highlanders of Canada,
December 1943," Ottawa: Directorate of History, Department of National
Defence, n.d., 3.
3. Forin, correspondence with Roy, 12.
4. Seaforth Highlanders of Canada War Regiment Diary, Dec. 1943, n.p., National
Archives of Canada.
5. Matthew Halton, CBC Radio broadcast, 7 Dec. 1943, CBC Radio Archives.
6. Hastings and Prince Edward Regiment War Diary, Dec. 1943, 33-N-5, National
Archives of Canada.
7. Forin, correspondence with Roy, 13.
8. Seaforth War Diary, n.p.
9. Forin, "Baranello to San Leonardo," 4.
10. Bert Hoffmeister, interview by author, West Vancouver, B.C., 23 Nov. 1998.
11. Anna Tucci, interview by author, Ortona, 9 Dec. 1998.
12. Farley Mowat, *The Regiment*, 2nd ed. (Toronto: McClelland & Stewart, 1973),
140–41.
13. Hastings and Prince Edward Regiment War Diary, 33-N-5.
14. Mowat, *The Regiment*, 141.
15. Hastings and Prince Edward Regiment War Diary, 33-N-5.
16. Mowat, *The Regiment*, 141.
17. Mowat, *And No Birds Sang* (Toronto: McClelland & Stewart, 1979), 226.
18. Hastings and Prince Edward Regiment War Regiment Diary, 33-N-5.
19. G.W.L. Nicholson, *The Canadians In Italy: 1943–1945*, vol. 2 (Ottawa: Queen's
Printer, 1956), 297.

## CHAPTER 8 / THE IMPOSSIBLE BRIDGE

1. Robert L. McDougall, *A Narrative of War: From the Beaches of Sicily to the
Hitler Line with the Seaforth Highlanders of Canada, 1943–1944* (Ottawa:
The Golden Dog Press, 1996), 114–15.
2. Reginald H. Roy, *The Seaforth Highlanders of Canada, 1919–1965.*
(Vancouver: Evergreen Press, 1969), 242.

3. Ibid., 241.

4. Ibid.

5. J.D. Forin, "Baranello to San Leonardo: The Seaforth Highlanders of Canada, December 1943," Directorate of History, Department of National Defence, n.d., 4.

6. J.D. Forin, correspondence with Dr. R.H. Roy, 19 Jan. 1968, University of Victoria Special Collections, 14.

7. G.W.L. Nicholson, *The Gunners of Canada*, vol. 2 (Toronto: McClelland & Stewart, 1972), 167.

8. Roy, *Seaforth Highlanders of Canada*, 242–43. Teece was awarded the Military Medal for his exploits. Carter won a Military Cross for his gallantry on Dec. 6–7, which included at one point calling an artillery barrage down on his own position to drive off attacking Germans.

9. Jerry Richards, interview by author, Victoria, B.C., 6 Nov. 1998.

10. Ibid.

11. Princess Patricia's Canadian Light Infantry War Diary, Dec. 7, 1943, sheet 6, National Archives of Canada.

12. Cameron Ware, interview by Dr. Reginald Roy, 23, 25 June and 10 July 1979, University of Victoria Special Collections.

13. G.W.L. Nicholson, *The Canadians in Italy: 1939–1945*, vol. 2 (Ottawa: Queen's Printer, 1956), 297.

14. Richards, interview.

15. Farley Mowat, *The Regiment*, 2nd ed. (Toronto: McClelland & Stewart, 1973), 144.

16. Hastings and Prince Edward Regiment War Diary, Dec. 1943, 33-N-6, National Archives of Canada.

17. Basil Smith, "Memoirs of a Quarterbloke" Directorate of History, Department of National Defence, n.d., 38.

18. Ibid., 37.

19. Ibid.

20. Hastings and Prince Edward Regiment War Diary, 37-N-7.

21. N.a., "Biographies Regarding Medals Won at Ortona," Directorate of History, Department of National Defence, n.d., 39.

22. Hastings and Prince Edward Regiment War Diary, 37-N-7.

23. "Biographies Regarding Medals Won at Ortona," 39. Nolan was awarded the Military Medal for his exploits.

24. Nicholson, *Gunners of Canada*, 298–99.

25. 1st Canadian Division Intelligence Summary No. 27, File RG 24 Vol. 10888 234C1.023(D1), National Archives of Canada.

26. Nicholson, *Gunners of Canada*, 298–99.

27. Bill Strickland, interview by author, Kelowna, B.C., Aug. 1989.

## CHAPTER 9 / INTO THE INFERNO

1. Peter Stursberg, *The Sound of War* (Toronto: University of Toronto Press, 1993), 52–56.

2. Matthew Halton, CBC Radio broadcast, 8 Dec. 1943, CBC Radio Archives.

3. Charles Comfort, *Artist at War* (Pender Island, B.C. Remembrance Books, 1995), 69–70.

4. Victor Bulger, correspondence with author, 22 Sept. 1998.

5. Comfort, *Artist at War*, 70–71.

6. Ibid.

7. Bill Strickland, interview by author, Kelowna, B.C., Aug. 1989.

8. Bulger, correspondence.

9. Halton, broadcast.

10. Comfort, *Artist at War*, 72.

11. Ibid, 71.

12. Kim Beattie, *Dileas: History of the 48th Highlanders of Canada: 1929–1956* (Toronto: 48th Highlanders of Canada, 1957), 419–21.

13. 48th Highlanders of Canada War Diary, Dec. 1943, 32-N-5, National Archives of Canada.

14. Beattie, *Dileas*, 421–22.

15. 48th Highlanders War Diary, 32-N-6.

16. Ibid.

17. N.a., "Biographies Regarding Medals Won at Ortona," Directorate of History, Department of National Defence, n.d., 12.

18. Major S.J. Simons, "Unit History, 2nd Canadian Field Park Company RCE, Campobasso to Ortona, Dec. 43/Jan. 44," Directorate of History, Department of National Defence, 10 Feb. 1944, 3.

19. "Biographies Regarding Medals Won at Ortona," 12.

20. 3rd Canadian Field Company, Royal Canadian Engineers War Diary, Dec. 1943, n.p., National Archives of Canada.

21. Matthew Halton, CBC Radio broadcast, n.d., CBC Radio Archives.

22. 3rd Canadian Field Company, Royal Canadian Engineers War Diary, n.p.

23. Kerry, Col. A.J., and Maj. W.A. McDill, *History of the Corps of Royal Canadian Engineers,* vol. 2 (Ottawa: The Military Engineers Association of Canada, 1966), 169.

24. 3rd Canadian Field Company, Royal Canadian Engineers War Diary, n.p.

25. Fraser's leadership example to his men this night earned him the Distinguished Service Order. Sapper McNaughton earned a Military Medal. When Matthew Halton tried to record an interview with McNaughton, the rough bulldozer operator from Manitoba was too shy to tell his story. So Halton did it for him in a memorable broadcast that made the sapper a nationally known hero.

26. Strome Galloway, *A Regiment at War: The Story of the Royal Canadian Regiment, 1939–1945* (n.p., reprint 1979), 108.

27. Strome Galloway, *Some Died at Ortona* (n.p., n.d.), 176.

28. The Royal Canadian Regiment War Diary, Dec. 1943, n.p., National Archives of Canada.

29. Galloway, *Some Died at Ortona*, 177.

30. The Royal Canadian Regiment War Diary, n.p.

31. Ibid.

32. J.T.B. Quayle, *In Action: A Personal Account of the Italian and Netherlands Campaigns of WW II* (Abbotsford, B.C.: Blue Stone Publishing, 1997), 15–16.

33. Ibid.

## CHAPTER 10 / YOU TAKE IT NOW

1. G.W.L. Nicholson, *The Canadians In Italy: 1943–1945*, vol. 2 (Ottawa: Queen's Printer, 1956), 300.
2. Ibid., 297.
3. 3rd Canadian Field Company, Royal Canadian Engineers War Diary, Dec. 1943, n.p., National Archives of Canada.
4. Daniel Dancocks, *The D-Day Dodgers: The Canadians in Italy, 1943–1945* (Toronto: McClelland & Stewart, 1991), 161.
5. 14th Canadian Armoured Regiment War Diary, Dec. 1943, n.p., National Archives of Canada.
6. A.K. Harris, "Account at Ortona," University of Victoria Special Collections, 4.
7. 14th Canadian Armoured Regiment War Diary.
8. N.a., "Biographies Regarding Medals Won at Ortona," Directorate of History, Department of National Defence, n.d., 14.
9. Reginald Roy, *The Seaforth Highlanders of Canada, 1919–1965* (Vancouver: Evergreen Press, 1969), 246.
10. N.a., "Biographies Regarding Medals Won at Ortona," 54.
11. Jock Gibson, interview by author, Vancouver, B.C., 23 Nov. 1998.
12. Roy, *Seaforth Highlanders*, 247.
13. Ibid.
14. Gibson, interview.
15. Captain A.G. Steiger, "Report #18: Historical Section Army Headquarters: The Campaign in Southern Italy (Sept.–Dec. 1943), Information from German Military Documents regarding Allied operations in general and Canadian operations in particular," Directorate of History, Department of National Defence, n.d., 53.
16. Harris, "Account at Ortona," 5.
17. N.a., "Biographies Regarding Medals Won at Ortona," 44, 50. There were many medals won this day at San Leonardo. Lt. McLean would win a DSO, as would Brigadier Wyman and 14th Canadian Armoured Regiment (Calgary Tanks) commander Lieutenant Colonel Cyril Noulton Neroutsos. Amy picked up a Military Cross. Price, McDougall, and Barss collected Military Medals.
18. Kim Beattie, *Dileas: History of the 48th Highlanders of Canada: 1929–1956* (Toronto: 48th Highlanders of Canada, 1957), 423–24.

## CHAPTER 11 / STERLIN CASTLE

1. Strome Galloway, *Some Died at Ortona* (n.p., n.d.), 179.
2. G.W.L. Nicholson, *The Canadians in Italy: 1939–1945*, vol. 2 (Ottawa: Queen's Printer, 1956), 302.
3. Galloway, *Some Died at Ortona*, 180.
4. W.R. Freasby (ed.), *Official History of the Canadian Medical Services, 1939–1945: Volume One: Organization and Campaigns* (Ottawa: Queen's Printer, 1956), 166.
5. Jerry Richards, interview by author, Victoria, B.C., 6 Nov. 1998.
6. Galloway, *Some Died at Ortona*, 181.
7. Hastings and Prince Edward Regiment War Diary, Dec. 1943, 33-N-8, National Archives of Canada.

8. N.a., "Biographies Regarding Medals Won at Ortona," Directorate of History, Department of National Defence, n.d., 40. Pemberton received the Military Medal.

9. Ibid., 16, 38. Hammond won a Military Cross, Yearwood a Military Medal.

10. Royal Canadian Regiment War Diary, Dec. 1943, n.p., National Archives of Canada.

11. Ibid.

12. J.T.B. Quayle, *In Action: A Personal Account of the Italian and Netherlands Campaigns of WW II* (Abbotsford, B.C.: Blue Stone Publishing, 1997), 12–17.

13. Ibid.

14. Royal Canadian Regiment War Diary, n.p.

15. Quayle, *In Action*, 20.

**CHAPTER 12 / AT ALL COSTS**

1. Captain A.J. Porter, "Report No. 165 Historical Section Canadian Military Headquarters: Operations of 1 Canadian Infantry Division and 1 Canadian Armoured Brigade in Italy, 25 Nov. 43–4 Jan. 44," Department of National Defence, n.d., 50–51.

2. Canadian 1st Division War Diary, Dec. 1943, n.p., National Archives of Canada.

3. Porter, "Report No. 165," 50.

4. Kim Beattie, *Dileas: History of the 48th Highlanders of Canada: 1929–1956* (Toronto: 48th Highlanders of Canada, 1957), 425.

5. Porter, "Report No. 165," 50.

6. Farley Mowat, *And No Birds Sang* (Toronto: McClelland & Stewart, 1979), 228.

7. Robert L. McDougall, *A Narrative of War: From the Beaches of Sicily to the Hitler Line with the Seaforth Highlanders of Canada, 1943–1944* (Ottawa: The Golden Dog Press, 1996), 120.

8. Porter, "Report No. 165," 47.

9. 14th Canadian Armoured Regiment War Diary, Dec. 1943, 5, National Archives of Canada.

10. Ibid., 51.

11. Anna Tucci, interview by author, Ortona, 9 Dec. 1998.

12. Antonio Di Cesare, interview by author, Ortona, 8 Dec. 1998.

13. Hastings and Prince Edward Regiment War Diary, Dec. 1943, 33-N-8, National Archives of Canada.

14. Maj. N.L.C. Mathers, "Lessons learned and experience gained during HQ 1 Canadian Division fighting for Ortona, 1st Canadian Division Intelligence Summary No. 29," National Archives of Canada, n.d., n.p.

15. Captain A.G. Steiger, "Report #18 Historical Section Army Headquarters: The Campaign in Southern Italy (Sept.–Dec. 1943), Information from German Military Documents regarding Allied operations in general and Canadian operations in particular," Directorate of History, Department of National Defence, n.d., 54.

16. W. Victor Madej (ed.), *German Army Order of Battle, 1939–1945* (New York: Game Marketing Company, 1978), n.p.

17. Mathers, "Lessons learned."
18. Karl Bayerlein, interview by Major Michael Boire, Heilbronn, Germany, 12 Jan. 1999.
19. Ibid.
20. Karl Bayerlein, diary.

### CHAPTER 13 / A LITTLE OLD HEART STARTER

1. Reginald Roy, *The Seaforth Highlanders of Canada, 1919–1965* (Vancouver: Evergreen Press, 1969), 250.
2. Jim Stone, interview by William S. Thackray, 13, 20 May and 3, 10, 17 June 1980, University of Victoria Special Collections.
3. John Alpine Dougan, interview by author, Victoria, B.C., 23 Oct. 1998.
4. G.R. Stevens, *A City Goes to War* (Brampton, Ont.: Charters Publishing Co., 1964), 267.
5. Captain A.J. Porter, "Report No. 165 Historical Section Canadian Military Headquarters: Operations of 1 Canadian Infantry Division and 1 Canadian Armoured Brigade in Italy, 25 Nov. 43–4 Jan. 44," Department of National Defence, n.d., 51.
6. Cameron Ware, interview by Dr. Reginald Roy, 23, 25 June and 10 July 1979, University of Victoria Special Collections.
7. Stevens, *A City Goes to War*, 268.
8. G.R. Stevens, *Princess Patricia's Canadian Light Infantry, 1919–1957*, vol. 3 (Griesbach, Alta: Historical Committee of the Regiment, n.d.), 131.
9. Thomas de Faye, interview by author, Victoria, B.C., 3 Nov. 1998.
10. A.K. Harris, "Account at Ortona," University of Victoria Special Collections, 6.
11. Ibid., 7.
12. Ibid., 7–8.
13. Bert Hoffmeister, interview by author, West Vancouver, B.C., 23 Nov. 1998.
14. Dougan, interview.
15. Ibid.
16. Princess Patricia's Canadian Light Infantry War Diary, Dec. 1943, 36-N-9, National Archives of Canada.
17. Ware, interview.
18. Porter, "Report No. 165," 52.
19. Ibid.
20. Harris, "Account at Ortona," 8.
21. Ibid.

### CHAPTER 14 / ALL WE CAN DO

1. G.W.L. Nicholson, *Canadians in Italy: 1943–1945*, vol. 2 (Ottawa: Queen's Printer, 1956), 305–6.
2. Captain A.J. Porter, "Report No. 165 Historical Section Canadian Military Headquarters: Operations of 1 Canadian Infantry Division and 1 Canadian Armoured Brigade in Italy, 25 Nov. 43–4 Jan. 44," Department of National Defence, n.d., 56.
3. Ibid., 57.

4. Nicholson, *Canadians in Italy*, 306.

5. Lex Schragg, *History of the Ontario Regiment: 1866–1951* (n.p., n.d.), 161–62.

6. Porter, "Report No. 165," 57.

7. Ibid.

8. Ibid.

9. West Nova Scotia Regiment War Diary, Dec. 1943, 42-N-3, National Archives of Canada.

10. Daniel Dancocks, *The D-Day Dodgers: The Canadians in Italy, 1943–1945* (Toronto: McClelland & Stewart, 1991), 165.

11. West Nova Scotia War Diary, 42-N-4.

12. John Matheson, correspondence with author, 24 Sept. 1998.

13. Major G.D. Mitchell, *RCHA — Right of the Line: An Anecdotal History of the Royal Canadian Horse Artillery from 1871* (Ottawa: RCHA History Committee, 1986), 110.

14. Waldo E. Smith, *What Time the Tempest: An Army Chaplain's Story* (Toronto: The Ryerson Press, 1953), 176.

15. Matheson, correspondence.

16. Thomas H. Raddall, *West Novas: A History of the West Nova Scotia Regiment* (n.p., 1947), 156–57.

17. Porter, "Report No. 165," 58.

18. Mitchell, *RCHA*, 110.

19. Ibid, 110–11.

20. Raddall, *West Novas*, 157.

21. West Nova Scotia War Diary, 42-N-5.

22. Raddall, *West Novas*, 157–58.

23. West Nova Scotia War Diary, 42-N-5.

24. George Garbutt, correspondence with author, 30 Nov. 1998.

25. June Thomas, interview by author, Victoria, B.C., 23 Oct. 1998.

26. Syd Thomson, correspondence with author, Dec. 1998.

27. Thomas, interview.

28. West Nova Scotia War Diary, 42-N-4.

29. Raddall, *West Novas*, 159.

## CHAPTER 15 / THE GERMANS AND THE MUD

1. Chris Vokes, *Vokes: My Story* (Ottawa: Gallery, 1985), 141.

2. Richard S. Malone, *A Portrait of War: 1939–1943* (Don Mills, Ont.: Collins Publishers, 1983), 214.

3. Ibid.

4. Vokes, *Vokes*, 143.

5. Matthew Halton, CBC Radio broadcast, 15 Dec. 1943, CBC Radio Archives. Dates are those when report broadcast in Canada. Some were recorded earlier.

6. Matthew Halton, broadcast, 15 Dec.. Different broadcast, same date.

7. Major D.H. Cunningham, "The Press in the Ortona Battle," National Archives of Canada, 1–2.

8. Ibid.

9. Captain A.J. Porter, "Report No. 165 Historical Section Canadian Military Headquarters: Operations of 1 Canadian Infantry Division and 1 Canadian

Armoured Brigade in Italy, 25 Nov. 43–4 Jan. 44," Department of National Defence, n.d., 60.

10. G.W.L. Nicholson, *Canadians in Italy: 1943–1945*, vol. 2 (Ottawa: Queen's Printer, 1956), 308.

11. Major G.D. Mitchell, *RCHA — Right of the Line: An Anecdotal History of the Royal Canadian Horse Artillery from 1871* (Ottawa: RCHA History Committee, 1986), 111.

12. Princess Patricia's Canadian Light Infantry War Diary, Dec. 1943, 36-N-13, National Archives of Canada.

13. West Nova Scotia Regiment War Diary, Dec. 1943, 42-N-5, National Archives of Canada.

14. Porter, "Report No. 165," 62.

15. Ibid., 61.

16. Ibid., 62–64.

17. Thomas H. Raddall, *West Novas: A History of the West Nova Scotia Regiment* (n.p., 1947), 161–62.

18. N.a., "Biographies Regarding Medals Won at Ortona," Directorate of History, Department of National Defence, n.d., 23–24.

19. Porter, "Report No. 165," 64.

20. June Thomas, interview by author, Victoria, B.C., 23 Oct. 1998.

21. Ibid.

22. Ibid.

23. Lex Schragg, *History of the Ontario Regiment: 1866–1951* (n.p., n.d.), 162–63.

24. Thomas, interview.

25. Nicholson, *Canadians in Italy*, 309.

26. John Alpine Dougan, interview by author, Victoria, B.C., 23 Oct. 1998.

27. Porter, "Report No. 165," 66–67.

28. Fritz Illi, interview by Major Michael Boire, Zuffenhausen, Germany, 20 Feb. 1999.

29. Willi Fretz, interview by Major Michael Boire, Sinsheim, Germany, 19 Feb. 1999.

30. Ibid.

31. Karl Bayerlein, diary.

32. Captain A.G. Steiger, "Report #18 Historical Section Army Headquarters: The Campaign in Southern Italy (Sept.–Dec. 1943), Information from German Military Documents regarding Allied operations in general and Canadian operations in particular," Directorate of History, Department of National Defence, n.d., 57.

33. Ibid.

34. W. Victor Madej (ed.), *German Army Order of Battle, 1939–1945* (New York: Game Marketing Company, 1978), n.p.

35. Steiger, "Report #18," 57.

## CHAPTER 16 / THE SAFEST PLACE FOR US

1. Gunner H.R. Martin, "Press Release Regarding Major Paul Triquet Winning Victoria Cross. Miscellaneous Biographies of Army Personnel, 1939–1945," Department of National Defence, 1944, 1–6, 1–4.

2. Major G.D. Mitchell, *RCHA — Right of the Line: An Anecdotal History of the Royal Canadian Horse Artillery from 1871* (Ottawa: RCHA History Committee, 1986), 112.
3. Jean V. Allard, *The Memoirs of General Jean V. Allard* (Vancouver: University of British Columbia Press, 1988), 59.
4. Ibid.
5. Martin, "Miscellaneous Biographies," 3.
6. N.a., *The Canadians at War, 1939/45*, vol. 2 (Montreal: Reader's Digest Association (Canada) Ltd., 1969), 362.
7. N.a., "Battle Drill and the PIAT," Appendix to Royal 22e Regiment War Diary, Dec. 1943, n.p., National Archives of Canada.
8. Captain A.J. Porter, "Report No. 165 Historical Section Canadian Military Headquarters: Operations of 1 Canadian Infantry Division and 1 Canadian Armoured Brigade in Italy, 25 Nov. 43–4 Jan. 44," Department of National Defence, n.d., 68.
9. Headquarters 3rd Canadian Infantry Brigade War Diary, Dec. 1943, 40-N-8, National Archives of Canada.
10. *The Canadians at War*, 362.
11. Ibid.
12. Allard, *Memoirs*, 60.
13. Porter, "Report No. 165," 69.
14. T*he Canadians at War*, 362–63.
15. Daniel Dancocks, *The D-Day Dodgers: The Canadians in Italy, 1943–1945* (Toronto: McClelland & Stewart, 1991), 169.
16. Mitchell, *RCHA*, 112.
17. Captain Lex Schregg, *History of the Ontario Regiment: 1866–1951* (n.p., n.d.), 164–65.
18. Ibid., 164.
19. Porter, "Report No. 165," 69–70.
20. Mitchell, *RCHA*, 112–13.
21. *The Canadians at War*, 365.
22. Ibid.
23. Schregg, *History of the Ontario Regiment*, 165.
24. Captain A.G. Steiger, "Report #18 Historical Section Army Headquarters: The Campaign in Southern Italy (Sept.–Dec. 1943), Information from German Military Documents regarding Allied operations in general and Canadian operations in particular," Directorate of History, Department of National Defence, n.d., 59–60.
25. Ibid., 59.
26. Ibid., 58.

## CHAPTER 17 / A NEW PLAN IS NEEDED

1. Hastings and Prince Edward Regiment War Diary, Dec. 1943, 33-N-12, National Archives of Canada.
2. Princess Patricia's Canadian Regiment Light Infantry War Diary, Dec. 1943, 36-N-13, National Archives of Canada.
3. Captain A.J. Porter, "Report No. 165 Historical Section Canadian Military

Headquarters: Operations of 1 Canadian Infantry Division and 1 Canadian Armoured Brigade in Italy, 25 Nov. 43–4 Jan. 44," Department of National Defence, n.d., 71.

4. Ibid.

5. Ibid.

6. PPCLI War Diary, 36-N-14.

7. Strome Galloway, *Some Died at Ortona* (n.p., n.d.), 188.

8. Carleton and York Regiment War Diary, Dec. 1943, 8, National Archives of Canada.

9. Robert Tooley, *Invicta: The Carleton and York Regiment in the Second World War* (Fredericton, N. B.: New Ireland Press, 1989), 189.

10. Porter, "Report No. 165," 72.

11. Headquarters 3rd Canadian Infantry Brigade War Diary, Dec. 1943, 40-N-10, National Archives of Canada.

12. Porter, "Report No. 165," 72.

13. N.a., *The Canadians at War, 1939/45*, vol. 2 (Montreal: Reader's Digest Association (Canada) Ltd., 1969), 365.

14. Ibid, 366.

15. N.a., "Biographies Regarding Medals Won at Ortona," Directorate of History, Department of National Defence, n.d., 26.

16. Major G.D. Mitchell, *RCHA — Right of the Line: An Anecdotal History of the Royal Canadian Horse Artillery from 1871* (Ottawa: RCHA History Committee, 1986), 112.

17. Mitchell, *RCHA*, 114.

18. Headquarters 3 CIB War Diary, 40-N-10.

19. Mitchell, *RCHA*, 114.

20. Headquarters 3 CIB War Diary, 40-N-10.

21. Jean V. Allard, *The Memoirs of General Jean V. Allard* (Vancouver: University of British Columbia Press, 1988), 61.

22. George "Duff" Mitchell, interview by author, Ottawa, 12 Sept. 1998.

23. Headquarters 3 CIB War Diary, 40-N-10.

24. *The Canadians at War*, 367.

25. Porter, "Report No. 165," 73.

26. Nicholson, *The Canadians in Italy: 1943–1945*, vol. 2 (Ottawa: Queen's Printer, 1956), 317.

27. Antonio Di Cesare, interview by author, Ortona, 9 Dec. 1998.

28. Antonio D'Intino, interview by author, Ortona, 8 Dec. 1998.

29. Americo Casanova, interview by author, Ortona, 7 Dec. 1998.

30. Fritz Illi, interview by Michael Boire, Zuffenhausen, Germany, 20 Feb. 1999.

**CHAPTER 18 / MORNING GLORY**

1. West Nova Scotia Regiment War Diary, Dec. 1943, 42-N-6, National Archives of Canada.

2. Headquarters 3rd Canadian Infantry Brigade War Diary, Dec. 1943, 40-N-12, National Archives of Canada.

3. 14th Canadian Armoured Regiment War Diary, Dec. 1943, n.p., National Archives of Canada.

4. West Nova Scotia War Diary, 42-N-6.
5. Thomas H. Raddall, *West Novas: A History of the West Nova Scotia Regiment* (n.p., 1947), 166.
6. Ibid., 167–68.
7. G.W.L. Nicholson, *The Canadians in Italy: 1943–1945,* vol. 2 (Ottawa: Queen's Printer, 1956), 316–19.
8. Captain A.J. Porter, "Report No. 166 Historical Section Canadian Military Headquarters: Administrative Aspects of the Operations of 1 Canadian Infantry Division in Italy, December 1943," Department of National Defence, 29 Nov. 1946, 76.
9. Major G.D. Mitchell, *RCHA — Right of the Line: An Anecdotal History of the Royal Canadian Horse Artillery from 1871* (Ottawa: RCHA History Committee, 1986), 114.
10. Porter, "Report No. 166," 76.
11. Ibid., 78.
12. Kim Beattie, *Dileas: History of the 48th Highlanders of Canada: 1929–1956* (Toronto: 48th Highlanders of Canada, 1957), 433.
13. 48th Highlanders of Canada War Diary, Dec. 1943, 32-N-9, National Archives of Canada.
14. Beattie, *Dileas*, 436.
15. Porter, "Report No. 166," 80.
16. Ibid., 80–81.
17. Beattie, *Dileas*, 437.
18. Ibid., 439.
19. Ibid., 438.
20. Ibid.
21. Nicholson, *Canadians in Italy*, 318.
22. Beattie, *Dileas*, 439.
23. Nicholson, *Canadians in Italy*, 318–19.
24. Strome Galloway, *Some Died at Ortona* (n.p., n.d.), 192–93.
25. G.W. Stephen Brodsky, *God's Dodger* (Sidney, B.C.: Elysium Publishing Co., 1993), 203.
26. Galloway, *Some Died at Ortona*, 192.
27. Ibid., 192–94.
28. J.T.B. Quayle, *In Action: A Personal Account of the Italian and Netherlands Campaigns of WW II* (Abbotsford, B.C.: Blue Stone Publishing, 1997), 22–23.
29. Galloway, *Some Died at Ortona*, 193–94.
30. Porter, "Report No. 166," 82–83.
31. Quayle, *In Action*, 23–24.

CHAPTER 19 / THE DRIVE TO ORTONA

1. J.T.B. Quayle, *In Action: A Personal Account of the Italian and Netherlands Campaigns of WW II* (Abbotsford, B.C.: Blue Stone Publishing, 1997), 24.
2. Charlie Prieur, "Chronicles of the Three Rivers Regiment (Tank) at War," n.p., n.d., 115.
3. Colonel Strome Galloway, *Some Died at Ortona* (n.p., n.d.), 195.
4. Captain J.A. Porter, "Report No. 166 Historical Section Canadian Military

Headquarters: Administrative Aspects of the Operations of 1 Canadian Infantry Division in Italy, December 1943," Department of National Defence, 29 Nov. 1946, 83.

5. Quayle, *In Action*, 24.

6. Royal Canadian Regiment War Diary, Dec. 1943, n.p., National Archives of Canada.

7. Galloway, *Some Died at Ortona*, 196.

8. Royal Canadian Regiment War Diary, n.p.

9. Strome Galloway, *A Regiment at War: The Story of the Royal Canadian Regiment, 1939–1945* (RCP, reprint, 1979), 115.

10. G.W.L. Nicholson, *Canadians in Italy: 1943–1945*, vol. 2 (Ottawa: Queen's Printer, 1956), 320.

11. Porter, "Report No. 166," 84.

12. Ibid.

13. Nicholson, *Canadians in Italy,* 323.

14. Karl Bayerlein, diary.

15. Americo Casanova, interview by author, Ortona, 8 Dec. 1998. It is unlikely the Germans destroyed the Casanova apartment because of American possessions. More probable is that the building, on Ortona's southern outskirts, was perceived as a threat to the defensive positions inside Ortona. Such a large building would have provided an excellent observation point for Canadian artillery forward observation officers and would have been virtually immune to German artillery or mortar fire.

16. John Alpine Dougan, interview by Tom Torrie, 27 July 1989, University of Victoria Special Collections.

17. Jim Stone, interview by William S. Thackray, 13, 20 May and 3, 10, 17 June 1980, University of Victoria Special Collections.

18. 12th Canadian Armoured Brigade War Diary, Dec. 1943, 108-N-27, National Archives of Canada.

19. Ibid.

20. Robert L. McDougall, *A Narrative of War: From the Beaches of Sicily to the Hitler Line with the Seaforth Highlanders of Canada, 1943–1944* (Ottawa: The Golden Dog Press, 1996), 151.

21. Ibid.

22. Jock Gibson, interview by author, Vancouver, B.C., 23 Nov. 1998.

23. McDougall, *A Narrative of War*, 151.

24. Ibid.

25. Reginald Roy, *The Seaforth Highlanders of Canada, 1919–1965* (Vancouver: Evergreen Press, 1969), 258–61.

26. McDougall, *A Narrative of War*, 153.

27. Charles Comfort, *Artist at War* (Pender Island, B.C.: Remembrance Books, 1995), 102–3.

28. Americo Casanova, interview.

## CHAPTER 20 / A BUNCH OF MADMEN

1. Jim Stone, interview by William S. Thackray. 13, 20 May and 3, 10, 17 June 1980, University of Victoria Special Collections.

2. Ibid.

3. John Alpine Dougan, interview by author, Victoria, B.C., 23 Oct. 1998.

4. Ibid.

5. Ibid.

6. Elwyn R. Springsteel, correspondence with author, fall 1998.

7. John Alpine Dougan, interview by Tom Torrie, 27 July 1989, University of Victoria Special Collections.

8. Dougan, interview by author.

9. Alon Johnson, interview by author, Victoria, B.C., 29 Sept. 1998.

10. Stone, interview.

11. Johnson, interview.

12. Loyal Edmonton Regiment War Diary, Dec. 1943, 38-N-8, National Archives of Canada.

13. 1st Canadian Armoured Brigade War Diary, Dec. 1943, 583-N-23, National Archives of Canada.

14. Dougan, interview by Torrie.

15. Ibid.

16. Seaforth Highlanders of Canada War Diary, Dec. 1943, n.p., National Archives of Canada.

17. Associazone Archeologica Frentana, *Immagini: Ottobre 1943–Giugno 1944, Nove mesi di martirio* (Ortona: Soc. Coop. Iniziativa Cristiana, 1993), n.p.

18. Captain A.J. Porter, "Report No. 165 Historical Section Canadian Military Headquarters: Operations of 1 Canadian Infantry Division and 1 Canadian Armoured Brigade in Italy, 25 Nov. 43–4 Jan. 44," Department of National Defence, n.d., 86–87.

19. Seaforth Highlanders of Canada War Diary, n.p.

20. Ibid.

21. 12th Canadian Armoured Regiment War Diary, Dec. 1943, 108-N-29, National Archives of Canada.

22. Reginald Roy, *The Seaforth Highlanders of Canada, 1919–1965* (Vancouver: Evergreen Press, 1969), 265.

23. Jock Gibson, interview by author, Vancouver, B.C., 23 Nov. 1998.

24. Karl Bayerlein, interview by Michael Boire, Heilbronn, Germany, 12 Jan. 1999.

25. Karl Bayerlein, diary.

26. Porter, "Report No. 165," 86.

27. Captain A.G. Steiger, "Report #18 Historical Section Army Headquarters: The Campaign in Southern Italy (Sept.–Dec. 1943), Information from German Military Documents regarding Allied operations in general and Canadian operations in particular," Directorate of History, Department of National Defence, n.d., 63.

### CHAPTER 21 / THEY ALWAYS MESS THINGS UP

1. Jim Stone, interview by William S. Thackray, 13, 20 May and 3, 10, 17 June 1980, University of Victoria Special Collections.

2. Daniel Dancocks, *The D-Day Dodgers: The Canadians in Italy, 1943–1945* (Toronto: McClelland & Stewart, 1991), 176.

3. Alon Johnson, interview by author, Victoria, B.C., 29 Sept. 1998.

4. Stone, interview, by Thackray. Stone was awarded the Military Cross for this exploit.

5. Ibid.

6. In fact, Stone never accepted that the attack probably would have failed at the rubble pile. He remained convinced that the tankers' timidity was the only reason the Edmontons failed to break resistance in Ortona on Dec. 22.

7. John Dougan, interview by author, Victoria, B.C., 23 Oct. 1998.

8. G.R. Stevens, *A City Goes to War* (Brampton, Ont.: Charters, 1964), 176.

9. Melville A. McPhee, correspondence with author, 21 Oct. 1998.

10. G.W.L. Nicholson, *The Canadians in Italy: 1943–1945*, vol. 2 (Ottawa: Queen's Printer, 1956), 327.

11. 12th Canadian Armoured Regiment War Diary, Dec. 1943, 108-N-30, National Archives of Canada.

12. Peggy Turnbull, correspondence with author, Feb. 1999.

13. Karl Bayerlein, diary.

14. Karl Bayerlein, interview by Maj. Michael Boire, Heilbronn, Germany, 12 Jan. 1999.

15. Ibid.

16. Captain A.G. Steiger, "Report #18 Historical Section Army Headquarters: The Campaign in Southern Italy (Sept.–Dec. 1943), Information from German Military Documents regarding Allied operations in general and Canadian operations in particular." Directorate of History, Department of National Defence, n.d., 64.

17. Bayerlein, interview.

18. Steiger, "Report #18," 63.

19. Major N.L.C. Mathers, "Lessons learned and experience gained during fighting for Ortona," National Archives of Canada, n.p.

20. Ibid.

21. Ibid.

## CHAPTER 22 / FIGHT FOR THE BULGE

1. Captain A.J. Porter, "Report No. 165 Historical Section Canadian Military Headquarters: Operations of 1 Canadian Infantry Division and 1 Canadian Armoured Brigade in Italy, 25 Nov. 43–4 Jan. 44," Department of National Defence, n.d., 94.

2. Ibid., 95.

3. Ibid.

4. Hastings and Prince Edward Regiment War Diary, Dec. 1943, 33-N-13, National Archives of Canada.

5. Frank McGuire eyewitness account, as related in note to author. June 1999.

6. Hastings and Prince Edward Regiment War Diary, 33-N-13.

7. McGuire account.

8. Basil Smith, "Memoirs of a Quarterbloke," Directorate of History, Department of National Defence, n.d., 42.

9. Ibid., 43.

10. Farley Mowat, *The Regiment*, 2nd ed. (Toronto: McClelland & Stewart, 1973), 154.

11. Lex Schragg, *History of the Ontario Regiment: 1866–1951* (n.p., n.d.), 170.
12. G.W.L. Nicholson, *The Canadians In Italy: 1943–1945*, vol. 2 (Ottawa: Queen's Printer, 1956), 334.
13. Daniel Dancocks, *The D-Day Dodgers: The Canadians in Italy, 1943–1945* (Toronto: McClelland & Stewart, 1991), 182.
14. Schragg, *History of the Ontario Regiment*, 170–71.
15. Mowat, *The Regiment*, 157.
16. N.a., "Battle of the Moro River: Hastings & Prince Edward Regiment," Directorate of History, Department of National Defence, n.p.
17. Smith, "Memoirs," 44.
18. Nicholson, *Canadians in Italy*, 334.

CHAPTER 23 / THE UNMUFFLED DRUMS OF HELL

1. G.W.L. Nicholson, *The Canadians in Italy: 1943–1945*, vol. 2 (Ottawa: Queen's Printer, 1956), 327.
2. Ed Boyd, correspondence with author, 11 Oct. 1998.
3. "Employment of Snipers in Sicily and the Italian Campaign," National Archives of Canada, 1–2.
4. Fritz Illi, interview by Major Michael Boire, Zuffenhausen, Germany, 20 Feb. 1999.
5. Jock Gibson, interview by author, Vancouver, B.C., 23 Nov. 1998.
6. Captain A.J. Porter, "Report No. 165 Historical Section Canadian Military Headquarters: Operations of 1 Canadian Infantry Division and 1 Canadian Armoured Brigade in Italy, 25 Nov. 43–4 Jan. 44," Department of National Defence, n.d., 89.
7. *Fighting in Built Up Areas, Part Two: Ortona* (London: Ministry of Defence, Britain, 1990).
8. Ibid.
9. Harry Rankin, interview by author, Vancouver, B.C., 15 Oct. 1998.
10. Charles Comfort, *Artist at War* (Pender Island, B.C.: Remembrance Books, 1995), 90.
11. Anna Tucci, interview by author, Ortona, 8 Dec., 1998.
12. June Thomas, interview by author, Victoria, B.C., 23 Oct. 1998.
13. Major D.H. Cunningham, "The Press in the Ortona Battle," National Archives of Canada, n.p.
14. Porter, "Report No. 165," 90.
15. Bert Hoffmeister, interview by author, West Vancouver, B.C., 23 Nov. 1998.

CHAPTER 24 / THE DARING GAMBLE

1. Kim Beattie, *Dileas: History of the 48th Highlanders of Canada, 1926–1956* (Toronto: 48th Highlanders of Canada, 1957), 459.
2. Ibid., 457.
3. Ibid., 458–59.
4. 48th Highlanders of Canada War Diary, Dec. 1943, n.p., National Archives of Canada.
5. Beattie, *Dileas*, 459–61.
6. 48th Highlanders of Canada War Diary.

7. Ibid.

8. The Royal Canadian Regiment War Diary, Dec. 1943, n.p., National Archives of Canada.

9. Hastings and Prince Edward Regiment War Diary, Dec. 1943, 33-N-16, National Archives of Canada.

10. Strome Galloway, *Some Died at Ortona* (n.p., n.d.), 205.

11. The Royal Canadian Regiment War Diary.

12. Galloway, *Some Died at Ortona*, 205.

13. Ibid., 206.

14. Royal Canadian Regiment War Diary.

15. 48th Highlanders of Canada War Diary, 32-N-12.

**CHAPTER 25 / IT'S CHRISTMAS EVE**

1. Jock Gibson, interview by author, Vancouver, B.C., 23 Nov. 1998.

2. Bert Hoffmeister, interview by author, West Vancouver, B.C., 23 Nov. 1998.

3. Ibid.

4. John Alpine Dougan, interview by author, Victoria, B.C., 23 Oct. 1998.

5. John Dougan, interview by Tom Torrie, 27 July 1989, University of Victoria Special Collections.

6. Dougan, interview by author.

7. Ibid.

8. G.W.L. Nicholson, *The Canadians in Italy: 1943–1945*, vol. 2 (Ottawa: Queen's Printer, 1956), 326.

9. Fred Mallett, "Carols and Bullets," n.p., n.d.

10. Wilf Gildersleeve, interview by author, West Vancouver, B.C., 14 Oct., 1998.

11. Syd Thomson, correspondence with author, Dec. 1998 and 25 Jan. 1999.

12. Dave Fairweather, correspondence with Dr. Reginald Roy, 10 Sept. 1967. University of Victoria Special Collections.

13. Seaforth Highlanders of Canada War Diary, Dec. 1943, n.p., National Archives of Canada.

14. Thomson, correspondence.

15. June Thomas, interview by author, Victoria, B.C., 23 Oct. 1998.

16. *Fighting in Built Up Areas, Part Two: Ortona* (London: Ministry of Defence, Britain, 1990).

17. Eileen Currie-Smith, interview by author, Coquitlam, B.C., 16 June 1999.

18. Gordon Currie-Smith, interview by author, Vancouver, B.C., 15 Oct. 1998.

19. June Thomas, interview.

20. Gordon Currie-Smith, interview.

21. Karl Bayerlein, diary.

22. Ibid.

23. June Thomas, interview.

24. Turnbull family, correspondence.

25. Seaforth Highlanders of Canada War Diary.

26. Ibid.

27. Ibid.

28. Captain A.G. Steiger, "Report #18 Historical Section Army Headquarters: The Campaign in Southern Italy (Sept.–Dec. 1943), Information from German

Military Documents regarding Allied operations in general and Canadian operations in particular," Directorate of History, Department of National Defence, n.d., 65.

29. Ibid., 64–65.
30. Ibid.; Bayerlein, diary.
31. Bert Hoffmeister, interview.

## CHAPTER 26 / AS MERRY AS CIRCUMSTANCES PERMIT

1. 48th Highlanders of Canada War Diary, Dec. 1943, 32-N-12, National Archives of Canada.
2. Kim Beattie, *Dileas: History of the 48th Highlanders of Canada: 1929–1956* (Toronto: 48th Highlanders of Canada, 1957), 467.
3. Ibid.
4. Ibid., 468.
5. Ibid., 469.
6. Ibid.
7. J.T.B. Quayle, *In Action: A Personal Account of the Italian and Netherlands Campaigns of WW II* (Abbotsford, B.C.: Blue Stone Publishing, 1997), 134.
8. Ibid., 134–36.
9. The Royal Canadian Regiment War Diary, Dec. 1943, n.p., National Archives of Canada.
10. Ibid.
11. Strome Galloway, *Some Died at Ortona* (n.p., n.d.), 208.
12. Seaforth Highlanders of Canada War Diary, Dec. 1943, n.p., National Archives of Canada.
13. Ibid.
14. Major Roy C.H. Durnford, diary, n.p., National Archives of Canada.
15. Ibid.
16. Wilf Gildersleeve, interview by author, West Vancouver, B.C., 14 Oct. 1998.
17. Durnford, diary.
18. Syd Thomson, correspondence with author, Dec. 1998.
19. Dave Fairweather, correspondence with Dr. Reginald Roy, 10 Sept. 1967, University of Victoria Special Collections, 4.
20. Ernest "Smoky" Smith, interview by author, Vancouver, B.C., 23 Nov. 1998. On October 22, 1944, during the battle for the Savio River bridgehead, Smoky Smith would win the third and last Victoria Cross awarded a Canadian during the Italian campaign when he knocked out a tank with a PIAT gun and then single-handedly broke up a heavy German infantry attack with fire from a Thompson submachine gun.
21. Ibid.
22. Loyal Edmonton Regiment War Diary, Dec. 1943, 38-N-10, National Archives of Canada.
23. Jim Stone, interview by William S. Thackray, 13, 20 May and 3, 10, 17 June 1980, University of Victoria Special Collections.
24. 12th Canadian Armoured Regiment War Diary, Dec. 1943, 108-N-35, National Archives of Canada.
25. Captain H.R. Heggie, "Three Rivers Regiment History of WW II" (n.p., n.d.), 69.

26. G.W.L. Nicholson, *The Canadians in Italy: 1943–1945*, vol. 2 (Ottawa: Queen's Printer, 1956), 332.

27. Melville McPhee, correspondence with author, 21 Oct. 1998.

28. Beattie, *Dileas*, 469.

29. 48th Highlanders of Canada War Diary, 32-N-12.

30. Beattie, *Dileas*, 471–72.

31. Ibid, 473.

32. Karl Bayerlein, diary.

33. Major General Chris Vokes, *The Red Patch: Canada's Front Line Newspaper*, vol. 2, no. 8, Dec. 1943, n.p.

## CHAPTER 27 / CARRY ON

1. June Thomas, interview by author, Victoria, B.C., 23 Oct. 1998.

2. Terry Copp, *Battle Exhaustion* (Montreal: McGill-Queen's University Press, 1990), 57.

3. Ibid.

4. Alon Johnson, interview by author, Victoria, B.C., 29 Sept. 1998.

5. Jock Gibson, interview by author, Vancouver, B.C., 23 Nov. 1998.

6. Melville A. McPhee, correspondence with author, 21 Oct. 1998.

7. Robert L. McDougall, *A Narrative of War: From the Beaches of Sicily to the Hitler Line with the Seaforth Highlanders of Canada, 1943–1944* (Ottawa: The Golden Dog Press, 1996), 158.

8. Seaforth Highlanders of Canada War Diary, Dec. 1943, n.p., National Archives of Canada.

9. Fritz Illi, interview by Major Michael Boire, Zuffenhausen, Germany, 20 Feb. 1999.

10. Dave Fairweather, correspondence with Dr. Reginald Roy, 10 Sept. 1967, University of Victoria Special Collections, 3.

11. Peggy Turnbull, correspondence with author, Dec. 1998 and Feb. 1999.

12. 12th Canadian Armoured Regiment War Diary, Dec. 1943, 108-N-37, National Archives of Canada.

13. Peggy Turnbull, correspondence.

14. Gibson, interview.

15. Ibid.

16. Bert Hoffmeister, interview by author, West Vancouver, B.C., 23 Nov. 1998.

17. Bert Hoffmeister, interview by B. Greenhous and W. McAndrew, Directorate of History, Department of National Defence, Ottawa, n.d.

18. Loyal Edmonton Regiment War Diary, Dec. 1943, 38-N-11, National Archives of Canada.

19. Melville McPhee, correspondence.

20. Karl Bayerlein, diary.

21. Kim Beattie, *Dileas: History of the 48th Highlanders of Canada: 1929–1956* (Toronto: 48th Highlanders of Canada, 1957), 475–77.

22. 48th Highlanders of Canada War Diary, Dec. 1943, 38-N-13, National Archives of Canada.

23. Beattie, *Dileas*, 478.

24. Ibid., 479.

25. 48th Highlanders of Canada War Diary.

26. Ibid.

27. Captain A.G. Steiger, "Report #18 Historical Section Army Headquarters: The Campaign in Southern Italy (Sept.–Dec. 1943), Information from German Military Documents regarding Allied operations in general and Canadian operations in particular," Directorate of History, Department of National Defence, n.d., 66.

28. Ibid., 66–67.

29. Ibid, 66.

30. Strome Galloway, *Some Died at Ortona,* n.p., n.d., 209.

31. General Bernard Montgomery, Personal message from the army commander, Christmas 1943.

32. Eric Morris, *Circles of Hell: The War in Italy, 1943–1945* (New York: Crown Publishers, 1993), 224, 236.

33. Galloway, *Some Died at Ortona*, 211.

CHAPTER 28 / THERE IS NO TOWN LEFT

1. Ed Boyd, correspondence with author, 11 Oct. 1998.

2. G.R. Stevens, *A City Goes to War* (Brampton, Ont.: Charters, 1964), 278.

3. Ibid.

4. Loyal Edmonton Regiment War Diary, Dec. 1943, 38-N-11, National Archives of Canada.

5. Seaforth Highlanders of Canada War Diary, Dec. 1943, n.p., National Archives of Canada.

6. Karl Bayerlein, diary.

7. 12th Canadian Armoured Regiment War Diary, Dec. 1943, 108-N-40, National Archives of Canada.

8. Ibid.

9. Gordon Currie-Smith, interview by author, Vancouver, B.C., 15 Oct. 1998.

10. 2nd Canadian Infantry Brigade War Diary, Dec. 1943, n.p., National Archives of Canada.

11. 12th Canadian Armoured Regiment War Diary, 108-N-41.

12. G.W.L. Nicholson, *Canadians in Italy: 1943–1945*, vol. 2 (Ottawa: Queen's Printer, 1956), 336.

13. Syd Thomson, correspondence with author, Dec. 1998.

14. Daniel Dancocks, *The D-Day Dodgers: The Canadians in Italy, 1943–1945* (Toronto: McClelland & Stewart, 1991), 180.

15. Matthew Halton, CBC Radio broadcast, 29 Dec. 1943, CBC Radio Archives.

16. Captain A.G. Steiger, "Report #18 Historical Section Army Headquarters: The Campaign in Southern Italy (Sept.–Dec. 1943), Information from German Military Documents regarding Allied operations in general and Canadian operations in particular," Directorate of History, Department of National Defence, n.d., 67.

17. Fritz Illi, interview with Major Michael Boire, Zuffenhausen, Germany, 20 Feb. 1999.

18. Karl Bayerlein, diary.

19. Alon Johnson, "The Last Patrol in Ortona," *The Forty-Niner: Official*

*Publication of the Fortyninth Battalion, The Loyal Edmonton Regiment Association*, n.d., 35–38.

### CHAPTER 29 / AFTERMATHS

1. Matthew Halton, CBC Radio broadcast, 4 Jan. 1944, CBC Radio Archives.
2. Ibid.
3. Ibid.
4. Jim Stone, interview by William S. Thackray, 13, 20 May and 3, 10, 17 June 1980, University of Victoria Special Collections.
5. Daniel Dancocks, *The D-Day Dodgers: The Canadians in Italy, 1943–1945* (Toronto: McClelland & Stewart, 1991), 179.
6. Major Roy C.H. Durnford, diary, National Archives of Canada.
7. Captain A.G. Steiger, "Report #18 Historical Section Army Headquarters: The Campaign in Southern Italy (Sept.–Dec. 1943), Information from German Military Documents regarding Allied operations in general and Canadian operations in particular," Directorate of History, Department of National Defence, n.d., 68.
8. G.W.L. Nicholson, *The Canadians in Italy: 1943–1945*, vol. 2 (Ottawa: Queen's Printer, 1956), 338–39.
9. Victor Bulger, correspondence with author, Oct. 1998.
10. Turnbull family correspondence.
11. Kim Beattie, *Dileas: History of the 48th Highlanders of Canada: 1929–1956* (Toronto: 48th Highlanders of Canada, 1957), 487–88.
12. Ibid., 489–90.
13. Jean V. Allard, *The Memoirs of General Jean V. Allard* (Vancouver: University of British Columbia Press, 1988), 66.
14. Carleton and York Regiment War Diary, Dec. 1943, 11, National Archives of Canada.
15. Robert Tooley, *Invicta: The Carleton and York Regiment in the Second World War* (Fredericton, N. B.: New Ireland Press, 1989), 194.
16. Americo Casanova, interview by author, Ortona, 8 Dec. 1998.
17. Antonio D'Intino, interview by author, Ortona, 9 Dec. 1998.
18. Antonio Di Cesare, interview by author, Ortona, 9 Dec. 1998.
19. Royal 22e Regiment War Diary, Dec. 1943, 13, National Archives of Canada.
20. Tooley, *Invicta*, 196.
21. Carleton and York Regiment War Diary, n.p.
22. Lex Schragg, *History of the Ontario Regiment: 1866–1951* (n.p., n.d.), 173.
23. Don Smith, correspondence with author, 12 Dec. 1998.
24. Ibid.
25. Jock Gibson, interview by author, Vancouver, B.C., 23 Nov. 1998.

### CHAPTER 30 / POINT 59

1. Don Smith, correspondence with author, 12 Dec. 1998.
2. Wilf Gildersleeve, interview by author, West Vancouver, B.C., 14 Oct. 1998.
3. Matthew Halton, CBC Radio broadcast, 11 Jan. 1944, CBC Radio Archives.
4. Loyal Edmonton Regiment War Diary, Dec. 1943, 38-N-11, National Archives of Canada.

5. Major General Chris Vokes, "Fighting State — 1 CDN DIV as of 2 Jan 44, Appendix A," University of Victoria Special Collections, 1.

6. Ibid.

7. Ibid., 1–2.

8. Ibid., 2.

9. Terry Copp, *Battle Exhaustion* (Montreal: McGill-Queen's University Press, 1990), 57.

10. Major General Chris Vokes, "Crossing of the Moro and Capture of Ortona," Directorate of History, Department of National Defence, 14 March 1944, 6.

11. Captain A.G. Steiger, "Report #18 Historical Section Army Headquarters: The Campaign in Southern Italy (Sept.–Dec. 1943), Information from German Military Documents regarding Allied operations in general and Canadian operations in particular," Directorate of History, Department of National Defence, n.d., 69.

12. Ibid.

13. Don Smith, correspondence.

14. Ibid.

## EPILOGUE / ORTONA IN MEMORY

1. G.W.L. Nicholson, *The Canadians in Italy: 1943–1945,* vol. 2 (Ottawa: Queen's Printer, 1956), 329.

# BIBLIOGRAPHY

**BOOKS**

Allard, Jean V. *The Memoirs of General Jean V. Allard.* Vancouver: University of British Columbia Press, 1988.

Ambrose, Stephen E. *D-Day June 6, 1944: The Climactic Battle of World War II.* New York: Simon & Schuster, 1994.

Associazone Archeological Frentana. *Immagini: Ottobre 1943–Giugno 1944, Nove mesi di martirio.* Ortona: Soc. Coop. Iniziativa Cristiana, 1993.

Barnett, Correlli, ed. *Hitler's Generals.* London: George Weidenfeld & Nicholson Ltd., 1989.

Beattie, Kim. *Dileas: History of the 48th Highlanders of Canada, 1929–1956.* Toronto: 48th Highlanders of Canada, 1957.

Bergerud, Eric. *Touched with Fire: The Land War in the South Pacific.* New York: Penguin Books, 1996.

Boissonault, Charles-Marie. *Histoire du Royal 22e Régiment.* Québec: Éditions du Pélican, 1964.

Brodsky, Gabriel Wilfrid Stephen. *God's Dodger.* Sidney, B.C.: Elysium Publishing Co., 1993.

*The Canadians at War, 1939/45.* Volume Two. Montreal: The Reader's Digest Association (Canada) Ltd., 1969.

Comfort, Charles. *Artist at War.* Pender Island, B.C.: Remembrance Books, 1995.

Copp, Terry. *Battle Exhaustion.* Montreal: McGill-Queen's University Press, 1990.

Dancocks, Daniel G. *The D-Day Dodgers: The Canadians in Italy, 1943–1945.* Toronto: McClelland & Stewart, 1991.

Davies, W.J.K. *German Army Handbook, 1939–1945.* Shepperton, U.K.: Ian Allan, 1973.

Del Ciotto, Nicola. *Per Non Dimentciare: Ortona, quel lontano Dicembre del '43.* Ortona: Editrice Soc. Coop. Iniziativa Cristiana, 1987.

Di Tullio, Saverio. Angela Arnone and Alex MacQuarrie, trans. *1943: The Road to Ortona.* Ottawa: Legas, 1998.

Douglas, W.A.B., and Brereton Greenhous. *Out of the Shadows: Canada in the Second World War.* (rev. ed.) Toronto: Dundurn Press, 1995.

Duquemin, Colin K. *Stick to the Guns: A Short History of the 10th Field Battery, Royal Regiment of Canadian Artillery, St. Catharines, Ontario.* St. Catharines, Ont.: Norman Enterprises, 1996.

Ellis, John. *The Sharp End of War: The Fighting Man in World War II.* London: David & Charles (Publishers) Ltd., 1980.

Freasby, W.R., ed. *Official History of the Canadian Medical Services, 1939–1945. Volume One: Organization and Campaigns.* Ottawa: Queen's Printer, 1956.

——. *Official History of the Canadian Medical Services, 1939–1945. Volume Two: Clinical Subjects.* Ottawa: Queen's Printer, 1953.

Gaffen, Fred. *Forgotten Soldiers.* Penticton, B.C.: Theytus Books Ltd., 1985.

——. *Ortona: Christmas 1943.* Ottawa: Canadian War Museum, 1988.

Galloway, Strome. *A Regiment at War: The Story of The Royal Canadian Regiment, 1939–1945.* Royal Canadian Regiment, reprint 1979.

——. *Some Died at Ortona.* n.p., n.d.

Granatstein, J.L., and Desmond Morton. *A Nation Forged in Fire: Canadians and the Second World War, 1939–1945.* Toronto: Lester & Orpen Dennys, 1989.

Hamilton, Nigel. *Master of the Battlefield.* London: Hamish Hamilton, 1983.

Hogg, Ian V., and John Weeks. *Military Small Arms of the 20th Century.* 6th ed. Northbrook, Ill.: DBI Books, n.d.

Jackson, Lt.-Col. H.M. *The Royal Regiment of Artillery, Ottawa, 1855–1952.* n.p., 1952.

Kerry, Col. A.J., and Maj. W.A. McDill. *History of the Corps of Royal Canadian Engineers.* Vol. 2. Ottawa: The Military Engineers Association of Canada, 1966.

Kesselring, Albert. Lynton Hudson, trans. *The Memoirs of Field Marshal Kesselring.* London: William Kimber & Co., 1953.

Kitching, George. *Mud and Green Fields: The Memoirs of Major General George Kitching.* Langley, B.C.: Batteline Books, 1985.

McDougall, Robert L. *A Narrative of War: From the Beaches of Sicily to the Hitler Line with the Seaforth Highlanders of Canada, 1943–1944.* Ottawa: The Golden Dog Press, 1996.

Machum, Lt.-Col. George C., compiler. *Canada's V.C.'s: The story of Canadians who have been awarded the Victoria Cross, a Centenary Memorial.* Toronto: McClelland & Stewart, 1956.

Madej, W. Victor, ed. *German Army Order of Battle, 1939–1945.* New York: Game Marketing Company, 1978.

Malone, Richard S. *A Portrait of War: 1939–1943.* Don Mills, Ont.: Collins Publishers, 1983.

Mitcham, Samuel W. Jr. *Hitler's Field Marshals and Their Battles.* Chelsea, Mich.: Scarborough House Publishers, 1990.

Mitchell, Major G.D. *RCHA — Right of the Line: An Anecdotal History of the Royal Canadian Horse Artillery from 1871.* Ottawa: RCHA History Committee, 1986.

Montgomery, Bernard Law. *El Alamein to the River Sangro: Normandy to the Baltic.* New York: St. Martin's Press, 1948.

Morris, Eric. *Circles of Hell: The War in Italy, 1943–1945.* New York: Crown Publishers, 1993.

Mowat, Farley. *And No Birds Sang.* Toronto: McClelland & Stewart, 1979.

——. *The Regiment.* 2nd ed. Toronto: McClelland & Stewart, 1973.

Nicholson, G.W.L. *The Canadians in Italy: 1939–1945*. Vol. 2. Ottawa: Queen's Printer, 1956.

——. *The Gunners of Canada*. Vol. 2. Toronto: McClelland & Stewart, 1972.

Pickersgill, J.W. *The Mackenzie King Record, Volume 1*. Toronto: University of Toronto Press, 1960.

Powley, A.E. *Broadcast from the Front: Canadian Radio Overseas in the Second World War*. Toronto: A.M. Hakkert Ltd., 1975.

Quayle, J.T.B. *In Action: A Personal Account of the Italian and Netherlands Campaigns of WW II*. Abbotsford, B.C.: Blue Stone Publishers, 1997.

Raddall, Thomas H. *West Novas: A History of the West Nova Scotia Regiment*. n.p., 1947.

Roy, Reginald H. *The Seaforth Highlanders of Canada, 1919–1965*. Vancouver: Evergreen Press, 1969.

Schragg, Lex. *History of the Ontario Regiment: 1866–1951*. n.p., n.d.

Smith, Waldo E.L. *What Time the Tempest: An Army Chaplain's Story*. Toronto: The Ryerson Press, 1953.

Stevens, G.R. *A City Goes to War*. Brampton, Ont.: Charters Publishing Company Ltd., 1964.

——. *Princess Patricia's Canadian Light Infantry, 1919–1957*. Volume Three. Griesbach, Alta: Historical Committee of the Regiment, n.d.

Stursberg, Peter. *The Sound of War*. Toronto: University of Toronto Press, 1993.

Tooley, Robert. *Invicta: The Carleton and York Regiment in the Second World War*. Fredericton, N. B.: New Ireland Press, 1989.

*The Tools of War: 1939/45 and a chronology of important events*. Montreal: Reader's Digest Association (Canada), 1969.

Vokes, Chris. *Vokes: My Story*. Ottawa: Gallery, 1985.

Wallace, John F. *Dragons of Steel: Canadian Armour in Two World Wars*. Burstown, Ont.: General Store Publishing House, 1995.

**Magazines and Newspapers**

Bradshaw, Mel. "The Legacy of Ortona: Street Fighting Experts." 1983. *Canadian Forum*, December: 12–15.

Greenhous, Brereton. "Would it not have been better to bypass Ortona completely. . . ? A Canadian Christmas, 1943." 1989. *Canadian Defence Quarterly*, vol. 18, 5: 51–55.

Johnson, Alon. n.d. "The Last Patrol in Ortona." *The Forty-Niner: Official Publication of the Fortyninth Battalion, The Loyal Edmonton Regiment Association*, 35–38.

Mallett, Fred. "Carols and Bullets." n.p., n.d.

"Ortona." 1982. *Infantry*, vol. 10, 15–16.

Thomson, S.W. "Christmas in Ortona, Italy 1943." 1993. *Canadian Military History*, vol. 2, 2: 25–28.

——. "Wounded in Sicily, 12 July 1943." 1993. *Canadian Military History*, vol. 2, 2: 109–10.

Vokes, Chris. "Major-General Chris Vokes Christmas Message." Dec. 1943. *The Red Patch: Canada's Front Line Newspaper* (First Canadian Division — Central Mediterranean Force), vol. 2, 8: n.p.

Film
*Fighting in Built Up Areas, Part Two: Ortona.* Britain: Ministry of Defence. 1990.

**Unpublished Materials**
"Battle of the Moro, The Royal Canadian Regiment." 145.2R13013 (D1A),
   Directorate of History, Department of National Defence.
"Battle of the Moro River, Hastings & Prince Edward Regiment." 145.2H1013(D1),
   Directorate of History, Department of National Defence.
"Biographies Regarding Medals Won at Ortona," Directorate of History,
   Department of National Defence.
Brown, Shaun R.G., The Loyal Edmonton Regiment at War: 1939–1945. MA
   thesis, Wilfrid Laurier University, 1984, Directorate of History, Department of
   National Defence.
Canadian 1st Division. War Diary and Intelligence Summary, December 1943.
   National Archives of Canada.
Carleton and York Regiment War Diary, December 1943. National Archives of
   Canada.
CBC Radio Correspondent Report, broadcast December 28, 1943. CBC Radio
   Archives, Toronto.
Cockburn, Robert Edward. Canadian Gunner Battle School 1943–1945: The
   Italian Campaign and the Employment of the 1st Canadian Infantry Division's
   Artillery. MA thesis, University of New Brunswick, Sept. 1981, Directorate of
   History, Department of National Defence.
Cunningham, D.H. (Major). "The Press in the Ortona Battle." National Archives
   of Canada.
Durnford, Roy C.H. (Major). Diary of Major Roy Durnford, Chaplain (Padre), the
   Seaforth Highlanders of Canada, June 1943–June 1945. National Archives of
   Canada.
"Employment of Snipers in Sicily and Italian Campaign." RG24, Vol. 10883,
   National Archives of Canada.
1st Canadian Armoured Brigade War Diary, December 1943. National Archives of
   Canada.
1st Canadian Infantry Brigade (Headquarters) War Diary, December 1943.
   National Archives of Canada.
1st Canadian Infantry Division Intelligence Summaries Nos. 28, 29, 30, 31, 32.
   File RG 24. National Archives of Canada.
1st Canadian Infantry Division Quartermaster Branch War Diary, December 1943,
   National Archives of Canada.
1st Canadian Infantry Division (Headquarters) War Diary, December 1943.
   National Archives of Canada.
Forin, J.D. (Lt.-Col.). "Baranello to San Leonardo: The Seaforth Highlanders of
   Canada, December 1943." 145.2S5013(D4), Directorate of History, Department
   of National Defence.
48th Highlanders of Canada War Diary. December 1943. National Archives of
   Canada.
14th Canadian Armoured Regiment War Diary, December 1943. National Archives
   of Canada.

Halton, Matthew. Broadcasts from December 7, 1943, to January 11, 1943. CBC Radio Archives, Toronto.

Harley, D.S. (Captain). Report of the Action Fought by 'C' Company on 20 Dec 43 before Ortona. 22 December 1943. 145.2S5013(D3), Directorate of History, Department of National Defence.

Harris, A.K. "Account at Ortona.' Dr. Reginald Roy Papers. University of Victoria Special Collections.

Hastings and Prince Edward Regiment War Diary, December 1943. National Archives of Canada.

Heggie, R.H. (Captain). "Three Rivers Regiment History of WW II." Unpublished manuscript. Michael Boire Collection.

"History 1 Anti-Tank Regiment (RCA) 5 Sept. 39–31 July 45, World War II." 142.7A1013(01), Directorate of History, Department of National Defence.

"Italian Campaign — Sicily and Southern Italy, July 1943–April 1945." Condensed from an Official Historical Sketch prepared by the Canadian Army Historical Section. n.a., n.d., n.p., Directorate of History, Department of National Defence.

Loyal Edmonton Regiment War Diary, December 1943. National Archives of Canada.

Martin, H.R. (Gunner), Press Release Regarding Major Paul Triquet Winning Victoria Cross. 000.9 Miscellaneous Biographies Army Personnel 1939/45. Directorate of History, Department of National Defence.

Major N.L.C. Mathers. "Lessons learned and experience gained during HQ1 Canadian Division fighting for Ortona, 1st Canadian Division Intelligence Summary No. 29." RG24, Vol. 10883. National Archives of Canada.

Notes on GOC Conference 0900 hrs., 28 December 1943. RG24, Vol. 10884, National Archives of Canada.

Porter, A.J. (Captain). "Report No. 165 Historical Section Canadian Military Headquarters: Operations of 1 Canadian Infantry Division and 1 Canadian Armoured Brigade in Italy, 25 November 1943–4 January 1944." Directorate of History, Department of National Defence.

——. "Report No. 166 Historical Section Canadian Military Headquarters: Administrative Aspects of the Operations of 1 Canadian Infantry Division in Italy, December 1943." 29 November 1946, Directorate of History, Department of National Defence.

Prieur, Charlie. "Chronicles of the Three Rivers Regiment (Tank) at War." Unpublished manuscript. Michael Boire Private Collection.

Princess Patricia's Canadian Light Infantry War Diary, December 1943. National Archives of Canada.

Royal Canadian Regiment War Diary, December 1943. National Archives of Canada.

Royal 22e Regiment War Diary, December 1943. National Archives of Canada.

Saskatoon Light Infantry Headquarters War Diary, December 1943. National Archives of Canada.

Seaforth Highlanders of Canada War Diary, December 1943. National Archives of Canada.

2nd Canadian Infantry Brigade (Headquarters) War Diary, December 1943. National Archives of Canada.

Simons, S.J. (Major). "2nd Canadian Field Park Company RCE Unit History, Italian Campaign, Campobasso to Ortona, Dec. 43/Jan. 44." February 10, 1944. 143.2F2013(02), Directorate of History, Department of National Defence.

Smith, Basil. "Memoirs of a Quarterbloke: Hastings and Prince Edward Regiment Canadian Army Overseas." n.p., n.d., Directorate of History, Department of National Defence.

Sprung, G.M.C. (Capt.). Account Regarding German Tactics at Ortona. January 3, 1944. National Archives of Canada.

Spry, D.C. (Lt.-Col.). Account regarding lateral move of RCR, 8 Dec. 43 from coast bridgehead to San Leonardo bridgehead. 145.2R13011(D3)RCR, Directorate of History, Department of National Defence.

Stacey, C.P. (Colonel). Report No. 129 Historical Officer Canadian Military Headquarters. Canadian Operations in Italy September–December 1943: Preliminary Report. Reginald Roy Papers, University of Victoria Special Collections.

Steiger, A.G. (Captain). Report #18: Historical Section Army Headquarters: "The Campaign in Southern Italy (Sept.–Dec. 1943), Information from German Military Documents regarding Allied operations in general and Canadian operations in particular." Directorate of History, Department of National Defence.

3rd Canadian Infantry Brigade (Headquarters) War Diary, December 1943. National Archives of Canada.

3rd Field Company, RCE War Diary, December 1943. National Archives of Canada.

12th Canadian Armoured Regiment (Three Rivers Regiment) War Diary, December 1943. National Archives of Canada.

Vokes, Major-General C., CB, CBE, DSO, biography. Directorate of History, Department of National Defence.

——. "Crossing of The Moro and Capture of Ortona." March 16, 1944. National Archives of Canada.

West Nova Scotia Regiment War Diary, December 1943. National Archives of Canada.

### Interviews and Correspondence

Bayerlein, Karl. 1999. Interview by Michael Boire. Heilbronn, Germany. January 12.

Boyd, Ed. 1998. Correspondence with author. December.

Bulger, Victor. 1998. Correspondence with author. September 22.

Casanova, Americo. 1998. Interview by author. Ortona, Italy. December 8.

Currie-Smith, Eileen. 1999. Interview by author. Coquitlam, B.C. June 16.

Currie-Smith, Gordon. 1998. Interview by author. Vancouver, B.C. October 15.

de Faye, Thomas. 1998. Interview by author. Victoria, B.C. November 3.

Dell'Osa, Fabio. Interview by author. Ortona, Italy. December 9.

Di Cesare, Antonio. 1998. Interview by author. Ortona, Italy. December 9.

D'Intino, Antonio. 1998. Interview by author. Ortona, Italy. December 9.

——. 1998. Interview by author. Victoria, B.C. October 23.

——. Interview by Ken MacLeod. Victoria, B.C. n.d.

Dougan, John Alpine. 1987. Interview by Tom Torrie. Victoria, B.C. July 27. University of Victoria Special Collections.

Fairweather, Dave. 1967. Correspondence with Reginald Roy. September 10. Reginald Roy Papers, University of Victoria Special Collections.

Forin, J. Douglas. 1968. Correspondence with Reginald Roy. January 19. Reginald Roy Papers, University of Victoria Special Collections.

———. Memo to Dr. Reginald Roy. n.d. Reginald Roy Papers, University of Victoria Special Collections.

Fretz, Willi. 1999. Interview by Michael Boire. Sinsheim, Germany. February 19.

Garbutt, George. 1998. Correspondence with author. November 30.

Gibson, Jock. 1998. Interview by author. Vancouver, B.C. November 23.

Gildersleeve, Wilf. 1998. Interview by author. West Vancouver, B.C. October 14.

Haley, John. 1998. Interview by author. Victoria, B.C. October 30.

Hoffmeister, Bert. M. n.d. Interview by B. Greenhous and W. McAndrew. Directorate of History, Department of National Defence.

———. 1998. Interview by author. West Vancouver, B.C. November 23.

Illi, Fritz. 1999. Interview by Michael Boire. Zuffenhausen, Germany. February 20.

Johnson, Alon. 1998. Interview by author. Victoria, B.C. September 29.

———. Interview by Ken MacLeod. Victoria, B.C. n.d.

Lochead, Tod. 1998. Correspondence with author. November.

McBride, Joe. 1998. Correspondence with author. December.

McGuire, Frank, via author's correspondence with Fred Gaffen.

McPhee, Melville. 1998. Correspondence with author. October 21.

Matheson, John. 1999. Correspondence with author. September 24.

Mitchell, G.D. 1998. Correspondence with author. August 30.

———. 1998. Interview with author. Ottawa, Ont. September 5.

Quayle, Jimmy. Interview by Ken MacLeod. Vancouver. n.d.

Rankin, Harry. 1998. Interview by author. Vancouver, B.C. October 15.

Richards, Jerry. 1998. Interview by author. Victoria, B.C. November 6.

Smith, Don. 1998. Correspondence with author. December 12.

Smith, E. "Smoky." 1998. Interview by author. Vancouver, B.C. November 23.

Smith, Herschell. 1981. Interview by Reginald Roy. Victoria, B.C. July 7.

Springsteel, Elwyn R. 1998. Correspondence with author. November.

Stone, James Riley. 1980. Interview by William S. Thackray. Victoria, B.C. May 13, 20; June 3, 10, 17. University of Victoria Special Collections.

Strickland, Bill. 1989. Interview by author. Kelowna, B.C., August.

Thomas, E.W. (June). 1998. Interview by author. Victoria, B.C. October 23.

Tucci, Anna. 1998. Interview by author. Ortona, Italy. December 9.

Turnbull, Peggy. 1998–1999. Correspondence with author. December 1998; January 4, 1999; February 8, 1999; February 10, 1999.

Ware, Cameron. 1979. Interview by Reginald Roy. Victoria, B.C. June 23, 25; July 10. University of Victoria Special Collections.

# General Index

# Index of Formations, Units and Corps